THE CREATIVIT

THE CREATIVITY
OF CRETE

*City States and the
Foundations of the Modern World*

MALCOLM CROSS

Signal Books
OXFORD

First published in 2011 by
Signal Books Limited
36 Minster Road
Oxford
OX4 1LY
www.signalbooks.co.uk

Published in association with The Greengage Press

A catalogue record for this book is available from the British Library

ISBN 978-1-904955-95-5 Paper

Design: Bryony Clark
Cover image: © Insuratelu Gabriela Gianina / Shutterstock

Printed in India

Contents

Tables

Maps

Plates

Preface and Acknowledgments

Crete is many things to many people but to one who enjoys walking in its stunning countryside, it is a land of tracks and paths. It is hardly possible not to be aware that many of these had the purpose of connecting one ancient site of habitation with another. This book is the product of thinking how these settlements grew up and why in many cases they are now no more than romantic ruins, sometimes well visited by scholars and tourists, but more often not. Like many before, I turned to John Pendlebury's *Archaeology of Crete*, first published in 1939. After all, the 'Cretan Lawrence' was as famous for his inexhaustible travels, and consequent discoveries of ancient sites, as he was for his detailed excavations.[1] While no one before or since has packed so much information on ancient Crete into one volume, it was disappointing to see that only twenty of the book's 380 pages were devoted to sites existing in the Classical and Hellenistic eras when many of the towns and cities whose remains one encountered were at their zenith.

While I am no match for Pendlebury in any regard, the idea took shape that it might be useful to survey what had become known since his day. Perhaps partly because of an inadequate knowledge of ancient history, classical studies and archaeology, I became increasingly aware of a disjuncture between what was being reported by scholars in these fields and by those from other disciplines who appeared to reach opposite conclusions. The normal, but by no means universal, picture painted by the former group was one of Dorian-dominated city states locked in never-ending rounds of warfare sustained by frozen Archaic cultures and unable to feed their people without turning to piracy. The latter, by contrast, contained experts in, say, political science, who praised Crete's early forms of democracy, or legal historians who saw in the inscriptions at Gortyn the earliest instance of codified civil law.

It would be surprising (indeed disappointing) if departing from the first view did not prove controversial. With luck, any resultant debates may prove a stimulus for further research. It needs to be stressed that this book is conceived as an essay in social science. Archaeologists and classicists may find it deficient in many respects, among them being the absence of the copious footnotes beloved by the former, and the plentiful abbreviations that are grist for the mill of the latter. More seriously, the mindset of the social scientist differs from that of the usual disciplines employed in understanding ancient societies. Whereas the former is always on the look out for commonalities in the hope of generalisation, the latter seeks understanding through the specifics of one or two cases. Neither has a monopoly of truth and

---

1 Patrick Leigh Fermor said of him that 'there was no part of the often harsh Cretan landscape that he would not or could not tackle; he covered over 1000 miles of the island's wild and steep terrain in a single archaeological season, discovering unknown ancient sites all the way' (Leigh Fermor, 2007: xii).

dangers of interpretation exist on both sides. What is self-evident difference to the classicist, for example, may be glossed over by the social scientist.

An attempt has been made to exclude impenetrable jargon, but the use of technical words is sometimes unavoidable. For this reason, I have included a glossary of terms that might prove useful. As far as transcriptions of Ancient Greek words are concerned, I have followed modern usage in excluding accents, but in spelling the 'modern' principle has been varied where necessary for ease of comprehension (e.g. Eleutherna and not Eleftherna). Where this is not an issue I have tended to follow the Greek (e.g. Knosos and not Knossos) but errors and inconsistencies undoubtedly remain.

The Gazetteer appended to the book is intended to provide a descriptive summary of the sites discussed in the text. It is no substitute for those that can be found elsewhere, but it may be useful for some since it summarises relevant research findings and sets each site in a spatial context.[2] Inevitably a survey sacrifices depth for breadth and those who wish to read further may find the extensive references of value. Some material is exceedingly difficult to find, even in the finest university libraries, while in other cases it is freely available on the internet. A short guide has been included immediately before the references themselves. Inevitably, I have missed much of value and suggestions, corrections or comments would always be appreciated.

Inevitably a book that depends on the work of others generates many debts of gratitude. Not being of their respective tribes allows me to acknowledge a major debt to the archaeologists, classicists and ancient historians whose works constitute the raw material from which much of the argument is constructed. A great deal of this research is truly outstanding. I am also most grateful to the 25th Ephorate of the Greek Archaeological Service in Chania, and in particular to its one-time director, Maria Andreadaki-Vlasaki, for permission to consult published and unpublished reports relating to the visited sites. It is a pleasure too to thank Dr Apostolos Sarris of the Laboratory of Geophysical – Satellite Remote Sensing and Archaeo-environment at the Institute for Mediterranean Studies, Rethymno, for his kindness and support in relation to mapping and data presentation. Rosie Chapman not only read the draft manuscript and made scores of valuable suggestions, particularly in relation to transcriptions of Greek words, but also generously shared with me her knowledge of the geography and geology of the 'Great Island'. Eirini Markoulaki very kindly helped to put me right on the spelling of many terms from Ancient Greek, and my wife, Jette Johst, provided much editorial advice. It is a pleasure too to thank James Ferguson of Signal Books and those whom he engaged to work

2 Others include Sanders, 1982; Perlman, 2004a; Sjögren, 2003; and the Barrington Atlas (Talbert, 2000). Unfortunately, all of these sources can only be found in esoteric publications that, even when in print, are often very expensive to purchase. A partial listing appeared in the summer of 2010 derived from entries in Wikipedia (Books LLC, 2010a; Books LLC, 2010b). This is certainly less costly than the others but demonstrates all the pleasures and pitfalls of such online sources being highly variable in content, accuracy and coverage with no apparent criteria for selection.

on the editing of the manuscript (Jonathan Derrick) and the design of the book (Bryony Clark). The manuscript was sent out for anonymous comment to a small number of people and extremely helpful and encouraging replies were received. Two specialists subsequently identified themselves, so it is possible for me to thank most warmly Dr Philip de Souza (Head of Classics, University College, Dublin) and Dr Manolis Stefanakis (Department of Mediterranean Studies, University of the Aegean) for their guidance. W.G. Runciman (Trinity College, Cambridge) read the manuscript and provided trenchant observations, although I think he might have preferred me to have written a different kind of book. I am very grateful to them all. I am alone responsible for the errors and absurdities that undoubtedly remain.

MALCOLM CROSS

(malcolm.cross@gmail.com)

For JJ

CHAPTER ONE

Introduction: Seven myths

On Wednesday 12 March 2008, a reception was held in the atrium of the Olympic Tower in New York City to inaugurate the opening of a spectacular new exhibition entitled 'From the Land of the Labyrinth: Minoan Crete, 3000–1100 B.C.'. Accompanied by a suitably impressive catalogue and guide, the exhibition of 281 artefacts from the Late Bronze Age marked the first occasion when these works had left their native island. In his opening address, the Greek Minister of Culture noted that for most people Hellenic culture started with 5th century Athens, yet here were examples of the highest artistic achievement dating from a much earlier period.[1] As other speakers remarked, on display was the material culture of the 'first European civilization', revealing communities at peace with themselves, able to engage in commerce and the arts thousands of years before these achievements were repeated elsewhere in the world.[2]

There is no question that the artefacts on display were of the finest quality and provided a dramatic introduction to the Minoan world. Given this illustrious past it is perhaps not surprising that Crete a millennium later looks positively dull and unexceptional. Moreover, as almost every contemporary commentator noted, Crete during the Classical era (500–330 BCE) was isolated from the Athenian world, both from the city itself and from the burgeoning Greek empire that sustained it. In addition, Crete continued as a backwater after the Romans brought the Classical and Hellenistic eras to an end in 67 BCE. Overshadowed by the past, largely ignored in its day and sidelined thereafter, it is perhaps understandable that by the beginning of the 7th century BCE Crete is usually regarded as entering a period of dormancy and cultural exhaustion.[3]

The central proposition of this book is that this conclusion is false. Before the

---

1 Unsurprisingly he did not point out that the Minoans were not Greek or that the Mycenaeans, who probably brought Minoan culture to an end, undoubtedly were.

2 A fine description of the exhibits and a review of the exhibition are available. See Robert B. Koehl 'Minoans in New York' *American Journal of Archaeology* 112 (July 2008) (Online Museum Review).

3 All dates are BCE (Before Common Era) unless otherwise indicated on the grounds that dating by reference to an event, whose date is in any case contested and which would have meant nothing to anyone alive at that time, appears unnecessarily clumsy. The 'Common Era' may be taken as synonymous with '*Anno Domini*' and thus 'BCE' with 'BC'. The term 'common' refers to the use of the Gregorian calendar, which is by far the most widespread dating system in the world. At the risk of some inconsistency, AD has been retained because of familiarity and because it would have had some meaning to the followers of all Abrahamic religions.

discoveries of the late 19th century by Arthur Evans at Knosos, Crete's achievements during the Archaic to Hellenistic periods (650–67 BCE) were widely recognised. Certainly, when it comes to material culture, there is very little to record that matches the Bronze Age on Crete, the Athenian Classical world or the wonders of imperial Rome. But culture and civilisation rest on foundations that extend further than the artistic realm. It may be true for obvious reasons, that archaeologists have not been as comfortable with, or as capable of recording, the achievements of human activity that lie beyond pottery, sculpture and the other plastic arts. But this says something about archaeology, not about the peoples whose lives it seeks to record. Part of the ferment in archaeology over the past three decades has been the attempt to draw the discipline closer to social and cultural anthropology; perhaps part of the purpose in this book is also to suggest a further move in this direction, drawing on the insights of the other social sciences.

An island apart

Crete is an island of superlatives, some positive and others less so. It is the southernmost land of Europe, the site of possibly the earliest European civilisation, and the European land most occupied by others, as the plaything successively of Rome, Byzantium, Venice and the Ottoman Turks for nearly two millennia. Yet any visitor who ventures beyond the artificial envelope of the tourist hotspots will be struck not only by its physical beauty but by a powerful sense of Cretan identity that seems to have been inspired rather than abraded by the presence of others.

Perhaps the most obvious feature of Crete is its topography. One is seldom far from a significant mountain and the balance between inaccessible mountain ranges, lower lying but nonetheless secure foothills and coastal plains defines its human occupation. The island is roughly 260km long running west to east and varies between 60km and not much more than a quarter of that between the north and south coasts. The obvious significance of three mountainous regions (the Lefka Ori in the west, the Psiloritis massif (Mount Ida) in the centre and the Dikti and Thryphti mountains to the east) has tended to be reflected in the way in which Crete has been interpreted. These geographical zones have formed what is almost a hierarchy of importance with the central region being predominant, followed by the east and then by the 'isolated' west. More recent archaeological discoveries, particularly in 'Minoan' Chania, have tended to cast doubt on the wisdom of this partition, and it is perhaps more appropriate either to consider the island as a whole or to focus upon more localised settings, depending on the purpose in hand.

That said, there are regional differences of possible importance. The climate, for example, is wetter and cooler in the north, and the east is more arid than the west. Both in the present and in the past, these facts may have helped shape settlement and relative prosperity. It should not be assumed, however, that today's climate is identical to that of the past. Studies of the vegetation suggest that since the Bronze Age, the climate of Crete may have grown more arid (Moody et al., 1996: 284).

Olive cultivation may have commenced very early in Crete, possibly as early as the Late Neolithic or 1,000 years before the mainland, although it was not until the Late Bronze Age that widespread cultivation of *Olea* occurred (Moody et al., 1996: 286). An observer today could be forgiven for thinking that no other crop had any economic significance.

If the mountains of Crete are the vital backdrop to human activity, then the sea in the foreground is no less critical. Indeed, almost every commentator has pointed to the role of the sea in the Late Bronze Age and probably much earlier. At one time the high point of the Minoan civilisation was referred to as a 'thalassocracy', as if to suggest that the control of the Aegean was the foundation of political life. The sea levels themselves have not remained steady, owing mainly to tectonic movements. These changes, most noticeable in the west, led initially to slow subsidence from the Early Bronze Age through to the Roman era. In the 4th century AD, however, the entire west end of the island appears to have risen by as much as 10m, a phenomenon evident from wave notches on rock faces at Phalasarna in the far west and elsewhere (Pirazzolli et al., 1992). Contemporary sources record a 'day of horror' as a massive tsunami struck the Egyptian city of Alexandria and the Nile Delta in July 365 AD, and recent research in western Crete has shown that this was produced by the same earthquake that lifted this end of the island to such a significant degree. The fault line lies in the Hellenic trench off western Crete where continued seismic activity suggests a possible recurrence as frequently as once every 800 years (Shaw et al., 2008).[4]

Insofar as the siting of major places of settlement was directly linked to the availability of arable land and pasturage, then climate and environment in general may well have played an important role, alongside safety and the security of boundaries, in shaping the island's human face.[5] At different points in time these calculations produce markedly different outcomes; the Minoans' enthusiasm for the sea affected where they built their palaces and towns while, after the collapse of this civilisation, the sea clearly took on a more sombre significance as the remaining population fragmented and fled to the mountains, only to return gradually over many centuries.

Cretan chronology

The length, complexity and richness of Crete's history are so astonishing that carving it into comprehensible slices is immediately appealing. It is also rather dangerous for historical divisions inevitably tend to be reified, and before long narratives appear that seem to suggest recognition on the part of those so classified with the appellations attached to them. Moreover, in the Cretan case, the most

---

4 This date has not gone unchallenged. An earlier study using radiocarbon dating locates the timing of the uplift approximately two centuries later (Price et al., 2002).

5 For an excellent overview of land use and the shifting balance between human activity and ecology see Moody and Rackham, 1996.

widely accepted chronologies are a mixture of architectural form, pottery types, phases of migration, external cultural events and foreign rule. In fact they are a mess, but have become so widely adopted that much of the secondary literature would be incomprehensible without some understanding of the labels and the years to which they refer.

Era	Dates
Neolithic	Before 3650 BCE
Late Bronze Age:	
Prepalatial/Early Minoan	ca. 3650 – ca. 1900 BCE
Old Palatial/Middle Minoan	ca. 1900 – ca. 1700 BCE
New Palatial/Late Minoan	ca. 1700 – ca. 1370 BCE
Postpalatial/Late Minoan	ca. 1370 – ca. 970 BCE
Early Iron Age:	
Protogeometric	ca. 970 – ca. 810 BCE
Geometric	ca. 810 – ca. 700 BCE
Orientalizing	ca. 700 – 650 BCE
Archaic	ca. 650 – ca. 500 BCE
Classical	ca. 500 – ca. 330 BCE
Hellenistic	ca. 330 – 67 BCE
Roman	67 BCE – AD 330
Late Roman/Early Byzantine	AD 330 – AD 824
Arab	AD 824 – AD 961
Late Byzantine	AD 961 – AD 1212
Venetian	AD 1212 – AD 1669
Ottoman Turk	AD 1669 – AD 1898

The central focus of this study is on the period from 650 BCE until the coming of Roman imperial rule (i.e. the Archaic, Classical and Hellenistic eras). There is almost no discussion of events beyond the middle of the 1st century and all date references are BCE unless clearly stated. Some comment is included, however, on earlier periods where this is necessitated by the discussion in hand and a very brief summary of this earlier history now follows.

Minos and after

It is an impossible task to summarise in a few sentences Cretan prehistory before 700 BCE. What can be said is that by far the greatest attention has been given to the Late Bronze Age (LBA) in general and to the Minoan period in particular. The scholarship on this period is impressive and, as the flood of books, articles and reports testifies, it continues to exercise a seductive hold over Cretan specialists.[6]

6 Just to illustrate this point consider the case of *Nestor*, an international bibliography of Aegean studies run by the Department of Classics at the University of Cincinnati, whose chronological limit is the Paleolithic to the Geometric period. The bibliography of materials on this topic currently lists 41,000 entries, although – of course

To the inexpert eye, however, it is hard not to be struck by the extent to which certain themes predominate while others are more rarely found. The first and most obvious of the former is the Minoan chronology itself. The term 'Minoan' to describe the civilisation of the Cretan Bronze Age is one of many inventions to have come down to us from the fluent pen of Sir Arthur Evans. His excavations at Knosos produced astonishingly rich layers of pottery remains and it was perfectly sound archaeological practice, then as now, to label these strata in terms of the characteristic features of the finds. This produced a relatively straightforward division into 'Early', 'Middle' and 'Late' periods, but differences *within* each of these categories persuaded Evans to introduce subdivisions that created a complex matrix as shown in the following table. What the table also shows is the relative chronology proposed by the Greek archaeologist Nicolas Platon (1966: 206–7).[7] Platon, excavator of the important Minoan site at Kato Zakros in south-eastern Crete, based his classification upon the evidence of the architectural remains of the so-called 'palaces' at Knosos, Phaistos, Ag. Triada, Malia and Kato Zakros. It can be readily observed that the relationship between the two chronologies is less than perfect, but Platon's scheme is perhaps more satisfactory because it was made to correlate with major physical structures across the island, rather than with the changing fashions of potters from one location.

Minoan Chronology

Prepalatial Period	Early Minoan I (EMI)	3650–3000 BCE
	Early Minoan II (EMII)	2900–2300 BCE
	Early Minoan III (EMIII)	2300–2160 BCE
	Middle Minoan IA (MMIA)	2160–1900 BCE
Old Palatial Period	Middle Minoan IB (MMIB)	1900–1800 BCE
	Middle Minoan II (MMII)	1800–1700 BCE
New Palatial Period	Middle Minoan III A (MMIIIA)	1700–1640 BCE
	Middle Minoan III B (MMIIIB)	1640–1600 BCE
	Late Minoan IA (LMIA)	1600–1480 BCE
	Late Minoan IB (LMIB)	1480–1425 BCE
Postpalatial Period	Late Minoan II (LMII)	1425–1390 BCE
	Late Minoan IIIA1 (LMIIIA1)	1390–1370 BCE
	Late Minoan IIIA2 (LMIIIA2)	1370–1340 BCE
	Late Minoan IIIB (LMIIIB)	1340–1190 BCE
	Late Minoan IIIC (LMIIIC)	1190–1170 BCE
Subminoan		1170 BCE

– not all of these are on Greece, let alone Crete. In 1994, however, a survey of Aegean prehistorians identified just under three hundred individual specialists, more than half of whom came from the US or Britain. Forty-eight per cent identified Crete as their area of greatest expertise and the vast majority (72 per cent) saw themselves as specialists on the Late Bronze Age.

7 Slightly modified to suggest an earlier date for the start of the Early Minoan/Prepalatial period.

At best, however, undisturbed deposits or the remains of buildings produce a *relative* chronology, in the sense that deeper layers are assumed to have been laid down prior to those above, but this does not, of course, tell the archaeologist *when* this occurred. In the case of the Cretan deposits, it was only the connection with Egyptian tombs and motifs, whose date was known, that enabled an absolute chronology to be attempted. Aegean pottery as a whole has been found in a number of sites in the Nile Valley dating from the period of the Middle Kingdom (2025–1650 BCE), although no Minoan wares have been found prior to the 12th Dynasty (ca. 1985–1773 BCE). Some of these items may have been carried there by workers on the pyramid of Sensuret II (1877–1870 BCE), since they were found in housing settlements set up for workers on this tomb. However, it seems highly probable that goods flowed in both directions since carved stone bowls that are not uncommon in Minoan deposits are usually regarded as having been inspired by Egyptian examples, some of which have also been found in Crete. Perhaps of far greater interest was the discovery of wall paintings at Tell ed-Dab'a on the Eastern Nile Delta, usually regarded as Avaris, the capital of the Hyksos, which have been shown to be remarkably similar to those found at Knosos and other palatial centres in Crete. They include fragments showing bull leaping and other friezes depicting bulls in pastoral settings (Bietak et al., 2007). The context in which these motifs have been found in Egypt is earlier than that thought to be true for Knosos, which may suggest that the *absolute* chronology shown above is ripe for revision since it is generally accepted that the wall paintings in Tell el-Dab'a were the work of Minoan artists.[8] Of course, the obvious alternative is that those we regard as 'Minoans' were in fact Egyptians, which is a thesis first put forward by Bernal (1987). Indeed, some genetic research, but by no means all, has also indicated an African origin for the Minoans. Arnaiz-Villena et al. (1999) suggest that Sumerians, Cretans and Iberians all possess common origins in waves of population movement of what are today Caucasoid Berbers from North Africa and the Sahara following the beginnings of desertification in the period between 8000 and 6000 BCE. On the other hand, King et al. (2008), using a sample from skeletal remains in Neolithic settlements in Crete, have shown a marked affinity in Y-chromosone haplogroups with peoples from north-western Anatolia and the border lands with Syria and Palestine. If this is true, then artists from these areas might have traveled to both Egypt and Knosos, albeit at different times.

Doubts about the absolute chronology also arose in relation to the eruption of the volcano that all but destroyed the island of Santorini (Thera) 140km to the north of Crete. Once thought to have been the main reason for the collapse of the Minoan civilisation in LMIB, it now appears from an array of scientific data that this event, and the enormous tsunami to which it gave rise, occurred nearly 200 years before, in approximately 1620 BCE. All of this emphasises the lack of clarity

---

8 Manfred Bietak and his co-workers have argued that the relationship between Knosos and Avaris is so plain that it may suggest a dynastic connection (Bietak et al., 2007).

over the *absolute* chronology, even though the *relative* chronology has provided the scaffolding of support for the whole edifice of 'Minoan studies'. This is clear in our understanding of the broad contours of the transitions suggested by the terms 'prepalatial', 'old palatial' and 'new palatial'. The 'prepalatial period' was marked by the emergence, or possible arrival, of a people capable of using copper and imported tin ores to produce bronze artefacts. Perhaps significantly, they used a hieroglyphic script. In time, as this culture developed, complex buildings were erected at Knosos, Phaistos and Malia that appeared to combine administrative, religious and ceremonial functions (MMIB–MMII). Over time records began to be kept using a new pictographic script known as 'Linear A'. The buildings had certain characteristic architectural features in common, including open courts and a 'U'-shaped layout. Around 1700 BCE, violent destructions occurred to these complex buildings, but they were swiftly rebuilt in more elaborate form with wide staircases to upper stories. This 'New Palace' period (from MMIII onward) marks the zenith of Minoan achievements both artistically and in terms of economic fortunes, particularly in relation to seaborne trade. As far as the former is concerned, the magnificent wall paintings made on smoothly worked lime plaster when soft date from this period. There were, however, numerous other settlements such as small towns (e.g. Palaikastro, Pseira), villages with small groups of houses (e.g. Tylisos, Ag. Triada, Mochlos, Kommos) and isolated houses, often with an obvious agricultural function (e.g. Vathypetro) (cf. Cadogan, 1991).

The 'New Palaces' were eventually destroyed by fire around about 1450 BCE (LMIB) with the exception of Knosos, although some destructions occurred there too, followed by a phase of rebuilding. Approximately two generations later (ca. 1375 BCE), the last 'palace' at Knosos was also destroyed. These events, together with linguistic innovations (the use of Linear B, an early form of Greek, on administrative tablets at Knosos, Chania and elsewhere) and cultural changes (the adoption of *tholos* tombs), have persuaded most commentators that this was a period during which Mycenaean Greeks from the mainland arrived on the island and in effect took over the major power positions. Certainly, towards the end of the Minoan period, significant changes did occur, most notably an increase in the number of 'warrior graves', images of chariots in frescoes and other suggestions of a more aggressive culture. The administrative records at Knosos also suggest to some that by the 'New Palace' period this city was capital of the island as a whole under the direction of an elite comprised of Mycenaean Greeks or their descendants (Cadogan, 1992: 36). The question of a Mycenaean physical presence in Crete, as distinct from cultural forms, is also the subject of continuing research in genetics and other scientific studies. King et al. (2008) have demonstrated higher frequencies of haplogroups typical of a mainland Mycenaean presence in skeletal remains, thus supporting the theory from material culture of mainland settlement in the late second millennium BCE. On the other hand, some doubt has been cast on how extensive the Mycenaean presence was, at least at Knosos, following strontium isotope ratio analysis ($87Sr/86Sr$) of human dental enamel and bone in chamber tombs hitherto thought to be evidence of mainland domination following the collapse of Minoan palace societies in LMIB. The results showed that all the individuals in the sample had been born locally (Nafplioti, 2008).

From this period onward, as the island entered the Early Iron Age, the picture becomes even less clear. For some years after the collapse of the social order in which the 'palaces' appear to have played a central role, some rebuilding appears to have occurred and some of the old sites were reused. But from circa 1200 BCE there are major changes in settlement patterns with large centres in coastal or low lying areas being abandoned in favour of small villages in upland regions, often extremely hard to reach. These may have numbered up to 150 different places, nearly all of them characterised by their height above sea-level, natural barriers to easy access and sight lines to lower level ground (Wallace, 2010: 61). Unsurprisingly, exploration of these sites has focused on their defensiveness, seeing them as places of refuge from severe dangers emanating, it is normally assumed, from outside the island (Nowicki, 2000). These dangers, whose origins and parameters remain a mystery, must have receded over the following three centuries, for by the 8th century most of the highly inaccessible defensible sites had been, or were in the process of being, abandoned in favour of the larger settings overlooking arable lands that are the focus of this study. This transition did not, however, occur before others from outside the island had spotted the opportunities for settlement created by the flight to the hills, thereby creating the multi-ethnic world of the Cretan *poleis*.

In assessing how plausible these arguments are, it is important to distinguish between the reasons for the decline in the Minoan civilisation on the one hand and the new forms of settlement on the other. For example, a recent contribution argues that persistent earthquake activity during the Late Bronze Age ruptured groundwater supplies, making life in typically low-lying palace complexes untenable (Gorokhovich, 2005). Saro Wallace takes this argument further by suggesting that the primary reason for the new settlements in the mountains was also the search for water (2010: 58). It is perfectly possible that natural and climatic causes made farming impossible in low lying areas. On the other hand, it is quite implausible to see this as the main factor in relocation to the typical refuge sites of the 12th–8th centuries. The mountainous regions of Crete contain an enormous number of high, well-watered zones that lack almost all of the properties of the 'refuge sites'. One has only to visit a sample of these sites, most of which do not have easily accessible springs, to appreciate that no one would opt to settle there if they felt they had other choices that would not put them at risk of annihilation.

In later chapters, much is made of the way in which the Cretan *poleis* over the course of the Classical and Hellenistic eras invented innovative ways of responding to the three challenges that all societies face: how to establish a community that coheres as an entity, how to make and implement decisions, and how to survive in a material sense. It is interesting to observe that, until very recently, attempts to answer these social, political and economic questions were conspicuous by their absence in the world of 'Minoan studies'. Of course there are numerous exceptions to this glib generalisation, but it is notable that only in the last decade, as the study of Late Bronze Age Crete enters its second century, have many old assumptions been seriously challenged. For example, the central feature of the Minoan world is the existence of the 'palace'. But this terminology suggests a leadership analogous to a monarchy and ruling family, and therefore a highly stratified social order. Moreover, it is a short step from this to imagine that the centres we know of were the capitals of large states. Gerald Cadogan, for example, feels confident enough to suggest there were 'four or five different states' during the 'new palace' era (1992: 35). But what if the 'palaces' did not have this function? What if they were in some sense 'public spaces' or more collegiate structures, housing multiple families? The 'postpalace' transition might then be seen as a growing individualism that would account for the well documented growth in separate housing units in LMIII and later (Driessen, 2010). Similarly, the usual assumption is one of gradual political centralisation, first to 'palace society' and later to a more highly integrated 'new palace' structure. But what if Crete was not like this at all? The island has always been 'regional' in the sense that political structures reflected local needs. Some critics have recently suggested how important such regional structures were, while others are challenging the notion of overarching Knosian power (Haggis, 2002; Knappet, 1999; Knappett and Schoep, 2000). Put simply, there may be far greater continuities between prepalatial and postpalatial society than was once thought possible, and the concept of the 'palace' may itself not be as significant in social and political terms as has hitherto been assumed.

What is clear is that Crete by the 8th century had experienced successive waves of migration and had become a multicultural world. Herodotus (7.173) describes how two periods of depopulation had led to migration from the Greek mainland. First the Sicilian adventures of King Minos created a demographic vacuum filled by Mycenaean Greeks (ca. 1350 BCE); then 'in the third generation after the death of Minos', Crete again lost population as a result of the Trojan War, which was followed by plague and famine at home. This prompted a second phase of inward migration by the so-called 'Dorians', probably throughout most of the Early Iron Age. The 'Dorians', composed of their three 'tribes' (*phylai*) the Hylleis, Pamphyloi and Dymanes, are normally distinguished by dialect and geographical origins from the four *phylai* of the Ionian Greeks. They are traditionally regarded as the conquerors of the Peloponnese moving south from their homelands in Macedonia and Epirus in the north of Greece during the period 1100–1000 BCE, putting paid in the process to the Mycenaeans and any vestiges of Minoan peoples. Their culture is normally thought to have provided the militarism in Laconia and in particular its capital Sparta. From there they are thought to have migrated eastward as far as Halicarnassus and Cnidus on the coast of what is today southwestern Turkey and onwards to Corinth and a number of cities on the Black Sea. Their southern migration went at least as far as the coast of north Africa (Cyrene) and included the islands of the southern Aegean (Melos, Thera, Cos, Crete and Rhodes).

By the time Homer wrote the *Odyssey* (ca. early 7th century BCE) he could argue that the occupants of Crete's ninety cities were truly multicultural and multilingual: 'there are Achaeans, stout-hearted Eteocretans, Kydonians, Dorians with their three tribes and god-like Pelasgians' (19.175–79). The ancient geographer Strabo suggests that these subcultures achieved a spatial expression with Dorians occupying the east, Kydonians the west and the Eteocretans (i.e. the original population) the south and far east (10.4.6–7) but, as we shall see, most commentators emphasise the overriding influence of the Dorians throughout the island. Colin Renfrew (1996) has argued that Greek migration may have been divided more by social class than ethnicity. The first to come, he suggests, were an elite speaking high Greek while later arrivals were the largely male artisans, labourers and foot soldiers with a working class dialect. The sheer numbers of the second group, together with their partnerships with local women, meant that it was their language that came to supplant both Eteocretan (Linear A) and high Greek.

Myths and fallacies

As a way of sharpening the argument each of the main chapters that follows addresses one strand of conventional wisdom concerning how Crete in the period after, say, 650 BCE is usually understood and sets out a case against this interpretation drawing on existing scholarship from a range of disciplines. These conventional wisdoms may be labelled as follows:

- Myth of cultural exhaustion
- Myth of internecine strife
- Myth of frozen time
- Myth of Dorian ascendancy
- Myth of aristocratic governance
- Myth of economic subsistence
- Myth of Roman liberation

These mythologies remain powerful and with them comes a failure to appreciate just how creative Crete was in forging an identity that was justly proud not only of an illustrious Bronze Age past but also of an equally impressive Classical and Hellenistic age present.[9] As Montesquieu wrote in the *Spirit of Laws* (1794), 'when the ancients wanted to express a people that had the strongest love for their country, they always mentioned the inhabitants of Crete'. In this important sense Crete has never been simply Greek, and is not so to this day.

If Crete reached its zenith in the Middle and Late Minoan New Palace era (1650–1375 BCE) and then collapsed, its nadir is usually interpreted as lasting for at least a millennium, first through a flight to small defensive sites high on perilous,

---

9 The use of the term 'myth' in relation to Cretan prehistory may evoke in some recollections of Zeus, Minos, Theseus, Daedalus, Icarus and a large cast of lesser characters, but here the reference is to a series of common assumptions found in both scholarly and popular texts.

inaccessible outcrops and later to the larger city states that form the focal point of this book (cf. Wallace, 2010). Throughout this long period, it is the *contrast* with the earlier splendour that is the hallmark of most studies. What is termed the 'myth of cultural exhaustion' has had two misleading consequences that are discussed in Chapter 2. The first of these is a disinclination to consider cultural continuities that admittedly are hard to study, but which nonetheless can be found, even when the original 'Eteocretan' population (thought to have been the descendants of Late Bronze Age people) may have been decimated and when the island became repopulated by migrants from the mainland. The second is a failure to appreciate the astonishing creativity of the new city state civilisation that emerged from the mid–7th century onwards. This chapter documents these arguments and offers an explanation based on the almost mystical hold that a 'Minoanised' prehistory has had on what have recently been termed the 'prophets of modernism', or those who sought to (re-)construct Western intellectual and artistic endeavour in the 20th century (Gere, 2009).

The third chapter offers a critique of the paradigms that have shaped our understanding of the Hellenic world from the Archaic period until the final domination of Rome. The most powerful image here is of an all-powerful Athens presiding over an expanding empire that extended for hundreds of miles beyond the Mediterranean Sea. This was a world of almost constant warfare, either to take over and control new lands or to struggle with Sparta, the only other member of the Greek world capable of subduing the mighty city. There is plenty in the historical record to support this perspective, but it has had the unintended consequence that what was going on elsewhere is regarded as either of no importance or merely a reflection in microcosm of the Athenian story. In recent years, this paradigm has been re-examined and what has emerged is a sense that the Hellenic world was much more complex than the theory of the struggling duopoly suggests. In the Cretan case, where contact with Athens was remarkably infrequent, it suggests the need for a reassessment of the myth of warring city states, acting out on a small scale the struggles on the larger Aegean canvas. While there is no question that examples of conflict occurred, the chapter considers theories of networks and 'peer polity interaction' as coming closer to capturing the main features of Cretan life at this time.

Chapter 4 can be read alongside the more detailed site descriptions contained in the appended Gazetteer. It makes the point that the earliest and most important city states occupied remarkably similar sites and that over time, as trade links developed, those that survived created, merged with or influenced the development of smaller coastal settlements that became a network of trading posts. Ever since Homer's wonderful description of Crete as 'a rich and lovely sea-girt land, densely peopled, with ninety cities and several different languages' situated in a 'wine-dark sea', the interpretation of these independent political entities has fluctuated between the assumption that each must be different from the other to the opposite proposition, encouraged by Aristotle's discussion of *the* Cretan constitution, that all were essentially the same. Looking from the perspective of human geography, however, we have inland settlements of one kind in a characteristic setting, all of which were *poleis* or city states, and settlements of another kind on the coast, only some of which were city states but many of which came to assume a major trade-related importance. The *relationship* between these two types became one of dependency of the coastal settlements on those inland, before eventually a reversal of fortunes brought greater success for some trading ports as the original city states declined into oblivion. The myth that is opposed here is that the city states inhabited an unchanging world rather than one characterized by an evolution from being dominated by rather isolated and traditional *poleis* towards a more complex pattern of winners and losers determined by a new economic logic that depended as much upon trade as it did on subsistence agriculture.

The second half of the book examines in turn the social institutions that were created in the first type of *polis*, or city state, but whose influence continued right to the end of our period. Chapter 5 focuses on the maintenance of social order, particularly through the very early adoption of written law. Cretans appear to have been very well aware that social stability depends not so much on equality as on a clarity of *expectation*, albeit with very unequal distribution, of rewards and punishments. More important, Crete at this time was composed of numerous groups that, while not sharing kinship identities, nonetheless saw themselves as having specific cultural origins. In modern parlance, Crete was from the origins of city states, or *poleis*, in the 7th century a multi-ethnic society, or – more correctly – a series of multi-ethnic societies. The form and even some of the content of written law are seen as deriving from this fact in the sense that it was written and displayed publicly to proclaim that no one ethnic group would ever monopolise power. It may even be true that the concept of the city state itself, small enough not to make secession possible but large enough to offer the benefits of co-operation, owes it origins to the necessity of coping with the potential threat to social order stemming from internal conflict between ethnic segments. The contrast with ancient Athens is instructive and important since in this case an alternative strategy was adopted in which individual loyalties to a common culture superseded early ethnic identities. This has led some to conclude that ancient Athens from the fifth century onwards was more an early form of nation state than a *polis*.

This approach differs from the very common view that Crete throughout the whole period under discussion was dominated by the 'Dorians'. The usual assessment of the Dorian influence contains a powerful paradox, possibly derived from the perennial struggles between 'Dorian' Sparta and 'Ionic' Athens. On the one hand, Dorian art and architecture are considered one of the main ingredients of the classical tradition, melding with the Ionic to form a unique synthesis (e.g. the simplicity and strength of the 'Doric' column contrasting with the grace and flourishes of the Ionic); on the other hand, in Sparta and Crete this artistic creativity is usually said to have been abandoned in favour of an arid militarism, because of a need to maintain supremacy over others. The argument here questions this paradox, at least as far as Crete is concerned, seeing in the island's later developments an emerging mercantilism more along the lines of the 'Dorian' cities of Corinth, Rhodes and Argos. More important, the chapter questions the proposition of the 'Dorian ascendancy', seeing in the evidence more support for the idea of a society comprised of communities with a more fluid social composition.

Chapter 6 focuses more specifically on the governance of the Cretan *poleis*, siding with those who, from Aristotle onwards, have preferred to accept that all or most adopted a set of political institutions that was recognisably 'Cretan'. Evidence from early inscriptions that appears to be concerned with the avoidance of tyranny is examined afresh and is seen as a way of avoiding the permanent dominance of one ethnic group over others, even where they may have been demographically and militarily superior. The forms of representation that emerged could in some senses be termed 'democratic' in that periods of office-holding were highly constrained, and those who assumed political roles were accountable to the body of male citizens. The proposition that forms of democracy emerged in the Hellenic world in a number of city states before Athens is no longer innovative. What is perhaps less well appreciated is that Crete should be bracketed with those elsewhere that have been recognised in this regard. More important is the suggestion that the particular *form* of democracy was both unusual and very different from that in Athens. The argument is that in both settings a form of democratic accountability evolved that reflected the tensions that lay beneath the surface. In Athens, these were largely the ever-present threat of a tyrannical aristocrat while in Crete, by contrast, the political system was designed to avoid the domination of one traditional *phyle* over all others.

Chapter 7 follows this logic and links back to the description of the Cretan *poleis*, identifying economic factors as having been instrumental in creating the ports that grew up in the period after 400 BCE and which ultimately surpassed their progenitors in importance. The discussion focuses on the early adoption of coinage but, more important, on the manner in which this was married to private property and the generation of a culture of acquisition. This took form in the shape of a very early monetary *system*. The argument is clarified by reference to the literature on political economy, rather than that which defines coinage as merely a convenient medium of exchange. While this is a topic on which the existing research on Crete is woefully thin, there are indications that economic development, particularly from the 4th century onwards, occurred within a framework of rules and institutions specifically designed to promote it. Despite the reliance of ancient Athens on trade in grain for its very survival, the comparison with Crete is again instructive, for arguably the former travelled less far down the road to a capitalist economy than the latter. As a result, it is a fallacy to regard Crete as an impoverished island by the late Hellenistic period; rather, it was moving towards assuming a role for which it was so suited by its geographical location at the cross-roads of burgeoning trade at almost all points of the compass.

If the previous argument has any validity, it is not possible to accept the usual conclusion that the Roman conquest of Crete was a by-product of a campaign to rid the eastern Mediterranean of piracy, and that it provided an opportunity to replace self-sufficiency and agrarian poverty with access to a great trading empire. Chapter 8 takes the opposite view, arguing that it was precisely the burgeoning wealth of Crete that made it such a prize for Rome's legions and that – far from benefiting – the island was reduced to the familiar role of serving someone else's economic needs. This chapter concludes with a very brief summary of the struggle by Cretans over two thousand years to rid themselves of these burdens.

Finally, in Chapter 9 an attempt is made to consider ancient Crete's achievements in the context of the modern world. It is certainly true that if one wished to trace *direct* connections to more recent debates on the rule of law, on forms of democratic accountability in multi-ethnic settings and on private property and personal acquisitiveness, then Crete would not provide much source material. The Roman conquest opened up a period of foreign control as a result of which the promise of Crete's early creativity was well and truly lost. That does not, however, make it irrelevant to today's world. The lessons that economic progress cannot be imposed from outside, that it can never succeed without accommodating ethnic divisions (where they exist) in some form of power sharing, and that all must be enmeshed in an agreed framework of rules, are not trivial. They may not be quite the same as those that flow from the individualistic cultures of Northern Europe and North America, but that does make them any less salient to the challenges of the 21st century. None of this gainsays the immense cultural chasm between the peoples of Crete in the period under consideration and today's world.

The point of the comparison with ancient Athens and elsewhere may now become clear. All societies from the simplest to the most complex face three challenges of overriding importance. They face the problem of social order and stability, the problem of direction, leadership and administration, and the problem of material survival. Ancient Athens solved these problems in one way, the *poleis* of ancient Crete in another. It is not a question of judging whether one set of answers was more or less 'right' or even more successful than the other. Rather, the purpose is to document the differences although – more contentiously – this study does argue that anyone looking from the vantage point of today's world at how these issues were resolved in the past ought not to ignore the evidence from ancient Crete, although, as far as *material* culture is concerned that evidence is not always very obvious.

Anyone visiting many of the sites included here is likely to be struck by the paucity of the remains when compared with either the Minoan sites or those from the Classical and Hellenistic eras in, say, Athens, Corinth, Thebes and Syracuse. The most obvious reason for this is the very patchy exposure of the sites to modern archaeology. Much remains hidden because it has never been systematically explored. This is very obvious in sites that are exceptions to this rule, such as Lato, but even where recent exploration has occurred, it has tended to be partial, exploring one or two features such as the necropolis at Itanos or the harbour at Phalasarna. That said, the poor state of much that remains is also the result of other factors. For the sake of convenience, we might term these 'early', 'systematic' and 'casual'.

Early destruction of ancient Cretan cities has arisen as a result of both nature and human endeavour. Regarding the former, far more important than the effects of sun, wind and rain is the propensity in Crete for major tectonic activity. Undoubtedly many Minoan buildings were destroyed by earthquake and the same must be true for later buildings as well. Crete lies on the Aegean Sea Plate that is moving more or less south-westerly, forcing down as it does so the African Plate that is moving gradually north. The boundary between them is the Hellenic Arc that ends off the eastern coast of Crete. The result is periodic exposure to major tectonic movement. No one can be quite sure what the intensity was of the quake of 226 BCE that toppled the Colossus of Rhodes, or even those of AD 66 or AD 365. Of these the former may have produced subsidence of up to 25cm in western Crete while the latter produced a dramatic uplift and one of the largest tsunami ever known (Papadopoulos et al. 2010).[10] Like that of AD 365, the earthquake of 1303 is thought to have been in the region of 8 in magnitude; the latter is recorded as devastating Herakleion with great destruction to buildings and loss of life. Similarly in 1810, where the epicentre lay to the north-east of Crete, the tectonic movement and subsequent tsunami again caused major damage in Herakleion and probably throughout the island.[11]

It is equally clear that the burning and sacking of buildings after a siege was another early cause of destructions. The Romans, for example, sacked Phalasarna, Kydonia, Knosos, Hierapytna and probably many other cities. Internal wars would have also taken their toll, but in many of these cases (e.g. Lyktos), cities were rebuilt unless their lands were absorbed into those of others (e.g. Hierapytna's destruction of Praisos in the early 140s BCE and the earlier conquest and division of Rhaukos). It is hard to estimate how much physical destruction was caused by these events, but they may not have been as significant as the taking of treasures (including statues, monuments and inscriptions) by foreign powers, or by the actions of domestic institutions such as churches and monasteries. Examples of the former abound in the report on the many ancient theatres of Crete by Onorio Belli, written at the end of the 16th century. Writing of the smaller theatre at Hierapytna, for example, he comments on the 'exquisite workmanship' of the capitals and entablatures of the building and how many had been removed to Venice by the Proveditor-General (Governor under Venetian rule) (Falkener, 1854: 12). He records 'statues of great beauty' being looted in the same way from Lyktos, while at Knosos, which at that time showed the remains of its Classical walls of four miles in circumference, 'many fine and perfect statues' also ended up in Venice (Falkener, 1854: 17; 24).

---

10 Studies recently completed at Balos, north of Phalasarna, suggest that boulders of 67 and 75 tons respectively were lifted up to 25m above sea level, possibly by the AD 365 tsunami (Papadopoulos et al. 2010: 4).

11 Other dates where earthquake damage is recorded on Crete include AD 1494, 1612, 1681, 1741, 1843, 1846, 1856 and 1870.

Perhaps of even greater destructive power were the local institutions, in particular monasteries and churches. Lumps of entablature and other structural features can be seen incorporated in the walls of churches at Lisos, Polyrrhenia, Lyktos and at numerous other sites. Federico Halbherr, writing about the site of Itanos at the end of the 19th century, refers to the monks of the Toplu monastery levelling the ground and retrieving building stone without regard for the ancient city. As he puts it, 'even here, although at some distance from any village, the work of slow destruction goes on, thus rooting up the last remnants of a city which, from its position, must have held an important place in the history of Cretan civilization' (1891: 242). To this seeming disregard for posterity must be added casual destruction wrought, particularly where villages are close to ancient sites, by villagers seeking building stone or clearing land for farming. It is no exaggeration to say that anyone with an interest in the above-ground fabric of ancient sites needs to look very carefully at stone-built village houses nearby. If for thousands of years there has been so little official interest in preserving the remnants of Crete's independent past, it is hardly surprising that local people should show an equal lack of concern.

CHAPTER TWO

Cultural exhaustion or renaissance?

Ancient Crete from the 7th century to its losing battle with the legions of Rome between 69 and 67 BCE has not fared well from the attentions of either specialists or the public at large. Nowhere is this more evident than in the importance that is given to the sites of major settlement. A visitor to the mysterious site of the urban centre of the city state at Dreros, for example, will find a small official brown sign once there, but no indication that here were promulgated the first written laws in the Western world and arguably the first articulation of an important form of democracy (Keane, 2009: 90). Anyone arriving at the largely unexcavated site of Lyktos (or Lyttos) will find it hard to differentiate between the remains of 19th century windmills and buildings that may have housed meetings of the city's administration in accordance with what was perhaps the very earliest political constitution in the world. The visitor to ancient Aptera appears to fare rather better, but most visitors probably leave with the conviction that this impressive site, at what once was termed 'Palaiokastro' to the east of Chania, owes its construction to the Romans. Plenty of people visit the site at Gortyn and most no doubt appreciate the fragments of the 'Great Law Code' on display, but their evaluation of it as the first known attempt to promulgate systematic public law will not be aided by the brochure they receive with their ticket whose text, helpfully in Greek and other European languages, fails to mention it. In fairness it must be said that this is not a criticism of either the Greek Ministry of Culture or of the Archaeological Service of the island. Without the latter we should know far less than we do, and the former will never have the resources to do justice to the wealth of ancient material that Greece possesses. It does, however, underline the fact that Crete during this period is not seen as comparing very favourably with what went before, with what was happening elsewhere at the same time (e.g. in Classical Athens) and with what came after (e.g. Imperial Rome).

Crete is justly famous for its extraordinary Bronze Age history. Despite the impressive volume of scholarly material already available on the Minoan world, there are countless theses and scores of archaeological lifetimes still to come devoted to further exploration of its undoubted wonders. One feature that is often the focus of comment is the seemingly peaceable nature of the Cretan communities at this time. After all none of the famous sites shows much attention given to defensive architecture and for many years it was unquestioned that evidence of widespread destruction was the result of natural causes. Not so the later centuries where classical literary sources testify to continuous internecine warfare between battle-hardened troops belonging to one or other of Crete's city states (*poleis*). In some near contemporary accounts, the Cretans were not even seen as being capable of fighting with honour:

> The Cretans are irresistible, both by land and sea, when it comes to ambushes and piracy and the tricks of war, night attacks and all engagements undertaken with fraud; but when it comes to the face to face assault of phalanxes fighting on equal terms, they are base and craven-hearted.
>
> Because of their congenital greed, they are engaged in constant upheavals, private and public, and murders and civil wars (Polybius, Histories, Book 2: 319ff).

The comparison with the noble, aesthetic life in a Minoan palace is uncomfortable and Susan Alcock was right to suggest that 'the later centuries were either neglected or interpreted through the lens of that Bronze Age past' (2002: 99).

A note on historiography

Since the evidence found in Polybius becomes rather important as the argument unfolds, it is worth pausing to assess the veracity of his account. Much has recently been claimed for Polybius. He has been hailed as the first historian to move beyond the study of individual states or events and to recognise 'the transnational interconnectedness of all parts of the globe' (Inglis and Robertson, 2005: 101). Polybius, the author of forty volumes of *Histories*, large parts of which have survived, was born around 208 BCE in the Greek city of Megalopolis, home to the Achaean League on the Peloponnese. He accompanied his father Lycortas who was ambassador to Rome in 189 BCE, and from that time onwards his sympathies lay with the burgeoning hegemony of the Romans over the Greek world. Angered by the Achaean League's apparent sympathies with Macedonia, with whom the Romans were at war, he was forcibly exiled to Rome in 167, and held there for seventeen years during which time three-quarters of the *Histories* were completed. Amounting to more than four times the volume of his illustrious predecessors, Herodotus and Thucydides, his *magnum opus*, or *Universal History*, is noted both for the care and precision of its historiography, but also for its unwavering pro-Roman sympathies.[1] He was eventually employed by Rome to help supervise some of the Greek cities that survived the onslaught, and statues were raised to him in Mantinea, Tegea and Olympia as well as his home city of Megalopolis.

Given his leanings, Polybius was no lover of either democracy or of city states,

---

1 Ortega y Gasset praised him as 'the clearest head as historian ... the ancient world produced' (1995: 22; quoted in Inglis and Robertson, 2004: 176)

preferring instead a mixed form of government combining as he saw it the benefits of monarchy, aristocracy and democracy – in other words the Roman imperial system of *respublica* (Inglis and Robertson, 2006: 7).[2] Later interpretations of Polybius have wavered between seeing him either as an apologist for a brutal hegemony or as an insightful analyst of a 'globalised' world, and thus as a precursor to postmodernism (Inglis and Robertson, 2004). His views on Crete were especially harsh, although he was writing well before the Roman conquest. This may have been partly because his vision of an interconnected world applied to the Hellenised lands around the Mediterranean, whose networks had undermined the traditional autonomy of the *polis*. From this vantage point, and notwithstanding the gradual adoption of federalist thinking, Crete – with its many autonomous city states – would have looked very backward indeed.[3] In short, Polybius's opinions are of interest but they are no match for his statements of historical fact which for the most part appear to have been correct.

A backward, impoverished world?

It is not entirely clear whether the 'Mycenaean' incursions towards the end of the Bronze Age and the 'Dorian' migrations later were as distinct as is sometimes supposed, or indeed whether the difference was more one of class than of ethnicity, but nonetheless by the 8th century BCE Crete was clearly Greek. Throughout the Archaic and Classical periods, however, little mention is made of Crete in major histories even though, as later sections will show, reference is often made to the island in the writings of Plato, Aristotle and others.[4] What is clear, however, is that Crete is seen as cut-off, isolated and backward. Certainly there has never been any suggestion that culturally there was anything to compare with the achievements of Athens. On the contrary, the normal view is that Crete was more like Athens's great rival Sparta, being rather rigid, militaristic, hierarchical and ascetic.

There are relatively few studies that focus on the social structure of Archaic, Classical and Hellenistic Crete. An exception is the work of the classicist Ronald Willetts whose numerous books brought to the attention of the English-speaking world a wealth of information on ancient Crete (Willetts, 1955; 1965; 1969; 1976). Willetts argued that the citizen-elite of the Cretan *poleis* shared a common 'Dorian' ancestry derived from waves of migration from the mainland and that there was an ethnic division of labour in which the remaining population of free peasants and slaves were for the most part descendants of the Minoan and Mycenaean eras.

2 It can be argued that the Durkheimian vision of a 'society' integrating and regulating its inhabitants was based on the Platonic or Aristotelian ideal of the city state. On this reading, Polybius is again a precursor to postmodernism in looking beyond the concept of 'society' to understand the sources of social order in the whole 'inhabited world' (*oikoumene*) (Inglis and Robertson, 2004: 165).

3 As Inglis and Robertson stress, 'Greek intellectuals more and more tended to see themselves as part of a general Hellenic universe, rather than primarily as citizens of particular city-states, as had their ancestors of the classical age of the *polis*' (2005: 106).

4 For example, the only references to Crete in the *Oxford History of the Classical World* (Boardman, Griffin and Murray, 1993) are to the myths and legends of Minoan Crete.

From his earliest work onwards, Willetts concluded that Cretan city states were aristocratic and backward looking:

> During the greater part of the first millennium BCE the Dorians governed the Cretan cities. This protracted stage of Dorian aristocratic society was comparable, in several of its main features, with other parts of the Greek world, such as Sparta, which failed to achieve the democratic institutions of Athens and similar commercial city states (Willetts, 1969: 49).

Although there were no monarchies in Crete during this period, the elites were similar, he suggests, to those of the English Middle Ages living off the tithes from landless serfs.

This seemingly medieval world of tribal castes was not only conservative but unchanging. In Willetts's view 'the Cretan city states were relatively conservative and backward, economically and politically' (1969: 49). Archaeologists too have shared these negative views. John Pendlebury, for example, who is still one of the few archaeologists to have surveyed the island as a whole, suggested that by the Hellenistic period there was nothing particularly 'Cretan' about the island. As he writes in his justly famous *Archaeology of Crete*, first published in 1939, 'Crete had entered the Hellenistic *koine* and its individuality is nearly lost' (1965: 358).[5] In support of this theme he argues that much of the pottery cannot be readily distinguished from Roman wares and that as a result 'it is exceedingly difficult to place many of the sites with any certainty on one side or other of the dividing line' (1965: 354). Later archaeologists from more local traditions, such as Costis Davaras, one of the first excavators of the Minoan site at Mochlos, also see this conservatism and lack of originality as both characteristic and counterproductive. The autonomous cities of Hellenistic Crete, he suggests, 'were plagued by the irreconcilable contradictions of their social structures; resistant to all change, they became more and more at the mercy of forces they could not hope to control' (1976: 138). In this judgment Davaras is merely echoing the views of other equally well known voices. In his examination of the Geometric pottery of Crete, the Italian archaeologist Doro Levi saw in this period the end of cultural creativity. He concludes his well known evaluation of this period's pottery output by saying that by the Archaic era 'we see the last flight of imagination of the old civilization of Crete before it settles into the darkness of its exhausted, lethargic sleep' (Levi, 1945: 18).

While there have not been any overall assessments of the economies of city states in Crete, what little there has been takes the side of the debate about the ancient economy as a whole made famous by Moses Finley (1981; 1999). This is the argument, following the work of the great German sociologist Max Weber, that identifies the city states as not possessing the culture of thrift and deferment of consumption deemed necessary for the eventual emergence of the capitalist spirit.

---

5 The reference here to '*koine*' is to 'Koine Greek' (Ελληνιστική Κοινή) which was the common form of the Greek language that emerged in the eastern Mediterranean and Near East about 300 BCE as a dialect distinct from that of Attic Greek.

The eminent classicist Angelos Chaniotis, writing of Cretan city state economies, argues that they were based on mere subsistence:

> Large-scale agricultural production and manufacture connected with exports seem to have played an insignificant part in the Cretan economy of the Classical period' (1999: 182).

Thus 'the numerous communities did not participate in a unified economic system; their concern for their subsistence led inevitably to conflicts' (1999: 192). From this perspective the expansionist tendencies of the Hierapytnians in the south-east of the island, for example, who towards the close of the second century achieved a threefold increase in their territory, were not a result of market pressure to use their comparative advantage of having a well-placed port to feed overseas markets in Egypt and North Africa, but were a product of population pressures because 'they were not in a position to maintain their subsistence within their original territory' (1999: 204). In other words, the dead weight of tradition simply precluded taking advantage of trade opportunities:

> Although the strategic position of the island on the trade routes of the eastern Mediterranean increased transit trade in Hellenistic Crete, this did not substantially change the traditional social and economic order and did not set aside the traditional ideal of economic status based on land ownership; the instability and the orientation towards subsistence and not towards trade hindered the formation of a strong group of manufacturers (Chaniotis 2005: 81–82).

Piracy tends to be seen in the same light, as a way of coping with population pressures on subsistence resources, rather than as a defensive strategy for the maintenance of lucrative trade routes.

The conventional view is also that money in the modern form of coinage came late to Crete. As it was an island outside the positive influence of Athens and bogged down in the non-commercial culture of Sparta, its Doric institutions failed to rise above a Hobbesian world where life was nasty, brutish and short. Interaction between the *poleis* was based on internecine conflict while failing economies produced legions of pirates and mercenaries to bolster their empty coffers. Crete, particularly in the Hellenistic era, is seen as 'a primitive, pirate-infested, aristocratic, Dorian ghetto, with nothing to recommend it beyond its ability to produce very effective mercenaries' (de Souza, 2000: 112).[6] There is no doubt that the 'Dorian ascendancy' is regarded as the twilight of Cretan prehistory. Richard Hutchinson in his well-known survey of this period is another example. In the Classical period, he suggests, the best artists emigrated and the island 'acted mainly as a recruiting ground for bowmen and slingers for the richer cities of the mainland' (1962: 350).

---

6 This is not a view held by de Souza and others too have noted the effects of these attitudes. Gondicas (1988: I) , for example, opens her study of western Crete by saying 'Cette attitude a malheureusement conduit à une négligence quasi complète de l'étude des époques antérieures et postérieures, d'où une image erronée de l'histoire de l'île.'

Dorian Crete when compared with what had gone before was 'less cultured and comfortable, a motherland of warriors, and sometimes of pirates, rather than of artists and architects' (1962: 31). This picture is frequently contrasted with what happened after the Roman invasion when Crete is seen as able to enjoy the benefits of the stability and prosperity of the empire.

The heritage of Minoa

In understanding the heritage of the Minoan past, a distinction must be made between what that heritage meant to the population in, say, the Classical era, and what it has meant to those coming later who sought to interpret Crete's past. It is notable that the occupants of Crete themselves at this time may have recognised the significance of the island's past but saw themselves as continuing these traditions. Susan Alcock, for example, documents twelve cases in the late Classical and Hellenistic Greek world where contemporary tomb cults were found in much earlier burials, and another thirty-eight where this was probably the case. Her argument is that these were expressions of the desire to invoke the spirit of past stability in periods of tension and stress in *polis* society (Alcock, 1991: 459–60). It could also have been that Cretan citizens in these later centuries saw themselves as true inheritors of the island's creative traditions.

As far as those interpreting Cretan prehistory in later centuries are concerned, a distinction may be drawn between those writing before and after the excavations at Knosos at the end of the 19th century. Earlier in that century most of the comments were very positive and focused almost entirely on the period prior to the Roman invasion. For example the entry for Crete in the 1823 edition of *Encyclopaedia Britannica* argued that the 'republic of Crete continued to flourish till the age of Julius Caesar. No other state has enjoyed so long a period of strength and grandeur'. The entry went on

> From that era to the present time, that is, for period of 1900 years, the Cretans have no longer formed a separate nation, or made any figure among the states and kingdoms of the world: their noble and ingenious manners, their arts and sciences, their valour and their virtues, are no more. They have lost these with the loss of liberty (*Encyclopaedia Britannica; Or A Dictionary of Arts, Sciences, and Miscellaneous Literature* Constable and Co, 1823: 738).

But why thereafter should the tone change so markedly? Was it simply because the discoveries of the Minoan Golden Age were simply more impressive and remarkable?

Without seeking in any way to diminish the achievements of the Cretan Bronze Age, there are a number of reasons why one unanticipated consequence of how they have been recorded has thrown the creativity of later generations into the relative shadows. First, any age requires its interpreters and champions to be fully appreciated. Where would the study of Rome be without Gibbon and what would Minoan Crete look like from the 21st century without Arthur Evans? The panoply of kings, palaces, courtiers, rituals and even the name 'Minoan' itself were interpreted through the fertile Victorian mind of Arthur Evans. Regardless of the position one takes on the strengths and weaknesses of his contribution, no one can deny that he opened up a field that has proved to be astonishingly productive. By the middle of the 15th century BCE, the 'new palace' societies were in decline and by ca. 1375 even mighty Knosos was transformed. The 'Golden Age' was over and what came next appeared to owe more to mainland influence, first Mycenaean and later Doric. The important point is perhaps that Evans and those who came immediately after him, such as John Pendlebury, created a paradigm for interpreting Cretan prehistory that inevitably cast a penumbra over the following centuries.

To understand why the interpretation of what came after the Minoan era was so negative, it is vital to appreciate how what came before was *constructed*. In recent years there has been a growing awareness in Mediterranean archaeology that the portrayal of the Aegean Bronze Age at the end of the 19th century said almost as much about its interpreters as it did about its creators (Papadopoulos, 2005; Hamilakis and Momigliano, 2006). The point has been made that Minoan archaeology, with its spectacular finds of a complex and seemingly noble civilization, creates a history 'from which modern Europeans should wish to imagine their descent' (Preziosi, 2002: 32). In this way Europeans can interpret their forebears, in peaceable, creative and co-operative communities, as illustrious pioneers of modernity (Gere, 2009). While there is no doubt that the Cretan and indeed, Greek, past has been moulded by the unseen hands of outsiders, the story is rather more complex. In contrast to the thesis of Yiannis Hamilakis (2002; Hamilakis and Momigliano, 2006) it is not so much that the 'Minoans' have been simply constructed and consumed as signifiers of modernity, but that their identity has been fashioned to fit the preoccupations of the period in which they have been discussed.

At the risk of over-simplification, it may be helpful to focus on three periods to see how the 'Minoanisation' of the present took place, since its creation in the ferment of the closing years of the 19th century. The first phase, evident at the *fin de siècle* although actually extending well into the 20th century, was the interpretation of the Cretan Bronze Age as a European civilization to match anything that could be discovered in the Valley of the Kings. The most powerful image is of the Bronze Age inhabitants of Knosos paying courtly dues to their monarch ensconced in his palace complete with its throne rooms and 'lustral basins'. But from the pens of Arthur Evans, R.C. Bosanquet and others, this was not just *any* monarchy, but one that looks today singularly Anglocentric. The opposition between this Golden Age and the barbarism of the Mycenaean and later usurpers tempted James Whitley (2006) to entitle a recent essay 'The Minoans – a Welsh Invention?' as he detected the early British protagonists drawing parallels between the events after 1450 BCE and the survival of a Celtic fringe following the Anglo-Saxon and Norman invasions.

But it was not just in archaeology that this imagery took hold. Arnold Toynbee saw the Minoans as formulating a set of religious ideas that led ultimately to Christianity. The economic historian Oswald Spengler meanwhile identified them as

early creators of a successful insular economy based on seaborne trade and therefore similar in kind to that of the British Empire (Sherrat, 2006). The 'Minoans' in
this sense were initially nationalised to become fair-skinned peoples whose culture
provided echoes of imperial might. Resistance to the idea that Crete's Bronze Age
population might have had an African or Middle Eastern origin, and the advancement of the concept of a 'thallasocracy' – or rule by those who commanded the
oceans – can be seen in this light.

The second interpretation can be found before 1918 but reached its zenith in the
inter-war years. This is the view that the 'Minoans' represented the pure efflores-
cence of a primitive cultural form. 'Primitivism' is not a reference to its simplicity
or lack of sophistication but rather to something primordial and essentialist. In this
reading Minoan civilisation reveals elements that come before the Fall, whether
this is seen in religious terms, or simply from the complexities and confusions of
industrialism. In art, for example, the Expressionists and Surrealists drew inspiration from the frescoes found in the rooms of the 'palace' at Knosos and elsewhere
(particularly Agia Triada and Amnisos) or from the figurines (such as Cycladic
heads) and images of female deities. So powerful was this influence that the eye of
the so-called 'Parisien' fresco from Knosos appears familiar to any lover of Picasso's
middle years. In the workings of the mind too, the Minoans appeared to Freud
as embodying the pre-Oedipal or feminine stage of the mind's evolution.[7] Cathy
Gere (2006) has shown how Freud uses the Minoans to represent the images that
became unearthed through the inherited memories discovered in his patients
during their psychoanalytic treatment.

A third stage in the 'Minoanisation' of European identities occurred in the post-
war period. The emphasis shows a different side of the Golden Age. The central role
of woman as mother-goddess, together with the seemingly non-militaristic culture
of the Minoans, provided a perfect peg on which to hang a feminist critique of
male domination. The apparent co-operative nature of Minoan communities and
their love of nature made them a perfect point of reference for those seeking to
build a European identity out of the ashes of World War II. This narrative has not
been confined to European bureaucrats searching for an appropriate iconography
to portray an earlier age of pre-nationalism, it has also been found in academic
discourse, particularly where an attempt has been made to argue for the importance
of cultural continuities (see e.g. Kristiansen and Larsson, 2005; cf. Sjögren, 2006;
Nördquist and Whittaker, 2007).

The Greeks themselves, and particularly the Cretans, have hardly been immune
from the tendency to define the Minoans as the starting point of European
civilisation. The opening ceremony of the 2004 Olympic Games at Athens, for
example, was replete with images of Minoanised youths with bronze torsos and
maidens with characteristic ringlets and eye make-up. A pilgrimage to Knosos is a
necessity for anyone visiting Crete and the island abounds with symbols and signs

---

7   See Freud's *Moses and Monotheism* first published in 1939.

of its illustrious forebears. In this way the 'Minoans' have become 'heritaged' or constructed as noble ancestors whose way of life contains the roots of European civilisation. One consequence is a reluctance to countenance the possibility that internecine conflict may have led to the eventual collapse of this civilisation (Nafplioti, 2008). Rather, the Mycenaeans and then the rougher Dorian 'tribes' are identified as the perpetrators of this ignoble aggression.

The Cretan archaeologist Stylianos Alexiou, reflecting on 'a far-off time of peace, wisdom and wealth when King Minos held sway', sees the post-palatial era as a 'dark, almost barbaric period of sad decline, devoid of artistic achievement, in which a sub-standard culture was evolved among the struggles for power of battling antagonists' (Alexiou, n.d.: 69). If the Cretan Bronze Age contained these wonders, the Iron Age and its aftermath were constructed to fit an opposite interpretation. Even though in Greek literature connections are increasingly made between the Bronze Age and the Classical and Hellenistic era, for the most part the 'Dark Ages' represent a cultural break in which the Mycenaeans are seen as the intruders who destroyed the wonders of the Golden Age, to be followed by the more pedestrian Dorians whose mishandling of Cretan society led inevitably to the long march towards rule by external powers (Beaton, 2006; cf. Roessel, 2006).

While the emergence of a 'Minoanised paradigm' for the interpretation of the Cretan past has been a powerful influence, it cannot be the sole cause for the neglect of later centuries in more recent scholarship. Three other factors may have played some part. The first is the assumption of the Dorian ascendancy itself. Particularly to those versed in the Ionian achievements of Athens, the Dorians were associated with the isolationist, ascetic and militaristic city state of Athens's greatest enemy, Sparta. The similarity of many social institutions between Cretan *poleis* and Sparta further strengthened this assumption. Leaving aside the issue of whether Dorian migrants necessarily thought and acted like 'Spartans' – rather than, say, like their brethren in Corinth – what if the Dorian ascendancy was a myth and Crete was actually made up of many peoples; that is, much more of a melting pot than a pale copy of the hierarchical, monarchic and warring state whose cultural energies were devoted to ever greater victories on the battlefield? As later chapters will make clear, there is ample evidence to doubt both the idea of 'Dorian Crete' and the notion that even where this influence can be seen that it was a facsimile of life in Sparta.

Second, all intellectual pursuits bring to bear the insights of their methods, theories and forebears. Archaeology, which has figured so prominently in interpreting Cretan prehistory, typically uses material remains as a portal for understanding the world of those who generated them. The overwhelming richness of finds from the 'Golden Age' of Minoa, their uniqueness, beauty and craftsmanship, has provided a perfect platform for demonstrating scholarly expertise. While there has been a period of ferment within the discipline concerning how 'materiality' can be understood, it has made only a modest impact on Cretan studies.[8] Reading much

---

8 There is a new generation of archaeologists working on Crete and happily many of these are Cretan. It is

of the vast literature on Cretan archaeology, one could be forgiven for thinking that it is only through *material* culture that culture itself is possible; that however sophisticated, innovative and original the social, economic, political and eventually literary components of culture may be, they are no match for those items that can be displayed in a glass case. Classicists by comparison have been far nimbler in recording the achievements of Cretans in the periods under consideration. They have observed the prevalence of rules governing the holding of political and administrative offices; they have faithfully documented the inscriptions recording the earliest codes of law, they have noted how from the 5th century onwards fines were assessed in monetary terms and how coinage became the dominant medium of exchange. Perhaps it is not unreasonable to note, however, that with some very distinguished exceptions, they have not yet used their often precise and exacting scholarship to offer a revisionist interpretation of the period under review.

Finally, the creativity of the Cretans is easier to see if one moves beyond commonsense definitions of familiar concepts in the social, political and economic realms. If the rule of law is seen to depend upon the division between a legislature and an executive, in which judgements are handed down after pleadings by professional advocates, and with reference to a written body of statute and case law; in other words, if the rule of law can only exist within the context of Roman law, then Crete may appear to some wedded to superstition and arbitrary judgments. If 'democracy' is simply defined as citizens voting in popular plebiscites, then Classical Athens outplays anything that the Cretans produced. If a monetary system is simply defined as possessing coinage as a medium of exchange, then Crete vies with many others for the honour of having the earliest such system. On the other hand, if we are guided by modern thinking in the social sciences and we think of the rule of law in its wider social context as a means of persuasion concerned with instilling the virtues of social order, then regardless of its intellectual roots, what we know of Cretan innovation assumes a wider importance. If constitutional governance is seen as only depending in part on voting, and crucially on the institutions and rules that serve to preclude tyranny (particularly by majorities) along with corruption and disorder, then the picture again changes. If a monetary system is thought of as including the institutions, regulations and systems by which basically free markets are managed, Crete during these periods appears in a new light. The argument that follows therefore turns in part on challenging commonsense assumptions about the meaning of key concepts. When this is done, achievements of the city states appear to be the opposite of 'cultural exhaustion'; rather, what is suggested is a period of vibrancy and vigour. This also throws a different light on the eventual destruction of the Cretan city states by Roman invaders. Often seen as a blessing in disguise for releasing the Cretans from their poverty, overpopulation, piracy and warmongering, it brings us back to the views widely held in the first half of the

noteworthy, however, that even where individual scholars have been pioneers in rethinking the foundations of their discipline, it has apparently been difficult for them to incorporate new perspectives into their Cretan writings as distinct from their commentaries on theoretical and methodological innovations in general.

19th century. For example, one of the protagonists in the debate in Britain over the threat of uncontrolled population increase argued:

> We know that (Crete) did not fall by the weight of its numbers but became another victim to the insatiable cruelty and avarice of Rome, which coveted the conquest of so noble an island (Sadler, 1830: 206).

Or again, noting the same demise, the 1823 edition of the *Encyclopaedia Britannica* argued that the island's legislature 'regarding liberty as the only sure basis of a nation's happiness, had instituted a system of laws, the natural tendency of which was, to inspire men with an ardent passion for liberty, and with such virtue and valour as are necessary to support and defend it' (1823: 738).

The divisions of the period between the foundation of city states in Crete in the middle of the 7th century and the subjection of the whole island to Rome are real events of sociological significance, whereas the subdivision of the period into the Archaic, Classical and Hellenistic eras has no explanatory value. Those eras are not reflected in cultural differences, nor do they signify clear distinctions in social structure. They are, in other words, examples of what W.G. Runciman has called the 'Fallacy of Pre-emptive Periodization' (2009: 202). On the other hand, transitions do occur where structures of belief and practice change. Thus it makes sense to speak of the 'Age of the *Polis*' to signify the whole period under consideration, since this was a period of autonomous city states with similar patterns of belief and social practices that did not exist before or after. More contentiously, within this period also there are changes that are here regarded as significant but which are seldom considered important. Inward-looking, militaristic communities based upon a simple division of labour between landowners and landless labourers gradually gave way to more outward-looking, more complex societies whose division of labour now embraced a larger mercantile class that in turn was manifest in the growth of 'secondary' centres more conveniently located for seaborne trade.

The architects of the Cretan *poleis* appear to have been very well aware of the dangers of conflict for the well-being of their communities. They went to enormous trouble to avoid internal disruption and their legal and political systems must be seen in that light. As far as we know, with one or two exceptions they were singularly successful in this endeavour, and this itself suggests that they may have all approached these issues in a similar way. They were also strongly disinclined to engage in foreign adventures, even though they undoubtedly had the resources so to do. This too suggests the presence of internal social stability, since coping with perceived external threats is a tried and tested strategy for papering over splits in the social fabric. They were, however, prepared for conflict within Crete itself, and this is reflected in how their communities were organised and where indeed the major cities were located. Such conflicts did indeed emerge from time to time, but much more rarely than is commonly supposed.

CHAPTER THREE

Internecine conflict
or peer-polity networks?

If the first myth surrounding Cretan *poleis* was that of cultural exhaustion, then the second is to suggest that what energies remained were channelled into continual squabbling and warfare. It would have been remarkable if over six hundred years in an island divided into ninety or more self-governing entities, often with no marked boundaries, there were not occasions when armed struggles occurred, especially when each possessed its own militia. The prevailing view, however, of inter-*poleis* relations has focused almost entirely upon warfare and conflict. Commentators appear to have taken rather too literally Polybius who suggested that 'acts of savagery practised against each other' were 'a spectacle of everyday occurrence' in Crete (Polybius *Histories* 24.4). The myth has persisted, as can be seen in this sentence from a popular history purportedly describing the whole period from the 7th century:

> The island was paralysed by an almost permanent state of civil crisis that was to mar its fortunes throughout the years of antiquity, until the Roman conquest (Detorakis, 1994: 47).

Again in a recent study of *War in the Hellenistic World*, the island is taken as one of four major examples and the author, Angelos Chaniotis, concludes that 'war was the most important feature of Cretan everyday life' (2005a: 12).

While it *is* true that the very existence of more or less independent mini-states with no buffer space between their unfenced territories was a recipe for discord, in fact major conflicts were rather rare. Close examination shows that inter-*poleis* conflicts were of three main types. First, there were the struggles for dominance between powerful rivals, the most important of which was the almost continual skirmishes between Knosos and Gortyn which erupted in 210 BCE, again in 189 and which rumbled on, despite periods of alliance, until the Roman invasion. By far the most frequent conflicts, however, were those between neighbours. Examples would include the sacking by Knosos of Lyktos in 343 BCE and again more than a century later in the war of 221–219. Expansionist ambitions with trade in mind were probably behind the attack by Gortyn against its neighbour Phaistos (ca. 150 BCE) because the former swiftly took over the latter's port at Matala. The same may have been true for the conflict between Lato and Olous at the end of the 2nd century. More basic territorial struggles, possibly linked to expanding population pressure, lay behind the obliteration of Rhaukos by its northern and southern neighbours, Gortyn and Knosos, in 165 BCE, while a rise in economic fortunes for Hierapytna in the east may have been behind the destruction of Praisos in ca. 144 BCE and subsequent disputes with her then neighbour, Itanos, after 122 BCE (finally resolved by treaty in 112–111).

The third category of conflicts is that of occasional raids for reasons that remain unclear. One of the most (in)famous was that by Kydonia against Apollonia in 171 BCE which, though victorious, was widely condemned by classical writers. There were a number of settlements with the name 'Apollonia' and it is probably unlikely that this was the one to the west of Herakleion that may have served as the port for Tylisos. Perhaps, therefore, there were a dozen or so major outbreaks of hostility over a period of more than three centuries. To set this in perspective, this compares with the same number of wars in Europe with a smaller number of independent states in the half century *after* the Second World War (Gantzel and Schwinghammer 1999: 81). That is not to say that other conflicts did not occur, but it is to agree with Spyridakis when he complained:

> One of the many myths perpetuated by tradition and accepted with few reservations in the scholarly world is that of the anarchic state of affairs in Crete resulting from the endemic inter-city wars which supposedly plagued the islands in classical antiquity (1970: 40).

Even Angelos Chaniotis, who makes much of the conflicts that did occur and includes both internal disorder (e.g. Gortyn in ca. 220 and Phalasarna ca. 185 BCE) and the involvement of individual cities in occasional conflicts outside the island, has to admit that most so-called 'wars' were 'no more than skirmishes, sudden attacks against forts, and raids in the more or less defenseless countryside' (2005a: 12). It would be wrong therefore to assume that stability was never the norm. Indeed, the vast majority of the *poleis* described in the Gazetteer never appear in epigraphic evidence relating to the cessation of hostilities or other matters dealing with conflict. Thus, it is quite clear that for the majority of city states, whole generations would pass without ever witnessing conflicts other than periodic squabbles with neighbours.

The propagation of this myth is not without implications. Aside from diverting attention away from the many attempts at collaboration, it has two other effects. It inevitably lessens the probability that commentators will focus on what city states actually achieved, and it also precludes an analytical approach. If all that is to be said is that separate communities were in a constant state of warfare, why try to ask whether they were all pretty much the same or the opposite? In other words, the assumption of unceasing, belligerent self-interest obfuscates more than it illuminates, even as regards understanding the conflicts that did occur.

What is a city-state?

It is tempting to define the *polis* in terms commonly characteristic of the city-state, notably an autonomous entity with an urban centre and a rural hinterland. But this descriptive focus is analytically unsatisfactory for there are other examples with these characteristics that cannot usefully be defined as *poleis* and at least one (Sparta) that did not possess rural possessions typical of city states elsewhere in the Hellenic world. Garry Runciman suggests two necessary conditions that are more satisfactory. The first is that a *polis* must be juridically autonomous or hold a monopoly of the means of coercion within the territory to which its laws apply. A second feature, he suggests, is that it must be founded on the distinction between citizens, who performed the political duties and who possessed the power, and dependent non-citizens (Runciman, 1990: 348). While it is fair to regard these as necessary conditions, a *sufficient* definition of the *polis*, as distinct from city states that might exist elsewhere, cannot exclude the presence of shared activities (e.g. *symposia*) that constitute the common domain (the *koinon*) which characterises city state life (Schmitt-Pantel, 1990: 201). In the Cretan case, these would include the system of common meals (*syssitia*) and the room(s) for male citizens in which they took place (*andreion*).

It is important not to consider the *polis* in terms that derive from modern political science with their inevitable focus on equality and human rights. All city states were profoundly hierarchic since they were communities where political rights depended upon citizenship and only some adult males (*politai*) qualified as full (voting) citizens. Citizens themselves, however, could influence events in one form or another. As Ian Morris has reminded us, 'if the citizens became subjects, their community ceased to be a polis' (1991: 27). Their political role was exercised over three other main groups – their wives and children (who were also citizens), free non-citizens (*metoikoi* or sometimes *xenoi*) and a peasantry of slaves (*douloi*) and serfs. The free non-citizens were often citizens of other *poleis*, drawn towards internal migration by economic opportunities, and therefore making up an intermediate social segment from which traders were often recruited. In Crete, slaves were mostly fellow Cretans taken through the conquest of other city states and serfs were landless agricultural workers paying part of their produce as tribute to the owners of the lands they farmed. Political power was mirrored in economic power since the citizenry owned the land on which landless peasants worked whose obligations stopped in theory with the tributes they paid to land-owning citizens, although frequently they were drafted to fight in inter-*polis* wars (Willetts, 1976).

The traditional view of the Greek city state is to regard it in terms used by the French sociologist Emile Durkheim in the late 19th century as possessing social solidarity based on the similarity of its component parts. It coheres as an entity because of the equality of the citizenry (but not, of course, of the entire population), each and every one of whom is expected to participate in the organization and running of the whole (Durkheim, 1961). The 'collective consciousness' of this 'mechanical solidarity' is expressed in the sacred sphere. Religion here reflects the collective will; it evolved to articulate an ethnic identity (de Polignac, 1995). The quest for social control in city states sits comfortably with Durkheim's depiction of societies with a rather minimal division of labour. Durkheim drew a distinction between integration, or the ties between individuals and their societies, and regulation, or a society's ability to control individuality. In pre-industrial societies, with a relatively undifferentiated division of labour, powerful support for the sacred has the effect of achieving both societal goals. Individuals are tied closely to others through a dense network of beliefs and the system is controlled through support for the sacred. It is not that strong ties exist between all individuals, but rather that common social goals are firmly embedded in the minds of all so that ties are strong because of their persuasive significance, not because of their frequency or duration (Durkheim, 1961: 313; cf. Segre, 2004: 222).

While it would be wrong to conclude that the transition to a more segmented division of labour with the coming of stronger trade relations amounted to a major change when compared with modern societies, nonetheless the transition would have entailed more competitive economic relations (in Durkheim's terms changes in society's material density) and a greater likelihood of ties between one city state and the next (in Durkheim's terms greater moral density). The role of government and administration would be enhanced at this point, so that it would not be coincidental to see greater social complexity occurring at the same time as enhanced political systems. In this sense, federal ambitions (e.g. the Cretan *Koinon*) become less a defence against external threats and more an attempt to build a 'network of networks' to enhance internal cohesion at a time of greater 'material density' or social complexity (Segre, 2004: 223).

Of course, there are dangers in using the *polis* as the unit of analysis (Vlassopoulos, 2007). This is especially true if the *polis* is taken as the only focus for the *whole* of the Greek world. Within Crete, however, it became in the course of the 7th century and thereafter the dominant social and political institution. But this is not to suggest that networks below the level of the *polis* were unimportant. Indeed, the *koinonia* or association is seen even in Aristotle's day as an important part of social regulation:

> But all *koinonia* are parts, as it were, of the *koinonia* of the polis. Travellers for instance associate together for some advantage, namely to procure some of their necessary supplies. But the *politie koinonia* too, it is believed, was originally formed, and continues to be maintained, for the advantage of its members.... . Thus the other *koinonia* aim at some particular advantage; for example, sailors combine to seek the profits of seafaring in the way of trade or the like; comrades in arms the gains of warfare, their aim being either plunder or victory over the enemy, or the capture of a city.... . All these *koinonia* then appear to be parts of the *koinonia* of the polis (Aristotle *Nicomachean Ethics* 1160a.4–6 quoted in Vlassopoulos, 2007: 12).

It would be entirely within Durkheim's theory of social structure that such forms of association would become more commonplace and important for social integration and regulation as trade relations impelled a more complex division of labour.

On the other hand, Max Weber took a far more 'modern' view of the Greek city state. He was impressed by the rationality of its decision-making structures and in particular by its capacity for excluding individual tyranny or any form of hereditary power structure. These are opposed judgments, for Durkheim focuses upon the moral or normative force of the city state while Weber is interested in rational decision making in political and administrative life. Perhaps one of the most interesting theoretical contributions to date is the attempt to combine the two approaches. Oswyn Murray (1990) rejects the tribal, pre-rational notion of the *polis* based on superstition and tradition but wants to accept the Durkheimian view that its collective consciousness was critical to its survival. What he suggests is that 'the *polis* as a rational form of political organisation is the expression of the collective consciousness of the Greeks' (1990: 19). From this perspective:

> we can see how it is that the *polis* dominates religion and the family and gentile structures, rituals of death, military organization and rites of commensality; we can understand how it is that the political life of the city develops as a set of ritual practices concerned with decision-making, why tradition counts and is yet manipulated as a rational tradition (1990: 19).

In other words, Durkheim is helpful for he reminds us that political life to the Greeks was different because it was not a separate institutional sphere, but the means by which the general will was known and acted upon. In the Western world, we are familiar with another tradition where politics is the art of the possible, the craft of compromise, but for the Greeks politics was concerned with the whole, 'the community (*koinonia*) was paramount: the purpose of politics was unity not compromise' (1990: 21). On the other hand, Weber's concern for the wellspring of rationality also applies since city states used tradition to shape and achieve progress, which is one of the reasons why *stasis*, or the incapacity to generate positive change and the tendency to slump into internecine discord, was so feared. The spirit of the city state is then one where ritual, belief and knowledge of the past are constantly applied to creating a sense of purpose and evolutionary development for the future. They are not traditionalist in the sense of being conservative but rather *radical* in their pursuit of the potential contained in the beliefs of the past.

The founding of city states

It would be natural to suppose that political development in Crete and other outposts and colonies of the mainland would be derived from precedents set in the core territories. In fact, most recent scholarship has suggested that things were the other way round. As Hansen has recently written 'the *polis* arose as a *result* of colonisation' and 'it was the rise of *poleis* in the colonies that was the efficient cause of their rise in Greece proper' (Hansen, 2006: 44; emphasis in original). Although certainty is elusive, it is probable that the *polis* itself was founded in Dreros in Eastern Crete and Hansen argues that the *terminus ante quem* for this event was ca. 650 BCE (Hansen, 2006a: 41). The early development of the *polis* and its constitution in Crete is further supported by the reference in Aristotle's Second Book of the *Politics* to the Cretan *politiai*, and by Plato whose book *Laws* imagines an ideal *polis* (Magnesia) and tellingly locates it in the Mesara Plain.

Why this vital institution, which was to spread through the mainland and colonies and eventually come to number more than a thousand cases around the Aegean, or like 'frogs around a pond' in Plato's memorable phrase, should have found such fertile soil in Crete is not clear. One possibility, for which no proof is ever likely to be forthcoming, is that it was a reflection and refounding of a city-state culture from the second millennium BCE. In any event, not only did the evolution of the *polis* start early in the Cretan case, it finished late in the sense that Crete was among the last outposts of the Greek world to fall to Roman domination. This is an important point: it is possible that the achievements of Cretan city states are partly the product of time – that is, the six centuries over which they evolved – rather than deriving from causes that were uniquely Cretan.

The establishment of inland city states on their characteristic sites did not occur in a vacuum. It has a very clear and coherent history that dates back to the Late Bronze Age. What could be called the 'Early Iron Age transition' (ca. 1200–700 BCE) was triggered by the abandonment of sites made famous by their 'palatial buildings', extensive rural lands, open undefended structures and frequently seaside locations, in favour of much smaller settlements on rocky, inaccessible and seemingly inhospitable summits. These atomised communities, although often in sight of each other, must have endured great hardship and inconvenience in eking out a life for themselves in these unpromising perches. The most logical motive for making this move was to escape annihilation by an aggressive opponent (Nowicki, 2000). Other than linking this phenomenon with the clear arrival of Mycenaean cultural forms, it is not entirely clear what this massive threat must have been, although it has been observed that rather than communities being defensive against each other, the evidence supports the existence of networks of co-operation (Nowicki, 2000: 249–57). In other words the threat must have come from somewhere else, presumably the sea.

Considerable debate has taken place on whether defence was the only motivation for this major transition. It is certainly true that the collapse of the centralised societies of the Late Bronze Age might have been expected to produce an atomised reaction, but that does not explain why it should have entailed what must have been an exhausting struggle into the mountains. It is also far from clear that the Minoan world was that centralised. Recent scholarship paints a picture of nodal points with many outlying settlements (Adams, 2006). As Saro Wallace observes, this was a 'harsh compromise' between self-sufficiency and defensibility that cannot be accounted for by new farming methods, climate change or a preference for ethnic solidarity, all of which at one time or another have been proposed (2007: 256).

At least 120 'defensible sites' of this kind have been located and there may have been as many as 150, although only nine have been excavated (Desborough,

1964: 191; Nowicki, 2000: 41–223; Wallace, 2007: 256). From the 10th century these scattered small communities began a process of concentration leading to the abandonment of more than half the total as gradual nucleation occurred and denizens of these eyries began to reform in those previously inhabited sites that offered less inconvenience and greater opportunities for successful cultivation (Wallace, 2003: 256–62). In other words, by about 700 BCE the sense of threat must have changed or diminished for by this time the need was felt for new institutions that could provide specialist services and a more productive use of arable land and permanent pasture. This was the time to abandon as places of habitation those places that had made life such a struggle for survival.

The '*polis*-transition' did not, however, mean an abandonment of the small, inhospitable locations altogether, nor did it entail a return to a world where threats were so minimal that defensiveness could also be a thing of the past. The search for the ideal site for the new order was again a compromise but this time more obviously a halfway house between security and prosperity. The *polis* was born out of a perceived need to move forward economically while at the same time maintaining autonomy and strength:

> The nucleated sites developing from the tenth century onward, all originally established in the initial shift (but representing less than 50 per cent of the original foundations), seem to have been selected for continued use according to specific economic and political criteria. They are large flat-topped hills with room for expansion, and have relatively easy access to sizable extents of arable land (in contrast to many of the abandoned sites): none belongs in the most extremely defensible class of post–1200 BC settlements. New drivers of social and economic complexity were clearly coming into play (Wallace, 2007: 253).

Although it is almost impossible to be certain, Wallace puts forward the plausible proposition that the residents of the defensive sites must have felt a strong degree of regional identity which could then be mobilised as nucleation occurred in the process of polity-formation. On the other hand, and perhaps paradoxically, she also argues that the clan identities forged in the centuries of clinging to the summits may have had a role in creating the extended family bonds that were indeed a hallmark of *polis* life (Wallace, 2007: 260). More plausibly, the old refuges continued to have symbolic salience as they can be shown to have been continuously used as cult sites, cemeteries and places of celebration.

It is certainly true that *polis* sites were usually chosen to have *both* a flat area for public and private habitation spaces *and* high places for worship and sacred spaces. Less in support of Wallace, however, is the fact that wherever possible the sites were chosen to have two acropolises (Lato, Dreros, Axos, Gortyn and numerous others). One possibility is that this too reflects a longer memory. Wallace interestingly observes that some 'landmark' sites (sites on visibly prominent rocky outcrops), such as Karphi, Kophinas and Youkhtas, were all 'peak sanctuaries' in the Middle and Late Bronze Age while Monastiraki (Katalimata) and Kavousi

(Vronda) (just inland and southeast of the Bay of Mirabello in Eastern Crete) had both been used as settlements in the Middle Bronze Age (Wallace, 2007: 265–66; cf. Kyriakidis, 2005). Perhaps the 'twin acropolis' is also a reflection of the Minoan past. It was Arthur Evans who first labelled the double-peaked image, found almost as frequently as the double axe in Minoan art, as 'horns of consecration', thereby connecting this stylised representation with the bull cult. It is noticeable, however, that this image was often used in architectural settings on the roofs of buildings, and it has also been suggested that it may be a reference to the Egyptian hieroglyph for the 'horizon', to which it bears some resemblance (MacGillivray, 2000: 129). A more plausible proposition is that it symbolises a dualism inherent in sacred observance. Such dualisms are ubiquitous in both cultic and more established transcendent forms of religious observance (obvious examples would include life/death, day/night, summer/winter, light/dark, good/bad, sacred/secular etc). It is not so clear whether the so called 'peak sanctuaries' possessed any such dualism (i.e. whether they were in any way 'paired') but this is not essential to the later interpretation. Certainly, iconic images of the 'horns of consecration' and the double axe are often found together in sacred spaces (Kyriakidis, 2005: 95). The double acropolis seems so integral to *polis* site selection that it is not implausible to see it as a way of connecting the new settlements with the distant past and thereby giving the new location legitimacy and a sense of the sacred. To establish whether this line of analysis is worth pursuing, the obvious strategy would be to examine *poleis* in other environments without a Minoan prehistory.

If the defensive sites established in the Early Iron Age were created by what might be termed a 'pre-*polis* transition', then by the end of the Archaic period (ca. 500 BCE) a second major phase of change had occurred. Although the early *polis* was always located on a site of earlier settlement, by this time the *polis* proper had emerged with very characteristic features. As Aristotle put it in the *Politics:*

> It should be difficult of access to the enemy, and easy of egress to the inhabitants.
> Further, we require that the land as well as the inhabitants of whom we were just now
> speaking should be taken in at a single view, for a country which is easily seen can be
> easily protected. As to the position of the city, if we could have what we wish, it should
> be well situated in regard both to sea and land (7: 11).

It is probable that Aristotle was thinking of Cretan examples when he wrote this, for there is no doubt that the transition from the defensive sites to what we will call the 'primary *polis*' was to a location with a high degree of similar features. This does not mean that relocation and nucleation were the only processes occurring at this time. Given the steady flows of inward migration from Greek speaking peoples from the mainland, it is probable that the early *poleis* were established by a mixture of old residents and newcomers, rather than only by those in their isolated, inaccessible settlements who had survived both the hardships of their location and the threats that must have driven them there in the first place.

Towards a typology

The German sociologist Max Weber, writing in the closing decades of the nineteenth century, proposed what he termed the 'ideal type' as an aid for comparing social institutions. He did not mean the same thing as Aristotle whose concern was for the philosophical problem of what would work *best*; rather, what Weber was trying to extract was an accentuation of the defining features that were critical to the institution itself. His purpose was to aid comparison and to be concerned with the explanation of non-conformity as much as with commonality (Weber, 1949).

The architects of the first settlements, termed here 'primary *poleis*', chose the sites for their location so carefully and with such common regard for the objectives of defence, administrative coherence and social solidarity that it is possible to isolate an ideal type that powerfully reflects almost all extant remains on the ground. The ideal type might be said to embody the following features:

- A steep-sided but flat-topped hill capable of being terraced to produce flat or gently sloping ground of 15ha–80ha or possibly more
- Either a natural defensive site or one capable of improvement (fortifications etc) to become one
- All round visibility over farm lands and access routes
- Fertile farm land immediately below and around the site
- Single or preferably double peaks for accommodating sacred areas
- Sufficient building stone of suitable quality for both domestic and public buildings and for defensive walls
- Close access to fresh water
- Access to the sea no more than a day's march away
- A safe distance from the next inland *polis*, preferably a day's march or more.

The degree to which these ambitions were innovative can be seen by comparing the sites of the 'primary' city states with both the settlements of the Minoan era and those of the Early Iron Age.

The ideal type Minoan settlement would have been in a low-lying, undefended coastal location such as Palaikastro, Kato Zakros, Petras, Mochlos, Malia, Kommos, Kydonia and possibly at Maleme, west of Chania.[1] Even Knosos, Phaistos, Agia

---

1 The existence of a *tholos* tomb at Maleme, dated to LMIII, long ago suggested the existence of a Minoan settlement west of the town and east of the Tavronitis River. Despite the construction of the military airport in the 1930s, whose eastern section at least lies right over the site, there is still evidence today of this settlement. Shadows of substantial foundations can be seen from satellite imagery just south of the eastern end of the runway beneath the fill that was used to construct the flat area for the runway itself. Heavily abraded sherds, mostly from *pithoi* and cooking wares that also appear to be Late Minoan, are evident in the field area just north of this end of the military zone and 50m back from the beach. This site was well known before the military installations were constructed. A report in the *Contemporary Review* in 1907, for example, spoke of a square mile area stretching from the eastern bank of the Tavronitis River to the village of Maleme, the whole of which when tilled yielded 'ancient finds, such as ordinary antique tombs, walls, pottery fragments, porcelain phials and various small articles, some of which point

Triada and Galatas, while further inland, were in no way defensive sites, nor were they fortified. In fact, when taken in the round, the many Minoan sites at different scales of importance and function, and the absence of clear boundaries, make it extremely difficult to consider an ideal type construction of what a 'Minoan' settlement was. In a recent and very thorough synthetic overview of the North-Central area (Knosos, Malia, Galatas, Tylisos, Archanes and many smaller sites), Ellen Adams found it impossible to apply either a theory of the state or a geographical approach using central place theory to the multitude of sites that she identifies:

> The fact that central places are so difficult to identify – or to tell where they were central places of – suggests that power relations were much more complex in the Minoan world than modeling, such as central place theory, allows (Adams, 2006: 6).

For example, it is simply not clear where the boundaries of Archanes, a very substantial Minoan site, and its neighbour Knosos, only approximately an hour's walk away, were situated. Even Knosos, important as it was in cultural, administrative and ritual terms, may not have held sway politically over a territory of its own.

In the second case, the flight to the hills after the collapse of the Mycenaean palace-societies was to small locations in extraordinarily inaccessible settings (e.g. Karphi) where considerations other than defence were secondary (Nowicki, 2000; Wallace, 2003; 2005). By contrast, the primary *polis* was based not just on the principle of survival but also on concepts of coherence and continuity. For example, *poleis* often had unoccupied areas within their fortification walls even though they may have had suburban areas or *proasteia* beyond (e.g. Aptera had eight suburbs in the Stylos valley to its south) (Hansen, 2006a). This may have been because of the need to accommodate hinterland dwellers in times of war or to allow for food production when under siege. It is likely that a combination of these reasons applied in most cases. In other words, the 'primary *polis*', although often functioning in a threatening environment, was *designed* not just for short-term survival but for long-term evolution.

The creation of the primary *polis* did not exhaust the phases of change. During the late Classical era (ca. 4th century BCE) the locus of human activity shifts again, almost certainly because of expanding trade opportunities. It is not that there were no other sites of settlements or human activity. As Lena Sjögren (2003) has shown so well, there were from the pre-*polis* era many hundreds of farmsteads, cult centres, burial grounds and other sites. What changes in this third transition is the gradual incorporation of ports into the structure of the primary *polis*. This did not necessarily proceed always in the same way. In some cases it was a question of

---

to a great antiquity' (Jannaris, 1907: 22). The same article, entitled 'Another Prehistoric City in Crete', reports on the find by the Katakis brothers in April 1906 of the large slab concealing the tholos tomb on the slopes above the main site that contained the skeletons of six individuals. Grave goods had been taken and only fragments of *pithoi* remained, but the author plausibly suggests that other Mycenaean tombs were no doubt nearby overlooking 'an important city' spreading below to the sea (1907: 23).

direct takeover (including by force), in others the creation of new entities and in others again the evolution of (usually unequal) political ties circumscribed by treaty obligations. In Aristotle's terms, cities were able 'to reap the benefit of intercourse with their ports' (*Politics* 7: 11). What may have been a residual defensive strategy, namely ensuring visibility to the sea, now became an opportunity for establishing networks of trade relations that had existed only in the Late Bronze Age before.

This third transition was not simply a geographical issue. It was accompanied, and perhaps in part caused, by changes in the division of labour. In the primary *polis* era the peasant, for example, would pay his dues directly to the citizen, but by the 1st century BCE at the latest, and in Crete probably much earlier, the dues were owed by all to the institutions of governance and not to individual citizens (Morris, 1991: 27). As Robin Osborne has also pointed out, as the 'new' *polis* evolved there was a demand for cash, and market relations themselves were clearly entailed in sustaining both the move to greater complexity and higher levels of connectedness (Osborne, 1991: 137).

In using the terms 'primary' and 'secondary' there is no intention of entering another debate that uses similar nomenclature. The concept of 'primary' and 'secondary' state formation, for example, has a considerable history in the study of Aegean societies, but this debate revolves essentially around *external* connections between Minoan and Mycenaean societies and the wider Mediterranean (Parkinson and Galaty, 2007: 118). Thus using the term 'primary' does not suggest that *polis* evolution had any particular impact on mainland Greece or the other way round, although network theory would suggest that both were possible. On the other hand, this debate is not entirely irrelevant. The use of the ideal type concept, whose major purpose is to permit categorisation and therefore commonalities, immediately highlights cases that fall outside the 'primary' versus 'secondary' distinction. That is, there are cases of *poleis* that are like 'primary' city states in terms of power and influence, but are not located on inland sites. These are ports, but unusually ones that lack relations of dependency on 'primary' city states. For this reason they are termed 'independent *poleis*', although this is not meant to imply that that they are without any ties of dependency. The point is that they are not owned or controlled *internally*, which means in turn that they came to possess properties that others did not. These 'independent *poleis*' were central to a network of contacts that were external, and their form and function came to be determined by this fact.

Space and social networks

We now turn to how we can understand the *spatial* distribution of city states in both the earlier and later periods. One classical perspective can loosely be called 'central place' theory and is a product of straightforward geographical mapping exercises in which nodal points are identified, their sizes measured and their importance in terms of transport links or trade routes assessed (Christaller, 1935; Wagstaff, 1987). Although based on a series of rather untenable assumptions, these perspectives lend themselves well to systems approaches since they readily allow mapping techniques showing the flow of goods and services, and the feedback effects that sometimes occur as functional specialisations arise over time. Models such as this are also readily adaptable to the cultural sphere and are the (often implicit) idea behind notions of cultural diffusion or the spread of ideas over time.

The critique of this perspective, developed in the late 1960s and 1970s, was derived from a more radical tradition in which what mattered more was not the existence of nodal points in space but the *nature of the relationship* between them. In particular the flow of goods, services and ideas was not equal; rather it was fundamentally altered by the differences of power between one node and the next. Thus the 'core-periphery' models of the so-called 'New Geography' suggested that nodal points were not simply of differing size and structure, they were also related by domination and dependence (Harvey, 1973; 1996). Such ideas led within nation states to the concept of 'global cities' (Sassen, 1991; Castells, 1983) and between them to 'world systems' theories, associated with the writings of Immanuel Wallerstein (Chase-Dunn and Hall, 1997; Wallerstein, 1974).

Archaeologists, particularly those of a more analytic bent, responded initially to these perspectives in two ways (Clarke, 1968, 1977). First, they adopted some of the central ideas, which led to some important revisions in the understanding of areas like the Mediterranean basin. Concepts of diffusion were replaced by a firmer grasp of the *politics* of space and, in particular, by a reassessment of the importance of imperial Rome (Peregrine, 1996; Stein, 1998). Aegeanists, whose focus lay in the pre-Roman era, were generally less persuaded by ideas of core-periphery, but they did tend to accept the importance of a more holistic perspective than the site-by-site investigations that had gone before (Kardulias, 1999; McGuire, 1996). There is no evidence to suggest that Crete in the Classical and Hellenistic eras felt in any way subservient to Athens, and for this reason core-periphery models, which stress bilateral relations of hierarchical control, are not as relevant as more 'globalised' models of multi-directional networks. On the other hand, *internally* the focus on inequalities of power and influence is salient for it permits an appreciation of how primary city states evolved from subsistence autonomy to trade-based economic surplus. Establishing coastal dependencies was part of that transition that in some cases led to the abandonment of inland sites.

More recent contributions to ancient history, however, have gone down the road of emphasising multi-directional networks. Horden and Purcell (2000), for example, reject the idea of focusing on the component parts of the Mediterranean region, preferring instead to stress the 'connectedness' of the totality (cf. Harris, 2005). In this approach an appreciation of human history cannot be divorced from the sea, coastlines, plains and mountains. This is a systemic view, in which the totality is viewed as an organic whole. It is perhaps a modern interpretation of the perspective that informed Braudel's classic study *La Méditerranée et le Monde Méditerranéen – l'époque de Philippe II* (1949) that in turn informed the world systems perspective. For Braudel, the unity of space is paralleled by the complexities of time. Everyday events, and even processes in the medium term, are less important than the *longue durée*, or the slow evolution of historical time fashioned by the interaction between socio-economic forces on the one hand and the environment on the other. City states (and later nation states) figure prominently in the *longue durée* since they are the focal points in the cycles of evolutionary change. This is history far removed from the antics of kings and generals; indeed, when considering the human component, Braudel focuses specifically on the daily lives of the working poor and dispossessed rather than members of elites.

Influenced by Braudel, the idea of utilising the Mediterranean as a whole has a particular appeal in the age of globalisation. The 'connectivity' of the Mediterranean can be seen in a distinctive 'regime of risk', a characteristic logic of production, an extreme topographical fragmentation and special forms of communication (Horden and Purcell, 2000; 2005). This idea differs markedly from core-periphery models precisely because there is no core, and therefore no periphery. Unlike the Finley approach, in which localism is stressed, the issue now is to create a macro-level paradigm in which the outer areas help create the whole; in other words they are not peripheral. Thus, for example, the role of the Delphic Oracle in creating a Greek identity is precisely through the *relationships* created with the geographically dispersed *poleis*. In this context, we should expect similarities of form and well-developed networks of communication. The concept of 'network', which was originally used heuristically to grasp the subtleties of 'pan-Hellenism', works equally well in approaching the relationship between primary settlements *within* one territory, or even between primary and secondary nuclei (Malkin, 2003: 56).

A theoretical concept from archaeology that also tries to move beyond the idea of atomised city-states enmeshed in a Hobbesian struggle for dominance and survival offers another perspective within this tradition. As long ago as 1986, Colin Renfrew and John Cherry first put forward the concept of 'peer-polity interaction' (1986) to focus attention on real and symbolic exchanges between polities in a more or less equal relationship, rather than relations of domination. These interactions, curiously including warfare and competition, also cover emulation, trade in commodities, transmission of innovations and symbolic exchanges, including language and ethnic identity. What those writers proposed was that the manner in which city states changed over time could not be appreciated without recognising their interactions with each other. Whether this was by treaty, by trade or by exchanges of population, such 'peer-polity interactions' (PPI) were central to the way in which the residents of the city state saw themselves and others. This was not just a question of exchanges between more or less equals; rather, it shaped memory and the cognitive map of territory. It is at first puzzling to note that warfare was included within the range of PPI, but when appreciated as a cognitive process this seems acceptable, since conflict clearly affects how others are understood. Within the Hellenistic world, peer-polity involvements were often at their strongest in mediation efforts between warring city states, but violence imprints itself powerfully upon memory (Ma, 2003).

Peer-polity interaction has proved a more powerful concept with ancient historians than with archaeologists, at least as far as the Aegean is concerned. One important point that has emerged is that the strength of horizontal ties, even where relatively weak, is not unrelated to issues of power discrepancy (Granovetter, 1973; 1983). As John Ma (2003: 30) has shown, peer-polity interactions are strengthened in a world where there are perceptions of external threats from others more powerful still, or where it is necessary to control the aspirations of potential tyrants within the *polis*. On the second issue he says that 'cities collaborated in creating a context of civic culture and locally meaningful honours, within which they could locate the identities of individual big men, and hopefully constrain them' (Ma, 2003: 33). It is normally claimed that Classical and Hellenistic Crete was made up of small autonomous aristocracies (Willetts, 1955). The available evidence does suggest that each *polis* contained quite clear divisions of wealth, political power and social esteem. It does not follow, however, that these divisions were the most salient in terms of social structure. Bonds of civic culture, even between entities that regarded themselves as autonomous and ethnically different from their neighbours, may well have been of greater significance. Moreover, this perspective might help us understand why the period under discussion saw a greater move towards *koinon* or collective and mutually supportive institutions. The threat from Rome was known about for at least a century before it became realised, and this itself would have had profound effects on network ties. When the final battles loomed, it was the 'Cretans' that the legions faced, not the citizens of one or other *polis*. In other words, the drift towards stronger peer-polity networks is not unrelated to a growing awareness of the wider world (cf. Karafotias, 1997).

One of the great strengths of a network approach is to make one aware of the levels of consciousness that are engendered as more complex social interactions occur. Individuals from different *poleis* may through trade relations come to comprehend their worlds in what have been called 'tripartite terms' – divided between where they live, within the Aegean and within the Mediterranean (Malkin et al., 2007: 1). It is particularly important to note that moving away from static structural approaches towards social networks permits a greater focus on major transitions. In this sense the establishing of a port opens up a conversation with other ports, with a result that will affect both.

If the 'new geography' brought the concept of power onto the spatial agenda, then the 'new archaeology' tended to remove it again in favour of an examination of what 'space' actually meant. Under the influence of a postprocessual rethink into intersubjectivity, it became more widely appreciated that space is not merely a geometric phenomenon (i.e. a synonym for distance). Space in these approaches is socially constructed and, in an important sense, relative to time, or times (Thrift, 1996; 2006). The idea that how something as seemingly fixed as location is actually mediated by changing interpretations of where individuals think of themselves and who they are relative to others, immediately brings on to the agenda a sense of 'place' and a sense of identity (Hetherington, 1996; cf. Lefebvre, 1991). For the archaeologist this means that landscape matters because it embodies *where* we are relative to others; similarly, how identity is proclaimed matters because it embodies *who* we are relative to others (Tilley, 1994, 2006). A visitor to any of the 'primary *polis*' sites discussed in the next chapter and described in the Gazetteer cannot avoid thinking about how these are connected. No one living behind the walls of, say, Aptera or Lato, overlooking their lands below that provided them with the means of survival, could avoid thinking of themselves as anything but members of these communities, regardless of whether they were rich or poor, landed or dependent upon others.

The other side of this phenomenon is also important. Firm identities of place are paralleled by equally secure notions of 'otherness'. In other words, it is important to focus both on nodal points in a spatial network and on the qualities of the relations between them. In the study of the Bronze Age Aegean, this perspective has been used to provide a new understanding of 'Minoanization' or the spread from Crete of typically Minoan cultural and material forms (Broodbank, 2000). Rather than a diffusionist model in which ideas and innovations are seen as spreading like a ripple on water, this approach allows an assessment to be made of the differential impact of relationships themselves (Evans et al., 2006; Evans et al., 2007). Since the network model can be constructed using quantitative variables, the effects of particular changes in the strength of relationships (e.g. the impact of the destruction of Akrotiri following the Thera eruption) can be identified, as can the centrality of particular sites (e.g. Knosos) (Knappett and Nikolakopoulou, 2005). Another example of even greater relevance is that of the two most powerful *poleis* in Crete, Knosos and Gortyn. They are normally seen as engaged in interminable squabbles for island-wide supremacy, but in fact each may have been struggling to promote alternative models of inter-*poleis* networks with the former favouring an integrationist strategy while the latter preferred a more open, federal structure (van Effenterre, 1948). These images of 'otherness' have repercussions more widely. Just as in the modern world, where there is a connection on the part of the United Kingdom between European integration as a loose union and ties to North America, so too there was a greater readiness by Gortyn to countenance strong links with the regional superpower of Rome.

The question arises, where does this discussion takes us in formulating an approach to analysing the distribution and role of city states? The first point to recognise is that central place theory is not without relevance. The perspective predicts that nodal points with the same status will tend to be distributed rather evenly, with larger centres further apart than those of a lower order. It also serves as a reminder that economic linkages are normally fundamental in networks. On the other hand, the theory is static and in an important sense unreal, since it takes no account of topography, which is an issue of major importance in a mountainous island such as Crete. What is useful, however, is the implication that there may be a *pattern* to settlement distributions and that economic and trade questions can help determine the categories into which city states fall.

Two other conclusions are relevant. First, the 'peer-polity' approach has much to commend it as a way of underlining the potential for networks to emerge from autonomous political units. Certainly, power relations both within and between city states are important, but the point is that the ancient Mediterranean prior to the Roman imperial presence cannot be said to have had a *centre* to which other sites could be 'peripheral' (Horden and Purcell, 2000). In fact, the 'peer-polity' perspective is not incompatible with Central Place Theory since one lays out a pattern and the other focuses upon how component parts relate to each other, and both do so at a middle-range level (i.e. one that is in principle capable of testing alternative hypotheses). Kosso and Kosso in their application of both Central Place Theory and the peer-polity perspective to Minoan Crete make the point that the former has a descriptive role since 'the archaeologist's project is to show interaction among states, and this requires as preliminary information a picture of where the states are and that they are distinct' (Kosso and Kosso, 1995: 586). The role of the peer-polity perspective enters the picture when we move from description to *explaining* patterns of interaction. Then the central question is, given that there are polities, how do they interact? (Kosso and Kosso, 1995: 593). In the past the answer has tended to be that the interactions were basically hostile. Indeed, there is powerful evidence to suggest that citizens of city states thought that this was highly probable. The reality, however, is that serious hostilities were rather rare, especially given the number of autonomous actors, their contiguous boundaries and ever-present rivalries. A whole series of outcomes may flow from this perception and reality, ranging from the famed rise of the Cretan mercenary soldier under contract to an overseas power to the greater likelihood that those on the 'realist' side of the question would want to branch out into wage labour rather than continue to worry overly about the state of their battledress. These two examples are possibly linked as overseas experience and capital become resources for a new breed of traders (Tandy, 1997).

The second point is that the peer-polity perspective was developed to examine socio-political *change*. As relational theory suggests, network relations must be considered temporally. Moreover, while this may not be apparent from *relations* themselves, if change is apparent this provides a link with institutional analysis. In other words, we may see *how* change occurs through spatial analysis but have to look inside city states themselves to understand *why* it emerges. What the foregoing suggests therefore is a focus on a typology of nodal points, a concern for the pattern of the interactions between them, together with a realisation of how these may change over time. Given (as far as we know) similarities in the populations and the environments they inhabited, it would be puzzling if the cultural traits that city states came to manifest differed greatly from each other. This in turn makes it likely that as ways of thinking become transformed into ways of being, all 'social spaces' will manifest adaptive variations around a common set of institutional practices. In this sense it is not just 'polities' that are 'peer' but also institutions dealing with modes of persuasion and material acquisition. In other words, what would really be surprising is not similarity but major difference.

What emerges from the attempt to link the institution of the *polis* with its spatial distribution is that change was endemic and endogenous. All societies face three problems of survival. They have to generate solidarity and social cohesion through persuasion; they have to establish security, order and direction through a political mechanism; and they have to survive in material terms. The quest for equity, order and income helps frame our understanding of the ancient city states as they evolved from a rather arid militarism to a richer preoccupation with making networks work in terms of generating greater wealth. It is not a question of the primacy of one of these 'three dimensions of social space', but rather of understanding how all three co-exist and co-evolve (Runciman, 2009: 152). Therefore, in choosing to select how the *polis* tackled the problems of order and persuasion first, there is no suggestion intended that modes of acquisition and coercion were somehow later in emerging. Nothing could be further from the truth: the early *polis* had a very characteristic way of solving the problem of material survival, and an equally typical leadership structure based initially on establishing the principle of autonomy. Internal cultural complexity, however, appears to have posed at least as large a 'coercive problem' as upholding independence. Similarly, placing the mode of acquisition as third in line for detailed discussion does not signify a wish to downgrade its importance. On the contrary, changes in the mode of production and acquisition transform both the social and spatial dynamic to the point where the traditional *polis* is itself largely superseded by the time the Romans arrive to cash in on the prosperity to which these changes had given rise. But before considering that we must examine in greater detail the settlements themselves and the way they evolved over six centuries.

CHAPTER FOUR

Frozen in time or an evolutionary transformation?

While it is an exaggeration to suggest that commentators have assumed an absence of evolution in ancient Crete over more than five centuries, the consensus is nonetheless that change was very gradual. Indeed, for some it is precisely the 'conservative and backward' nature of the Cretan *poleis* that appealed to Plato and Aristotle, dismayed as they were by the vicissitudes of Athenian democracy (Willetts, 1969: 49). As others have noted 'there remains a readiness to recognize continuities in Cretan life, to expect conservatism in Cretan behaviour', and nowhere is this more true than in the belief that the institutions moulding and shaping that behaviour, the *poleis*, were themselves resistant to change (Alcock, 2002: 100).

As a precursor to what later became called the 'nation state', the single most important defining characteristic of the city state was its autonomy from others. But that is not the same as saying that each was unique. On the contrary, they shared many features and in the Cretan case, the argument has been advanced in the previous chapter that they could be divided into three broad types. The first was the *polis* proper while the second was a more dependent type of settlement, usually established after the passing of some centuries, which became ever more tightly bonded to one or other of the founding city states. The third category contained a small number of *poleis* as powerful as many members of the first group but nonetheless sharing with members of the second type port functions and an external orientation. The previous discussion of network theory has also suggested that while autonomy for 'primary city states' would always be central, we should be alive to the possibilities of 'peer-polity' interactions; in other words that we can draw a distinction between bonds of equivalence and bonds of dependence, according to which type of relationship we seek to understand.

This chapter is concerned with whether the proposed classification makes sense of what we know about where the bulk of the population of Crete was located during the six centuries before the Roman invasion. The classification is based upon the concept of the 'ideal type'. It was never intended that this would describe an empirical reality, but rather that it would enable distinctions to be drawn, whose features would themselves be reflected in the real world. It is therefore appropriate to ask whether this is true or not, as far as we can tell from the evidence available to us. Another central implication of this approach is to focus attention on those instances that fall *outside* the classification, for this may point to historical differences of potential importance.

Hansen's recent studies on the size of all city states throughout the Hellenic world suggest that the vast majority were rather small, with four-fifths controlling a territory of 200km² or less (Hansen, 2006b: 29). Hansen uses what he calls a 'shotgun approach' to estimate total population sizes on the basis of the density in the known urban core and the rural hinterland. With this approach, approximate population sizes can be deduced for each of five categories of *poleis*. These results are shown in Table 4.1.

TABLE 4.1   Estimated Population sizes of *poleis* from territorial extent

Area (hectares)		Population		
		urban	*hinterland*	*total*
Type 1	<2,500	600	300	900
Type 2	2,500–10,000	2,025	1,010	3,035
Type 3	10,000–20,000	3,675	1,840	5,515
Type 4	20,000–50,000	7,725	7,725	15,450
Type 5	> 50,000	9,100	18,200	27,300

Source: Adapted from Hansen (2006b: 24).

Overall only 10 per cent of the known *poleis* exceeded 50,000 hectares but they contained 40 per cent of the population. Translated into the Cretan case, only Knosos and Gortyn might have been Type 5 *poleis*, and possibly only the latter, after it had taken over some adjacent communities. It is probable that most primary *poleis* fell into types 3 and 4. For example, Lato, a primary *polis* of considerable importance at an elevation of more than 300m overlooking the Bay of Mirabello in eastern Crete, was described in inscriptions in the 2nd century BCE as possessing lands whose circumference was approximately 66km. This might therefore equate to a territory at the lower end of type 4 and a total population of perhaps 10,000 or more, of which maybe half lived within the walls of the urban centre. Simply on grounds of apparent importance and topography, other primary *poleis* in Crete falling into this size category may have included Aptera, Arkades, Axos, Dreros, Eleutherna, Lappa, Lyktos, Phaistos, Polyrrhenia, Praisos and Sybrita or twelve (43 per cent of the total discussed here) with perhaps two being larger and the remaining fourteen possessing territories below 20,000 ha.[1] When secondary settlements are considered in size terms, the estimates are much harder. We know

1 These locations do not exhaust the total number of primary city states (Perlman, 2004a). See the Gazetteer for further details and for an explanation of why others have not been included.

rather less about them, they appear to be more diverse and they changed in size rather rapidly in both directions. Most probably fell into Hansen's Types 1 and 2, with only Itanos and Phalasarna likely to have been larger in the Classical era, but later joined by Hierapytna and Kydonia (Type 3 and above). Indeed, these four, all of which may have been founded as what we are terming 'secondary' settlements, soon outgrew this categorisation, so that over time a third type emerged that are referred to as 'independent *poleis*'.

The primary poleis

The 'primary *poleis*' share many features in common besides the standard requirement for an urban core and a rural hinterland. Their location had to be well separated from their neighbouring city states, while the site of the urban centre had to oversee and control its agricultural lands. Above all it had to be secure from both belligerent neighbours and overseas invaders. The setting itself was especially important. There had to be places for the gods to dwell, well above the fray of everyday life, and there had to be space for public buildings, meeting places and domestic households arranged in such a manner that they engendered a sense of security and social solidarity. More practical considerations too were important, particularly the availability of building stone and fresh water.

As Paula Perlman (2004a) makes clear, we can never be entirely certain about the number of *poleis* that existed in Crete during the period of her main focus (the Archaic) or later. Some city states appear to have been overrun by others and new ones may have been formed. We know a number of toponyms so far unattached to particular sites and, of course, the other way round. How much more difficult, therefore, to attempt a subdivision of those we do know. And yet any visitor to those sites where we do have a reasonable knowledge of their original name, and which are located away from the sea, will be struck by a number of overwhelming similarities. These have been summarised in the characterisation of the 'primary *polis*' contained in Chapter 3. Table 4.2 lists them in alphabetical order along with some of these characteristic features.[2] The table includes an estimate of the size of the urban area, an indication as to whether it was founded before 500 BCE and its period of later occupation up to 67 BCE, the elevation of the highest point of the site above sea level, the approximate sight line from the same point and the straight line distance to the next *polis*.

There are three main points to be made. First, most of these sites date from the Archaic period or before. Those that appear to belong to a later period *may* have existed earlier but further exploration will be required before this can be ascertained with certainty. Second, nearly all are at a considerable elevation with clear lines of visibility over much of what can be assumed to be their original lands and, finally, they are well dispersed so that the urban core is not adjacent to that

---

2 Rather more detail on each of these locations is contained in the Gazetteer.

TABLE 4.2   Primary *poleis* and their basic characteristics

Poleis	Size[a] (ha)	Period[b]	Elevation[c] (m)	Sight line[d]	Distance[e] (km)
Anavlochos	40+	A/C	625	360	7.0
Anopolis	20 (?)	A/C/H	682	270	26.0
Aptera	>60	A/C/H	230	360	15.5
Arkades	50	A/C/H	672	360	8.0
Axos	40	A/C/H	587	360	16.5
Biannos	30–40?	A/C/H	339	200	8.0
Dreros	40	A/C/H	482	360	7.0
Eleutherna	40	A/C/H	372	270	8.0
Elyros	20	C/H	559	270	4.5
Gortyn	100+	A/C/H	220	180	12.5
Hyrtakina	40	A/C/H	907	300	4.5
Kantanos	20	A/C/H	550	190	3.5
Keraia	20 (?)	A/C/H	380	90	6.0
Knosos	100+	A/C/H	76	—	12.5
Lachania	20	A/C/H	321	300	4.5
Lappa	30	C/H	367	360	15.0
Lato	30	A/C/H	357	360	9.0
Lyktos	60	A/C/H	623	360	12.5
Malla	20?	A/C/H	460	220	11.5
Oleros	20–30?	C/H	358	270	11.5
Pelkis	30	A/C/H	459	270	3.5
Phaistos	—	A/C/H	85	—	12.5
Phalanna	15 (?)	A/C/H	593	360	15.0
Polyrrhenia	30	A/C/H	381	360	21.5
Praisos	50	A/C/H	331	360	34.0
Priansos	60	A/C/H	396	360	10.0
Sybrita	50	A/C/H	608	360	8.0
Tylisos	30+	A/C/H	160	270	12.5

a   This refers to the estimated size of the urban area not the *polis* as a whole.
b   In almost all cases this is the period suggested in the *Barrington Atlas* unless otherwise referenced. It excludes settlement prior to 650 BCE or to continuity beyond 67 BCE.
c   This is the elevation above sea level at the highest point unless otherwise stated.
d   'Sight line' is an approximation of the visibility from the highest point in the urban centre.
e   This refers to the straight line distance between one primary *polis* and its nearest primary *polis* neighbour. Given the topography it can be safely multiplied by two or three to give a marching distance on the ground.

of a neighbour. When taken with the similarity of the physical features that are described in the Gazetteer, the primary *poleis* do appear to have a considerable amount in common in terms of the site that was identified by their builders. They are nearly all located on a flat-topped hill at an elevation that averages about 400m; they have visibility on at least three sides, while the fourth is usually protected by higher land that would also have fallen within their territory, and they are not easily accessed by neighbours, so that even the forces of the closest would take a day or more to reach them and would therefore be known about well in advance.

Map 1 shows the distribution of the urban centres of 'primary *poleis*' included in the Gazetteer superimposed on the island's topography. Certain common features are immediately apparent even at this very general level. The first is the degree to which the urban centres were located not just on high ground but on ground constituting the foothills of the three mountain ranges that are such a hallmark of the island's topography. This is seen most clearly in the case of the Dikti range where no less than nine urban centres have, as it were, their 'backs' to higher lands forming almost a complete circle around the mountain range. A similar pattern, though not as clear, can be seen with the other two main mountain ranges around which a further twelve urban centres can be found.[3] This means that the vast majority of urban centres used the higher ground behind them, probably as part of their defensive strategy. The other seven fall into three distinctive categories. First, Polyrrhenia and Praisos occupy typical urban centre sites, but far to the west and east respectively of the really high lands. It is tempting to suggest that their relatively isolated positions themselves served to act as a defence, but another factor would certainly have been the compensation of ample fertile arable lands within easy reach of their control and utilisation. A second category is that of the two urban centres (Aptera and Anopolis) that occupied typical sites on high ground commanding their hinterland and port but unusually close to the sea. Aptera is in a truly unique setting for not only is the site of the urban centre easily defended, but it also commands fertile lands in the Stylos valley to the south and looks directly over perhaps the finest natural harbour in the Mediterranean. The extraordinary energies that went into its defence suggest that Aptera's original builders believed the benefits of this position outweighed the costs of its monumental shielding walls (see Plate 1). Anopolis too was probably at one time walled but was also more adequately defended by its location more than 600 metres above the sea, over which it had commanding views.

The third case is that of Knosos, Phaistos and Tylisos which, as far as we know, occupied sites that were adjacent to or indeed right over the Minoan settlements for which they are rightly famous. In one sense they are the exceptions from prehistory that prove the rule for the ideal type of *polis* urban centre. They are all relatively low-lying, are closer to the sea than is usual and appear to have minimal

---

3 This is on the assumption that Gortyn in the Classical and Hellenistic eras lay above rather than in the Mesara Plain, as was later to be the case.

defences either through the benefits of topography or through man-made bastions. An examination of Map 1 also suggests the peculiar absence of 'primary *poleis*' on the high ground to the east of the Psiloritis (Idaion) range, which can be explained by the position of Knosos and Gortyn to the north and south of the central valley. The fact is that attempts were made to establish primary *poleis* in exactly these locations. The two most important examples are Rhizenia (Rhitten) and Rhaukos. In the former case, the most probable location for the urban centre was near modern-day Prinias, just over ten kilometres north of Gortyn and on a typical flat-topped plateau on the eastern side of the Psiloritis range where to this day impressive ruins remain. Paula Perlman (1996: 265–66, 2004a: 1186) cites evidence to suggest that Rhizenia had its own assembly, council and public officials, but also that it was a dependent *polis* of Gortyn whose autonomy was constrained by its southern neighbour. The archaeological evidence also suggests that the *polis* (if indeed Rhizenia ever was one) may have disappeared by the beginning of the 5th century (Rizza and Rizzo, 1985: 166; Rizza, et al., 1994).[4] In the second case, that of Rhaukos, there is no doubt that this was an important *polis* in the Hellenistic era and probably before. It is reputed to have possessed both an *agora* and *prytaneion* or meeting/council chamber, and it struck coins on the Aiginetan standard from the beginnings of the Hellenistic period (Sanders, 1982: 154; Perlman, 2004a: 1185). The urban centre was located near and probably beneath modern-day Ag. Myronas on the eastern side of the Psiloritis range and north of Rhizenia at Prinias. The urban centre was destroyed by Gortyn and Knosos in the middle of the 2nd century and its land partitioned between them, but very probably its autonomy was heavily compromised before this date. A similar fate befell Phaistos around 150 BCE when its urban centre was sacked and its lands taken over by Gortyn. Thus, the pattern of settlement is maintained even though, for the reasons suggested above, these additional settlements are not included in this study.[5]

The location of the primary *poleis* is also remarkable for the evenness of their distribution. The history of inter-*poleis* conflict, while frequently exaggerated, was clearly a sound reason for trying to maintain this principle, as was the need for the urban centre to be centrally located within its lands. Another feature is their remarkably similar distance from the sea. To some extent this is dictated by the mountain chains of the Lefka Ori in the west, the Oroseira Dikti in the centre and to the east, and the Asterousia range to the south of the Mesara Plain, but nonetheless there appears to have been a common need for defence on the one hand and access to the sea on the other.

4 Paul Faure (1963: 23–24; 1993: 70) has suggested that an unexplored site lying between Gortyn and Lebena on the northern side of the Asterousia range of mountains near to the modern village of Apesokari is that of Rhizenia, and the *Barrington Atlas* also prefers this location. Given the distance between Gortyn and its port at Lebena, it is more likely that these remains were from some kind of staging post just before the ascent into the mountains.

5 There are other candidates whose fate was to be within easy striking distance of either Knosos or Gortyn. Eltynia, for example, is listed in the *Barrington Atlas* as lying to the east of the Minoan town of Archarnes and therefore six kilometres south of Knosos near to the modern village of Kounavi. Sanders (1982, 6/12) believed it still existed in Roman times, but in earlier eras it must have been either destroyed by Knosos or subsumed by its neighbour.

The careful location of urban centres of *poleis* dating from the Archaic period, or in some cases probably before, can be seen in the examples shown in Map 2. In the case of Dreros the urban centre is located on a double summit overlooking fertile lower lands to the south. Praisos, far to the east and beyond the Thryphti mountain range, is similarly on a double summit facing north just above the confluence of two river valleys. With the modern roads stripped out of the map, the similarity of position – in particular the seeming importance of all-round visibility – is very apparent. Sites with double summits, possibly in order to accommodate temples to more than one protecting deity, can be seen at Sybrita (Plate 3), Polyrrhenia (Plate 4), Axos, Hyrtakina, Lachania and Kantanos and possibly also at Biannos and Oleros. Even at Eleutherna (Nisi and Pyrgos spurs) and Gortyn (either side of the river) the architects of the original *polis* appeared to consider twin peaks a positive feature in choosing an appropriate site for development. Official buildings at Lato (e.g. *prytaneion, exedra,* theatrical area etc.) were located on the saddle between the twin peaks (Plate 5) and a similar layout can be seen at Praisos (Plate 6). Other *poleis*, where the archaeological evidence is less developed, had a similar strategy (e.g. the *agora* at Dreros or the possible *prytaneion* at Hyrtakina).

Some exceptions

One of the great virtues of ideal type construction, other than in aiding comparison, is to focus attention on 'outliers', or instances that do not fit the pattern. These are of two main types. The first are instances within the data presented that differ from the others in possibly significant ways; second, there are those that have been excluded on the grounds that they do not appear sufficiently similar for inclusion. A case of the former is Anopolis and Araden which lie either side of the famous Aradena gorge in Sphakia south-west Crete. Neither site has ever been adequately explored, but on the evidence of the remains that do exist, it would appear that the urban centre at Araden is late when compared with the others. It is also very close to the urban centre of Anopolis which lies 3km to the east. Stephanus Byzantius argued that the different names were alternatives for the same place, but Perlman (2004a: 1150) is more likely to be correct in suggesting that Araden may represent a refounding of Anopolis, which is located in a particularly inhospitable setting more reminiscent of the defensive sites of the Early Iron Age. Hierocles mentions Phoinix as the harbour of both but says it belongs to Araden (Perlman, 1995). In this discussion, therefore, they have been assumed to be the same place, at least for the later part of the period under consideration.

Second, the inclusion of somewhere termed 'Lachania' will seem an apparent eccentricity to anyone familiar with Crete. Paul Faure (1988) identifies the site at Kastelos, 7km south-south west of modern-day Chania, as that of 'Lachania' (sometimes referred to as 'Alchania'). This designation is followed by Perlman (2004) but she does not find evidence of *polis* status for the site, at least during the Archaic period. Sanders and others have commented on the size of the remains and Richard Pococke, writing in the first half of the 18th century, thought they were those of ancient Kydonia (Pococke, 1745: 603; Sanders, 1982: 168). Given the move of the main *poleis* to their ports in the Hellenistic period, and the subsequent rise to prominence of some of these, it is not fanciful to speculate that this is what occurred in this case. Captain Spratt may have been right to suggest that there were 'two Cydonias' – the one referred to by Homer (*The Odyssey* 19: 176), which 'may have stood upon some inland eminence' and another right on the sea (Spratt, 1865: 140). Spratt may have been wrong, however, to believe that the inland city was at Vryses. The archaeologist Nicolas Platon believed that 'Alchania' was a *kome* or suburb of Kydonia and that this was the origin of the city's modern name, but the site at Kastelos is too far south to have been contiguous with the port settlement. *Kome* might mean a dependent village, and this is what it would have become as the economic importance of 'Kydonia by the sea' grew in parallel with similar transformations elsewhere. Although the site has never been fully excavated, the total area of late Classical and Hellenistic remains at Lachania/Alchania may be greater than 20ha and there is evidence of monumental public buildings of this period comprised of ashlar masonry, as well as later remains.[6]

The inventory provided by Paula Perlman (2004a) includes twenty-eight inland *poleis*, of which twenty-one are included in Table 4.2.[7] Of the remaining seven, the reasons for their exclusion can be summarised as follows. First, there are those *poleis* that appear to have failed a test of autonomy, in the sense that their freedom of manoeuvre was compromised by a more powerful neighbour. Aulon, a satellite of Gortyn and possibly less than two kilometres from the latter's urban centre, is a case in point. Of the remaining six Eltynia, Rhaukos and Rhizenia/Rhitten have been mentioned above. The remaining ones are Allaria, Datala and Dragmos. Perlman opts to put Allaria close to Chamelvri just east of modern-day Rethymno and just inland from the coastal settlement at Stavromenos (Pantomatrion). As the discussion in the Gazetteer clarifies, there are no persuasive reasons for this decision and on the balance of probabilities this city state lay further east at an unknown location.[8] Perlman locates Datala at Aphrati (Prophitis Ilias). This is approximately 5km to the east of where she places Arkades (east of the village of Ini). It is most unlikely that two *poleis* would have their urban centres this close and there is nothing at the Ini site that is suggestive of a *polis*. Arkades has

---

6 If any of these could be shown to be a *prytaneion* or *bouleuterion* then it would be evidence of *polis* status (Hansen, 2003: 271).

7 In two cases a site is not included as a *polis* (Anavlochos and Lachania) by Perlman and in a third it is included at a different location (Arkades). The reasons for the decision to include each site are set out in the Gazetteer.

8 Smith in the mid–19th century and Belli in the 16th century both place Allaria east of Oleros and close to Praisos (see Gazetteer). Svoronos suggests that it might have been near the modern village of Messalare (Meseleri), which lies between Hierapytna and Istron (1890: 1–2). On the other hand, more modern interpretations point to an affinity in coin weights between Allaria and Kydonia, suggesting a site for the *polis* in the west (Stefanakis, 1997: 239–40). Svoronos discusses one coin, attributed to Allaria by some numismatists, which he believes to be a false attribution. Its design is similar to four others but it bears the letter ΛΛ, which might suggest that was in fact from Lachania, if indeed it was from Crete at all. This possibility would certainly explain an affinity with Kydonian coinage.

been included, therefore, at the Aphrati location following the original Italian archaeologist and epigraphist Federico Halbherr, the excavator of the Gortyn Law Code, who doubted the attribution of Arkades to the site at Ini, preferring instead the hill at Prophitis Ilias west of Aphrati, which he says 'corresponds far better to the importance which this city is known to have had in ancient times' (Halbherr, 1896: 564). Dragmos, in the far east of Crete, was absorbed by Praisos probably in the late 3rd century, but its whereabouts is in any event unclear.

Secondary settlements

The primary *poleis* do not exhaust the settlements in Crete during the period under consideration. Particularly from the last quarter of the 4th century BCE settlements emerged on the coast of a markedly different type from the earlier communities. Some of these also possessed their own lands and were referred to as *poleis* in inscriptions in either a political or urban sense (Perlman, 2004a). Since the major urban centres in the modern era are all on the sea, they include settlements that went on to become dominant centres for administration and commerce. In their origins, however, they nearly all emerged as ports and were either established by a primary *polis* or developed independently but soon fell within the ambit of one or other primary city state as trade relations become more central.[9]

The coastal settlements identified in this study are shown in Table 4.3. Since under half of the thirty-three settlements included have been identified as *poleis*, an immediate question arises as to why those in the other half have been selected. The answer is that in almost all cases, these locations are thought by others to have served as ports for primary *poleis*. Where known, the way in which they became established as having this function is detailed in the Gazetteer. A second feature is their probable small size, sometimes with an 'urban' core under one hectare.[10] The most important point, however, is the date of their foundation as far as we can judge from the remains of material culture. While one appears to have been founded early, all the others were established in the Classical and Hellenistic periods and usually after 400 BCE.

Map 3 shows the location of all the secondary settlements and it can be seen that these are themselves similar and totally different from the primary *poleis*. Where possible the architects of the urban centres of secondary settlements chose higher ground than sea level, but access to fresh water as well as to the sea was a critical issue. Again the relatively even distribution is evident around the coastline with the exceptions of the far east and the far west. This is mainly because these centres were in many cases established to serve the needs of inland city states. Those that were also *poleis* themselves, and many of the others, would have had lands of their own. It is true that the links with inland *poleis* are not always clear from inscription

---

9 The reasons why this occurred are discussed fully in Chapter 7.
10 These estimates are based on a variety of sources but largely the evidence of the physical remains.

TABLE 4.3   Secondary settlements with period of foundation, approximate size and status

Name	Period	Size (ha) [a]	Status
Ag. Georgios	C/H	2	—
Amnisos	C/H	2	—
Amphimalla	C/H	3	—
Apollonia	C/H	—	*Polis*
Arvi	C/H	1–2	—
Bionnos	C/H	<2	—
Chersonisos	C/H	10	*Polis*
Herakleion	C/H	—	*Polis*
Hydramia	H/R?	<3	—
Inatos	H	3	—
Istron	C/H	<3	*Polis*
Kalami	H?	<3	—
Kalamydi	H/R?	<2	—
Kamara	H	—	—
Kasteli	H	—	—
Kastri	C/H?	2	—
Kytaion	C/H	3	*Polis*
Lebena	C/H	2–3	*Polis*
Lisos	C/H	3–5	*Polis*
Matala	C/H	2–5	*Polis*
Milatos	A/C/H	10–15	*Polis*
Myrtos	C/H	1–2	—
Olous	C/H	<5	*Polis*
Pantomatrion	H	3–5	*Polis*
Phoinix (Loutro)	C/H	<1	—
Phoinix (Sellia)	C/H	2	—
Platanias	H?	2–3	—
Rhithymna	C/H	—	*Polis*
Soulia	H	—	—
Stalai	H	1–2	*Polis*
Syia	H	2–3	—
Tarrha	C/H	2	*Polis*
Trypitos	C/H	2–3	—

a   This refers to the size of the urban area only.

evidence but the probability is, nonetheless, that there were many more linkages than these, particularly as trade links grew in the Hellenistic period. The general pattern is of settlements that were smaller and of later foundation than their inland cousins. It has to be admitted, of course, that the evidence on which this proposition is based is not as strong as in the case of the primary *poleis*. This is partly because so little excavation work has taken place, but also because in at least six cases the ancient sites have been buried beneath modern coastal towns.[11] Even in cases where evidence of material culture still exists, the growth of villages for residence and tourism often makes the extent of ancient settlements very uncertain.[12]

Map 4 shows both types of settlement and it is immediately obvious what the links might have been in the sense of a topographical connection between a primary and secondary centre. Of course, straight line connections have little bearing on actual pathways, but a striking feature of the connection between the primary and secondary settlements is the existence of a visible sight line, two examples of which are shown in Plates 7 and 8. Where this was not possible, the original architects appear to have wanted to find a landmark feature to identify the route to the sea. The unique 'U'-shaped opening at 'Fortetsa' above Arvi which can be seen so clearly from ancient Biannos is an excellent example. Maps 5, 6, 7 and 8 give much more precise information of the topography for eight representative case studies. Sometimes the path that an ancient track must have taken is rather obvious. For example, it must have run around the contour westward in the case of Eleutherna and thence north-west down the river valley past modern-day Pikris and Ano Viran Episkopi towards the sea at Pantomatrion (Stavromenos) (Map 5). A long haul down the Amari valley is the only way that the ancient track could have gone in the case of Sybrita's access to the sea at Soulia (Map 6). In some cases the proximity of very high land meant that primary *poleis* were relatively close to the sea and in these cases, the ancient routes are both clear and relatively straightforward. The neighbouring primary *poleis* of Hyrtakina and Elyros are clearly connected by river valleys to their respective ports at Lisos and Syia (Map 8). In some cases the possible connection is not quite so clear. In the case of Praisos, for example, a primary *polis* that is thought to have had sea access both to the north and to the south, the possible northern port at Trypitos lies a little to the east of the linking river valley of the modern day Pedelis River (Map 7). On the other hand, the coast is more or less flat at this point and it could have been that the adjacent fresh water source (the modern day Asproughas River) flowed for more of the year. There are two cases – Axos and Kytaion (Map 5) and Gortyn and Lebena (Map 6) – where the routes are reasonably clear but impressively difficult. In the former case, the track must have gone north and slightly east to pass the massive

---

11 Chersonisos (Limin Chersonisou), Herakleion (Iraklio), Kamara (Agios Nikolaos), Kasteli (Kasteli-Kisamos), Matala and Rhithymna (Rethymno).

12 For example, at the following six locations residential sprawl, coastal erosion and tourism make it very difficult to be certain about the size and shape of ancient settlements – Apollonia (Gazi), Hydramia (Dramia), Inatos (Tsoutsouros), Kastri (Keratokambos), Olous (Elounda), Pantomatrion (Stavromenos).

height of Sofiani Koryfi (892m) and then north past modern-day Aloidhes and onwards to modern-day Sises and the coast. In the second case the arid uplands of the Asterousia mountains bar the way of any traveller and it remains unclear which way the path would have gone, particularly in its southern section.

Map 4 and the list of secondary settlements excludes four coastal locations of great importance. In the case of two of them (Kydonia and Hierapytna) this is because what little evidence we have suggests that these were secondary settlements early on, but that both rapidly outgrew their 'primary *poleis*' or larger settlement and absorbed them. The reasons for this are not entirely clear in either case, but the possibility is that two factors played a part: first, their inland 'partner' was relatively weak (Lachania and Oleros) and, second, each grew to become a major trading centre. Again the date for these transformations is not entirely clear, but probably in the former case this could have been as early as the 5th century (some time after Aiginetan traders had settled) and in the latter during Hierapytna's rapid expansion phase in the 2nd century (Perlman, 2004a: 1166). They are joined by two other *poleis*, Phalasarna and Itanos, to constitute a third category that have features in common with both primary *poleis* and secondary settlements. They are like the former in size, period of founding and importance but like the latter in their location and in being in a relationship, or a series of relationships, with more powerful partners. They have been termed 'independent *poleis*' to emphasise these differences and to stress that they were able to act on their own in terms of treaties and agreements with others. The term is not entirely accurate because at various times they certainly had relations of dependence, but in each case these were with external powers.

The first point to notice is their physical location as is shown in Map 9. In a real sense they commanded each of Crete's four coasts. Not unnaturally they invested heavily in their port installations and focused their trading relationships on those parts of the Aegean, North Africa and the Near East to which they were closest. These specialised relationships, shown in Table 4.4, affected in some cases how they were constructed, as in the case of Phalasarna's harbour, how they were governed, as in the Ptolemaic control of Itanos, and how they behaved towards their neighbours, particularly in the 2nd century when trading reached its zenith. Kydonia's aggression against Phalasarna, which it conquered in 184 BCE, and Hierapytna's struggles with first Praisos (overrun in 145 BCE) and subsequently Itanos – which it never conquered, but which continued the dispute, rumbling on with Roman mediation, until 112–110 BCE – are almost always put down to a simple wish to expand territory. It is more plausible, however, to conjecture that these hostilities were trade-related. Kydonia undertook a major issue of coinage between 189 and 184 BCE to help finance her campaign against Phalasarna which occurred at the same time that Roman involvement in North Africa was forcing the latter to compete more strongly with Kydonia in trade with the Greek mainland (Stefanakis, 2002: 236). Itanos lost Ptolemaic protection in exactly the same period as Hierapytna's eastward expansion (145–140 BCE) with the death of King

TABLE 4.4 Independent *poleis* with period of foundation, approximate size, status and trading relationships

Name	Period	Size (ha) [a]	Status	Trade relations
Hierapytna	A/C/H	50+?	*Polis*	Rhodes, Cyrene
Itanos	A/C/H	30–40	*Polis*	Ptolemaic Egypt, Rhodes
Kydonia	A/C/H	80–100?	*Polis*	Peloponnese, Attica
Phalasarna	A/C/H	50–60	*Polis*	Phoenicia, Cyrene, Egypt, Peloponnese

a This refers to the size of the urban area only.

Philometer, which would have meant more competition over the Crete-Rhodes trade connection (Spyridakis, 1970: 59).

Map 10 shows the detailed topography of Phalasarna in the far north-west and Itanos in the far north-east where the position of one is almost a mirror image of the other.[13] The map shows very well the care with which protection from the north was sought in establishing the harbours on which the seaborne fleets depended (Plates 9 and 10).

There is another possibility concerning Phalasarna's undoubted wealth during the Hellenistic period. This is that it had become a centre for piracy, and it has even been suggested that this was the main reason why the town was destroyed by the Romans in 67 BCE (Hadjidaki, 2001). There is very little evidence for either of these arguments. It is certainly true that Polybius and others made frequent mention of Cretans and piracy in the same sentence, and it would be foolish to suggest that this never occurred. On the other hand, what looks like piracy to one party is often an attempt to take over or retain trade routes to another, and it is not easy to imagine a town of Phalasarna's importance being founded upon a practice that almost by definition is likely to elicit a violent response (de Souza, 2000). Phalasarna was constructed with enormous care over a very long period and, without any clear evidence to the contrary, these stories appear more likely to be fiction than fact. So too does the parallel proposition that the Romans targeted Phalasarna because they wished to eliminate piracy. The Romans probably opened their second offensive to take over Crete at Phalasarna because the closest points of entry were either there or at Kydonia where they had previously been rebuffed. As a fuller discussion in Chapter 8 makes clear, their objectives were the domination of the island and the use of its resources as one of the final parts of the Greek world remaining unconquered (Sanders, 1982). If they had selected Phalasarna for special attention, it is more plausible to propose that this was in retaliation for the city state's history a century before of sending 3,000 mercenaries to assist Perseus in his

13 The Greek numismatist J-N Svoronos (1890: 200) put it well when he wrote, '*De même que Phalasarna était la ville principale de la côte occidentale de Crète, Itanos était la plus importante de la côte orientale*'.

battles with Rome, as well as because – as proved to be the case – it was less easy to defend than Kydonia.[14]

Kydonia and Hierapytna were also linked to *external* powers and it is perhaps this that stimulated their early development. It is as if their connection with a 'primary' centre was with one that happened to be overseas. In the case of Kydonia, it was with the Aiginetan settlers at the very end of the Archaic period that used the settlement as a trading post for links onwards to North Africa. Hierapytna's connection – sometimes conflictual – was with the mighty trading power of Rhodes, almost the parallel case to Kydonia, one controlling the flows across the north and the other across the Libyan sea to the south and to the east (Halbherr, 1893: 10).

The preceding argument has outlined a model of location and setting for three types of settlement in the period covered by the Archaic, Classical and Hellenistic eras. Setting out the geography in this manner, however, loses sight of history, and it is vital to stress that this period of more than five centuries was *dynamic*. Patterns of settlement changed critically over these centuries, largely in response to a shift in economic fortunes. The details of these changes will be discussed in later chapters but their repercussions for the size and importance of urban settlement are included here.

Network links

It is important to stress that network links between the coastal sites and the primary *poleis* are in some cases very clear while in others they are no more than probable, and in others still the relationship is only plausible. The last category is indicated by placing the possible port in parenthesis in Table 4.5. The argument presented later proposes that the driving force for all these associations was fundamentally economic, but the spatial associations were not by any means uniform. In other words, the primary city states found various ways to meet the imperative to strengthen their network ties to the coast. A city state could establish its own settlement, as in the case of Lato and Lato pros Kamara. It could take over another settlement by treaty, often a *polis* in its own right, as in the case of Lyktos and Chersonisos, or thirdly it could do so by force, as in the case of Gortyn whose subjugation of Phaistos brought with it access to the *Kolpos Mesaras* at Matala.

The network relations themselves were also diverse. The table proposes five types of connection as follows:

- (Type A) the *straightforward connection* between a primary city state and a port, usually in its own territory.
- (Type B) a *sequential* connection in which an early port is replaced or supplemented, normally in the Hellenistic era, by another usually close by but better placed.

---

14 This issue is considered in more detail in Chapter 8.

- (Type C) a *double connection* in which a primary *polis* establishes port functions to the north *and* south of the island at the same time.
- (Type D) a *federal* solution in which small city states combine to provide a treaty-based association
- (Type E) the *independent* solution in which the port comes to operate independent of a Cretan primary *polis* and where power relationships are subsequently reversed.[15]

TABLE 4.5 Possible and known inland-coastal network links

Primary *polis*	Secondary settlements	Distance (km)[a]	Relationship	Type
Anavlochos	(Milatos)	4.5	Unknown	?
Aptera	Kalami	1.5	Owned	A
Anopolis	Phoinix	3.0	Owned	A
Arkades	(Kastri)	13.0	Unknown	?
Axos	Kytaion	11.5	Treaty?	A
Biannos	(Arvi)	6.5	Unknown	?
Dreros	(Olous)	9.0	Unknown	?
Eleutherna	Pantomatrion	10.0	Owned	B
	Rhithymna	19.0	Owned	A
Elyros	Syia	4.5	Treaty	D
	Poikilasos	9.0	Treaty	
	Tarrha	16.5	Treaty	
Gortyn	Lebena	14.5	Owned	B
	Matala		Owned	
Hyrtakina	Lisos	5.5	Treaty	D
Kantanos	(Kalamydi)	7.0	Unknown	A
Keraia	(Platanias)	13.5	Unknown	A
Knosos	Amnisos	5.0	Owned	B
	Herakleion	5.0	Owned	
Lachania	*(Kydonia)*	*7.0*	*Unknown*	*E*
Lappa	Amphimalla (N)	12.0	Owned?	C
	Hydramia (N)	7.5	Owned?	
	Phoinix (Sellia) (S)	11.0	Unknown	

continues >

a Straightline distance. Marching distance would have been at least twice as long.

15 Shown in Table 4.5 in italics

TABLE 4.5   *continued*

Primary *polis*	Secondary settlements	Distance (km) [a]	Relationship	Type
Lato	Kamara	5.5	Owned	A
Lyktos	Chersonisos	12.0	Treaty	A
Malla	(Myrtos)	7.0	Unknown	?
Oleros	*Hierapytna (S)*	*7.5*	*Treaty?*	*C/E*
	Istron? (N)	6.0		
Pelkis	(Ag. Georgios)	3.0	Unknown	?
Phaistos	Matala	9.0	Owned	A
Phalanna	(Bionnos)	14.5	Unknown	?
Polyrrhenia	Kasteli	4.5	Owned	B
Praisos	(Trypitos) (N)	9.0	Treaty?	C
	Stalai (S)	14.0	Treaty	
Priansos	Inatos	7.0	Owned	A
Sybrita	Soulia	18.5	Unknown	A
Tylisos	(Apollonia)	6.0	Unknown	?

a   Straightline distance. Marching distance would have been at least twice as long.

Each strategy has its merits and demerits. To move away from an old port and establish a new location, or to push south and north to benefit from both major trade routes, suggests a strong commitment to economic development. Type D is interesting for it represents a coming together of rather small city states for both defensive and trade-related reasons. The best known case is the Confederation of Oreioi in western Crete, which brought together Hyrtakina and Elyros with the coastal settlements at Syia, Tarrha, Lisos and probably Poikilasos in a form of association that lasted for at least two centuries from the late Classical period to the beginning of the 2nd century BCE (Sekunda, 2000). The final Type (E) is of great interest, even though it contains only two city states. Kydonia was probably a minor settlement until links with Aiginetan traders at the end of the 6th century initiated a process of development that transformed its fortunes and led swiftly to inward migration from Aigina and probably from elsewhere in Crete. A similar process appears to have led to the emergence of Hierapytna as a powerful trading port. Once a port for Oleros, Hierapytna's early connection with Rhodes soon gave this *polis* the economic muscle to reverse this power relation and to become eventually the most economically powerful city state in the east.

Evolutionary transitions

That the dynamics of change impinged on individual settlements in unique ways is beyond doubt, but it is also true that more general processes were at work, largely as a result of initiatives and developments instituted by the citizenry themselves. The rise and fall of Cretan city states was evolutionary rather than revolutionary. Indeed, the evidence for *internal* disorder or discord is notable by its absence. Nonetheless, change was not continuous; there were transitions from one phase to another, such that it is helpful to think of stages that could be termed 'foundation', 'integration' – with ports but also with other city states – and 'consolidation' as the primary *poleis* declined and in many cases were eventually abandoned. It would be far too glib to suggest that all went through these phases at the same speed or at the same time, and it is certainly not true that they can be simply equated with the Archaic, Classical and Hellenistic periods, yet the *polis* of the 6th century, with its emphasis on military and communal autonomy, was a very different place from that after ca. 330 BCE when a more complex division of labour existed both *within* the *polis* and *without* as networks of trade relations demanded ever more specialist skills and functions. While variations are important, this typology does capture some more general characteristics:

Foundation phase (ca. 8th–6th centuries). This is the period when the large *poleis* were established on their defensive and commanding sites some way back from the sea. The date at which this phase starts is unclear and contested, and undoubtedly varies from place to place, but it is probably fair to argue that the origins of some city states go back to the Geometric period (8th century BCE) or even earlier. By the 7th–6th centuries, the pattern of inland settlement appears to have been well established. What is less clear is who these people were and how they were related to the population who, centuries before, had seemingly fled to inhospitable sites even higher up the mountain sides than the creators of *poleis* society (Nowicki, 2000).

There is little doubt that the development of defensive sites in the 12th–10th centuries forced their occupants into small-scale self-sufficiency. What is less clear-cut is the reason for the transformation out of these often inhospitable settings towards larger, more nucleated and, in agricultural terms, easier nodes of settlement. If threat was the original motivation for flight into atomised communities at high elevations then it is attractive to propose that growing self-confidence may have led to the abandonment of these communities. The reality is probably more complex and would include an economic imperative to control a larger hinterland (Wallace, 1997–2000: 91). It is almost impossible to know which weighed more heavily in the minds of those who lived in these communities at this time, nor is it possible to clearly separate these possible causes. For example, one factor behind an imperative to reconfigure economic organisation may have been the growth of population numbers, but that itself could be caused by an ebbing of hostilities and a sense of greater optimism.

An alternative hypothesis is that this transformation did not occur at all, in the sense that those in refuge sites did not voluntarily relocate and found city states at a lower level. From the 12th century or before, and certainly for centuries after, Crete was subject to steady inward migration. Whether this was an ethnic succession (e.g. Mycenaean followed by 'Doric') as many have believed, or whether it was peoples of similar culture but variable wealth, is not the point (Renfrew, 1996). In the Late Bronze Age Crete was not Greek but by the 7th century, when city states began to emerge, it most certainly was. Given the tenuous hold over survival that refuge sites must have implied for those forced to live there, it is implausible to believe that they were occupied by migrants or their descendants. In other words, it is more plausible to suggest that city states were founded by comparative newcomers who may certainly have used their military prowess, greater numbers and possibly greater wealth to subjugate, and possibly enslave, the 'Eteocretans' still ensconsed in their rocky eyries.

Integration phase (ca. 500–300 BCE). In the early part of this phase, city states were ultra-conservative, highly disciplined, militaristic and hierarchical (Willetts, 1955). Gradually, however, they appear to have become less rigid and more interested in cultural participation with their neighbours and in the Hellenic world in general. The founding, incorporation or takeover of small coastal settlements is an indication of this maturation process. It is also marked by a greater division of labour, the consolidation of a monetary economy and through that the building of an infrastructure of trade, with specialist officials and new rules and regulations. Once polities come to rely on taxation rather than the duties of citizenship, it is but a small step to greater social complexity and higher levels of social fluidity. Over time 'primary' settlements, austerely located on their commanding bastions, were unable to contain these political, social and economic forces and the locus of human activity began to move inexorably towards the coast.

The creation of a monetary system was not uniform, nor was it created overnight. By the last third of the 4th century, however, at least 40 *poleis* (including nearly all of the inland city states) had established their own currencies, and with them trade relations took on an entirely different character (Wroth, 1886). Economic imperatives demanded the integration of inland and coastal settlements but there was no standard pattern by which this was achieved.

Consolidation phase (ca. 300–67 BCE). The consolidation phase gained momentum in the second half of the Hellenistic period. Largely shaped by economic and trade relations, it entailed two powerful processes. First there was a gradual shift in population from the inland *poleis* to the coastal settlements, and second, a commensurate shift in political relations as power ebbed from the inland *poleis*, particularly to those coastal settlements that were well placed to exploit emerging trade routes. Although the city state concept lasted well into the Roman era, its overwhelming rationale, to ensure survival through autonomy and autarchy, began to fade – a process that was exacerbated by sharing with one's neighbours the destiny of now being part of a pan-Mediterranean empire. Consolidation took a number of forms. Nodal points in the networks of primary centres disappeared.

Their points of access to the sea sometimes followed and, in any event, the need for specialist services and more complex infrastructure brought with it coastal consolidation too. The logic of this evolutionary transition may have been fertilised by Roman *imperium* but was not dependent upon it, having been well established for many decades before the successful campaign of 69 BCE.

These processes were by no means achieved in a common manner. For example, in the early years of the 2nd century Lyktos absorbed Chersonisos which thereafter became officially 'Lyktos by the sea' (Perlman, 2004a: 1155). In Lato a major population shift took place to Lato pros Kamara (modern day Agios Nikolaos) and the upland polis declined in importance. In Praisos, the *polis* provided guarantees to the coastal *poleis* of Stalai (S) and Siteia (Trypitos) (N) in return for shipping and trade relations (Perlman, 1995). The important analytical point, however, is that the integration phase brought about similar outcomes whereas in the consolidation phase, by contrast, the process was one of concentration and rationalisation. Broadly speaking, those coastal sites best placed to exploit trade routes to the north and west (e.g. Kydonia, Phalasarna) or the south and east (e.g. Hierapytna and Itanos) grew rapidly, while others held steady or declined in relative importance. As some settlements grew in economic importance their political power led to the reverse of what had occurred two centuries before. As Perlman (1995: 135) notes, towards the end of the 2nd century the Hierapytnians commemorated their restoration of the sanctuary of the goddess Athena Oleria at Oleros, suggesting that by then the latter was a dependency of the former. Similar processes of political reversal occurred elsewhere, but they were accompanied by adaptive pressures of *selection* since trade always requires a concentration of roles in those places where competitive advantage is most evident.

The purpose of this chapter has been to locate the Cretan *poleis* and other settlements in both space and time. What is suggested is that during the Archaic period of the 7th and 6th centuries BCE there emerged a desire to found secure, independent upland communities of some size with their own lands and institutions. Chief amongst these were sacred spaces that gave purpose and coherence to the populace and public bodies that gradually developed recognizable political institutions. In turn these led to legal systems both internal, governing how redress for grievance and social control could be achieved, and external, seeking to control the ever present threat of internecine conflicts with neighbouring city states. As these processes took place they had spatial consequences, particularly the wish to consolidate a link with the only major highway of transport available, the sea. Thus pressure developed to ensure that the closest point of contact with the sea could become a part of the political, legal and above all economic network that would facilitate greater prosperity. Places that could become, or were already, ports were linked by treaty, brought into being or taken over by conquest. The result was the networks that have been described and mapped above. What remains to be done is to analyse in more detail the *content* of the legal, political and economic achievements that the foregoing suggests.

CHAPTER FIVE

Dorian ascendancy
or an ethnic mosaic?

Aristotle noted the apparent contentment of subordinate classes in Crete and the absence of social unrest, especially when compared with the 'perpetually revolting' helots of Sparta, but he could think of no other explanation for it but geographical location outside the mainstream of the Hellenic world (*Politics* 2: 11). The argument here will differ, stressing the early evolution of a written language and the codification and enactment of publicly displayed laws.[1] The central point, however, is to stress what it was that these laws were intended to achieve. We are used to considering law in terms of social justice, but early Cretan law makers had a quite different goal; they were seeking to achieve a resolution to what could be called the problem of social cohesion. In this they were remarkably successful, managing to create rules of conflict resolution, sanctified by appeals to the gods and proclaimed for all to see, that both sustained a conservative social order and impeded fissiparous tendencies that might at any time have threatened to engulf them.

In terms of social structure, there were certain features that Crete shared with the rest of the Hellenic world. These were clearly agricultural communities and as such rather conservative and inward-looking. There were also marked social divisions between the owners of large estates at one end of the social scale and serfs at the other. Landowners were undoubtedly powerful and it was they who possessed an unchallenged right to citizenship and the duty of military service in defense of the *polis*. But throughout the Greek world from the 7th century onwards, there were also independent farmers who owned their land and claimed some political and economic rights as a result. There were also free labourers possessing fewer rights. Initially these may have subsisted purely through paying a tribute in the form of produce to landowners, but it is also probable that later, in the Hellenistic period, they became more dependent upon wage labour. The military orientation of city states and their periodic engagement in conflict produced many opportunities for

---

1 This is compatible with W.G. Runciman's point when he writes, 'In cultural evolution, the big transitions are first, the emergence of language and symbolism, and second, the emergence of literacy' (2009: 202).

enslavement and it is possible that this element, as elsewhere thousands of years later, restricted the evolution of more productive labour systems. Similarly, the dominance of landed classes inhibited the emergence of traders and in Crete, as elsewhere, there was an initial tendency for these to be drawn from the ranks of citizens who had migrated from one *polis* to another.

Then, as now, soil conditions and the relative scarcity of open spaces suitable for grain production meant that cash crops in the form of olive oil or grapes for wine production took precedence over subsistence farming for food crops. This in turn led to an early interest in markets and a market-based economy. Markets prompt the emergence of urban areas and this is one reason why the two pillars of the city-state, an urban core and rural hinterland, emerged as they did. Once urban populations grew in size, this stimulated greater complexity in social divisions and a greater challenge to those wishing to maintain social solidarity and cohesion.

Social stratification

The work of the classicist Ronald Willetts (1955, 1965, 1976) is possibly the most influential in characterising the society of ancient Crete from the Archaic through to the Hellenistic period. His stress lay on the rigidity of social divisions and he appears to have had in mind the history of Britain in the medieval era in suggesting that the *kosmoi*, or those in leadership roles, had a monarchic function while the rest of the population of each city state was divided into four classes. At the top was an aristocracy comprised of members of the *hetaireia*, or exclusive association of landowning male citizens from elite families exercising political power, beneath them were the *apetairos (perioikos)* or free men excluded from the *hetaireia*, who were in turn above the bonded serfs and chattel slaves.[2] Although this has no parallel in the medieval world, it was the tributes of serfs to their 'lords' that maintained the system of common meals (*syssitia*) for the men folk of the *hetaireia* meeting in the men's houses (*andreia*).[3] Willetts argues that these tributes, together with the 'incessant' warfare 'which ravaged the cities from the middle of the fourth century BCE until the Roman occupation, the subjection of weaker by stronger states, the absorption of surplus manpower in large-scale piracy and in mercenary service within the same period, all helped to stave off the application of drastic reform' (1990: 229). In contrast to the economic advances in 'democratic city states', Willetts sees Crete as locked in a cycle of conservatism based on an archaic serf-based system of land tenure:

---

2 Strictly speaking the *perioikos* were the free citizens of dependent *poleis* such as Aulon, Rhytion and Kaudos (Gavdos) that were all satellites of Gortyn. They had self government but paid dues to their dominant ally. The treaty between Gortyn and Lato shows that the *perioiki* could be sued in the same courts as citizens but they were required to pay taxes in the state that controlled them (Larsen, 1936: 18).

3 Chaniotis sees the rewards from warfare as essential to the life of the *polis*, even arguing that the captured booty funded the *syssitia* in the *andreia* (2005a: 135–136).

The economic and social history of Crete, over a period of more than two thousand years before the Roman occupation, was such that it could never emancipate itself from the abiding influences of age-old traditions (1990: 229–30)

With such a backward-looking, traditional and static conception, it is perhaps unsurprising that many have missed the signs of dynamism that are documented in what follows. First, however, there is the issue of an alternative conception of social structure to that which Willetts presents.

AN 'ARISTOCRACY'?

There is no doubt that the term 'aristocracy' from the Greek *aristokratia*, meaning the rule by the best suited, has an immediate appeal in rather rigidly hierarchical societies. Moreover, it was applied to military elites, and the citizens of all Greek *poleis* had military matters high on their agenda. Although Plato and Aristotle both used the term, it was with approbation when compared with what they saw as the alternative; namely 'democracy' or rule by those least capable of making sound political decisions. In the *Republic* Plato argues the case for decision-making by those capable of selflessness and rational thought, while in the *Politics*, Aristotle stresses educational excellence and moral superiority as additional qualities.

The term, however, has evolved to refer to landed elites with a birthright to rule, although other criteria such as wealth in general (e.g. medieval Venice) or ethnicity (e.g. Brahmins in India) are also known. From the Middle Ages onwards it came to be used almost invariably alongside monarchy to refer to a class of hereditary nobles whose role, while still military, was largely to sustain the crown. Following the French Revolution and the founding of the US Constitution, the preferred mode of government was one in which an elite was democratically elected periodically in accordance with a set of written rules, thus seeking to avoid the weaknesses of direct (Athenian) democracy and the alternative of a hereditary ruling class. In the case of ancient Crete, as we shall see in later chapters, there was no monarch, there was constitutional government and those in power were severely restricted in terms of the period they could serve. Therefore to label these communities as 'aristocratic', and as simply composed of a landed ruling class and serfs, has served to create a mythology of inflexibility and conservatism.

A RIGID HIERARCHY?

Although it is true that differential rights and duties attached to differing statuses, the social system was far more dynamic than is often supposed. This capacity for change became more pronounced over time and sprang from both internal and external sources. Internally, for example, the seemingly rigid social divisions were actually much more fluid than is often thought. John Davies's work on the Gortyn Code, which is discussed below, suggests that this crucial indicator of the prevailing social structure in the early Classical period identified in practice only two statuses, free and unfree, and that the latter were more correctly seen as having a 'serf' status (*woikea*) rather than that of a slave. On the one hand, this large, dependent population could be sold and inherited, and therefore possessed characteristics of slavery; on the other, 'the law provided for some protection against violence even if the monetary compensation went to the master, not to the injured person, and did in certain circumstances recognize the "serf" as a juridical person' (Davies, 2005: 316). Moreover, they could also own property, marry, divorce and remarry under the same rules as those who were free. Critically for social mobility, a male 'serf' marrying a free woman had offspring who were also free. In addition, there are solid reasons for thinking that the normal elision of citizen status with that of a landowner did not always hold. Paula Perlman's investigation into ancient Eleutherna demonstrates that as early as the 6th century inscribed laws did not concern only agriculture and land holding but were also focused on craftsmen and artists (Perlman, 2004b). In other words, from before the time that the 'Great Code' at Gortyn was inscribed, what was emerging was a more complex division of labour that was more 'urban' than is often assumed.

This fluidity was also sustained by networks of contacts from outside the archetypal Cretan *polis*. As with *poleis* elsewhere, there were considerable numbers of *metics* or foreigners in most urban centres and, in many cases, these were the responsibility of a magistrate designated for that purpose and they were subject to the jurisdiction of special courts. Freedmen, or those granted freedom from the bonds of servitude, were classed with *metics* who were not normally ranked as members of the *apetairos* (Larsen, 1936: 18). All the evidence suggests that *metics* played a pivotal role in trade and trade-related services.

The classic division of labour was also affected in major ways by the growth in use of mercenary soldiers. Willetts himself reports on the employment of mercenaries by Egypt, Syria, Sparta, the Achaean League, Pergamon, Macedon, Syracuse and Rome (1976: 212). In 219 BCE, the Polyrrhenians sent 500 men to serve with Philip of Macedon's army and Knosos also sent the same number of mercenaries. A mercenary force of 1000 served in Alexandria in 221 BCE and 'at the battle of Raphia in 217 B.C. there were 3000 Cretans with the Egyptian army and 2500 (perhaps mercenaries) in the opposing army of Antiochos III' (1976: 212). The famous treaty of 183 BCE between thirty-one Cretan city states and Eumenes II of Pergamon was based on making available Cretan archers and infantry. Willetts writes:

> Trained Cretans were so much in demand for foreign service that the Cretan cities had sometimes to employ mercenary troops to make good the drain on manpower caused by their willingness to allow their own citizens to be recruited by others (1976: 212)

There is no doubt that mercenary service was a Cretan speciality. This could be interpreted as simply a reflection of economic and demographic pressures. As Chaniotis (2005a: 81–82) argues, 'when food and land shortages occurred, solutions were not sought in reforms, but in the conquest of a neighbor's territory and in migration'. But a great deal of mercenary service was organised through treaty arrangements by city states acting individually or collectively. This being so a more plausible proposition is that administrators saw in the export of military specialists (e.g. Cretan archers) a way of removing a potential source of trouble at home and a strategy for earning money abroad. In other words, mercenary soldiers were a form of organised migrant labour. Their wages are often seen as sustaining an agrarian way of life by providing an additional revenue stream, but their effect is usually anything but conservative. Entry to a cash economy, higher levels of economic return and exposure to foreign cultures are but three likely consequences of mercenary service.

A CLASS-BASED SOCIETY?

Even greater rigidity has been added to the 'aristocracy thesis' by the supposition that the ruling elite shared a common 'Dorian' ancestry, and that there was a neat cultural division between them on the one hand and serfs and slaves of Minoan and Mycenaean descent on the other. While it was certainly true that those captured in conflicts between city-states were frequently forced into dependency, the idea that the 'Dorians' were migrants with a unitary culture whose legacy from the Early Iron Age had enabled them to maintain dominance over an equally unitary cultural heritage of Mycenaean or earlier origin is implausible. Indeed recent scholarship has argued the opposite; that the 'Sea Peoples' of ancient legend were highly complex both linguistically and in other ways (Woudhuisen, 2006: 74 *passim*) and they were not alone in contributing to a complex ethnic mosaic in Crete.

This ethnic complexity was noted by Homer in the speech that the disguised Odysseus makes to his wife, Penelope. He famously depicts Crete as 'a rich and lovely sea-girt land, densely peopled with ninety cities and several different languages. First there are the Achaeans; then the genuine Cretans, proud of their native stock; next the Cydonians; the Dorians with their three clans; and finally the noble Pelasgians' (*Odyssey*, 19, 174–78). Writing perhaps seven hundred years later, Diodorus (5.80) also mentions 'the peoples who have become intermixed with the Cretans' who include Homer's list together with 'a heterogeneous collection of barbarians who in the course of time adopted the language of the ancient Greeks'. It is unlikely that this was a smooth process of acculturation; ethnic boundaries are engendered, created and recreated through contact. In other words, 'ethnogenesis' is more probable than the melting pot. As Jonathan Hall argues, the ethnic boundary (the *Dorians*) may have arisen as result of intermingling with others each possessing a foundation myth (Hall, 2002: 88–89).

There is no doubt that members of the three Dorian *phylai* or ethnic groupings (Dymanes, Hylleis, and Pamphyloi) did migrate to Crete, probably over a period of many centuries starting in the Early Iron Age.[4] They also came to be found on other Aegean islands, as well as in many locations on the Peloponnese

---

4 Hall is surely right when he suggests that 'the notion of a one-time massive influx of Dorians into the Peloponnese from a single, defined area of Central Greece, is belied by the composite nature of the tradition that purports to describe it' (2002: 82).

(e.g. Megara, Corinth, Sikyon, Phleious, Epidauros, Troizen, Argos and Sparta). The central point, however, is that Dorian *phylai* never came to dominate the island as Willetts and others have suggested. For example, as far as the three Dorian *phylai* are concerned, their associations are never all referred to in the same *polis*, and only in Hierapytna and possibly Olous is there any evidence of two of the three existing in the same place. On the other hand, twenty *phylai* have been identified amongst the thirteen public organisations documented in Crete, which means that there were substantial numbers of non-Dorian Greeks on the island, often no doubt descended from earlier migratory movements or coming from the Attic or Ionic *phylai* (Jones, 1987: 219–20).

TABLE 5.1   Selected Cretan *poleis* by attested ethnic groups (*phylai*)

	Axos	Dreros	Gortyn	Hierapytna	Knosos	Lato	Lebena	Lyktos	Malla	Oleros	Olous	Praisos
Aithaleis		X	X		X				X			
Ainaones			?				X					
Aischeis						X						
Archeia			X		X		X	X				
Autoletai			X				X					
Diphyloi								X				
Donokeioi	X											
Dymanes			X	X				X			X	
Echanoreis					?	X						
Hyakinthioi								X				
Hylleis	X											
Latosioi	X											
Kamiris				X								
Pamphyloi				X	X					X		
Synaneis						X						
Tharkaris												X
Waxioi	X											

Source: Jones, 1987

The ethnic complexity of Crete during the late Classical and Hellenistic periods can be seen from Table 5–1, which has been derived from Jones's work on the epigraphic evidence (cf. Perlman, 2004a). The analysis of dating formulas from Gortyn, for example, suggests the presence of at least six *phylai* from the middle of the 4th to the middle of the 1st century. These possibly include the 'Ainaones' (perhaps a reference to the Ainianes from Thessally, indicating a pre-Dorian people) and the 'Autoletai', both found elsewhere only at Lebena, suggesting a very specific Gortynian presence. The evidence confirms, therefore, that the Dorians at Gortyn shared the *polis* with possibly four other *phylai*. Where reference to a *startos* is found, this appears in a military context suggesting that these may have been regiments of the individual *phylai* (Jones, 1987: 226). Similarly at Knosos four *phylai* are attested (Aithaleis – also found at Dreros; Archeia – also at Lebena and Lyktos; Pamphyloi and one other in fragmentary form, possibly the Echanoreis, also found at Lato where it is assumed to be of pre-Dorian, Argive origin). The same number is found at Lyktos where the most prominent *phyle* appears to have been the Diphyloi who appear in two texts where the preamble refers to the 'upper city' and 'the city on the sea' (Chersonisos). Others were the Archeia, the Hyakinthioi (a restoration from a fragmentary text) and the Dymanes.

It is probable that the *phylai* played an important constitutional role from the earliest days of the Cretan city states. In Dreros, the famous fragment of law dating from the middle of the 7th century limiting the tenure of the *kosmoi*, opens with a reference to a consultation with the *phylai*, while a later oath refers to the Aithaleis (found also at Gortyn, Knosos and Malla) who were thought to be of Achaian (i.e. pre-Doric) origin (Jones, 1987: 228). Other evidence suggests additional migratory routes. In Lato, for example, two of the three *phylai* found in dating formulas from between 250 and 100 BCE were pre-Dorian, and the 'Aischeis' may have been of Samian origin. The reference to the 'Kamiris' at Hierapytna and the name of Lato's port at Kamara suggests the presence of Rhodian migrants, while at Praisos the inscription from the early 3rd century to a *phyle* called 'Tharkaris' is thought by some to be a reference to peoples originating in Thessaly.

Paula Perlman's work on toponyms and the names of the *kosmoi* in nine Cretan *poleis* also shows that chief magistrates belonged to both Doric and non-Doric ethnic groups. This, she says, 'makes it difficult to accept the picture of the socio-political organization of the Cretan city states with their Doric aristocracies and pre-Doric serfs which is commonly entertained' (Perlman 2000: 65). Extending this argument more recently, she writes:

> … contrary to what is often assumed about historical Crete, the island's communities were not in fact overwhelmingly Doric; nor is there any reason to conclude that the inhabitants constructed their own identity as Dorians (Perlman, 2005: 282).

Although each constituent grouping in this multi-ethnic world would probably have wished to ensure its frequent access to power, the rotation of the chief magistrates amongst the *phylai* was clearly designed to avoid monopolisation by any one group.

Thus, far from the chief societal characteristic of the Cretan *poleis* being their aristocratic structure, it is more plausible to argue that the dominant cultural form was concerned with constraining and ordering power. There were rigid social divisions, but these were never as caste-like as is often assumed. It is indeed significant that no Greek *polis* ever displayed the extreme oligarchy that propelled the Romans, the Turks and the Venetians to super-power status (Runciman 1990: 364). This point can also be revealed in aspects of material culture. The domestic architecture of Cretan city states is almost invariably modest and even public buildings were simple and unpretentious. The classical Greek house at this time is the 'courtyard house' where a single entrance opens into a vestibule from which there is access to an inner courtyard from which other rooms open. Ruth Westgate's (2007) study of domestic space in Crete in the 5th to 1st century BCE, which examines spaces within households as an indicator of social differentiation, shows that houses here were more open and unilinear and often very simple. Rooms open into other rooms and then into a central 'hearth room' with an opening to the outside which appears to have been the centre of social interaction. This makes the seclusion of women less probable and also suggests what we know from literary sources, that many 'domestic' functions were organised at a communal level. The education and training of children, food acquisition and male and female commensality were organised by the *polis*, at least for citizens and possibly also for the *perioeci*.[5] There is no doubt that state-run education for citizens involved a strong military component and oath ceremonies suggest that completion of military service was obligatory for young men (Chaniotis, 1996: 12–13; 2005: 21–22). Whether this reflected an unchanging military culture, as Chaniotis would have us believe, is much less clear.

Crete and written Greek

The overwhelming reason that communities can resolve the problem of social order is the emergence of a culture of compliance, or the acceptance of a system of rules. Many societies of the past achieved this through an oral tradition, but Crete is remarkable for being both the earliest place within the Greek world with *written* laws and for bringing them together into a formal code. To achieve this it was obviously necessary to be amongst those places within the Hellenic world that pioneered the use of *written* Greek.

It is important to differentiate between early writing systems and the evolution of a true alphabet, although it has to be said that Crete appears at the forefront of both.[6] In the second millennium BCE there emerged three writing systems on

---

5 Aristotle had suggested that Cretans who were not citizens had the same rights as those who were except for access to *gymnasia* and the right to bear arms (*Politics* 1264a).

6 This is not to suggest that *only* in Crete did such early systems emerge. There were simple syllabic scripts used in the Sinai in the 15th century BCE which may have also sprung from Caananite (i.e. Phoenician) sources (Millard, 1986: 392). Other scripts emerged, particularly Aramaic, which replaced the earlier cuneiform, but in all cases they were recorded only through scribes.

Crete; first a hieroglyphic system unique to the island, followed by 'Linear A' and 'Linear B'. The hieroglyphic system, as used, for example, on the Phaistos Disk, had a very limited number of signs, only forty-five in this case, and was a very simple syllabic script. 'Linear A', like the hieroglyphic system not so far deciphered, spread to some other Aegean islands (Kea, Kythera, Melos and Thera) and to Laconia on the Greek mainland and appeared for the last time at the end of the 'Neopalatial' era (1450 BCE) (Olivier, 1986: 377). 'Linear B' was found in the postpalatial period (after 1350 BCE) at Knosos and Kydonia on Crete and at Pylos, Mycenae, Thebes and Tiryns on the mainland, appearing for the last time around 1200 BCE. Olivier maintains that Linear B was adapted by the Mycenaeans from Linear A as a way of writing their own language, Greek (1986: 378; cf. Schoep, 1999).

It was not, however, until Crete came under the influence of Phoenician traders from what is now the Mediterranean coast of Lebanon, starting in the 10th century, that its Greek-speaking population developed a true alphabet, in particular one with vowel sounds. There has been much debate about how this Phoenician influence arose, although most contributors adhere to one or other of the following positions. The first is the argument for a permanent presence as shown by the evidence of Phoenician burials at the Tekke tomb near Knosos and 'Temple A' at Kommos in the south of the island. It has been claimed that 'the Kommos temple is the earliest Phoenician cult place found so far in the Aegean' (Negbi 1992: 609). It is certainly true that the Phoenicians were formidable sailors and ventured westward at least as far as Sardinia (Stampolides and Kotsonas, 2006). The other proposition is that it was Greek traders, including those from Crete, who went in the other direction:

> Some time in the second half of the eighth century Greeks from several cities were trading and residing at Al Mina and perhaps other towns of Syria and Phoenicia. These Greeks were dealing with literate peoples, and some of them found it convenient to become literate themselves. One individual or group may have made the innovation of using certain Phoenician letters for vowels, and others immediately grasped the idea (Cook and Woodhead, 1959: 178).

A similar argument for the source of this inspiration identifying Al Mina in Northern Syria (possibly the site of ancient Posideion) has been advanced by Jeffery (1990: 11–12). This might account for the fact that the Greek alphabet that emerged, probably as early as the 8th century, was not consistent in the letters it included, depending on where it was found. Whichever process was at work the person(s) who adopted the Phoenician script as a way of recording Greek vowel sounds 'apparently saw the problem and made the changes in a single move, for every one of the oldest specimens of Greek writing, scattered from Sicily to Rhodes, employs the classic vowels, except omega' (Millard, 1986: 396). The most likely explanation for Phoenician influence is that both of these processes occurred simultaneously.

These advances opened the door to a wider level of literacy and effectively broke the monopoly of scribes as the arbiters of written recording. The new fusion occurred in a number of places in the southern part of the Greek world, but there are certainly those who believe that Crete became 'the region where the oldest known version of the Greek alphabet originated' (Haarman, 1995: 133):

> It is most likely that knowledge of the vocalic-consonantal alphabet, specifically knowledge of how to replace Phoenician semi-consonants with Greek vocalic values, spread from Crete throughout the Aegean and subsequently to the Greek mainland (1995: 135).

Arguably, therefore, the first complete alphabet (that is one with both consonants and vowels) and the earliest elaboration of a European alphabet was a Cretan rather than a Greek invention, deriving in part from the heritage of the Minoan world.

The literacy debate

The link between levels of literacy and the evolution of democracy has proved far more controversial in the Cretan case than one might imagine. At the risk of over-simplifying a debate that is still far from being concluded, there are two positions that are currently advanced, although the first comes in two variants. It denies the proposition that widespread literacy existed in Crete, at least during the Archaic period, and that there was any identifiable move towards democratic governance. The two variants of this position can be identified according to the explanations that are offered for the abundance of written law in the island. As Perlman argues, as far as we are aware at present, 'the practice of writing down laws for public display began in Crete' (2002: 187). In addition to Dreros and Gortyn, seven of the Archaic *poleis* of Crete are known to have inscribed laws for public display before the end of the 6th century: Axos, Eleutherna, Eltynia, Knosos, Lyktos, Phaistos and Prinias (Rhizenia) (2002: 187). The second argument is essentially the reverse, suggesting higher levels of popular literacy *and* a connection between this and more popular forms of governance. The debate gives rise to a quite different perspective on the importance of written law.

The first position, in its first variant, was initially set out eloquently by the archaeologist James Whitley and associates (Stoddart and Whitley, 1988; Whitley, 1997; 1998a; 2009). Whitley finds little evidence for supposing that literacy was widespread in Crete, despite the island's early role in the development of written Greek. He argues that the use of inscriptions is rare in the Archaic period, that there are few cases of graffiti, few dedications and basically few instances of the written form. Because of this, he suggests that rather than having taken over the Phoenician vowel sounds, the actual import from the east and south was the continuation of a scribal class preserving declaratory rule over a largely illiterate population.

Evidence in support of this argument has been adduced from the so-called 'Spensithios decree'. This decree was found on a '*mitra*', or abdominal guard worn by a Greek warrior, that was unearthed near Aphrati (Arkades).[7] Two specialists from the British Museum, where it is now located, dated it to 500 BCE (Jeffrey and Morpurgo-Davies, 1971). The decree is in the form of a contract of employment, outlining the terms for one Spensithios:

> To be for the city its scribe and recorder in public affairs both sacred and secular. No one else is to be scribe and recorder for the city in public affairs, neither sacred nor secular, except Spensithios himself and his descendants.

Therefore, in Whitley's argument whatever literacy existed is likely to have been 'scribal literacy' where the skill is confined 'to a small, specialist group, for whom the practice of writing is a specialist (and sometimes hereditary) skill' (Whitley 1998a: 322). It is worth noting that this was not the position advanced by the two authors who first analysed the Spensithios *mitra*. For them Spensithios simply had the job of formulating decisions taken by the *kosmoi* and council in a proper manner. Hitherto the city of Arkades (or Datala) 'may not have had enough public business to need the services of a paid, full-time official' (Jeffery and Murpurgo-Davis, 1971: 28). They argue that Spensithios was the equivalent to the other 'anonymous experts' who performed the same function in Dreros, Axos, Eleutherna, Gortyn and elsewhere.

Whitley's argument is stronger when it comes to the relative absence of written material, other than legal inscriptions. The comparison he makes is between early Cretan *poleis* and both Athens and Sparta where in both cases there were many instances of inscriptions used in commemorating heroic feats, and even more cases where craftsmen signed their works particularly in relation to narrative scenes on pottery. Yet 'Crete is unique in Archaic Greece in this respect: there is no narrative scene accompanied by any inscription in any medium that can confidently be dated to either the seventh or the 6th century' (Whitley, 1997: 652).

On the other hand, Whitley has also made an important assessment of the prevalence of written law on Crete and on the mainland. He has shown that in Attica there were no written laws before 550 BCE and only eight cases are known for the period from 550 to 480 (1998a: 314). This compares with twenty-eight from Crete over the same period and a further ten in the century before. What then can have been their function if they could not have been read by the population at large, even though they were inscribed on stones prominently erected in public spaces? The answer he gives is that the laws as declared at Gortyn were not meant to be read by the population at large. Rather they were:

> The Gortynian equivalent of the marble temples of mainland Greece, a Gortynian counterpart to the Parthenon. Like the Parthenon, it was partly a means of representing in symbolic form that for which the community as a whole stood. It was there to represent the majesty of The Law, and to represent the law to a population that was

---

7 The fact that the *mitra* refers to 'Datala' has led some to argue that this urban centre, whose whereabouts is otherwise unknown, must have been at Aphrati.

largely illiterate. It was intended to present the particular regulations and practices of a small city-state as eternal and immutable – permanent and beyond criticism, like some platonic form existing above and beyond the day to day concerns of the average Gortynian (1997: 660).

In other words, what Whitley suggests is that these laws should be seen as monuments and not as texts: 'there to represent the majesty of the law to a population that was largely illiterate' (1998a: 322). Moreover, the unfree or partially free resident would not therefore be able to notice that the restitution offered by the code was so unequal and biased towards the interests of a conservative citizen elite.

The other variant of this argument is forcefully presented in the work of Rosalind Thomas (1996; 2005) whose main interest of relevance to this debate has been in assessing whether the presence of *written* law in Crete is indicative of a major difference when compared with the stronger *oral* tradition in Athens in the same period. For Thomas the argument presented by Whitley goes someway towards an explanation but not far enough:

> The massive inscribed wall at Gortyn holding the Code emphasizes the authority of the laws, the grandeur of the Code, and the power of its creators. But is that all? If Crete is so different from the rest of Greece, why precisely is it different, and what is the context that could make it so different? (2005: 48).

She argues that written laws may have been used to control the scribes like Spensithios or to 'control and stabilize' the *mnemones* (recorders) and judges and to enable 'officials to check up on each other' (2005: 49) or to control rival aristocrats who had 'perhaps been taking it in turns to seize power or twist the top office to their own ends and where their peers got together to try a permanent settlement' (2005: 54). It is by no means clear, however, how the huge effort to erect laws in public would achieve this goal, or why this strategy was adopted in Crete and not to a similar extent elsewhere. The closest she comes to an explanation of this is to posit the possibility that Crete may have possessed political elites peculiarly disposed towards squabbling among themselves:

> It is most likely ... that communities in tense circumstances would be trying to give the new laws as much authority as they possibly could; and if such laws were effectively agreements reached by the ruling elite, as was surely true in Dreros and most archaic cities, in an attempt to limit the ambitions of one's peers, then the same pressures might exist (2005: 56).

Thus written laws were not simply codified versions of previous customs, but new departures created to cope with tensions and stresses in the social fabric of the *polis*. She writes of the 'probability that for most communities the laws that went up in writing were particularly special: these were not the ones agreed by all, but the contentious ones, the rules that constantly caused trouble, like the laws on heiresses, perhaps, listed at such length in the Gortyn Code' (2005: 54). Others too have believed that the written laws were somehow connected with resolving of conflicts among unelected elites. For Karl-Joachim Hölkeskamp, for example, the Cretan laws were not *codes* but ad hoc responses to periods of crisis (*stasis*). They emerged as 'an immediate and direct response to challenges which consisted in new, sensitive, basically very concrete problems and tangible demands arising in a community in a phase of growth, external pressure, internal tension and increasing complexity' (1992: 74). But neither he nor Thomas says what these 'concrete problems' were or why they should have been particularly found in Crete. There is a mass of evidence to suggest that tensions within elites were commonplace – but then why did they not lead to similar outcomes in the form of written laws elsewhere?

Where Thomas does not disagree with Whitley is in a refusal to accept anything democratic in the Cretan *polis*, which she sees as being run by a privileged elite or aristocracy. The Gortyn Code and other written laws in the island were 'not upheld by egalitarian or protodemocratic organs' since the Cretan *poleis* were 'not democratic in character or intention' (2005: 49). Even evidence that might be taken to suggest some system of popular consultation is dismissed. In Dreros, for example, the phrase that opens the famous inscription 'it has been decided by the polis' may not indicate 'widely based popular decision making' (2005: 58) and, for this reason, 'Crete cannot provide a model of the way written law *may* promote equality or even democracy' (2005: 47).

The second line of argument in this important debate opens from the proposition that the written laws in Crete were actually *intended* to be read. On Dreros, for example, Michael Gagarin makes the valid point that the written laws (fragments of eight have been found) were on the temple's eastern wall, which formed one side of the main gathering space, which meant that 'the law had a prominent place in the public life of the polis' (2008: 46–47). Moreover, he argues, the original text uses dividing lines as a rudimentary form of punctuation and to make the text easier to read. In other words:

> Those who inscribed early laws were concerned to make these texts as easy to read as possible for an audience that would have included some whose reading skills were rudimentary. Dividing lines would be less necessary if these archaic inscriptions were intended solely for display or were meant to be read by only a small group of elite members of the community (2008: 48).

Although the full content of the seven laws in addition to the famous statute of limitation is unclear, it is possible to conclude that they cover a wide range of topics and not just those dealing with the possible abuse of political power.

A similar story was true for the early laws at Gortyn. They were inscribed on the temple of Apollo Pythion rather than in the *agora*, presumably to stress the sanctity of the laws themselves. They would have extended 30–40m in length along the temple walls and, given that they are in sections and that a number of procedures were included to make them more legible and comprehensible, Gagarin concludes that there is little doubt that they were intended to be read. This is similar to an argument contained in Paula Perlman's analysis of the early statutes from Gortyn (2002: 196) where she also comments on the mason's attempt to stress the penalties for particular infringements. Perlman concludes that private writing actually increased after 600 BCE, suggesting that reading and writing were not confined to the elite members of the community, and that a significant number of people outside the ruling elite could have read the archaic legislation of Crete (Gagarin, 2008: 69; Perlman, 2002: 195). This does not mean that all those to whom the laws applied could read them, but the laws at this early period were clearly intended to underpin social stability by making it known that it was *law* rather than arbitrary power that would determine a particular outcome. As Gagarin concludes, 'we cannot exclude the possibility that ordinary citizens, and even slaves, read these texts too' (2008: 70).

Similarly, Gagarin is unimpressed by the proposition that the massive slabs containing the laws at Gortyn were simply intended to impress the lower orders. He points out, for example, that careful inspection of these stones shows that some of the blocks reveal the remains of erased texts, probably also laws, beneath the new, and Gagarin says quite rightly:

> If the primary reason for inscribing laws was to impress an illiterate population, there would have been no need to erase obsolete laws; one could much more easily write the new law separately, which would make an additional visual impact. If the laws were displayed in order to be read and used by the community, however, then the removal of obsolete laws would be imperative (2008: 128).

In addition, what the laws actually had to say was often to do with the rights and duties for different socio-economic categories of the population. There is very little that could be called oppressive or even frightening about the *content* of the laws. According to Gagarin, the opposite is the case; namely, that these laws formalise rules that represent the wishes of the population as a whole, and not just the elite. For this reason, he sees a connection between Cretan law codes and emergent representative political institutions since 'by the end of the 6th century, if not earlier, a civic body referred to as "the Gortynians" or "all Gortyn" was almost certainly enacting legislation and making other decisions for the community' (Gagarin, 2008: 126).

The laws and law codes of Gortyn

The most famous and outstanding examples of written laws in the ancient Greek world are those inscribed on various monumental stone slabs at Gortyn. The Gortyn laws are not confined to the famous Great Code (Davies 2005) (Plate 11). In fact the inscriptions cover a period of more than 150 years up to the mid–4th century. The earliest group, from about 600 BCE to ca. 525, comprises the texts inscribed on the temple of Apollo Pythios.[8] These are so fragmentary as to be difficult to interpret. A second group appears to have been inscribed on the walls of a number of buildings around the *agora* and to date from a period before 400 BCE. These include the 'Great Code' but there is a third group of apparently later date (up to 350 BCE) (Davies, 2005: 306). The Great Code was inscribed *boustrophedon* (alternating left/right) on the inner face of a curving wall that dates from the 5th century, the stones of which were reused by the Romans in building their Odeion. An earlier set of blocks (the 'Second Code') was reused in a Hellenistic building, part of which is also found within the structure of the Odeion.

The 'Great Code' itself was unearthed in 1884 by the Italian epigraphist and archaeologist Federico Halbherr, on a series of stone slabs beneath alluvial deposits from the Mitropolianos (*Lethaeos*) River and on other material embedded in the walls of a water mill nearby. Earlier, in 1857, Perron and Thénon had found part of a slab dealing with the laws of adoption, and in 1879 another piece was discovered by the Frenchman Haussoullier in the wall of a house near the mill (Roberts, 1888: 10). Halbherr's efforts, supported by Cretan associates but often opposed by the Turkish administration, marked the beginning of an association between this site and the Italian School that continues to this day (cf. Greco and Lombardo, 2005). Halbherr and his associates continued to find numerous other fragments at Gortyn, the texts of which were mostly published in a series of reports for the *American Journal of Archaeology* soon after their discovery (Halbherr, 1896; 1897; 1898; Xanthoudidis, 1898). It is important to note that although the Gortyn Code is justly famous, it fits into a pattern of other laws dating back to those at Dreros, all of which were also erected for public display and most of which appear to have been incorporated into the walls of temples or other public buildings (Perlman, 2002: 187). Indeed, the Gortynian laws cannot be interpreted as a single body of statute. Of the 159 inscriptions found so far at Gortyn, comprising about a quarter of those in Crete as a whole, 73 are sufficiently well preserved to be capable of interpretation, and they cover a period of nearly two and a half centuries from the early 6th century to the middle of the 4th century. Perhaps unsurprisingly, they are highly variable both in their coverage and in the degree to which they could be considered a unified 'code' (Davies, 1996: 32). John Davies has contrasted the highly codified laws on adoption with those on rape, seduction and adultery that are so poorly articulated in terms of definitional clarity and applicability as not to resemble a 'code' of any description (1996: 39 *passim*).

Because the so-called 'Great Code' is the fullest legal text ever found in ancient Greece, it has been subject to intense academic scrutiny and debate. There has been, for example, a long discussion as to its major purpose. There are those like Whitley who argue that its role was primarily symbolic and others like Paula Perlman (2002b) who take a very different view, arguing that the inscriptions on

---

8 The Temple to Apollo Pythios was built during second half of the 7th century but the Gortynians appear not to have inscribed its walls until early the following century. Its location, 700m from the agora and integrated into the Roman Praetorium complex, suggests that it may have been moved by the Romans from a higher site (cf. Perlman, 2002; 2004c).

Apollo Pythios and elsewhere were very carefully inscribed to aid legibility. John Davies (2005) argues that they were intended for an administrative purpose, to make clear how the affairs of the *polis* would be conducted. Michael Gagarin, on the other hand, suggests that the laws were meant as a practical guide in actual litigation, a role that is similar to modern statute (Gagarin, 1995, 1999, 2001, 2004). There are also those who believe the 600 lines of inscription cannot be considered a 'code' because the focus is so narrow and fragmentary (Kristensen, 2007: 2). In fact, a more telling observation would be that the text does not constitute 'law', at least as commonly understood. There is almost no reference to criminal law; no provision for violence or offences against the person (with the exception of rape for which fines alone are suggested); none for theft or dishonesty and none for fraud or deception. In fact this is not so surprising. Criminal matters were dealt with very differently since offences falling into this category were regarded as being against the community itself and were therefore dealt with by the citizenry or, more probably, their representatives in the Council. As Headlam observes 'murder especially was treated in this way; not only because the community was injured by the lawlessness, but because bloodshed involves religious impurity' (1892–93: 69). Other matters, such as adoption, had to be proclaimed in the *agora* (earlier a meeting place, later a market place as well) suggesting that here too the issue concerned a matter of civic interest.[9]

The code deals with a series of rights and duties relating to family life and the disposition of property. It is as important for its *assumptions* as it is for the provisions of the rules it outlines. It makes clear, for example, that Gortyn operated on the principles of private property and a money economy, as early as the 5th century and probably much earlier. Land, for example, is considered in the code as alienable, thereby indicating the rights of private land ownership. In addition the code confirms the hierarchical nature of Cretan society by making it clear that fines for various offences are subdivided according to the category of the population in which a defendant is included. For example, payments due as fines for rape vary according to whether the assailant or victim was a free citizen (belonging to a *hetaireia*), a free citizen with no political rights (*apetairos*), a serf or a slave. It is particularly important, however, that just as citizenship rights might be granted to foreigners, so too it was possible for manumission to occur and, under some circumstances, for the children of slaves to be free (e.g. when a male slave married a free woman and went to live in her household). Westermann, for example, observes:

> The laws of Gortyn in Crete present a situation in which the rights accorded to slaves assimilated them even more closely to the free population than was the case at Athens (1974: 22).

---

9 The Code says that a declaration of adoption 'shall be made in the market-place, when the citizens are gathered, from the stone from which proclamations are made'.

Overall, the rules, while focusing on a number of specific rights (e.g. those of the divorcee, the heiress, adopted children etc.), underpin three important aspects of Gotynian society. First, they sustain a male dominated concept of family honour. For example, in the rules relating to adultery, the ensuing penalty will be higher if the event occurs in a male relative's household. Second, the rules relating to the rights and duties of an heiress make it clear that 'tribal' endogamy must occur, thereby sustaining ethnic divisions; and third, the rules apply rights and duties differentially according to gender. For example, in the case of inheritance all houses wherever situated will pass to sons and other property will be 'fairly' divided in the ratio two to one between sons and daughters. As John Davies has pointed, out the heiress is seen above all else as a 'conveyor of property' since 'every detail is directed toward maximizing the likelihood that she will marry the closest available paternal relative, thereby ensuring that property stays firmly within the paternal lineage, while minimizing the role of maternal relatives' (Davies, 2005: 322). Although this appears horribly inequitable to modern eyes, as Schaps reminds us 'it must be remembered (that) Gortyn was unique in the Greek world in giving daughters *any* inheritance rights in the presence of equally close males' (Schaps 1975: 57). Also, as Miller has observed this is an important step in affirming the rights of women over their own property as 'neither (a wife's) husband nor her son could alienate or promise her property' (2009: 305). If on divorce a women can prove that her spouse is at fault, then, in addition to the property she brought to the marriage, she is entitled to half the family's production plus half what she has produced herself (e.g. by weaving) and a modest penalty of five staters. It is clear, therefore, that a primary purpose of the 'Code' is to cement a series of rather conservative obligations and thereby help to preserve an ordered agrarian community based on private property and accepted social inequalities.[10]

It must be remembered that it was probably the magistrates who promulgated the laws (i.e. the *kosmoi* and *gnomones* with or without their subordinates the *mnemones* or recorders) and that judges (*dikastai*) were only magistrates when assuming this role. As elsewhere, all officials were precluded from serving again for a period of years and Davies advances the plausible hypothesis that the variability in the quality and extent of codification can be explained if we assume that what was inscribed were the *changes* in the law proposed or approved by a magistrate, or board of magistrates, at the end of his or its period of office (1996: 52).[11] In other words, rather as with English common law, there were two processes going on simultaneously: the first a process of systematization and the second one of continuous amendment through judicial interpretation.

Davies comments that criminal statutes (other than those dealing with rape) are almost absent, and also that the provisions for the *syssitia* are only referred to indirectly. Overall, 'it is a system of protecting privilege, of safeguarding the

---

10   The most detailed English translation and commentary are contained in Willetts 1967 but cf. Willetts 1976.
11   At Gortyn the periods were three years for a *kosmos*, five for a senior *kosmos* and ten for a *gnomon*.

ownership and transmission of property (including "slaves"), and of ensuring the continuance of male lineages' (2005: 327). One problem, of course, is that we cannot know for sure whether other laws, either as yet not found or not capable of interpretation, covered other issues but, as Davies argues, the more likely situation was one where magistrates were intended to interpret the law as they saw fit within general parameters. In his words '...the possibility should at least be aired that we are dealing with a form of case law' (1996: 44).

The unity of Greek law?

The evidence presented thus far does suggest that Cretan law had some special characteristics, but that is not the same as saying that there is no such thing as ancient Greek law as a whole. In the nineteenth and early twentieth centuries it would have been assumed, especially among European specialists, that it made as much sense to speak of 'Greek law' as it did to refer to 'Roman law', even though they differ greatly one from the other. What has subsequently come to be referred to as 'Athenocentricity' suggested that what appeared to be variation was simply a question of the evolutionary stage to which regions of the Greek world had progressed. It was Moses Finley who first argued against the proposition that the Gortyn Code represented merely an 'an early stage of Greek law'. Indeed, he called this argument 'equivocal and misleading' (1951: 83) and went on to ask:

> Did the law of *all* the Greek communities go through this stage? If so, why was fifth-century Athens no longer in that stage, when fifth-century Gortyn was? What evidence is there that Gortyn ever transcended that stage; if not, why not? (1951: 83; emphasis in original).

Moreover, if we take a work like Plato's *Laws*, the whole point is a debate between a Cretan, a Spartan and an Athenian, indicating that 'the legal conceptions of the three communities were worlds apart, in spirit as well as in concrete application' (1951: 83). Finley cites other examples, such as the divergent practices on the sale of land between different *poleis* and the range of procedures regarding the recovery of debt. These are powerful points but the argument is perhaps taken to extremes. If his statement that 'never in antiquity was there a Greece in the sense in which there was a Rome' meant anything, it tended to imply that the division was between an atomistic and acephalous dominion and one of complete uniformity and unity. The reality lay somewhere in between.

Gagarin agrees with Finley that 'differences in the substantive laws of Greek cities are so great that we cannot speak of substantive unity in any meaningful sense' (2008: 243). On the other hand, Gagarin detects great similarities in what might be termed the 'legal process'. Greeks everywhere, he suggests, wrote in non-technical language and displayed it for public scrutiny; they relied upon a defendant making an oral plea without professional assistance so that 'we can meaningfully speak of a unity of Greek law which we might call *procedural* in the broad sense that all Greek cities (except in Egypt) share a similar attitude to the purposes and general methods of legislation and litigation' (2008: 243; emphasis added). Thus, he suggests, there appears to have been a shared understanding of the judicial process, even though the *content* of substantive rules may vary from *polis* to *polis*. This extends beyond the process of litigation and includes the organisation of justice, and above all can be seen in the practice of writing laws down so that 'features commonly considered characteristically Athenian, are not just Athenian or democratic, but Greek' (2008: 8; 244). Gagarin is not alone in supporting this contention. Gerhard Thür (2007), for example, has stressed that the commonalities (e.g. the use of oaths, divine sanctions and the similarities in procedural law) far outweighed the variations.

The role of written law

Broadly speaking, there are two opposing views on the functions of Greek law in general and *written* Greek law in particular. On the one hand, there is the argument recently articulated by Zinon Papakonstantinou (2002; 2008), but with a long pedigree, that views Greek law as a tool which the powerful use to suppress class-based dissent and which, *per contra*, the weak use to try and outwit and control the powerful. Regarding the Archaic law from Dreros, for example, Papakonstantinou argues that the text represents a negotiated settlement of class-based divisions evident from the fact that three separate groups of officials are required to swear the oath (2008: 63; cf. 2002). Similarly the *dikastai* in Athenian courts were not, as others suggest, simply citizens whose turn had come to perform this judging function, but rather elite legal specialists. Even Spensithios is thought on this analysis to represent a member of the elite (2008: 78), rather than, as is often thought, a foreigner selected precisely because he was more likely to be objective and above local rivalries and interests.

Hölkeskamp, too, argues that we have to look for the stresses that led to written law being constructed. Clearly it was seen as a solution, but to what? He suggests that aristocratic conflict and competition was a critical issue leading to 'ever-increasing exploitation of the common people' but that this and other pressures such as population growth were not sufficient to explain the emergence of bodies of law (1992: 66):

> In the increasingly densely populated, economically differentiated, socially stratified and politically autonomous 'polities' in the city state culture of Archaic Greece, it must have been the steady demand for a new quality of internal consolidation which generated such a framework of 'civic' institutions of more than ephemeral stability' (1992: 70).

This, he argues, lay behind the emergence of written law since 'there was an inherent drive towards the development of genuinely "institutionalized" rules and solutions for the most obvious and urgent problem of guaranteeing the rather precarious internal stability of the community' (1992: 71).

This does not, of course, resolve the problem of why Crete pre-eminently was the place where these rules emerged most clearly and in a form providing a visible standard of internal justice. The answer, he suggests, must lie in the peculiar propensity among the Cretans for in-fighting and discord. On the Dreros inscription, for example, Hölkeskamp says that 'the emergence of this sort of legislation and of law-making ... was an immediate and direct response to challenges which consisted in new, sensitive, basically very concrete problems and tangible demands arising in a community in a phase of growth, external pressure, internal tension and increasing complexity' (1992: 74).

The approach taken by Michael Gagarin is almost the opposite. On the reasons for the written display of the laws at Dreros, his argument is that they represent an attempt by members of the *polis* to ensure their involvement in the installation of a new *kosmos* and to reinforce the feeling in the population at large that it was they – and not the elites – that had imposed these rules of conduct on their officials. As he writes, 'the law was an expression of (the people's) authority as a group and it was thus in their interest to have that authority memorialized in a publicly displayed text' (Gagarin, 2008: 78). In other words, the existence of written laws, the way they were displayed and the references in the texts to collective organisations of the people (*polis, damos/demos*, the 'Gortynians') convince Gagarin that there is 'stronger support for the view that non-elites were responsible for early legislation than that the elites were regulating their own competition by means of legislation' (2008: 88). The laws are thus an important landmark in the evolution of a representative system, albeit an inchoate one; they demarcate permanent rules of the political game, separate from traditional mores, that are accessible to all (even though *all* could not read them) and which possessed the authority of the *polis* as a whole backed by the ultimate wisdom of the gods. In this way writing created the idea of law itself, since 'henceforth a law would be any rule that belonged to this special body of written rules backed by the authority of the *polis*' (2005: 92).

Gagarin's answer to the obvious question as to why they should have been displayed in this form at this time (from the middle of the 7th century) is that the typical Cretan *polis* was expanding to embrace geographically dispersed communities. These might not share the customs and traditions of the urban centre, which would throw doubt on what the rules actually were when possible violations occurred:

> In sum, the increasing need for detailed rules in cities that were growing larger and more diverse and the desire of a body of ordinary members of the community to confirm their own authority were the most important factors behind the rapid spread of publicly displayed, written legislation (2008: 86).

These were the reasons for the prominent display of the written laws in a public setting, he suggests, and they were therefore made as readable as possible for those with perhaps limited literacy. Gagarin extends this argument to embrace the Greek world as a whole, except in certain colonies such as those in Ptolemaic Egypt.

Moreover, he sees these features as not only 'Greek' but *only* Greek, in the sense that other cultures wrote down codes of laws but these were used for academic study or for reasons of persuasion, they were not intended to be available in a form suitable for utilization by members of the population at large. This is clear, he suggests, when a comparison is made between the Gortyn Code and the Babylonian Code of Hammurabi.[12] The latter was a written guide to procedure, whereas the former is a guide to practical action to redress grievances. In his words 'the Greek use of writing in law – writing legislation but keeping procedure unwritten – was just the reverse of Near-Eastern practice' (2008: 174). This profound difference makes it very unlikely that the Gortynians were influenced in developing their written statutes by the Code of Hammurabi or any other Near Eastern precedents.

Athenian and Cretan law

Any explanation for the extensive use of written law in numerous Cretan *poleis* from the Archaic period onwards has to consider whether this was simply a reflection of practices elsewhere in the Greek world. On the face of it, this does not seem very likely. More than half of the entries in Koerner's (1993) listing of written laws in ancient Greece are from Crete, while in a parallel study by van Effenterre and Ruzé (1994–5) the figure is 40 per cent. However:

> Since we probably have only a small fraction of the texts originally inscribed on stone from this period, and nothing written on more perishable materials such as wood or papyrus, we cannot necessarily conclude that the Cretans wrote more laws than other Greeks; they may simply have inscribed more of them on stone, or (less likely) archaeologists may just have found more legal inscriptions on Crete than elsewhere (Gagarin, 2008: 43)

Also, Gortyn's laws, and those of many (perhaps most) city states in Crete might just have been earlier than those elsewhere, possibly as a consequence of the early adoption of a more or less fully formed Greek alphabet. While the enormity of the task and a lack of evidence make it impossible to compare Crete with *every* city state at the time, it is possible to examine this question in relation to ancient Athens.

As Michael Gagarin (2004, 2005a, 2005b, 2008), David Cohen (1995, 2005) and others have argued, there are important similarities that must be mentioned. Of these the following appear to be particularly prominent. The first is the lack of a separation of powers between the legal function and the political. The early Cretan laws clearly dealt with constraining political leaders, whatever the origins and functions of subsequent laws may have been. Many commentators who support the 'elite conflict' theory for the origins of written law have noted this point – so

---

12 The Code of Hammurabi, which dates from the middle of the second millennium BCE, contains 282 laws written on 12 tablets. It was found in 1901 on a *stele* at the site of ancient Susa in western Iran. It is now in the Louvre in Paris.

much so, in fact, that some want to suggest that there was no autonomous realm in Greek law. For example, as Foxall and Lewis put it in their introduction to a collection of essays on law in ancient Greece (largely Athenian), 'law, for the Greeks, was a tool not a master' (1996: 6). The second similarity perhaps flows from the first. As Gagarin and others have argued, what actually took place in the courts themselves, insofar as we can tell, made little reference to written statute and the citizenry had no reason therefore to encourage or evolve a body of professionals whose job it was to act on behalf of a plaintiff or defendant. Looked at through the modern lens of largely Roman law and jurisprudence, with its separation of legal from executive functions, its caste of specialists and its dependence upon written statute and case law, legal processes in the ancient *polis* seem arbitrary, unhealthily linked to rhetoric and intensely politicised. This opens the question whether it makes any sense to speak of the 'rule of law' in ancient Greek courts, for that implies a dispassionate application of impartial rules.

Finally, there is the claim concerning the similarity of legal process throughout the ancient Greek world. Referring to Michael Gagarin's work, Cohen notes his support for Finley's view on the variability of substantive law, but also the existence of 'underlying common ideas in the realm of procedure, understood in the broadest terms as legal process' (Cohen, 2005: 4). An important commonality of procedure is the freedom for litigants to present their cases as they wished, while another is the 'openness' of the system with judges filling in the gaps in the law as they saw fit. In recognising these similarities, can it then be claimed that there is a fundamental unity in the way that Greek-speaking peoples evolved, practised and utilised their laws? With only Crete and Athens more easily available as exemplars, any answer has to be tentative but it would have to address three very important topics: the way that justice was defined and delivered, the exact nature of the link between law and administration, and the wider social functions of law. If there was a commonality on these issues we could, at least on the basis of the most researched cases, indeed speak of ancient 'Greek law', while being conscious of major differences in the *content* of individual statutes according to the *polis* from which they had evolved. My answer will be that this case has not yet been shown and that Crete still remains *sui generis*, albeit not hermetically sealed from ideas pertaining elsewhere.

THE DELIVERY OF JUSTICE

It would be inappropriate to spend time on the philosophical underpinnings of justice in the Athenian world, but the manner of its delivery is so peculiar as to make it for all intents and purposes unique.[13] The first point to note is the intimate connection between the evolution of *polis* law and the emergence of a formal political system. This is a phenomenon shared across all city states and it follows that if political systems varied then so too would the legal processes that emerged

---

13 There is a large and growing literature on how the concept of justice was interpreted in ancient Athens. See, for example, Havelock (1978), Farenga (2006) and Lanni (2006).

alongside them (Thomas, 2005: 42–43). As we shall see in the next chapter, Athens and Crete developed singularly different forms of democracy – one direct, egalitarian and focused on the individual, the other representative, hierarchical and focused on group rights.

Decisions in 5th and 4th century Athens were the result of deliberations by the people (*demos*) in two parallel democratic institutions, the Assembly and the courts. In the words of Harvey Yunis 'the purpose of both institutions was to express the will of the *demos* – that is, the mass of ordinary citizens who made up the vast bulk of the citizen body and wielded power in the state – in a fair, open, institutionally stable way' (2005: 191). Whatever emerged from both forums was in the hands of individuals who, in the sense that they were competing for influence, were engaged in political acts. Although procedures differed in the two bodies 'the same underlying process operated in both institutions and gave them both democratic integrity':

> A large audience of ordinary, anonymous citizens, effectively representing the *demos* as a whole, listened to a debate among individual citizens on whatever question was to be decided. At the conclusion of the debate the audience voted and the question was decided. (In the Assembly the debate was open-ended; in the courts the debate pitted prosecutor against defendant) (Yunis, 2005: 192).

Individual citizens were influential in determining outcomes in precisely the same way; namely, how persuasive they were in accruing votes in their favour.

A second feature in the legal process is the absence in the Athenian case of professional expertise. As a consequence of the egalitarian ideology, not only did the individual present his own case, which was also true in Crete, but judgments were made by an individual's peers without the possibility of intercession by a legal specialist. Yunis writes very clearly on this point:

> In an Athenian trial only three parties were involved: prosecutor, defendant, and a panel of citizens, known as *dikastai* (literally 'judges'), who, combining the functions of judge and jury, determined the outcome. All three parties functioned without training, expertise, or supervision in the law. Prosecution and defense spoke in turn for an equal amount of time. When they were finished, the *dikastai* voted by secret ballot for either the prosecutor or the defendant; simple majority ruled (Yunis, 2005: 194).

The term '*dikastai*' is sometimes translated as 'jurors' rather than 'judges', but this is misleading since in the absence of anyone in the court with legal training, or for that matter with knowledge of the law, the decision and sentencing took place without judicial direction, with no guarantee that formal deliberation would take place and without recourse to precedent or case law.[14] There was no provision for leave to appeal (Todd, 2005: 100). All that we know about Cretan procedures

---

14 To be one of the *dikastai* it was only necessary to be a full citizen, to have reached the age of thirty and to be free from debt to the state.

suggests a considerable difference. While individuals represented themselves, they did so before magistrates acting as judges, whose role was to interpret traditional laws, whether written or not, assisted by those like Spensithios, whose job was to record the law and, presumably, previous cases that had been decided upon it. Unlike litigants in an Athenian court, it does not seem probable that opposing sides in a Cretan court had free rein to say and act as they wished, unrestrained by any reference to appropriate jurisprudence.

As Harvey Yunis suggests the only constraint on Athenian litigants was rhetorical in the sense that they 'would constrain themselves from saying anything that might alienate their audience, the *dikastai*' (2005: 195). The use of oratory, not simply as the means of presenting a case based on fact but as a means of persuasion in lieu of fact, appears to have reached a high point in Athens after 420 BCE. Athenians did not use the distinction we are familiar with between civil and criminal cases; rather, they used the division between *graphai*, or cases that anyone could bring, and *dikai*, or those that could only be initiated by an interested party (Osborne, 1985: 40). *Graphai* prosecutions are sometimes thought to be democratic in nature because they can be brought on behalf of those who could not defend themselves, but as Robin Osborne reminds us:

> Equal opportunity to prosecute is only an effective means of furthering democracy if accompanied by equal capacity to prosecute, and it is clear that the way in which all prosecutions are in fact embedded in social relations precludes this (1985: 41).

The risks of bringing a case in the *graphai* category were considerable if the plaintiff was unsuccessful, and for this reason an individual might use the services of a logographer or someone who either wrote, or wrote and presented, a case in court (Osborne, 1985: 43). Again, however, the rhetorical tradition was paramount. David Cohen, referring to its importance, calls it the 'organizing category for both forensic oratory and legal thought' (2005: 10). Much of our evidence for the way Athenian courts worked comes from the written versions of speeches made by the most famous of the Attic orators, although not all specialists would agree on the centrality of the oral process. Michele Faraguna (2007), for example, has recently argued that the operation of the 'rhetorical phase' was always set within tight constraints imposed by written documents, so that one cannot conclude that ancient Greek law was dependent only upon orality. The critical issue, however, is that we have no evidence suggesting that the system at Gortyn, or in other Cretan courts, was even remotely similar.

Michael Gagarin too refers to the 'complete orality of Athenian trials' (2008: 196) and to the 'long tradition in the orators that oral communication of important information is superior to written communication' (2008: 200), and he certainly manages to establish a fundamental point concerning the role of writing in all known courts of the Greek world: what he refers to as the 'fundamental duality' between the use of writing for legislation but restricted use of writing in litigation (2008: 197). In Crete too the proceedings were primarily oral, although not dependent upon oratory alone as he contends. Gagarin, however, wishes to go further than this and suggest two other points of consistency.

The first is the denial of any link between the political realm and the legal process. He is obliged to proceed down this path because he accepts the traditional view that all Cretan *poleis* were non-democratic oligarchies (2008: 197). To admit a link, therefore, would be to accept a cause of variation in the legal process. Yet the whole point about the informality of the Athenian legal process was to restrict what was written so as not to militate against those with restricted or non-existent literacy (2008: 206). By restricting the use of writing the 'Athenians prevented any possibility of the law becoming more formal. Litigants remained free to present their arguments and proofs in court in any way they wished, using ordinary language familiar to the untrained jurors' (2008: 207). This made the law itself malleable in practice since either the plaintiff or defendant could use any law or part of a law they wished and they controlled which clauses were read to jurors, and in which sequence, in order to enhance their case. Moreover, it is clear that proposing new laws was open to any citizen. They were simply required to publicise them before they were considered by the '*nomothetai*', whose role was to consider all proposals, along with their own, and offer them to the council for consideration. Decrees, as distinct from laws, were proposed orally in the assembly which alone could accept or reject them (2008: 188). This meant, in theory at least, that anyone thinking of a legal action but not finding laws that might adequately support him could propose them in advance of proceeding to court. No wonder Todd refers to the Athenian system as one 'in which legal statutes played a relatively minor rôle as sources of law' (Todd, 2005: 98, note 5).

All this is clearly a reflection of the *particular* individualistic ideology of Athenian democracy. From what we know it simply did not and could not work like that in Gortyn where a body of more or less coherent law was applied by an authoritative figure to each case presented before the court. The presentation may have been oral, and made without recourse to professionals, but it was set within a much more formal context. This is not to deny the close link between the political realm and the legal, but simply to suggest that just as the former was based upon a formal set of constitutional principles, so too were the proceedings in court.

The second point concerns the attention given to the displaying of laws in public settings as monumental indicators of the authority of the *polis* itself. Although Gagarin is at pains to point out that 'from its very beginning in the late seventh century, Athenian legislation was written down and publicly displayed' (2008: 206), and there is no doubt that some laws in Athens were set up for public display, no one has been able to demonstrate the existence of anything resembling in coverage the Gortyn codes or possibly those from other Cretan *poleis*. Gagarin supports his argument by reference, in the Athenian case, to Draco's law on homicide of the late 7th century, reinstated and reinvigorated in the late 5th century. This was indeed a case of written law adopted more or less unchanged in the Kleisthenic reforms but it is only one law whose use was rare and unusual. Others may indeed have been written down on perishable fabric but, with the possible exception of Solon's famous wooden *axones*, they were not intended for public display. As Rosalind Thomas confirms, 'Athens has left us no archaic laws on stone' (2005: 44):

> Our evidence provides large numbers of laws on stone from Crete, quite a few on bronze from Olympia/Elis and the Argolid, especially Argos, but none or only the scantiest fragments from Thebes, Catana, Sparta, Athens, and Locri, which were famed for their lawgivers (2005: 44).

No wonder then that Plato in the *Laws* was so insistent on referring to the laws of Crete as 'famous among the Hellenes' for conferring 'every sort of good' (Plato *Laws* Book 1).

LAW AND ADMINISTRATION

Probably one reason why Plato and other philosophers were so enthusiastic about the laws of Crete is that they saw in them a legal process that was not prey to the vicissitudes of such an open, and to some extent arbitrary, system as that which operated in 5th century Athens. When Robin Osborne remarks that 'much of the work of the Athenian law courts was at the level of regulating conflict' he is referring not to political struggles at a group level but to the resolution of individuals' quarrels; or, as he puts it, 'the Athenian law courts were a public stage upon which private enmities were played out' (1981: 52). It is not then just the 'open texture' of the Athenian system but its individualistic and unpredictable nature that sets it apart from other legal frameworks (cf. Hart, 1961: 124–32). As Osborne writes, 'the capacity to fit actions to men was a primary quality of Athenian legal procedure' (1981: 48). If that was the case, is it possible to conclude that in Athens there was anything we could call the 'rule of law'?

As with almost every aspect of the ancient world, this question has been subject to intense debate. It is possible, for example, to define the 'rule of law' in a minimalist sense to simply mean that courtroom procedures operated in accordance with the law. One argument in previous historical investigation into Athenian law was that other principles, such as an appeal to 'equity', could be found in the speeches of the Attic orators, and that this suggested that conformity with the law could not be guaranteed. More recently, a counter argument has emerged that suggests appeals to 'equity' are not suggestive of a departure from law, but simply imply judgments that are provable and therefore conform to the principle of the 'free evaluation of evidence' (Meyer-Laurin, 2007: 139).[15] Another argument with a similar conclusion has been advanced by Edward Harris (2000; 2005). What has impressed him, through an analysis of actual cases, is that litigants did not in fact 'invent law'; rather they stuck closely to it even when the law itself was noticeably imprecise, and with no clear definitions of the substantive concepts it

15 Further arguments that draw parallel conclusions on the 'modernity' of Athenian law can be found in Ostwald (1969) and Sealey (1994).

employed (2000: 78). This was a community, he argues, that 'took the rule of law very seriously' (2000: 79).

On the other side of the Atlantic, things do not look the same. In his study entitled *Law, Violence and Community* (1995), David Cohen suggests that Athenian trials were characterised by a confrontational struggle which was the result of an agonistic ethic. This makes it difficult to speak of the 'rule of law' in a general sense since the Athenian legal process was embedded in 'a democratic political culture defined by participatory institutions on the one hand and the recognition of the power of persuasive speech (rhetoric) on the other' (Cohen, 2005: 14–15). The majesty of the law does not therefore figure very prominently.

Adriaan Lanni (2005) takes a more nuanced approach. In her study of the Athenian courts she finds numerous categories of evidence in the popular courts that were considered relevant but which a modern court would immediately dismiss. These include background information relating to a dispute but not contained in the action itself, appeals by a defendant for pity on account of the potential impact of a negative judgment and material relating to the character of either party to the dispute (2005: 114 *passim*; 2006). Her work is, however, much more subtle in three ways. First, these 'extralegal pleas' were not intended to take the place of a proper evaluation of the evidence, but were made in order to contextualise it properly and therefore to understand it. This brings her to a criticism of Cohen's concept of the courts being a zero-sum competition over honour and esteem, since extra-legal submissions were not intended to fuel the feud, but to reach an equitable resolution (2006: 44). Moreover, in certain categories of case (e.g. maritime laws or *dikai emporikai* and those relating to homicide or *dikai phonou*), there seems to have been a far greater acceptance of the need to follow law more closely. Thus, while the legal system in Athens 'cannot be characterized as embodying a rule of law, the participants nevertheless viewed the process as aiming for recognizably "legal" rather than social ends' (2005: 128). Moreover, the courts were not irrelevant in helping to sustain a remarkably stable society that operated without any obvious means of coercive control. So while we cannot speak of a 'rule of law' in the sense that an abstract body of principles guided everyone's conduct, the courts nonetheless helped sustain social order through enforcing social norms (Lanni, 2009). Some of these may well have figured in laws unrelated to the case in hand while others (including 'the treatment of friends and family and private sexual conduct') were essentially extralegal (2009: 694).

SOCIAL FUNCTION OF THE LAWS

Evidence on the wider social functions of the law is not easy to discern even in the modern era, let alone with such inadequate information as we possess in the present comparison. Yet the close integration of political and legal systems, common to both but differing in form between the Athenian and Cretan cases, should make us alive to the possibility that law itself functioned differently in each setting. At an abstract level we are familiar with the common distinction between individual and group rights, the former integral to traditional notions of law in Western democracies, the latter integrated uneasily in recent years following attempts to overcome centuries that saw the systematic exclusion of minorities. This argument will be elaborated further in the final chapter, but if we can accept the existence of a continuum from one to the other, then it may be that Athens and Crete are on different points along it.

There is no doubt that Athenian democracy was highly individualised in the sense that all the institutions of society were moulded to enhance personal engagement and individual rights. This is what Lanni means when she says of submissions in the popular courts that they reflected 'a highly individualized and contextualized notion of justice' (Lanni, 2005: 128). To put it in social science terms, the function of law, aside from the quest for justice, was to bind the individual citizen, *qua* individual, into the institutions of the state. As many commentators have noted, politics and the law helped to bring order to a society divided by wealth and status. Fearing divisions along these lines from the days of Solon, the operation of the courts served to belittle social divisions in favour of the individual's rights to justice and participation. An individual bringing an action in the popular court would frequently claim the good of the *polis* as one of their motives for so doing. Similarly, the decisions of jurors were often perceived as a choice between alternative visions as to how Athenian citizens should live (Christ, 1998: 190). The critical categories were the individual and the society as a whole.

One should not be too surprised at this individualism. After all Kleisthenes may have wanted to overcome the Attic divisions between city, countryside and coast, but by destroying any lingering ethnic attachment to *phylai* and creating administrative ones in their place, he made it clear that attachment was intended to be through personal and not group obligation. We can speculate on what his motives may have been but Robin Osborne probably comes very close when he supports Herodotus in believing that the intention was to weaken Ionian ethnicity in favour of civic pride, and possibly thereby to bolster anti-Spartan sentiment (Osborne, 1996: 300).

In Gortyn, and possibly in other Cretan *poleis*, the law appeared to function in a very different way. In contrast to Athens, the laws lay out obligations and duties in class terms, making frequent references to the different penalties for the same offence according to the social origins of the defendant and the context in which the alleged offence arose. At the same time the rights accorded to women were less divisive. For example, whereas in Athens women citizens could not inherit, could control only a small amount of property and marry only other citizens, in Gortyn they could inherit in their own right, retain property if divorced and could pass it on within their families as men could (Gagarin, 2005: 31). They could also marry slaves and pass on their free status to their children. It is as if the architects of these institutions feared completely different kinds of conflicts. In the Athenian case, the absence of reference to social class bears silent witness to its salience; in Gortyn the seeming preoccupation with social divisions belies the real concern which appears to have been with potentially disruptive consequences coming from elsewhere in the *polis*.

There is no compelling evidence that differing levels of literacy were the reason for the predominance of written law and, even if there were, it is just as persuasive to hypothesise that levels in Crete, where the laws were on public display, would be higher than where they were not. A possible reason why written laws emerged so powerfully in Crete soon after or coincident with the establishment of systems of political representation is that they were seen as an integrative force in a multi-ethnic society. What the Gortyn law does very clearly is lay down the implications of particular situations for each horizontal or class category of the population; what it equally clearly does *not* do is indicate that differences of treatment will flow from particular membership of a constituent *phyle*. This would suggest that the greater fear of the political leadership was of *stasis* between *phylai* and not between groupings by social class. The law therefore functioned alongside the system of representation itself as a means of social integration across ethnic groups. Written law, which made crystal clear which social categories would be accorded differential treatment, was defusing the potential for ethnic conflict. By way of contrast, other seemingly similar *poleis* turn out on inspection to have been rather different. Sparta, for example, did not display laws publicly and possibly never wrote them down at all. But Sparta's ethnic composition had one important similarity to that of Athens. As Jones (1987) demonstrates the Dorian *phylai* gave way early on to territorial divisions (*obai* or villages), as was the case in Athens with the transformation of the ancient *phylai* into 'artificial' categories of association based on *deme* or physical location. The danger in Sparta would have been one of ethnic secession had it not been for the powerful ideology of militarism and the even more significant structure of political control.

Without using these terms, Michael Gagarin comes close to the proposition that Cretan laws were intended to signify and promote ethnic unity. For example, the bilingual text from the fragmentary eighth law at Dreros suggests the presence of at least one Eteocretan community within the *polis* as a whole. As he argues:

> In such circumstances, towns like Dreros faced the challenge of creating a unified sense of community. The prominent display of this law with its enactment clause would advertise this accomplishment and would strengthen the sense among the members of the community who constituted this polis, including perhaps some members of these neighboring communities, that they comprised a single unified group, the polis of Dreros (2008: 79).

Given the content of these laws, he may also be right in suggesting that pressure from below was an important ingredient in encouraging the political leadership to take these actions.

In the Gortyn case, as well as that of Dreros, references are made to some form of democratic accountability in the formulation of the written laws. As John Davies notes the use of the term 'Gods' and the phrase 'these things were decided by the Gortynians voting' (*Inscriptiones creticae* 4.78.1, Guarducci, 1950) 'encourages the assumption that the simple invocation "Gods" elsewhere reflects other assembly decisions' (2005: 309). He goes on to say:

> Because the Great Code also begins thus, states its start date in public terms, and regulates the behavior of public officials, it too must have had some public validation (2005: 309).

But public validation does not mean that the initiative for Cretan laws came directly from the people. It is much more probable that the leadership of the individual *phyle*, on behalf of those they felt they represented, argued the case for the preparation of written laws and for their public display. There are frequent references in the Gortynian laws to the phrase 'as is written' as a cross reference to other laws, and Gagarin is right to suggest that they 'were all part of a single, unified body of texts, "what is written", which comprised the laws of the city' (2008: 143). He captures the probable context well when he writes that:

> the sight of dozens of texts displayed all around (the Gortynians) in public areas of the city must have made members of the community, especially but not only those who could read them, feel themselves part of a group that acquired special authority by being the possessors of, the beneficiaries of, and (probably) ultimately the authority behind "the things that are written" (2008: 144).

This is precisely the sense of unity that any representative system of validation seeks to instill into the minds of all those who make up the political entity.

Others too have noted the apparent quest for equity and balance in the Gortyn Great Code. Alberto Maffi (2005), for example, argues this case, but in terms of the relations between social classes. Given the code's firm strictures on the differential rights and duties of citizens and others, this seems improbable. Ethnic segments of a population contain members of all or most class positions, although not necessarily in the same proportion. There is, therefore, no contradiction in accepting the proposition that democratic accountability may have existed alongside a hierarchy divided in ethnic terms. This also means that those who discern in the written laws of Crete the expression of political tensions are not necessarily wrong. Rosalind Thomas rightly argues that the fact that as many as eleven Cretan cities show evidence of archaic laws inscribed on stone cannot be dismissed as 'merely an accident of evidence' (2005: 43–44). She senses in the first Dreros law that because the focus is on what it is forbidden for a chief official to do this implies:

> That written law might often have been turned to in times of political and social upheaval and represented an attempt in some places (like Dreros) to limit or regularize the power of the politically active elite, perhaps by their very peers (2005: 46).

But she does not suggest what the basis for the political tension might have been. Had this been Athens, then undoubtedly it would have been the threat of another tyranny, but there is no evidence from any Cretan *polis* that power was ever usurped on an individual basis. On the contrary the system allowed for the *rotation* of offices on behalf of a *phyle* or ethnic grouping. It is certainly probable that this itself was linked to laws in written form. As Sara Forsdyke argues, 'by putting these laws in physical form and by invoking the authority of the gods either explicitly on the stone or by placing the stone in a sanctuary, communal and divine support were brought to the fragile public offices of the early polis' (Forsdyke, 2005: 26). In this sense *rotation* was a form of power sharing. Crete did not need a procedure for individual banishment through exile to avoid tyranny since the publicly proclaimed laws, sanctioned by a popular assembly, meant that this could not occur.[16] The early Gortynian laws include a number concerning the sacrificial calendar and, since individual ethnic groups had their own gods, these would have been particularly important to preserve in stone (Gagarin, 2008: 81).

The issue of literacy may have had very little to do with this, since what is at stake is a different concept of the social functions of law. Law in Crete performed an integrating function across *phylai* and was written in monumental form to make it clear to all constituent ethnic groups that this was so and that the dominance of one was temporary. In Athens by contrast, this need was not there and law remained largely oral. In both settings there were clear links with political institutions but these did not function in the same way either. There were, of course, ethnic groupings in 7th and 6th century Athens that paralleled those in Crete. But the latter never had a Kleisthenes whose reforms pushed Athens along the road from a *polis* to an *ethne* (or nation). Aristotle in his *Constitution of Athens*, writing of the reforms of Kleisthenes, says that the redistribution of the population was done 'with the object of intermixing the members of the different tribes, and so securing that more persons might have a share in the franchise' (21.2). Quite clearly this was in the place of the old divisions for Aristotle goes on to say 'from this arose the saying "Do not look at the tribes", addressed to those who wished to scrutinize the lists of old families' (21.2–3). As Thür has put it:

> The democratic regulations include: the most equitable allotment possible of jurors from all ten tribes (*phylai*) of the citizens on the day of the trial and their distribution among the *dikastēria* (2005: 147).

This is an alternative to rotation and strict rules of succession in ensuring that tyrants did not emerge. In place of the ethnic groupings in Crete, Athens manufactured non-ethnic associations in the form of the artificial *phylai*, and in place of principles of rotation they upheld the concept of ostracism.

It is interesting to note that if there is validity in these arguments, they may also throw some light on one puzzle surrounding the Spensithios decree. As Gorlin (1988) has observed the decree is the earliest record of a high procedural office

16 In addition to Dreros and Gortyn, on some interpretations a fragmentary inscription from Eleutherna appears to be similar (van Effenterre and Ruzé, 1994–5: 83; cf. Forsdyke, 2005: 26, n. 50). The principle of rotation has also been shown in other multi-ethnic settings containing at least the three Dorian *phylai* (Jones, 1980).

holder in any Greek *polis*. The role Spensithios assumed was hereditary and the authors of the original publication of the text felt it very probable that the office holder must have been a citizen (Jeffrey and Murpurgo-Davis, 1970). Henri van Effenterre argued against this on the grounds that the rewards and privileges that are declared as due to Spensithios were typical of those identified in other Cretan inscriptions for foreigners (not citizens of the *polis* in question) working in the service of the *polis* (van Effenterre, 1973: 38). Van Effenterre is careful, however, not to suggest that Spensithios remains a foreigner, but rather that the office he holds and the honours he receives grant to him the equivalent of citizenship through naturalisation. The original authors point out that no mention is made of Spensithios belonging to a particular *phyle*, *startos* or *hetaireia* (Jeffrey and Murpurgo-Davis, 1970: 149), but Gorlin thinks the rewards he receives are simply to prevent him losing his citizenship status through debt or misfortune, while others have argued that he is identified without any ethnic association because he is well-known there (Beattied, 1975: 22). But if van Effenterre is right then an obvious conclusion may be drawn that Spensithios was recruited precisely *because* he was not a citizen and therefore above the fray of potential inter-ethnic feuding. Spensithios was concerned with noting and recalling the law for *kosmoi* in their role as judges and it would have been critical that he brought some objectivity to this task, for if Cretan law codes evolved through a combination of written statute and case law, it would be imperative that an official charged with this responsibility was not in the pocket of any sectional interest.

Crete and the rule of written law

Although Michael Gagarin wants to argue that both Athens and Crete showed evidence of the rule of law, his evidence is more compelling in the latter case. He takes a more onerous definition of the 'rule of law' than one based simply on the argument that statutes were followed in court. He identifies three criteria that take us far closer to a modern understanding (2004). First, disputes must be resolved by law, rather than by violence; second, no one person may be above the law, and third, legal decisions must not be subordinate to political or other extraneous considerations. Gargarin cites Herodotus and Thucydides in support of the first principle, but he might equally have included Plato's comment by the 'Athenian stranger' in the *Laws* that :

> [the] state in which the law is subject and has no authority, I perceive to be on the highway to ruin; but I see that the state in which the law is above the rulers, and the rulers are the inferiors of the law, has salvation, and every blessing which the Gods can confer (Book IV).

Gargarin finds this general principle evident in the first line of the Great Code of Gortyn when it says, 'whosoever may be likely to contend [in court] about a free man or a slave is not to seize him before trial' – in other words, the law and not personal retribution should be the first resort (2004: 178). Similarly, the Great Code makes it quite clear that the *kosmoi*, the most powerful individuals in the *polis*, were subject to its rules and that legal decisions should depend upon evidence and argument in court rather than hearsay or personal standing (2004: 179–80). How different this is from Harvey Yunis's summary of the typical Athenian trial where 'it was impossible to separate law, politics, ideology, and the litigants' style and personality. All were on trial simultaneously' (Yunis, 2005: 196).

It must be admitted that not all scholars would agree with this judgment on the Gortyn codes, let alone those elsewhere in Crete. Indeed, it is perhaps not too much of an exaggeration to suggest that what Crete is famous for in the spheres of legal scholarship is sometimes thought of as unimpressive precisely because it came from outside the normal (Athenian) ambit. Thus Rosalind Thomas, noting the Cretan precedents in written law, wants to argue that this does not make its legal system more just:

> I find it hard to believe that seventh century Dreros was particularly enlightened despite its fine inscibed law, let alone that all or even most of its citizens could read the inscription (1996: 9).[17]

This lack of 'enlightenment' is also evident, she suggests, in relation to the remedies on offer in ancient Greece. Here the argument turns on oath taking and appeals to the gods rather than the application of impersonal rules. But as the Drerian law on the circulation of *kosmoi* makes abundantly clear, on issues to do with the constitution, the remedies in Crete were anything but airy-fairy and ad hoc. It is hard to imagine a clearer and more draconian ruling than being banned from office for a period of years on pain of very heavy fines and the annulment of all prior decisions. In a further attempt to downgrade the Cretan laws, Thomas goes on to say that 'while Crete is famous for its extensive inscribed laws, it was precisely Cretan officials that Aristotle criticized for their use of arbitrary judgment' (1996: 9), yet a close reading of Aristotle's comment shows that this remark was directed not at the *kosmoi* acting in their judicial role as magistrates, but at members of the Council of Elders in Cretan constitutions, whose powers were in any case severely constrained. Aristotle is critical of the election of *kosmoi*, because they were drawn from a limited number of *phylai*, but not of their use of discretionary or arbitrary power in court.

This chapter argues the case for rethinking the traditional idea of Cretan society from the early Archaic period as a rigid, Dorian aristocracy in favour of a more flexible social order but one identifiably 'multi-ethnic', in the sense that many, perhaps all, city states had populations whose members considered themselves as belonging both to a traditional *phyle* and to the political entity in which they resided. Although our knowledge is sadly deficient in many respects, the argument

---

17 While offering no evidence Thomas argues that 'we can probably assume that the seventh century law about *kosmoi* was the only written law of Dreros at the time' (1996: 25–26 but cf. Demargne and Van Effenterre, 1937a, 1937b; Van Effenterre, 1946, 1961).

that Crete's written laws were intended to be read at least by some is regarded as more persuasive than that the giant slabs of text were simply meant to instill fear and compliance in a subordinate population. The early, and possibly pioneering, role that the island played in adopting a written Greek alphabet only adds weight to this conclusion. It is far less clear, however, whether practice elsewhere can uphold the general proposition that *all* inscribed law in the contemporary Greek world was equally intended for widespread public consumption. Gagarin (2008), for example, argues that the inscribed laws from Chios, Eretria and Cleonae must be bracketed with the Gortyn Code, but as Zinon Papakonstantinou has indicated in reviewing Gagarin's book, all these examples were written vertically and, as far as we can tell, often low to the ground. It would seem reasonable, therefore, to agree with his conclusion that 'even though in several archaic Greek communities publication of the laws and dissemination of their content was deemed important, accessibility and readability of the inscribed texts was not always a primary concern' (*Bryn Mawr Classical Review* 2009.06.49).

The present argument parts company with Michael Gagarin's well-known thesis on the underlying unity of Greek law. This is not to return to the famous argument put forward by Moses Finley on the wide diversity of substantive law in the Greek world. Rather it is to suggest that because Crete and Athens evolved laws strongly linked to their political systems, which were quite unlike each other, so too did the legal function vary. In Athens, the popular courts functioned to express a citizen's individuality both in terms of the reliance upon rhetoric and in the subordinate role this gave to law itself in determining outcomes. In Crete, by contrast, the law was independent of both the plaintiff and defendant, which necessitated court officials to determine its applicability, regardless of whether the proceedings themselves were, as in modern courtrooms, largely oral. It is possible to agree with Gagarin that in Gortyn the legal process 'was in some respects even more open to all the city's inhabitants than the legal process at Athens, for the female citizens of Gortyn could themselves bring suits (as well as own property), and even slaves could give testimony and swear oaths' (2008: 214) without accepting that law thereby possessed similar functions. Put another way, in addition to substance and procedure, we have to ask what did the law seek to achieve? In Athens it was to avoid tyranny by drawing the citizen into a nation with equal rights and duties; in Crete it was to avoid the tyranny of sectarian domination.

Two conclusions arise from this perspective. The first concerns the prevalence of *written* law in Crete when compared with anywhere else in the Hellenic world. The clue comes from the earliest known written law in Greece. The Dreros law establishes a system of power sharing which suggests that writing law down and displaying it in a public setting on the walls of the temple was meant as an affirmation of political unity in a society that was divided vertically into ethnic segments. The way in which the Gortyn codes identify remedies according to social class further supports this interpretation by focusing the political spotlight on social divisions that were manageable, rather than those that might easily destroy the *polis* itself. None of this confounds the argument that these laws gained their legitimacy through a form of representative government.

The final conclusion is to suggest that on most meanings of the phrase the 'rule of law', ancient Athens again differs from ancient Crete. Law did not rule in Athens except in the case of homicide, when Draco's injunctions appear to have retained an independent status from before the 5th century heyday of direct democracy, and in specialised fields such as maritime law when without the clarity of fixed rules commercial contracts would not have been viable. In Crete, by contrast, laws *did* rule in the sense that all – however mighty – were subject to them even though the treatment they received could only be considered equitable in the context of recognised social differences. Critically, the laws of Crete were not written to apply differentially according to ethnic origin, only to social standing.

CHAPTER SIX

Aristocratic governance
or a new form of democracy?

The central argument of the previous chapter was that the laws of at least some of the Cretan *poleis* from the Archaic period onwards were intended for a particular purpose, to reflect the ethnic composition of the island by ensuring that no one *phyle* came to dominate others. The early adoption of written law set parameters to the oral proceedings in court which were carefully constructed and proclaimed in order to reflect the rights and duties of individuals within a hierarchical social order, and thereby to play their part in ensuring that the interests of ethnic groups were seen as irrelevant for the maintenance of social cohesion. These were 'political' goals and the link between law and politics is therefore intimate and profound, as is also evidenced from the fact that the first laws written down were those that controlled access to political office.

This chapter explores the issue further by looking at the operation of political institutions themselves. The first issue to be examined after some preliminary observations is the nature of the 'Cretan constitution' and, indeed, whether in a land containing at least fifty *poleis* it makes any sense to employ the definite article. The second issue concerns the degree to which the political institutions could be said to be 'democratic'. The term itself has many meanings but it is usually agreed that by the end of the Classical period, many *poleis* throughout the Hellenic world had adopted some form of 'democracy'. What is argued here, however, is that in Crete a particular form of popular accountability had been assiduously pursued from very early on, and possibly from the foundation of the *poleis* themselves. This raises the issue of *representation*, which in the Cretan case had two meanings: either the representation of the *phylai* through the process of 'rotation', or a form of accountability to the citizens of the *polis*. While there is no certainty as to how these features operated in practice, some stress is laid on the issue of 'time limitation' as an important feature of early Cretan governance. The chapter then considers the issue of inter-*poleis* relations which are normally depicted as thoroughly conflictful. In examining this claim, features of co-operation are also highlighted. Finally, the discussion shifts to ancient Athens to point out major differences in the manner in which all these issues occur in these two locations. The conclusion is that it would be a mistake to assess Cretan progress towards *demokratia* in terms of an Athenian yardstick; rather the island pursued a form of representative democracy that was possibly earlier than that of Athens but, more important, of an entirely different type.

It is worth noting that arguing this case represents a clear break from conventional wisdom. As we have seen already the myth of antiquated Dorian aristocracies is very much alive and well in recent scholarship. For example, in Eric Robinson's (1997) important study on popular government outside Athens, which sought to reconsider the 'Athenocentric' notion that only with Kleisthenes's reforms can we see the beginnings of democracy, he lists sixteen cases of *poleis* that possessed similar features, many of which predate 508 BCE, but does not even consider the Cretan case as worthy of consideration.[1] It was not always thus. As we shall see, classical authorities gave much greater attention to Cretan initiatives, although by no means necessarily approving of them. Again, in the early 19th century, prior to the discoveries at Knosos, the general tone was much more enthusiastic. A good example is the entry in the 1823 edition of *Encyclopaedia Britannica* which, noting that 'the republic of Crete continued to flourish till the age of Julius Caesar', went on to explain:

> No other state has enjoyed so long a period of strength and grandeur. The legislature, regarding liberty as the only sure basis of a nation's happiness, had instituted a system of laws, the natural tendency of which was to inspire men with an ardent passion for liberty, and with such virtue and valour as are necessary to support and defend it.[2]

Another good example is the book written by the American lawyer Lewis Cass, who was later to be the Democratic Party's nominee for President. He enthused, after visiting the island, that Crete was unique in being the only republic that had lasted for a thousand years and had never untaken an offensive war:

> Happy will our country (USA) be, if in following this example, we shall be able to equal the Cretan republic in moderation, and to exceed it in longevity (1839: 3).

There is more than a hint here that what was admired was something other than an Athenian-type *demokratia*. The general point is not that Robinson should have included the Cretan constitution as an example of *demokratia*, since Aristotle did not do so and he is one of Robinson's major sources. Still less is it to argue that Crete evolved a democratic constitution *before* that of Athens as he manages to do successfully in some other cases. Such arguments depend on the definition of democracy that is employed, as well as agreement as to when *demokratia* started in Athens (now often accepted as before the reforms under Kleisthenes of 508–7). Rather, it is to suggest that some of the criteria used to justify the conclusion that a particular *polis* should be added to the 'pre-Athens' list (e.g. the existence of a council and assembly) would also have applied to Crete.

---

1 These were in alphabetical order Achaea, Acragus, Ambracia, Argos, Chalcis, Chios, Cnidus, Cos, Cyrene, Elis, Heraclea Pontica, Mantinea, Megara, Naxos, Samos and Syracuse.

2 *Encyclopaedia Britannica; Or A Dictionary of Arts, Sciences, and Miscellaneous Literature*, London, Constable and Co, 1823: 738.

The Cretan constitution

A settlement was not a *polis* unless it had the capacity for internal self-government. In the early days at least this was also accompanied by external autonomy (*autonomia*) but over time internecine conflicts led to the emergence of dependent *poleis*, particularly in the Cretan case when geographical misfortune placed a small *polis* near to either Knosos or Gortyn.[3] It is important to note the two major uses of the term '*polis*'; the first was to denote the urban centre of a self-governing community and the second the whole community, including its rural hinterland. As Hansen and Nielsen (2004) explain in the introduction to their unique survey of 1035 *poleis* in the Greek world:

> It follows that in most *poleis* (in the sense of state) there was only one urban settlement which was called *polis*. Such a *polis* had a hinterland, called *chora* or *ge*, and a *polis* lying on the coast would have a harbour, called *limen* or *epineion*, often including an *emporion*, i.e. a special market for foreign trade. The port of a large inland *polis* could itself be a major urban settlement which occasionally was considered a *polis* in the urban sense, and could be a *polis* in the political sense too (2004: 138).

It has been argued earlier that in Crete, the distinction between an inland urban centre and one on the coast was of major importance because the latter either was, or came to be, part of the mechanism by which the more powerful 'primary' *poleis* entered the trading world.

The need for self-government necessitated specialist buildings in which citizens or their representatives could meet. It is probable, for example, that each primary *polis* had a *prytaneion* with a dining space where the principal officers entertained eminent guests and recipients of the city's honours (e.g. victors in Panhellenic games), although in only nine cases have these buildings been excavated. The *prytaneion* usually contained an altar to Hestia and a hearth with an eternal flame, signifying the continuity and coherence of the city.[4] Most *poleis* also had a *bouleuterion* or a building where the elders, or more usually their representatives (*boule*), met. The physical remains of these two structures, normally characterised by their size and relatively expensive construction methods, can be seen in many of the inland *poleis* sites, even where little or no excavation has taken place. Throughout the Hellenic world it was rare for a *polis* to have a separate building (*ekklesiasterion*) for meetings of the Assembly (*ekklesia*), presumably because it would have had to be too large for the masons to construct from local materials. Sometimes these meetings were termed '*agora*', which suggests that they were held outside in a flat area of the same name. Later in the Classical period there are a

---

3 It is not entirely clear whether the concept of *autonomia* emerged later than the first *poleis* or whether dependency was a later development. Ostwald (1982: 14–26) holds to the former view while Perlman (1996) stresses dependency as a later development. Either way, it is self-government, rather than complete autonomy, that is a necessary condition for *polis* status.

4 The existence of a central hearth is one way by which a *prytaneion* can be identified.

number of references to meetings in the theatre (e.g. at Lato) and the *agora* would have then assumed its more common function as a market place (Hansen and Nielsen, 2004: 140). Given the climate, it is unlikely that the *agora* ever lost its civic role entirely and there are a number of references in the Gortyn Code to the 'stone' in the *agora* from which proclamations were made.

It would be anticipated that a society comprising fifty or more self-governing city states would be unlikely to possess a set of *common* political institutions. The classical historians, however, argued for a single Cretan *politeia*, in particular Plato in the *Laws*, Aristotle in Book 2 of the *Politics*, Ephorus in his *History* and Herakleides the Cretan (Perlman, 1992). Of these Aristotle has, perhaps, the most to offer in terms of understanding how the political institutions operated. This was partly because of his comparative perspective, which is reputed to have covered 158 Greek constitutions, as well as the period in which he was writing, which was right at the end of the Classical era (ca. 330 BCE). It is widely believed that his comparison of the Cretan and Spartan (Laconian) constitutions was based in fact upon knowledge of only one Cretan case, that of Lyktos (Lyttos), which was probably most like that of Sparta.[5] Nonetheless, he points out a number of key features. Aristotle accepts the argument that the Spartan constitution was derived from the Cretan precedent since the architect of the former (Lycurgus) is said to have visited Crete to learn about political institutions and the island's laws. In Plutarch's *Life of Lycurgus* there is reference to this visit and Plutarch also records that 'of some things he heartily approved, and adopted some of their laws, that he might carry them home with him and put them in use; for some things he had only contempt' (Plutarch: 215). Strabo too argues that 'the truth is that they (political institutions) were invented by the Cretans and only perfected by the Spartans' (10.4.17). The Spartan constitution, in its early formation from the ideas of Lycurgus and long before the *polis* became the totalitarian, ascetic and repressive creature of later years, initiated regular assemblies of citizens possibly as early as the late 7th century, or a century or so before the time of Kleisthenes in Athens. As Hornblower writes, 'the history of European democracy begins, arguably, not in Athens but in Sparta' (1993: 1). But it was Cretan ideas that lay behind those of Sparta and although Phoenician influences may also have been important, the principles that were developed, possibly first at Lyktos, were clearly early in their incorporation into a viable political system.

Aristotle notes the parallels, in particular the practice of providing meals in common for male citizens, usually referred to as *syssitia*, but in Crete and Sparta as *andreia* (a reference to the *andreion* or 'men's house' in which the meals took place). Moreover, each had similar arrangements to allow representatives of the citizen body to adopt executive and legal functions on behalf of the whole. In Crete these are referred to as *kosmoi* (*cosmoi*) while in Sparta they are named as

---

5 Since it was widely held that Lyktos/Lyttos was a colony of Sparta, although there is little evidence to support this belief.

ephor; the only difference being that there were ten of the former in Crete and five of the latter in Sparta.[6] Those over a certain age, thought to be 50 (*gerontes*), had a legislative role forming a council in the Cretan case, whereas all citizens joined in the *ekklesia* or general assembly to ratify the decrees of the elders and the *kosmoi* (Strabo 10.4.22). Strabo's comments are important here for he recognises that :

> On matters of highest moment (the *kosmoi*) have recourse to the counsel of the Gerontes, as they are called. They admit to this council those who have been thought worthy of the office of Cosmi (*Kosmi*), and who were otherwise of tried worth (*Geography*: 22, 206).

Aristotle's argument for the similarities is, however, very deceptive. Although it is probable that the Cretan precedent did influence the legislators of Sparta, the differences are very great. As Aristotle himself recognised, the 'subject population', who were the equivalent to the helots of Sparta, paid their dues into a common pool in proportion to their wealth, half for the *polis* funds and the remainder for the provision of common meals.[7] As payments were proportionate, no one could be excluded from any of the benefits of citizenship in Crete on grounds of wealth. In Sparta these payments were made at a standard rate and those who failed to comply were deprived of citizenship rights. Moreover, Crete had abandoned the institution of monarchy whereas Sparta had not, so that the citizenry was genuinely more powerful and did not have to compete, as in the mixed constitution of Sparta, with the wishes of a much more powerful king(s).

While the institutions of the Cretan *poleis* were not strictly speaking 'Spartan', nonetheless it would be quite wrong to conclude that they did not have some features in common. The most important was the commitment to a militaristic culture in which adult male citizens were brought up in a communal environment where they ate and drank together, and shared the bonds of intimacy that come from having to rely on each other in battle. Perhaps the major purpose of the political institutions and structures of the Greek *poleis* was to ensure that when required to do so, the citizen would become a hoplite, or warrior, to promote and defend the honour of the city state itself. Runciman (1998) borrows the term 'meme' from Richard Dawkins to suggest that in the case of the Greek *polis* four such strands were welded together to produce the culture of warfare on which the *polis* system depended, at least in the period through to the end of the 5th century. The 'ready to go to war' meme underpinned a readiness to be killed in close combat, the 'commemorate the fallen' meme celebrated those who did not return alive, the 'dedicate spoils to the gods' meme showed how central religion was to military success, and the 'avoid shame and guilt' meme indicated how achieving status was

---

6 In fact the number of *kosmoi* varied from *polis* to *polis*.

7 Aristotle defines the *Perioeci* as the 'subject population of Crete' but it is probable that this term only referred to those who were citizens of dependent *poleis* rather than to all those who were non-citizens (cf. Larsen, 1936).

the way by which deviance was avoided. Runciman is particularly adept at showing the intimacy of these bonds of loyalty:

> The sons of men who had themselves served as hoplites grew up not only hearing historical as well as mythical tales of bravery in battle but seeing in the behaviour of their fathers or other role models exemplification of all four of the 'memes'. Young boys could not fail to be aware of their fathers' arms and armour hanging on the walls of their houses, the periodic absence of their fathers on campaign, the casualty lists inscribed on stone, the helmets and shields of fallen enemies on display in the temples, the public commemorations of the dead in battle and the praise or, alternatively, shame and guilt, attaching to the performance in battle of men including their own neighbours, kinsmen and friends (1998: 743).

These cultural strands were characteristic of the *polis* model itself but they were applied with different degrees of intensity and conviction. The lack of foreign adventures and internal class-based conflict, and rather low levels of *inter-poleis* conflict (on which more later in this chapter), all suggest a difference in the level of militarism between Crete and, say, Sparta. Certainly, Aristotle when comparing Cretan and Spartan political institutions, castigates the latter for having a constitution that 'has regard to one part of virtue only—the virtue of the soldier, which gives victory in war' *Politics* (2.10). When victory had been achieved the Spartan leadership, in contrast to that of Crete with its heritage from the 'laws of Minos', could not rule with success 'for of the arts of peace they knew nothing, and had never engaged in any employment higher than war'.

Thus, although military service was an accepted part of a citizen's duties in Crete, the individual *polis* nowhere resembled the Spartan model. For example, although magistrates (*kosmoi*) may have been selected from an elite group of families, a major principle was that of *rotation* so that no one *startos* (probably the panel or college of *kosmi*) or *phyle* (ethnic group identified by territorial origin) could hang on to office for longer than a designated period (de Sanctis, 1901). In most cases this was a year but *poleis* differed in the time that had to elapse before a return to this position of authority could occur. In the case of Gortyn it was three years, while the earlier constitution of Dreros stipulated that repeat service could not occur for a decade on pain of exclusion from office, fines and the threat that all rules and edicts introduced by an individual would be null and void (Ehrenberg, 1943: 17). The exact inscription from Dreros (Plate 12), dating from approximately 650 BCE, reads:

> This has pleased the Polis. When a man has been kosmos, the same man shall not be kosmos again within ten years. Should he be kosmos again (*within this period*), he shall himself be liable to fines double the amount of those inflicted by him as a judge; and he shall himself be unemployable (*probably as kosmos*) as long as he lives and his acts as kosmos shall be null and void.

According to Perlman (2004a), the laws of Dreros were probably inscribed on the east wall of the temple to Apollo Delphinios, which was located on the saddle between the double acropolises of the urban centre, and would have been visible to all those occupying the adjacent agora. Perlman follows the early excavators in believing that it was here that political life was also located (Demargue and Van Effenterre, 1937a; 1937b). The Dreros inscription formed part of a collection of thirteen blocks found in 1936 in the large partially filled cistern adjacent to the temple.[8]

In Ehrenberg's judgment the opening phrase of the inscription is a reference to the assembly of citizens or constitutional authority. He emphasises the degree to which the interests of the *polis* lay above those of the political elite:

> It is very important to understand that even in this small aristocratic state of the seventh century, the Polis was stronger than any family or any union of families (1943: 170).

After the body of the text there appears another line which says that 'the oath shall be taken by the kosmos and the damioi and the Twenty of the Polis' (Demargue and Van Effenterre, 1937a: 333; Ehrenberg, 1943: 14). Although the meaning of this sentence is not entirely clear, the one plausible explanation is that the 'Twenty' were the council of elders, while the '*damioi*' were the leading financial officials of the polis.[9] The one *kosmos* identified must then have been the president or chairman of the board (*protokosmos*). Others, however, would disagree with this interpretation of the *damioi* seeing in this term a reference to the full assembly of the citizenry whose job it was to elect the board of *kosmoi* (Beattie, 1975: 20). The case for the *damiorgoi* being officials of some sort is, however, stronger. Sherk (1990: 268) points out that there is inscription evidence in the case of Olous and Polyrrhenia that identifies some of the *damiorgoi* by name, and in the latter case they are referred to as a five-man college. Guarducci (1935–50; II: 241) insists that this reference is to a group or board of *kosmoi* and she is probably correct.

Although he does not offer any proof, Van Ehrenberg assumes that Dreros at this time was an aristocracy; but, he says, 'even if the ruling class of the population was represented only by a few families, they were subordinate to the Polis, to its claims as well as to its formal constitution. The last decision was with the assembly, but real power ... rested with the council.' (1943: 18). If that was indeed the case, as seems perfectly plausible, then it is hard to see how this could be seen as simply an oligarchy. If the ruling class was that strong why did it not use its power to change the rules to suit its interests? One answer may be that this was because the laws were established to ensure rotation of power amongst ruling families, but even so the implication must surely be that even at this early date the voice of the citizenry counted, because it was they whose representatives made up the council. As Forrest observes, the *agora* adjacent to the temple was not simply a market place but a

---

8 After going missing for many years following its (re)-discovery in the 1930s, this important text can now be seen in the small museum of Neapoli, the town close to the site of ancient Dreros.

9 Van Ehrenberg uses evidence from Sparta to support this interpretation on the plausible grounds that the Spartan constitution was derived from those in Crete (1943: 18).

place where people spoke: 'Not much to start with but something: that is, there is a debate going on, with a plurality of opinion expressed on a regular basis' (2000: 288). In the Gortyn Law Code there is reference both to the limitation on repeat service and later to the concept of *rotation* so that members of each *startos* held office in succession, a system that ensured, even within an oligarchic structure, that political power was widely distributed. It is probable that the *syssitia*, or system of meals taken in common (usually referred to in Crete as '*andreia*' after the buildings in which it took place), together with a common education experience amongst the free population of citizens, also helped to produce what was a remarkably stable political life (Link, 1994: 124–30).[10]

Polybius, writing in the middle of the 2nd century, although notoriously hostile towards Cretan institutions, argues not only that Cretan and Spartan institutions were different but that they were *opposite* in many respects. Thus in respect of the constitutional arrangements, Polybius confirms that in Sparta the position of magistrate was hereditary and that members of the Council of Elders (*Gerousia*) were elected for life, whereas in Crete 'magistracies were annual and elected on a democratic system' (Polybius *Histories* 6: 373). As Strabo also says:

> [T]hey elect ten Archons (magistrates). On matters of highest moment they have recourse to the counsel of the Gerontes, as they are called. They admit to this council those who have been thought worthy of the office of Cosmi, and who were otherwise of tried worth (*Geography*: 22, 206).

It is hard to see how a political system such as this could be called 'aristocratic' if these two ancient commentators are correct, although as with all political systems this does not mean that each citizen has the same probability of being chosen for high office as the next. Wealth, social standing and previous political experience will undoubtedly have played the same role then as now, but the system would appear to have been a world away from one dominated by a hereditary elite (Link 1994: 124–30). This is a point to which we shall return.

There is still the question of the degree to which the definite article can be applied to the constitutional arrangements of the Cretan *poleis*. Perlman (1992, 2005) is certainly right to question whether this is probable. On the other hand, the archaeological evidence suggests that material culture was very similar in all the primary city states, so it is not implausible to assume that the differences that undoubtedly existed were variations on a common model, rather than of fundamental importance. It must be remembered also that the *polis* system itself had many commonalities as well as differences:

> Most *poleis* had the same set of institutions: an Assembly (*ekklesia*), a Council (*boule*), sometimes a Senate (*gerousia*), courts of law (*dikasteria*) and magistrates (*archontes*), either elected or picked by lot. It was the way in which power was divided between

---

10 Strataridaki (2009) has suggested that the *syssitia* was also as a mechanism for generating social solidarity by caring for some of those in a vulnerable economic condition (e.g. male orphans).

institutions, and the limited access to some of them, that distinguished one type of constitution from another (Hansen, 2006a: 113).

In the Cretan case, even if we cannot be certain as to the exact processes of selection, it would appear that in most if not all *poleis* an assembly of the citizenry contributed to the decision-making process, there was a board of magistrates with powers of leadership in both war and peacetime and an advisory board of elders filled on an honorary basis for life (Papakonstantinou, 1996). In other words, in the absence of evidence to the contrary, the classical case for commonalities is still strong, even if the argument for a unitary system is weak.

George Huxley argues that Aristotle's assumption of there being a single Cretan polity, rather than a large variety, is because the 'Achaean and Dorian incomers responded in a concerted manner to the problem of absorbing the indigenous population into the society'; but he ties this with the proposition that these incomers were clearly in the ascendancy (1971: 506). There is rather little evidence of this. First of all, as Huxley accepts, Aristotle points out that the *perioikoi* use the laws of Minos unchanged. If the incomers were clearly in the ascendant then why did they take over, seemingly without question, the indigenous laws as those by which a large proportion of the free population was governed? This is not how dominant incoming settlers behave. The arrival of the Romans some centuries later was not accompanied by respect for Minoan traditions. Second, of the twelve Cretan *poleis* where we have inscription evidence identifying some at least of the constituent *phylai*, in no less than five instances none of the three Dorian 'tribes' are attested (Jones, 1987).[11] In Dreros, where the principle of ethnic succession and rotation is first proclaimed, no Dorian groups are referred to in inscriptions, and why bother with rotation in the first place if one or two groups are always in the ascendant? Huxley argues that the reason the *perioikoi* did not revolt (unlike the Spartan helots) was that they retained their ancestral customs, but this again is an implausible proposition since ethnic subjection is even more likely to lead to revolt than that based simply upon class criteria, because by definition there is a consciousness of a shared identity with which to arouse people into action to defend their common interests.

Early democratic governance

We are left with the question of the degree to which Cretan constitutions were 'democratic'? They were clearly non-democratic in excluding women, non-citizens and slaves from political life. The key issue is the degree to which they offered citizen representation and limitations on the exercise of arbitrary power. It is by no means easy to be certain here because there is so little evidence to go on, but what there is suggests that from the outset Cretan city states possessed rule-bound

11 Dreros, Lato, Lebena, Malla and Praisos.

administrations with some form of restriction to prevent the emergence of tyranny or rule by reason of birth rather than the rule of law. The system may have developed from one where the oligarchic elements prevailed to one with closer adherence to democratic principles, but it is equally possible that elections were the way that representatives of each *phyle* were selected from the outset. This is not to say that each citizen member of a *phyle* had an equal chance of standing for election; it is very plausible to suppose that certain families would be over-represented among the candidates for office, but if the three systems of representation operated together (annual office holding; limitations on return; rotation of *phylai*) then political power would have been very widely shared. In other words, not only did the *kosmoi* apparently have a restricted tenure of office with strict limitations on a return to power, but individually they were also liable for removal from office for dereliction of duties, presumably by other magistrates and possibly after consultation with the *boule*.

ETHNIC REPRESENTATION

When Aristotle says that 'in Crete the Kosmi are elected out of certain families, and not out of the whole people, and the elders out of those who have been Kosmi' (*Politics:* 92) he sees this as a weakness when compared with Sparta. From this statement, it has always been assumed that the political structure of Crete was fundamentally aristocratic. On the other hand, a few paragraphs later, he complains that because in Sparta the equivalent category of office holders, the *ephoralty*, is open to anyone 'the office is apt to fall into the hands of very poor men, who, being badly off, are open to bribes'. His comment on Crete, however, is entirely consistent with the proposition that the candidates for *kosmoi* were drawn from and elected by those *phylai* who made up the population of citizens as a whole. In other words, all citizens participate in the election of the main executive board of *kosmoi*, but since each of them represents one ethnic segment voting is organized on a *phyle* basis.

There are two major variants of this segmented model. Either the whole board was elected by one *phyle* in turn (through the principle of rotation) or the board was composed of *kosmoi* each representing one *phyle* and it was the chairman (*protokosmos*) who was elected according to the principle of rotation. At first sight the second system may seem more probable, since the former sounds rather dangerous.[12] One major function of the board of *kosmoi* was to agree treaties and decrees with other *poleis*, sometimes at the close of hostilities. These lasted longer than the (one year) tenure of the individual serving as *kosmos*, so it was a considerable risk to devolve this power to one *phyle*. Moreover, it was the board of

---

12 Although there are parallels in the modern world as, for example, with the constitution of the Lebanon that specifies that three groups (Maronite Christians, Sunni and Shiite Muslims) shall share the highest offices of state while the current constitution of Bosnia-Herzegovina stipulates that one 'co-president' shall be drawn from Muslim, Croat and Serbian sections of the total population.

magistrates that determined whether the *polis* went to war. It must be admitted, however, that this is not entirely clear, and those who have studied the relevant epigraphy also appear to be uncertain. Robert Sherk (1990), for example, fully recognises the significance of ethnicity in the political life of Cretan *poleis* and notes that 'in each of the cities, the kosmoi were elected, the tribes of each city taking turns in providing them', which appears to be suggesting the first system. On the other hand, his major concern is with 'eponymous officials' or those whose name is mentioned in inscriptions as indicating a period of office. It is the chairman, or chief magistrate, who is eponymous, and the most common formula refers to his ethnic group plus his name. While this could indicate either system, the very power and importance of the *protokosmos* might suggest that it is this role that rotates and not the whole board of *kosmoi*. Against this judgment is the fact that all serve for one year only, thereby underscoring the temporary nature of the board and thus the possibility that it was drawn entirely from one ethnic group. Aristotle's point concerning the supposed deficiency of the Cretan constitution is not much help either. The whole population would only vote if the board was representative of each *phyle and* elections took place simultaneously. If each *kosmos* was replaced by an election within his *phyle* when his year was up, then only one small segment of the total electorate would be active at any one time. The remarkable study by Martha Baldwin-Bowsky of Lato and its port Lato pros Kamara perhaps provides the strongest evidence yet that the board of *kosmoi* did indeed rotate between the *phylai*. Her study traces family names on two major inscriptions from Lato pros Kamara towards the end of the 2nd century. It shows what she considers a democratic deficiency in that some families appear to dominate the important roles in both *poleis*:

> It is clear that a relatively small part of the population of Lato dominated public office. There is clear evidence of an annual magistracy, yet there were as many as six years in the last twenty of the 2nd century when the same clan may have supplied six different boards of elders (Baldwin-Bowsky 1989b: 343; cf. 1989a).

It is quite possible, as in all political systems to this day, that ethnic groups (*phylai*), brotherhoods (*phratriai*) and clans (*gene*) might each attempt to undermine open access to power, but these findings are entirely compatible with a population divided into three *phylai*, the number that is suggested by the table in the previous chapter (Table 5.1). On balance, therefore, it seems most likely that the executive and legal functions of the Cretan *poleis* did rotate between *phylai*, which would have meant that only a third or quarter or whatever fraction of the electorate of male citizens would have been called upon to vote in any one year. While this accounts for Aristotle's objection, it does not necessarily undermine the principle of democracy as we shall see in the final chapter. This would depend on how open the voting was in the election of *kosmoi* for the *phyle* coming into its period of office. It does, however, suggest a considerable level of trust between ethnic groups. For example, in a modern context, this system was rejected in Northern Ireland in favour of continuous power sharing because the necessary level of trust was not present.

A number of authors have come close to recognising this system of rotation, without perhaps realising the centrality of the principles that it embodies. For example, Beattie (1975), in commenting on the popular assembly or *ekklesia*, notes that it would have been 'organised in ten *phylai*' and that it would have been part of the assembly's role to elect the ten *kosmoi* (Beattie, 1975: 13). Moreover, he suggests that the Dreros inscription is compatible with the proposition that the Council too was composed of 'tribal representations' (1975: 15). Papakonstantinou (1996) identifies the two possibilities outlined here for the manner in which the board of *kosmoi* was composed, and goes on to say:

> The exact process by which the *kosmoi* were elected is also unknown but surely it had to do with the division of the Cretan society in tribes and clans and it must have reflected the particularities of the body of the eligible citizens (1996: 95–96).

He does not, however, identify the fundamental difference between populations divided horizontally into social classes and those further segmented vertically into ethnic groups, which allows him to agree with Aristotle that elections which were not open to the entire citizen body necessarily provided 'an oligarchic nuance to Cretan politics' (1990: 96). A similar conclusion is derived from Stefan Link's analysis of the Gortyn Code when he argues that the 'principle of rotation thereby ensured that even though not all citizens were eligible those that were regularly changed', thereby incorporating a democratic principle into an oligarchic structure (Link 1994: 124–30). It is more plausible to suggest that Polybius was right; the system of electing magistrates was democratic from the outset but quite different from the Athenian system of democracy in ways that are discussed below.

Inter-poleis *relations*

It has been known ever since Cretan epigraphy was first established that interstate treaties were relatively common, but the general assumption has been that these were occasioned only by the need to avoid war or establish a truce. In fact, the prevalence of treaties in Crete can be interpreted as indicating either that treaties were required because of regular conflict, or that independent states were more comfortable when they were in stable agreements with their neighbours. Of course both may be true, but it is difficult to agree with Chaniotis's assertion that because half of the treaties between Cretan cities in the Hellenistic era were treaties of alliance 'one immediately recognizes how seriously Greek states took their right to fight defensive and offensive wars' (2005a: 20).

Recent scholarship in the Classical Greek world as a whole has begun to question whether the external politics of the *polis* were really so embedded in opportunism and advantage. Polly Low, for example, writing on the interstate treaties in the whole Classical Greek world suggests otherwise:

... closer inspection reveals that there is a coherent, even logical, origin for these superficially confusing entanglements: namely, the pervasive influence of an ethics of reciprocity (Low, 2007: 253).

Oswyn Murray goes even further and argues that the creation of the concept of inter-state relations was one of the *polis*'s greatest achievements:

> If there is one thing that persuades us of the relationship between ancient polis and modern state it is the similarities between the polis conception of inter-polis relations and our own apparently modern concept of the *Staatsvertrag*, international law and the whole apparatus of international relations (Murray, 2000: 240).

This is precisely what is suggested by the Cretan evidence, which suggests that inter-state treaties were designed for two main purposes; first to codify the settlement of conflict, but second to underscore co-operation in military, religious and political fields. In the majority of cases where some form of conflict is referred to it falls short of out and out warfare.

Perhaps the most thorough examination of Cretan interstate treaties, at least in the Hellenistic era, is by Angelos Chaniotis (1996). The first point to note is that, in this period at least, treaty arrangements between *poleis* are more numerous in Crete than anywhere else in the Greek world. There are 74 known cases of treaties between individual cities and a further seven covering more than two cities. Rising populations and increasing wealth, often in the form of enlarged stock levels, increased the likelihood of border disputes and the attempted resolution of these is one of the major topics within interstate treaties. Not only is this evidence of a will to overcome inter-city state rivalries, but there is also a suggestion of a wish to combine in the face of a common aggressor, possibly coming from overseas (Chaniotis, 1996: 6–7).[13] Chaniotis (2005a: 28), for example, cites a treaty between Eleutherna and Lato in the first part of the 2nd century that includes the provision that:

> If an enemy invades the territory of the Eleutherneans or cuts off parts hereof, or occupies forts or harbours, or destroys the lots of the serfs, or wages war, the Latian shall help in land and on sea without any pretext with all his might.

Another between Gortyn and Lappa has very similar provisions:

> [I]f someone wages war against the Gortynians or occupies a fort or harbours or cuts off part of the territory, the Lappaians shall help the Gortynians on land and on sea, with all their might, to the best of their abilities.

Other themes are, perhaps, of greater importance in underlining the principles of reciprocity that the treaties suggest were an important feature of Cretan *polis* life.

---

13 Population growth during the Hellenistic period, itself a sign of prosperity, combined with the necessity of transhumance (animal movements between summer and winter pastures), increased the probability of trespassing on the territory of a neighbouring *polis*. It is possibly that the former fed mercenary recruitment while the latter may account for the preoccupation in many treaties with land-related issues.

The first is the kind of treaty that grants citizenship rights (*isopoliteia*) to members of another *polis*. This was a privilege in its own right, but in some cases it was accompanied by other reciprocal arrangements such as *epigamia*, or the right to marry across state boundaries; transhumance, or the right to graze stock on the territory of the other; or the right to participation in the festivals and assemblies of the other. The granting of citizenship rights was usually based on a qualifying period of residence or other device to prevent wholesale migration from one city state to another. One example would be the treaty of *isopoliteia* between Hierapytna and Priansos. A second form of treaty was the *sympoliteia* which prescribed the arrangements of alliance between one *polis* and another. Sometimes these were dependency relationships, as for example in the agreement between Praisos and Stalai, or could become a prelude to an eventual merger as between Lato and Lato pros Kamara (Chaniotis, 1996: 101–7). Chaniotis lists five cases of agreements of this kind from the total of 81 that he documents overall.

These internal arrangements were also supplemented by external treaties that tended to be of two kinds. First there were those in which another state would add its name to a Cretan agreement seeking to resolve conflicts. This mediating role was played increasingly by Rome towards the end of the Hellenistic period, but earlier Egypt under the Ptolemies was involved in a similar way. For example, Ptolemy VI Philometor (180–145 BCE) was invited by Gortyn to mediate in a peace treaty with Knosos and an inscription from Itanos records that its people received military help from Ptolemy VI against the people of Praisos. It is probable that Ptolemy V (205–180) played a similar role at an earlier date (Bagnall, 1976: 118). Certainly Gortyn and Ptolemy IV Philopator (221–205) had a close military and diplomatic alliance (Morkot, 2005: 228). These treaties are particularly important for they signal the probability of longstanding and entrenched conflicts. After all, turning to an outside arbiter may reasonably be seen as an indication that local solutions have been found wanting. Despite the examples noted above, however, they were not that common. Sheila Ager (1996), for example, documents 171 cases of interstate arbitrations in the Greek world from 337 to 90 BCE, of which less than 8 per cent concerned Cretan *poleis*.

The second kind of external treaty was trade-related. For example, the treaty between Rhodes and three *poleis* from East Crete (Hierapytna, Olous and Chersonisos) at the end of the 3rd century BCE, which gave the former access to the harbours and naval stations of the Cretan cities, was thought by some to have concerned the control of piracy, but was more probably a decree designed to enhance Cretan involvement in trade (Vogeikoff-Brogan and Apostolakou, 2004: 425).

The Cretan Koinon

During the Hellenistic period, there was a general tendency for *poleis* to seek a greater degree of unity than hitherto. The reasons for this were many and included a sense of external threat from Macedonia and elsewhere and also the growing importance of trade relations that tended to break down political barriers in search of market opportunities. The most famous instances were the Aetolian League in Central Greece, founded in 370 BCE, and its arch enemy, the Achaean League in the Peloponnese, that reached the zenith of its powers in the 3rd century. Two Cretan *poleis* were actually members of these associations, Kydonia in the former case and Gortyn in the latter, but the most important principle that underlay them was that of the *koinon*, or the concept of league or association. Hitherto, the focus has been largely on the warring nature of these two large groupings, both between themselves and with, first, Macedonia and, second, the Roman legions. More recently, studies have shown the extent to which a sense of ethnic identity fostered the co-operation that led to the *koina* becoming established. Emily Mackil (2003), for example, shows the interaction between economic, religious and political co-operation and how this was itself a response to the extremes of fragmentation in the *poleis*. What she argues is that *koina* were functional in that they institutionalised 'states of interaction' and interdependence. Although it is undeniable that from time to time they were at each other's throats, nonetheless, when bound by the rules of a functioning *koinon*, they were remarkably resilient. Mackil concludes her study of *poleis* on mainland Greece by saying:

> … while the Greek poleis were extraordinarily vulnerable as physical, political and social entities, they were also remarkably resilient because they operated as a tightly inter-connected system (Mackil, 2004: 512)

In other words, the *koinon* institutionalised a network of interdependence. These mainland examples were matched by the Cretan experience, although as in other areas, new and different elements were added. As the treaties suggest, the idea of the move towards alliances was not new; moreover, there were instances of long-term associations as in the 4th century Confederation of Oreioi which linked six small *poleis* in the Sphakia region of the south-west (Elyros, Lisos, Hyrtakina, Tarrha, Syia, Poikilasos).

There are also reasons for supposing that as early as the 5th century, Cretans could on occasion act in concert. As Forrest (2000) has pointed out, Herodotus records the occasion in 480 when the Athenians appealed to Crete for help against the Persians. The islanders consulted the oracle at Delphi and the Pythia (oracle) replied, 'Foolish men, was not the grief enough which Minos sent upon your people for the help given to Menelaus, out of anger that those others would not help to avenge his death at Camicus, while you helped them to avenge the stealing of that woman from Sparta by a barbarian?' (Herodotus 7. 145.1). In other words, the Athenians did not help the Cretans to avenge the death of Minos, but the Cretans helped to avenge the carrying off of Helen, so why give them support now? Forrest aptly asks 'to what body had the Greeks made their appeal and what body with what authority decided to turn to Apollo?' (2000: 283). It must have been some form of association or *koinon*. Moreover, long before the formal establishment of the Cretan *Koinon* networks and commonalities are found at a number of levels. For example, in terms of the sacred, the cult of Apollo Pythios is found at Allaria, Dreros, Eleutherna, Gortyn, Hierapytna, Itanos, Lato, Lyktos, Malla, Phaistos, Praisos, and Tylisos and, if images on coins can be relied upon, probably also at Aptera, Axos, Chersonisos, Kydonia, Lappa, Rhithymna, and Sybrita (Davies, 2007b: 60). Paul Faure (1978: 640) has noted the similarities in geographical terms both between what is found in sacred caves from Lato in the east to Polyrrhenia in the west and, over time, between Minoan cultic practices and those evident in the city states.[14]

The Cretan *Koinon* in a more formal sense was a general union of city states that developed from the 3rd century. Chaniotis (1996a) suggests that the origins of the *Koinon* can be seen in the first reference to a pan-Cretan identity which occurs in 267 BCE. Subsequent inscriptions suggest that in practice this was often masking a major division between pro-Spartan and pro-Ptolemaic forces on the one hand and those more responsive to the claims of Philip of Macedonia on the other. This correlates to a considerable degree with the rivalry between Gortyn and Knosos, with the former leading the *Koinon* in the first half of the 2nd century BCE and the latter taking over this role until the Roman succession.

The *Koinon* may have had its own officials, constitution and currency. Spyridakis reports on a Delian inscription that identifies some religious offerings to Isis as a gift of the Cretan people as a whole, which must refer to the *Koinon*. It seems possible, he argues, 'that, in addition to granting asylia rights and honors to foreigners, the loose Pan-Cretan Federation had some jurisdiction over religious matters as well' (Spyridakis, 1970b: 255). Quite reasonably he surmises that in turn the purchase of gifts must have meant the existence of a federal treasury and officials in charge of it. The *Koinon* existed primarily to give institutional recognition to the wish for political unity among Cretan *poleis*. It was never a federation as such, if this is defined as a single state with its own army, but it was able to enter into diplomatic relations with overseas administrations. The most notable case of this was the signing by the *koindikion* or political and legal authority of the *Koinon*, of a treaty in 183 BC with Eumenes of Pergamum on behalf of thirty-one city states.[15] The evidence suggests that this treaty, and another with Ptolemy IV Philometor, were for the provision of mercenary soldiers – a service which both reduced population pressure and boosted income for the Cretans, a topic that is discussed in the following chapter (van der Mijnsbrugge, 1931: 28).

In a manner reminiscent of the European Union, the individual *polis* retained a high degree of autonomy, and because of this and the overweening power of Gortyn and Knosos within the union, the *Koinon* was never totally stable. The rights of membership were codified under the Cretan *diagramma* which was a list of edicts with associated penalties for infringement existing mainly to prescribe

---

14 Faure calls them 'des facteurs d'unification considérables, avant même la formation du Κοινόυ crétois' (1978: 640).

15 The role of the *koindikion* is disputed. It certainly acted as a court but it may have had a very limited function in resolving inter-*poleis* disputes when it appears that appeals to foreign powers (Ptolemaic, early; Rome, later) were more common (Ager, 1994: 18).

rules of arbitration for the settlement of disputes between *poleis* (Chaniotis, 1996a). Both epigraphic and literary sources attest that the major rivalry between the two 'super-*poleis*' affected overall political stability. As van der Mijnsbrugge puts it, 'when they acted together they had all the other Cretans as subjects, when they disagreed, however, there was rebellion on the whole island' (1931: 21). The two large *poleis* came into conflict on various occasions, partly because of territorial ambitions but partly also because of a major disagreement over the role of the *Koinon* itself, with Knosos favouring a move towards a unitary state and Gortyn preferring a federal solution (Van Effenterre, 1948). Although the evidence is not unambiguous, there is a possibility that the Cretan *Koinon* evolved to embrace a wider concept of citizenship than that enjoyed by citizens of individual *poleis* (Brulé, 1978; Ager, 1994: 2).

It must be assumed that the majority of meetings of the Cretan *Koinon* took place in either Gortyn or Knosos, depending on which was predominant at the time. It is however possible that other, less partisan *poleis* also housed the council. For example, van Effenterre (1991) suggests that a large sanctuary building (*peribolos*) on the Nisi promontory at Eleutherna was also used as the meeting place of the Cretan *Koinon*. Unfortunately, there is no additional archaeological evidence to support other possible meeting places.

Can we then conclude, against conventional wisdom, that the political system in Crete was never an aristocracy and that the island may have pioneered one variant of democracy, differing considerably from that in Classical Athens? Clearly an answer depends in part on how we understand the Athenian variant and it is to that experience that we now turn. It is worth noting, however, that the Greeks themselves were ambiguous in their usage of the term. For many from the intelligentsia who preferred aristocracy or rule by the few, *demokratia* suggested the domination of the masses or those least equipped to exercise power. For its advocates, it suggested the devolution of power from ruling families and clans to the citizenry of the city state (Cartledge, 2007: 155).

The Athenian comparison

The conventional view is that the Athenian precedent represents the earliest form of democracy. For most of the years from 508–507 BCE until the death of Alexander in 322, Athens possessed a constitutional system that gave a considerable voice to the citizenry and the success of Athens in the Persian Wars (490–479) brought wealth and influence that enabled Athens to entrench and propagate the idea of democracy. Also, there is no doubt that the original initiative, associated with the enlightened aristocrat Kleisthenes, was indeed an important precedent, particularly the Council of 500 with rotating membership and restrictions on re-election (Hornblower, 1993: 9). Judgments concerning Athenian democracy, however, are especially perilous since almost all aspects of the system were attacked by contemporary critics and some modern commentators have been over-eager to praise a form of governance that differs markedly from anything that has been attempted since. Moreover, the literature on the subject is vast and appears to be expanding exponentially with the demise of European state socialism. In focusing on one or two particular features of the ancient Athenian democratic state, it is not the purpose to make any contribution to the secondary literature on this astonishing system.[16] Rather, it will only be necessary to draw out some key features and compare them with those that have been discussed for Crete.

It is usually recognised that Solon's reforms at the very beginning of the 6th century laid the groundwork for the construction of Athenian democracy. By adding four new census classes, graded by wealth rather than by birth, Solon's reforms enfranchised a significantly larger proportion of the agrarian population and created what has been termed 'a "grand design" for a comprehensive new communal order' (Stahl and Walter, 2009: 142). Largely to create a hierarchy with different levels of military commitment, Solon divided the citizen body into four classes according to the wealth they generated from the land. Thus the *pentakosiomedimnoi* (>500 bushel men) were distinguished from the *hippeis* (>300 bushel horsemen) but both could become *archontes* or the major executive office holders. Below them were the *zeugitai* (>200 bushel farmers with a team of oxen) and below them again were the *thetes* with little or no land and a product of less than 200 bushels. All four of these property classes were entitled to become members of the popular Assembly but only the first three could contribute to debates. In practice the role of the Assembly was to review and approve measures taken by the *archontes* (Ober, 1989). The role of the Council of 400, on which members of the first three groups could serve, was largely to draw up motions for debate in the Assembly. Former *archontes*, meanwhile, comprised the membership of the *Areopagus*, a body whose primary purpose was to review and advise the *archontes* on the laws governing the *polis*.

Thus, although the 6th century system was highly elitist in favouring wealth and those with the largest landed estates, nonetheless all citizens had a political role in repayment for their contribution to the military necessities of the state. Although this system did not avoid the tyranny of Peisistratus and his sons (546–510 BCE), it remained largely intact for many decades, but by the closing years of the century there was a real threat of a resurgent aristocracy and it was this, and the possibility of civil disorder and tension (*stasis*), that led to the reforms of Kleisthenes in 508–7 when faced with demands by the Athenian citizenry for a greater say in the running of the state. As Stahl and Walter put it:

> What had been prepared by Solon's reforms and – although inadvertently – matured under Peisistratid tyranny now bore fruit. The civic self-awareness of broad sections of the populace had asserted itself for the first time politically and was to become the decisive factor in the further evolution of the Athenian political order in the classical period (2009: 154–55).

---

16   But see Ober (2008) for an excellent review of recent research.

The greatest threat lay not so much in what was happening in the urban centre but in the continued coherence of the whole state. It must be recalled that Athens was exceptionally large by city-state standards. The southern border of Attica lay 50km south of Athens, while the northern boundary was more than 100km away. Population density was relatively high, which meant that agrarian communities of different sizes were spread over a huge area. The problem, therefore, was how to bring order, stability and a sense of identity to such a large terrain.

Kleisthenes' proposals were essentially managerial. He took the community organisations or demes as a starting point, revising and adding to them where they had fallen into abeyance. Each citizen was then listed by deme and identified as coming from that local community. Each deme in turn, which could have ranged from a few dozen individuals to many thousands, was given its own assembly under the auspices of an elected magistrate (*demarchos*) and sanctified by its own festivals and cults. The second level of organisation then shifted from 139 local demes to vertical divisions of the whole, so that ten new *phylai* were created each with a third of its members from the urban centre (*asty*) a third from the coastal regions (*paralia*) and a third from the inland areas (*mesogeia*). Although these new *phylai* were of similar sizes each possessed demes grouped into thirds (*trittyes*) which came together in a second tier of governance with its own assembly and three officials (*phylarchoi*). The idea was clearly that hierarchical and territorial loyalties would be cross-cut by an overarching membership of a very mixed and diverse entity which itself would constitute one-tenth of the *polis*. It was at this artificial 'tribal' level that recruitment to the army was organized, so that approximately 1,000 hoplites were recruited from each 'tribe' together with a small number of horsemen.

The *phylai* were also the basis of the new Council of 500 (*Boule*) at the third and final administrative level, because each sent 50 men chosen by the constituent demes in proportion to their size. This meant that some very large demes had more than 20 members of the *Boule* while others shared one member between them (Stahl and Walter, 2009: 157–58). Terms of service on the Council were limited to two and it has been estimated that at least a third of Athenian citizens who lived longer than the qualifying age of 30 would have served one term at least (Ober, 2008: 74). The Council, like its predecessor, was largely charged with drawing up the agenda for the popular assembly, but no longer were property or wealth criteria determinative of membership. Similarly, in 487 BCE the drawing of lots replaced the electoral system for choosing *archontes*, and in 462 a movement led by the Athenian Ephialtes succeeded in curtailing the power of the *Areopagus* which hitherto had been able to refuse motions passed by the assembly, thereby decreasing still further the role of landed wealth. The equality of the citizenry was further advanced by the extension of the right to speak on state matters to the *thetes* and by the progressive opening up to all of the right to be chosen as an *archon*.

As far as the Athenian system of citizen participation is concerned, most attention has focused on the Assembly, the day-long meetings of which could occur up to forty times a year and involve perhaps a (different) third of the citizens at any one meeting (Hansen, 1987). Its modern defenders make bold claims for this potentially anarchic arrangement:

> The system as a whole promoted the development of substantial agreement across a diverse population of citizens on core values, while encouraging debate on particulars. It sustained decision making practices that enabled effective policy formation and timely implementation (Ober, 2008: 73).

It is perhaps in North America that this enthusiasm has been maintained in the modern era, possibly because of an apparent affinity between the values of Classical Athens and the US Constitution. For example, Hannah Arendt is said to have believed that the *polis* 'offered an arena for action among equals in a realm of freedom, transforming man from a laboring animal to a human being giving expression to his individuality' (Saxonhouse, 1993: 488). The conservative political scientist Donald Kagan goes further in suggesting that:

> [I]n their commitment to political freedom and individual autonomy in a constitutional, republican and democratic public life, the Athenians of Pericles' day are closer to the values of our era than any culture that has appeared since antiquity (Kagan, 1991 quoted in Saxonhouse, 1993: 489).

Arlene Saxonhouse reminds us that contemporary commentators were much less sanguine than these 'modern mythmakers'. Leaving aside the well-known critics of 'rule by the mob', such as Plato and Aristotle, more subtle observers, such as Thucydides, felt that the benefits of the popular assembly lay not in capturing the will of the people but in bringing together men from a variety of backgrounds and having them engage in communal decision-making, or, in other words, in the integrative effects of individual participation (Saxonhouse, 1993: 490).

The actual success of this pioneering experience in civic participation is a source of continuing debate. Supporters can point to the early years after the revolution of 508 BCE when Athens successfully outmanoeuvred the Persian attacks in 490 and 480–79, most famously at the battles of Marathon and Salamis. Later in the century, after the widening of popular involvement in the institutions of governance under Ephialtes and Pericles, the critics' voices became louder, reaching a crescendo with the disasters of the Peloponnesian War (431–404) and the temporary suspension of *demokratia* in 411 and 404. As Edward Harris has observed:

> In 431 B.C.E. the Athenian democracy controlled a large empire, possessed the largest fleet in the Aegean, and had over 6,000 talents in its treasury. A mere twenty-seven years later the democracy was bankrupt, and had lost its fleet and empire. The next century was no better: the Athenians were able to rebuild their fleet only by accepting Persian gold, and their attempt to revive their empire ended in failure at Chaeronea. These blunders and many others gave the critics of Athenian democracy plenty to write about (2006: 509).

The death of Socrates and the ill-considered and panicky trial and execution of all eight generals after the naval battle of Arginusae in 406 are usually also regarded as low points in this experiment in empowerment.

Although a number of attempts have been made to explain the underlying reasons why *individual* involvement occurred rather than a system of representation, the most compelling argument is the one that can be found in contemporary commentators such as Thucydides – the need to integrate a territorially extensive and diverse entity through maximizing individual participation.[17] Edward Cohen's (2000) impressive study, arguing the case for considering ancient Athens as more of an *ethnos* or nation than a *polis*, demonstrates this very clearly. Although the book is an attempt to counter the normal concentration on the *politai*, or male politically active citizens, rather than the population as a whole, what it also shows is that Athens was totally unlike the face-to-face and hierarchical society that is often associated with the ideal type of *polis*. Rather it was a complex social order of cross-cutting loyalties in which the division between the *astoi* (or those considered 'local' or part of the society) and the *xenoi* (or those not so considered) was more important for the construction of Athenian identity than that between citizens and others. In other words, ancient Athens constructed its 'imagined' past in terms very reminiscent of a 'nation'. Although ethnic homogeneity and freedom from the massive changes wrought elsewhere through immigration became part of the myth of this nation, in fact ancient Athens was not an autochthonous, exclusionary world but 'actually offered relatively easy access into political participation to the progeny of immigrants who had assimilated into Athenian life' (Cohen, 2000: 50).

Therefore the divide between *astoi* and *xenoi* became critical, and only some of the *astoi* were *politai*. This was an assimilationist society in which, even where genuine ethnic differences existed, they were not reified into multi-ethnic or multicultural institutions. Cohen provides an excellent instance:

> (T)he Plataians, for example, are known to have been present in Attika in such profusion that even well into the fourth century they gathered monthly as a recognizable ethnic community at the "cheese market". But divided among the various demes spread throughout Attika, they functioned fully and were recognized fully as *politai*, even in routine litigation (Cohen, 2000: 67).

From this vantage point, *demokratia* can be seen as part of the assimilationist myth; a method of empowering *individuals* to participate and to consider themselves 'Athenians'. As he writes, 'personal involvement (and hence absorption into the community) was largely a matter of the realization of individual inclination over an extended period' (2000: 72). The construction of the idea of autochthony, or indigenous belonging, was assisted by the poor communications and size of ancient Athens, as well as by the fact that there was only a rather loose connection between

---

17 Some economists have argued that the democratic concessions were made to stimulate individual investments in an economy lacking the resources of other comparable city states (e.g. Sparta) (Fleck and Hanssen, 2006).

membership in a deme and where people actually resided. Paeans to Athenian nationalism and devotion to the fatherland (*patris*) were mobilised in particular at times of potential disintegration as, for example, at funeral orations to the fallen soldiers during the long years of warfare (Cohen, 2000: 91).

A form of democracy

In one sense Aristotle was right that Crete evolved a different politics from Athens because of its isolation. Perhaps the clearest indication of this is in the completely different meaning of the term '*phyle*' in these two locations. In the early years as the city states evolved from the 'Dark Ages' the meaning was similar. The 'tribal' groups were in two major divisions: the Attic-Ionic (Geleontes, Argadeis, Aigikoreis, and Hopletes with the addition of the purely Ionic Boreis and Oinopes) and the three 'tribes' speaking the Dorian dialect (Dymanes, Hylleis, and Pamphyloi), whose identity may have been burnished by their movement into the Peloponnese, but whose origins probably lay in North-Western Greece and ancient Macedonia. Certainly Pausanias describes them as descending from the mountains of Thessaly (Aeolia). With the reforms under Kleisthenes at the end of the 6th century, the old Ionic *phyles* were abandoned in favour of the ten artificial groupings intended to provide political integration and coherence in the newly defined democratic constitution. As Nicholas Jones has suggested, they were created in response to a perceived need for a 'relatively small-scale forum for political activity, leadership, and achievement' (1995: 538). Unsurprisingly, his detailed analysis came to the conclusion that this artificial construct 'did not in fact maintain a particularly intimate associational life' (1995: 521). Although we have no means of knowing precisely why Kleisthenes constructed these new *phylai* as he did, it is probable that they were the closest that the Athenians came to having mechanisms of representation (Jones, 1995: 539–40). What they were clearly not were *ethnic* groupings, since they lacked a collective sense of identity through a perception of cultural affinity and common origins.

In Crete by contrast the arrival of new waves of population stimulated the opposite process, one of ethnogenesis rather than 'ethno-destruction' (Jones, 1987: 220). This process is clearest in Gortyn and, in particular, in some of the provisions of the Great Code. For example, the clauses concerning the marriage of an heiress come close to total prohibition on marriage outside the *phyle*, thereby sustaining a principle of endogamy that is unknown in any of the other Greek *phylai* that number nearly two hundred (Jones, 1987: 224). As Jones puts it, 'for Gortyn, the conclusion seems inescapable that the membership of the *phylai* as late as the mid–5th century retained (or had reacquired) a significant degree of internal solidarity' (1987: 224–5). The political significance of these ethnic groupings was immense, for they formed the basis for the Cretan system of constitutional governance. The greater part of the inscription evidence in Crete relating to the *kosmoi* comes in the form of formulas from the preambles of decrees in which reference is made to the annual boards of *kosmoi* who served in a fixed, or widely known, sequence in office. The boards themselves were identified as coming from a particular *phyle* (Jones, 1987: 222). Each constituent *phyle* had its own internal hierarchy, at the top of which was the *startos*, which may originally have comprised the 'officer class' but which came to mean a board of *kosmoi*, possibly including former office holders. The political leadership of the *polis* was then subject to the constitutional principle of rotation, or, as Jones puts it, 'as the magistracy rotated among the *phylai*, from it were drawn the *kosmoi*' (1987: 226).

The difference from ancient Athens is very clear. In Athens there was a principle of rotation, but this applied as an administrative device to ensure that all the units from which the state was constructed were represented in the most powerful organs of governance. In the board of the nine *archontes*, for example, different posts within the board were assigned to members from different *phylai* in rotation (Jones, 1987: 42). In Crete, at any one time, one particular ethnic group provided the governance of the *polis*, while in Athens there was a system for ensuring participation of all (or most) geographical 'constituencies' in each administration. Put another way, in both the stability and social coherence of the city state was of paramount concern. This could only be achieved if other pre-existing loyalties could be neutralized or accommodated. In the Athenian case they were *neutralised*, but in Crete they were *accommodated* (and probably sustained) by the construction of the ideal of community as possessing multiple segments. In both, however, there was a price to pay for these attempts at overcoming the Hobbesian problem of order. In Athens 'the price the city-state paid for its stability was the creation of a new plurality – which, though politically inert, of necessity guaranteed its continuing disunity' (Jones, 1987: 22). In Crete, on the other hand, there was always a threat that the more powerful or larger *phyle* could attempt to monopolise the magistracy. That is the reason for the draconian penalties in the laws on rotation discussed in the previous chapter. It may also go some way to explain the pattern of relationships with other *poleis* whether through the distractions of inter-*polis* wars or through the opposite tendency to explore the benefits accruing from a Cretan *koinon*.

It is beyond the scope of this study to examine why, at least since the early 18th century, Athenian democracy is usually praised so highly.[18] It is at least plausible to argue that a system of direct engagement may give the *appearance* of responding to the popular will when in fact power was concentrated in the hands of one or a few. This certainly appears to have been Hobbes's view in his translation of Thucydides' *History* (1627) when he refers to the Athenian system as working best when it appeared democratic but was in fact monarchic under Pericles (Saxonhouse, 1992; 1993). According to Hobbes, what Thucydides admired was a system that *took account* of the multitude rather than one that was governed by it. His preference was for the benefits of *debating* alternative policies in the Assembly rather than for

---

18 For example: 'Athenian democracy was transformed in the political imagination. From a regime that turned the mob into a tyrant, it became the glorious vision of nobility, freedom, and equality to which politicians, theorists, and journalists could turn' (Saxonhouse, 1993: 488).

hearing the voice of the multitude. On this reading a representative system would even more readily 'take account' of the majority because, unlike the Athenian citizens in their *Pnyx* or Assembly, the representatives depended for their position on so doing. If Hansen (1983: 18) is correct in his estimation that the *Pnyx* in the 4th century could not have held more than 6,000, or possibly under a third of those entitled to attend, then it is indeed hard to see how discontinuity – and possibly chaos – could have been avoided.

The tendency to see Classical Crete as a unitary culture only divided horizontally by rank and status also fails to appreciate the significance of public associations in the life of the emerging *poleis*. In Athens, for example, every citizen belonged to a deme (inheritable membership of an area of origin, but not necessarily residence, through which citizenship status was conferred) and also to the *trittys* (thirds) and the *phyle* of which his deme was a component part (Jones, 1987: 1). Public organisations were not function specific but cut the other way so that the associations carried out all administrative tasks.[19] Members of a deme were descendants in the male line of the original registrants of a particular territory, but as *poleis* became established there was a gradual movement away from personal associations (e.g. the Dorian and Attic-Ionic *phylai*) towards territorialism, first with a hereditary affiliation then to a place of residence (Jones, 1987: 11).

Some further light can be shed on the important contrast between the Athenian and Cretan strategies of political survival. In Durkheimian terms a central theme in Plato's *Laws* is the threat to the *polis* of 'anomie' or an absence of a sense of belonging to a social unit that can offer both stability and order. In the *Republic*, Plato had supposed that the problem could be solved by supplanting loyalties to the family and household by overriding attachment to the state itself, but in the later work, where he imagines a new or reborn *polis* in the area between Gortyn and Phaistos in the Mesara (the city of the *Magnetes*), he is less sanguine, arguing instead for the mediating role of face-to-face associations as the way of binding the individual to the state (Jones, 1990: 473 but cf. Morrow, 1960 for a full treatment). What Plato attempts is a depiction of a city state that does not suffer from the inadequacies of either the Athenian system as he saw it or the system of Crete itself. Since an important part of the work deals with these intermediate associations, it can be read as a commentary on the degree to which each resolved the Durkheimian problem.

The *Laws* can be seen, therefore, as a blueprint for an ideal city state. The text is in the form of a discussion set in Crete between Plato himself in the guise of the 'Athenian Visitor', Megillus, a Spartan, and Kleinias, a Cretan, thereby indicating which precepts he regards as worthy of comprising part of the scaffolding of the new edifice. It becomes apparent that the Cretan location is intended to suggest a return to the source of good law (the laws that Minos bequeathed to the Cretans),

---

19 The nearest modern equivalent is perhaps the religion-based associations in the Netherlands. Schools, trade unions and many other public associations are organised in the Catholic south and the Protestant north on religious lines.

rather than the possibility that Plato saw in the Crete of his day anything worthy of emulation.[20] This point is made clear by the setting of the dialogue which takes place on a walk from Knosos to the 'cave and sanctuary of Zeus', which is probably a reference to the Idaean cave on Mount Ida to the southwest of Knosos where Zeus was said in legend to have been raised as a child. All of this, and the themes within the discussion itself, have been the subject of many years of scholarly debate; the point here is the issue of how fealty to the state can be generated.

Despite important differences, the first point to note is that Plato's image of a good *polis* is thoroughly Athenian in its proposal to adopt the artificiality of the post-Kleisthenes *phylai*, so much so in fact that some have considered Plato the father of town planning. That is to say, the twelve *phylai* and twelve equal units into which they are to be divided (demes) are territorial and not ethnic in construction. In Nicholas Jones's words the 'bias towards territorialism mirrors the widespread tendency, most clearly evidenced at Athens, to abandon the personal disposition of inherited social groupings' (1990: 480–81). Not only that, but Plato envisages each settler living both in the urban centre and in the rural area of his appropriately allocated territory, which is a perfect reflection of the attempt to integrate the city, inland area and coast in Kleisthenes's use of the concept of the *trittys* (thirds) in Athens. Where Plato's ideal departs from the Athenian model is largely in the area of *individual* democratic participation in favour of a more representative function of the *phyle* itself.[21] But there is no enthusiasm either for the alternative Cretan model that would have existed for perhaps as long as two hundred years when Plato was writing the *Laws*. The Athenian visitor makes it quite clear that power can never be granted to any individual or group because of either their wealth or their origins:

> We must not entrust the government in your state to any one because he is rich, or because he possesses any other advantage, such as strength, or stature, or again birth: but he who is most obedient to the laws of the state, he shall win the palm (Book IV).

In other words, the main criterion must be their adherence to the constitution itself.

Plato is then left with a dilemma. There will be a problem of social coherence and a sense of belonging amongst the citizens of 'Magnesia' that cannot be resolved by the *phylai* or by any other of the artificially created associations that Plato envisages. Plato then turns to the Spartan traditions, and the one above all others that was Cretan in inspiration, namely the *syssition* or the system of publicly funded messes that the Spartans used so effectively to instill and maintain their military prowess. Rather than retain its solely military purpose, Plato argues for a *syssition* for each gender which would be carefully controlled by an overarching centralised state. What Plato tries to do then is steer a course between the atomised solution of the

---

20 In fact it is almost certain that Plato had never been to Crete and there is little suggestion in any of his writings that he knew that much about how it had evolved since Minoan times, although he was well aware of the island's history and appears familiar with its topography (Morrow, 1960: 25 *passim*).

21 Jones speaks of it as the 'official promotion of the isolation and solidarity of the local community' (1990: 487).

Athenian city state and the segmented form in Crete. On the one hand, he keeps the artificial nature of the Kleisthenic *phyle* as the mechanism of administration, but since this does not overcome the problem of belonging, he suggests that the Cretan (or Spartan) concept of the *syssition* should be rethought and, when extended beyond its solely military function, introduced for both men and women (Jones, 1990: 489). The central point is that the author of the *Republic* has no use for the uncontrolled individualism of the Athenian model of democracy, however participatory, or the potentially conflictful model of the 'plural society', however equitable the Cretans tried to make it.

Although there are one or two other possible claimants, it can be said that Crete invented the city state; it was amongst the first to establish the constitutions by which they were governed, and in so doing introduced a form of representative democracy that, while there from the outset, grew in importance during the period of greater prosperity and population increase that marked the Classical and Hellenistic periods. It may be objected that we should look to Athenian democracy for the roots of this system, but no other political institution has borrowed from the direct form of democracy that Athens created, whereas almost universally some form of representation is the norm, albeit often rather different from the Cretan model. If ancient Crete's system was hierarchical and unequal in terms of citizenship rights, so were all other political systems. It is worth recalling that it was not until 1928 that women in Britain were granted the right to vote on the same terms as men. Suffrage was extended to women in France by 1944, and in modern Greece women voted for the first time in the parliamentary elections of 1956. Even now, EU citizens other than the British cannot vote in UK general elections, even if they are married to British citizens and have lived in the country for decades. The theory of *jus sanguinis*, or ties of blood, prevents modern Germany extending full citizenship rights to former *Gastarbeiter* of Turkish origin, even if German is the only country they have ever lived in and German is the only language they speak. When assessed alongside this litany, the record of multi-ethnic ancient Crete is remarkable for the civilisation of its underlying values. As Cherry put it:

> The city states of Classical Greece were small-scale autonomous territorial units, self-governing, subject to unique constitutions, issuing their own coinage, and so on; yet they were bound together by spoken language and written script, by the structure of religious belief, by comparable political institutions, by competition in international religious games and military co-operation against common threats – indeed by a cultural conception of Hellenism which amounts, in material terms, to what archaeologists normally call a 'civilisation' (1987: 155).

Cretan *poleis* did see themselves as part of a Hellenic world but they also saw themselves as apart from it, perhaps fourth in importance after their *phyle*, their *polis* and their island.

The concept of 'democracy' is nowhere near as straightforward as it may at first appear. While it is perfectly true that the vast majority of democratic polities elect those who make policy decisions, rather than the referendum system or direct decision making made famous by Classical Athens, there are major deficiencies in this system in those settings where representatives are returned to power not because of what they espouse but because of who they are. These weaknesses have become very obvious as Western democracies in today's world have sought to export their electoral systems into multi-ethnic societies where long-standing loyalties of a religious, linguistic or cultural nature take precedence over ideological persuasion. This is compounded where literacy rates are low and where conservative communal values have been sanctified by tradition. These are, of course, precisely the circumstances of Crete in the period under consideration, and in this setting rules for the avoidance of tyranny and corruption through the circulation of power, together with the opportunity to give assent to proposed laws and policies, may count for as much as the right to decide who governs. In any event, within the *phylai* male citizens could determine by voting who their representatives would be.

As the possible founder of the *polis* concept, Crete was also a leader in codifying a system of links and associations that made this system of power sharing work. Over time, treaties and alliances emerged that began to express an impulse towards a pan-Cretan identity. This would only have been possible if each *polis* had achieved a measure of internal social coherence and relative prosperity. The following chapter explores how this was achieved.

CHAPTER SEVEN

Fractured subsistence
or an emerging mercantalism?

The debate surrounding the ancient economy over the past three decades has generated a great deal of heat but rather less light than its chief protagonists might have wished. In an earlier formulation, it was simply a discussion of how advanced or 'modern' the ancient economy was when judged by the standards of the day. If one could trace the footprints of *homo economicus* in the texts of the ancients, then this suggested that the fortunes of the present and past differed only in degree. This perspective was fundamentally altered by Karl Polányi's reinterpretation of Max Weber's writings on Greece and Rome in which he had noted the peculiarities of how these economies worked (Polányi, 1957; Polányi et al., 1957). Individuals pursued 'profit' not in order to maximise financial gain, but for the purposes of social standing and esteem. Polányi added that this made exchange dependent upon reciprocity or redistribution, so that free markets did not operate in accordance with impersonal rules. Ancient Greece had not been subject to the 'rationalizing' forces that Weber detected in Western Europe after 1600 and therefore 'had little in common with modern capitalism, not because of the scale of economic activity, but because economic interests were subordinated to or absorbed within politics, honor, and war' (Morris, 1994: 353). These ideas, termed rather clumsily the 'substantiveness' argument, found their later champion in the work of Moses Finley and they are still actively debated in the pages of scholarly journals to this day (Cartledge, 1998; Davies, 1998; Finley, 1999). While it is perhaps unwise to seek to capture the subtleties and complexities of these debates in simple categories, it might be argued that three topics of particular interest have emerged. The first, largely focused on ancient Athens, is what might be termed the 'Finley debate': the debate on how far modern scholarship revises his main conclusions. The second raises the question of whether there were commonalities in the economies of the ancient Mediterranean that were characteristic of there and nowhere else. The third concerns the ancient economies outside Athens and how their differences might be reassessed in the light of the other two debates. The Athenian debate represents a useful yardstick for comparison with Crete, but the chapter opens with an assessment of where the island might fit in the 'commonalities' / 'differences' debates. Unfortunately Crete has not yet inspired an adequate economic history, but some treatment will be given to the usual 'negative exceptionalism' case, or the view that the island was simply retarded in most of the main indicators of economic activity. This is followed by an overview of some of the main characteristics that would need to be addressed by anyone seeking to dig deeper than is possible here. Consideration of the 'Athenian debate' allows for a provisional assessment of the case for 'positive exceptionalism', or the proposition that ancient Crete during the long evolution of its relatively stable city states fulfilled at least some of the potential for advancement that Aristotle predicted (*Politics* 2: 11).

The Aegean context

Earlier approaches to the economic history of the Classical and Hellenistic world have captured its most obvious features – the widespread culture of agrarian self-sufficiency and a concomitant absence of high levels of specialisation. Indeed, it was these features above all others that allowed Finley to identify a phenomenon that could be called 'the ancient economy' (1999: 34). What has been added since, however, is the realization that there was not one ancient economy but rather at least two. This is not a reference to geographical variation but, more fundamentally, to the existence of a parallel economic realm predicated upon a much more complex series of exchanges than has hitherto been accepted. As Léopold Migeotte puts it in the closing words of his review of the economies of ancient Greek cities, we are dealing with a dualism between, on the one hand, the more or less self-sufficient production of rural agriculture and craftsmen's workshops and, on the other, a complex pattern of trade-based exchanges (Migeotte, 2009: 178). As early as the late 4th century, it has now been recognised that there was a complex flow of Mediterranean exchanges whose main channels were, in John Davies's words:

> (a) between the Egyptian, Syrian, and Phoenician ports along the south coast of Turkey to the major ports of the Aegean; (b) between Aegean Greece and the heel and toe of Italy, eastern Sicily, the northern Adriatic, and Etruria; (c) between the Phoenician city-states, especially Tyre, and their colonial states of the western Mediterranean, above all Carthage; (d) between the Aegean and the Black Sea through Bosporos; and (e) between Syracuse and the Adriatic (2006: 78).

While we may not yet know precisely *what* was exchanged and in what quantities, it certainly included 'iron from Etruria, timber, salt, and silver from Iberia, grain from Egypt, the Black Sea, and Sicily, slaves from the Black Sea, silver (as coin or plate), ceramics, and wine from the Aegean, and spices and luxury craftsman goods from Arabia, the Levant and further east' (2006: 78). If this was so, then, as Migeotte has concluded, some regions of the ancient world were stuck in very primitive modes of accumulation' while others were far more trade-oriented, and therefore more recognisable in modern economic terms (Migeotte, 2009).

Recent evidence on rates of economic growth in the ancient world tends to support this conclusion. The Finley perspective suggests a rather static world but Ian Morris (2004) has argued that per capita consumption in the Greek world as a whole possibly doubled in the period from 800 to 300 BCE, thereby suggesting that economic growth, although slight, was a real phenomenon. This appears to have been correlated with a concomitant growth of population over this period, which rose by a factor of ten between 800 and 300 BCE (2004: 727). By using very creative methods involving demographic data, morbidity inferences and household remains, Morris is able to come to the conclusion that living standards increased by between 0.07 and 0.14 per cent per annum over a period of 500 years from 800 BCE. This compares with 0.2 per cent per annum in Holland during its 'Golden Age' (AD 1580–1820) and 1.2 per cent per annum for the UK as it reaped the benefits of the Industrial Revolution (AD 1820–1920). As Morris comments:

> The performance of the Greek economy in the first millennium BC was a whole order of magnitude lower than that of post-Industrial Revolution Britain, but it bears comparison with some of the most dynamic pre-industrial economies that we know of (2004: 726).

Aggregate consumption with a growing population obviously advanced faster than that per capita but, even so, rates of growth of 0.6–0.9 per cent per annum are significant, and are similar to those in European countries prior to the Industrial Revolution.

Morris asks what it was that drove this improvement. One factor was climate change that produced a 'Sub-Atlantic' pattern with high summer temperatures but more reliable winter rains. Morris also mentions coinage, property rights, and the lowering of transaction costs. Economic growth allowed populations to grow which in turn generated a need to exploit market opportunities and geographical advantages in terms of trade links (Morris, 2004: 736). To this extent, therefore, the entire Greek world appears to have changed fundamentally during the late Archaic, Classical and, above all, Hellenistic eras. But if trade was a critical factor, this begs the question in one sense, for why did trade itself become so firmly entrenched in one place and less so in another? Perhaps one starting point in addressing this question can be derived from trade theory itself. At a theoretical level, we can postulate a continuum from an autarchic model at one end of a spectrum, in which trade is minimal and unimportant, to an open economy approximating to the Ricardian model in which an economy trades in accordance with its comparative advantage. The latter will tend towards specialisation since the comparative advantage is unlikely to be spread across a wide range of commodities or services. In between these extremes lie economies with a more complex pattern of advantage and disadvantage in which trade is more likely to be governed by political rather than purely economic considerations. From the vantage point of the state these considerations might be both negative and positive. A negative consideration might, for example, include the necessity of ensuring adequate food supplies, while on the positive side they could include the desirability of using specialist knowledge and expertise in the service of others, together with a wish to exploit opportunities for generating tax revenue.

The former is negative in the sense that in a culture that values autarchy, trade may occur but as a necessary evil. Under these circumstances, the political ramifications may be highly significant. For example, Alain Bresson suggests that 'Athens managed to secure themselves a regular supply of grain by means of political control, either via the occupation of other territories or via the creation of checkpoints on the main sea routes' (Bresson, 2005: 104). He stresses that in Plato's and Aristotle's writings the autarchic city was not defined as completely closed but as one that organised by any means the provision of basic needs, often through primitive barter (e.g. through the exchange of wine for grain).

In any event, it is not just the happenstance of geography that determines a dependence on trade, although in the Mediterranean access to the sea might be considered a necessary precondition. The latter is a central feature of the idea that the Mediterranean is in some senses *sui generis*:

> [O]ne of the characteristics best suited to identifying the Mediterranean as a distinctive object of reflection is provided by the sea itself as the medium and focus of a network of communications which renders the mobility of people and things relatively easy (Purcell, 2005: 203).

In other words, responding to surpluses and shortfalls is facilitated when primary producers can access with relative ease markets that would be impossible to reach over rugged terrain. It is the decisions of politicians and administrators, however, that determine how spatial advantages are exploited. Nicholas Purcell makes this point well when he suggests that:

> The place did not somehow spontaneously generate the entrepôt: Bacchiad Corinth, post-synoecism Rhodes, Delos after 166 BC were in suitable places, but their response to the advantages was the result of the political choices of elites, inside or outside the community (2005: 209).

Those decisions are themselves not merely the result of a calculus based upon personal preferences, unrelated to the economic and social context in which leaders found themselves. Without falling into the trap of determinism, one may agree that trade-oriented strategies are more likely to be preferred in monetarised economies than in those that are not. Indeed Davies argues that monetarisation was the most powerful determinant of economic development in the ancient world, and was itself dependent upon the need to pay troops:

> Though some Greek and Macedonian soldiers came to accept payment for military services in the form of land by becoming settlers, most remained mercenaries, recruited for shorter or longer periods into a professional army and hoping to return home intact and wealthy (2006: 80–81).

Monetarisation may indeed proceed from the need to pay troops, but mercenaries having returned home with money to hand are perhaps an even greater stimulus to monetarisation (Cook, 1958). It is then not unreasonable to argue that one source of possible variation in the relative strength of the agrarian economy when set alongside the 'trade-economy' was, first, the importance of mercenaries as a traded service and, second, the extent to which payment was in land or money. Moreover, the linking of land to military service is not just a question of payment for mercenary service; it also raises the issue of land divisions whose sole purpose was to maximise available manpower for military activities. For example, one strand in the myth of equality in some *poleis* of the Hellenic world, most notably in Athens, lay 'in the military need of each state to maximise its heavy armed field force, a need that in turn had shaped inheritance rules and land-owning patterns so as to maximise the number of minimally viable land-holdings' (Davies, 2006: 87). In other words, *ceteris paribus*, a *polis* whose economy was highly dependent upon traded military service rewarded in monetary terms, and that also allowed for private property rights and the amalgamation of landed estates, might be economically more dynamic than one with the opposite characteristics.

If monetarisation was a factor in the level of *polis*-support for trade then, of course, trade would have also stimulated monetarisation, but trade had at least one other vital impact. It became a major source of public revenue. From the beginning of the Hellenistic period, the evidence from shipwrecks suggests a massive rise in sea-borne trade (Archibald et al. 2001: 279). The legendary wealth of Rhodes, for example, was generated both by the profits of shipping itself but also by the customs levies imposed by the state. Indeed, Purcell has advanced the claim that not only were customs dues vital for state revenues, but that the manner of their imposition had uniquely 'Mediterranean' features:

> Strange as it seems to modern fiscalities, the taxation of *exports* was a crucial element in pre-modern Mediterranean practice (2005: 206, emphasis added).

It was not just that cities on the sea, or with access to it through a dependent settlement, gained an important part of their income from taxing trade; in addition, duties were levied on anything coming or going. Although transit trade might escape, which may be one reason for its importance, even small vessels 'with mixed cargoes hopping from one anchorage to the next, survived both the notorious unpredictability of route in Mediterranean navigation, and the propensity of every harbour, however small, to charge customs dues' (Purcell, 2005: 221).

Purcell argues that the centrality of customs dues, together with differences of wealth and influence between Aegean ports, created opportunities for granting privileges which could be utilised in building networks of cooperation and dependency. Autarchy was almost impossible under these conditions because the rights and responsibilities that were engendered within these networks meant that every port, however small, had a place. In this sense the customs duties were, in his phrase, 'a levy on interdependence' (2005: 217). It was, he argues, 'a remarkable world of maritime interconnectedness' in which clusters of consumers and producers used their outlets to the sea to build exchanges and the opportunities and obligations to which they give rise. These went beyond the economic realm, generating in turn a cultural orientation or:

> [T]he ethical concerns with economic issues of the community and its leaders, the sometimes diffident but always potent orientation of early Greek culture toward the sea, that intensity of community self definition through the interplay of individuality and imitation which we think of as characteristic of the early history of the *polis* (2005: 218).

In other words, the form and content of the life of the *polis* cannot be divorced from the embrace of the Mediterranean itself that – for good or evil – provides both a structure of opportunities and a web of constraints.

But where does Crete fit within this picture? In the most general terms, it is quite clear that many of the commonalities, such as the centrality of the sea in the self definition of the life of the *polis* and the increasing dependence of governance on the revenues from trade, were as true for Crete as for anywhere. As we shall, in the *pattern* of trade, there are peculiarities, most notably the absence of a link between militarism and visible trade on the one hand and the balance between visible and invisible trade on the other. Before exploring these issues in greater detail, it is important to examine the claims made by adherents of what has been termed here the 'negative exceptionalism' case, or the proposition that in the centuries prior to the Roman conquest, the island was in economic terms simply backward, primitive and inward-looking.

Negative exceptionalism

Adherents of this view argue that because Crete stood apart from most of the struggles and foreign adventures that comprise the standard fare of Aegean prehistory, this meant that it did not share in the surge of economic prosperity that followed in the wake of a new era of traded goods. The most consistent proponent of the argument can again be found in the work of the distinguished classicist Angelos Chaniotis, whose writings, in the almost total absence of alternative voices, have proved to be very influential.[1] Since they reach opposite conclusions to those advanced here, it is important to consider why these differences occur.

The first point to note is that Chaniotis is clearly convinced, as was Ronald Willetts before him, by the innate conservatism and traditional orientation of all Cretan city states. As he suggests, 'the adequate economic system for such a social organization is a subsistence economy based on farming and animal husbandry,' so it is perhaps not surprising that this is what he finds (1999: 182). Although he notes the comments of ancient authors on the fertility and richness of Cretan

---

1 For example, in a recent review of Aegean economies in the Hellenistic period John Davies, citing Chaniotis, concludes, 'although some regions such as northern Egypt, western Syria, or Asia Minor showed significant economic transformation, others such as Crete showed little or none' (2006: 90).

lands, he then chooses to draw inferences for the economy as a whole by examining those that are most barren and infertile, the mountainous uplands. He recognises that most inland *poleis* did not occupy the highest ground, 'yet the territory of almost all the independent cities consisted of mountainous terrain, which could be exploited from the main settlement' (1999: 186). Therefore, he focuses on those Cretan agricultural activities that took place on the high plains and summer pastures which, then as now, suit only the seasonal grazing of goats and sheep. While it is perfectly true that there are relatively rich epigraphic sources that refer to resolving what must have been defined as problems of trespass over grazing lands, and there is no doubt that the exploitation of higher terrain (in particular the high plains of Lasithi, Omalos, Askyfou, Nida and others) has always played an important role in economic survival, no one visiting the sites of the 'primary *poleis*' can be in any doubt about the greater importance of the fertile plains and valleys that they invariably overlook.

Moreover, Chaniotis rules out from the start any suggestion that the extraction of surplus in the Cretan case could lead to economic reform. Rather, he suggests, it simply culminated in 'the conquest of the neighbour's territory and in migration' (1999: 183). So, although by the Hellenistic period he recognises an intensification of trade, this had no effect on the traditional social and economic order (1999: 184). Even though no Cretan *polis* was ever involved as a belligerent in an external war, Chaniotis suggests that for the Cretans 'trade was to a large extent a side-effect of war: bringing home luxury items, selling captives, trading with booty, and transporting these goods abroad on their ships' (1999: 185). There is a clear link between the conclusion that only subsistence was possible in Crete at this time and the argument concerning constant inter-*poleis* strife. He suggests that war was functional for without it 'many Cretan cities were not in a position to maintain their subsistence' (1999: 205). In fact, not only were Cretan wars rather rare but there is good reason for believing that environmental conditions also were propitious for levels of productivity above subsistence. For example, starting in about 650 BCE, there is a dramatic fall in the strength of the El Niño-Southern Oscillation signal affecting Crete, which did not show a very significant tendency to rise until the early years of Roman occupation, suggesting that the rise of the city states correlates well with a period of greater rainfall, and thus a greater likelihood of a surplus beyond subsistence (Tsonis et al., 2010: 539).

Moreover, if different starting points are likely to lead to different conclusions, then this is no less true in terms of how trade itself is understood. Most economic commentators in today's world recognise the limitations of a simple Ricardian view that emphasises comparative advantage as a determinant of trade. Based on an analogy with Newton's law, which considers both mass and distance as critical variables, the so-called 'gravity model' tries to come closer to the real world by incorporating the size of economies that trade and the distance between them. Thus units of similar size that are close together will be more successful trading partners than those that diverge greatly on these two variables. Comparable income levels, effective diplomacy and compatible trade-promotion policies have all been added to make an even stronger prediction of likely trading success. In the Cretan case, this should make us sensitive to the role of inter-*polis* trade. Chaniotis, on the other hand, dismisses such movements as having no economic importance. Even where there is epigraphic evidence for inter-*polis* trade this is not taken as indication of surpluses, but rather these agreements are seen as an 'alternative to the direct storage of food' (1999: 184). Citing the work of Marangou-Lerat (1995; Marangou, 1999) he agrees that wine was produced locally in significant quantities and traded within the island, but because it was not exported in massive amounts, it made little impact on economic development (2005b: 99–100). This is despite the fact that much 'internal' trade would have been carried by sea from the ports that the inland *poleis* were so careful to establish, and therefore prone to customs dues and thus the enhancement of public wealth.

If 'real' trade is only long-distance, there is also the assumption that goods concerned have to be produced or manufactured locally. This means that carriers, shippers, financiers and all the myriad services that support maritime trade, which Chaniotis recognises were a Cretan specialty, are ruled out, and thus he concludes that the evident forces of integration in the Hellenistic era are not seen as upsetting 'the traditional ideal of economic autarchy' (1999: 185). Above all, the provision of specialist military service, in which all agree that Crete excelled, is not seen as having any economic role even though, as the previous section argued, this was one of the major factors in monetarisation. Indeed, Chaniotis does not mention the fact that on the best survey ever conducted, Crete had 43 mints, some of them producing for four centuries before 67 BCE (Svoronos, 1890). Just to give an idea of the contortion which the exclusion of invisible trade produces, it is worth noting that at the present time two-thirds of the US economy is based on services and service workers make up four out of five workers. So-called 'transit trade' and the specialised services associated with the redistribution, insurance, financing and facilitation of goods emanating from elsewhere are as much a part of the economy as productive endeavour in tangible goods themselves. To deny this is like saying in today's world that the activities of the city of London have no bearing on the British economy. It is equally unacceptable to deny that the state-sponsored provision of mercenaries has any part in generating economic wealth. This is equivalent to denying the economic significance of tourism in modern-day Crete, when it is in fact the single most important element in the island's GDP. Moreover, this could have been a major reason why there is so little evidence of private wealth of the kind that was seen, for example, in ancient Athens and which Chaniotis misses in Crete (e.g. dedications of public buildings, financial contributions to festivals, elaborate funerary documents and honorific decrees to benefactors) (1999: 210). A combination of public wealth from customs dues and widely spread private wealth from mercenary service is unlikely to produce this outcome.

A critical part of the evidence adduced for the poor showing of the Cretan economy during the Hellenistic period in particular is the apparent failure of Crete to compete with Rhodes in the wine trade and in the production of the amphorae in which oil and wine were transported by sea. The evidence certainly suggests that this is true, since Rhodes was by far and away the leader in this field. On the evidence of the stamps that were sometimes applied to the handles of amphorae, the dominance of Crete's neighbour is impressive: [2]

> Of 113,469 handles reported by Sherwin-White, no fewer than 98,047 (86.4%) are Rhodian, and of them about 80,000 were found in Alexandria. No other state begins to approach such figures, though Cos, with 1,925 handles reported, shows a similar proportion from Alexandria (1,480, or 75.9%). In contrast, stamps of the second biggest supplier, Cnidus – 6,222 in all reported — gravitated towards Delos (4,525, or 72.7%, found there). Given the preponderance of amphorae in known shipwrecks of the Hellenistic period, it is fair to see in these and other figures a reflection of one of the main components by bulk (perhaps the principal one) of eastern Mediterranean trade in the Hellenistic period (Davis, 1984: 274).

But this does not mean that Cretan amphorae were not found outside the island. Even early on there is evidence of Cretan involvement in Mediterranean trade. For example, one of the earliest wrecks investigated (ca. 310–300 BCE), that of the *Kyrenia*, contained more than 400 amphorae, the vast majority of them from Rhodes but with examples also from Samos, Paros, Crete and Palestine (Rauh, 2003: 108). It has been shown that Hierapytnian amphorae have been located in Egypt, but the assumption has always been that these were the personal property of Cretan mercenaries rather than evidence of trade (Viviers, 1999). Similar evidence also tends to be discounted. For example, Chaniotis notes also that so called 'Hadra vases' were exported from Crete in large quantities and were 'certainly one of the most important products of Cretan pottery in the Hellenistic period' (2005b: 100). They were used as funerary urns and their name comes from a cemetery near Alexandria where they were initially found, but they have also been unearthed in Eretria and Rhodes. For Chaniotis, however, this is not indicative of trade relations because these were places where Crete sent mercenaries (2005b: 100). In other words, mercenary service has no positive economic role but has a negative one in enabling us to discount what otherwise might have appeared as a significant export.

While there is no question that the Cretan wine trade did not match that of Rhodes there is evidence of workshops producing amphorae in Crete, and it is quite likely that many more will be discovered since investigations have been conducted only in coastal regions where it appears that most of these vessels were produced in the years of Roman domination (Empereur et al. 1991: 51l; Empereur et al., 1992). Recent archaeological work has suggested the widespread production of amphorae in every region of the island, particularly in or near coastal coastal ports. Studies at Mochlos, Myrtos (Pyrgos) and Knosos, using modern petrographic methods,

2 The stamping of amphorae was part of a bureaucratic process, possibly particularly found in major producing territories, whereby their manufacture and progress were monitored and controlled (Rauh, 2003: 116).

have shown that the fabric for many amphorae was local and not imported (Eiring et al., 2002). Further studies at Trypitos near Siteia and at Lato pros Kamara in Eastern Crete showed '... substantial evidence of a significant production of local transport amphoras in East Crete from the third century BC' (Vogeikoff-Brogan and Apostolakou, 2004: 417). The authors also found a considerable variety of imported amphorae, suggesting that Crete was part of a wine trade originating in the south-east Aegean and ending in Egypt.[3] Moreover, it is most unlikely that the land-based wine trade, whose size and importance we simply do not know, would ever have used clay vessels. As Empereur et al. (1991: 522) suggest it is much more likely that animal skin containers would have been used. Also, as Chaniotis himself observes, trade networks involve both imports as well as exports. Even where wine is concerned 64 stamped amphorae of the 3rd century BCE were found at Trypitos, 43 from Rhodes and twenty from a range of other areas (Chaniotis, 2005b: 98; cf Papadakis 2000). At the 'unexplored mansion' at Knosos, 54 per cent of the stamps are from Rhodes with the rest coming from a range of places, including Corinth, Thasos, Knidos and Kos (Sackett et al., 1992: 138–41). This may not be significant in terms of Rhodian trade but it shows clearly that Crete at this time was firmly enmeshed in widespread trade relations with its neighbours (Chaniotis, 2005b: 97; cf. Perlman 1999).

A central feature of the 'negative exceptionalism' case is the comparison not only with other *poleis* in the Hellenistic period but with what came after. With the coming of the Romans what is suggested is that all appears to change: cities no longer fought each other, piracy was extinguished and the symbols of an archaic social order (common meals, military education and the *andreia*) were swept away as trade flourished (1999: 211):

> The peculiarities of the Cretan economy in the Hellenistic period becomes evident when we compare the Hellenistic evidence with that of Roman Crete (c. 50 BC – AD 250). It is only from the late first century B.C. onwards that we have evidence for a specialized production, for standardisation and for a mass export of local products, especially of wine (2005: 101).

Certainly, there is no denying the evidence that the long-distance wine trade, mainly to Rome, was massively expanded in the years after 67 BCE. Studies of amphora workshops do indeed show a preponderance of examples from the Roman era and there are many references in Roman authors to this trade.[4] But for Chaniotis, there are no doubts. We see for the first time 'the standardisation and commercialisation of production, massive export trade, and the integration

---

3 They also remark '... that the absence of evidence for Hellenistic Cretan amphora production was more a problem of recognition than a historical reality, particularly given the paucity of published Hellenistic deposits from Crete' (Vogeikoff-Brogan and Apostolakou, 2004: 417).

4 Even though the major study by Empereur et al. (1989) on the western end of the island argues that this could be due to an absence of comparable literary sources when compared with the Roman authors, since the bunches of grapes seen on the coins of Kydonia, Eleutherna and Sybrita among others hundreds of years before the Roman invasion may suggest a much earlier trading system (Empereur, 1989: 551).

of the island's production in economic networks that extended across the entire empire' (2005b: 102). The Roman conquest heralded the birth of economic growth and export-led production (2005b: 107).

The critical question that must be raised at this point is not whether the Cretan economy in the Roman era was reorganised to provide for Rome's needs. As Rauh argues, 'the history of the Roman conquest of the Mediterranean world was to no small degree a history of Roman domination of foreign trade' (2003: 133). And it is argued that there was now growth in the need for containers to carry the cargo, since in shipwreck data amphorae account for nearly half the cargo and '...commodities conveyed in amphorae formed the bulk of Roman commerce' (2003: 106). The real issue turns on the extent to which this process of extraction translated into benefits for the local population. The answer is that we do not know, but the evidence on Rome's use of its possessions elsewhere is not particularly encouraging. What Rauh (2003) shows is that the incursion of Roman imperial power into the eastern Mediterranean did indeed lead to a massive expansion of economic activity, but not for the purpose of indigenous economic development. Thus:

> Emerging amphora evidence indicates that Roman goods expelled Greek goods from the western Mediterranean and the Aegean in much the same manner that Roman armies crushed the maritime populations in their path (2003: 201).

Although attitudes may have hardened with the end of the Republic and the coming of the Empire, Roman traders simply took over from those decimated by military power. For example, in the case of Corinth and Carthage, Rauh writes that 'what changed was the disappearance at these places of once-thriving communities offering livelihoods for thousands of people' (2003: 201). Moreover, the export of primary produce from colonial enclaves has been shown on many subsequent occasions to be both highly inequitable and often transitory. In Crete, there are many examples of the remains of luxurious Roman villas but, as Empereur et al. argue for the wine trade, colonial production only lasted until wine production was established at home and elsewhere in the empire, whereupon local profits fell dramatically (1992: 648).

In short, Chaniotis simply looks in the wrong places – he looks up in the mountains when he should be looking down on the fertile plains, he thinks only of goods when he should also be examining services, and he focuses on private rather than public wealth. Moreover, he clearly believes, in the face of substantial evidence to the contrary, that colonial exploitation produces economic development across the board, rather than for a privileged elite of foreigners. On the other hand, if the overall evidence points in the opposite direction then the negative view is functional, for it clearly implies the need to focus on features of the Cretan economy that have been overlooked, such as the remarkable story of the island's mints, the reasons why they arose and the vital role they came to play.

Parameters of Cretan economies

In rejecting the case for 'negative exceptionalism', it is important to restate that the purpose is simply to argue that Cretan city states were not dissimilar in terms of their development to those elsewhere in the eastern Mediterranean. John Davies writes of an overall impression that:

> the economic interplay and exchange among the seaboard communities of the eastern Mediterranean did increase in intensity during the Hellenistic period and did go some way towards making one world out of what had been hitherto an assemblage of economic zones less intimately and more superficially connected (1984: 284–285).

One window into this connectivity lies perhaps in the evidence of the widespread adoption of coinage. Faced with a paucity of other sources, however, the economic historian of the ancient world may invest evidence of the circulation of coinage with greater significance than is justified. In this regard John Davies is right to warn that imagining a simple link between coinage and trade relations 'is not safe enough to allow it to dominate whatever model of circulation we hope to construct' (Davies, 1984: 280). Coins have to be defined as currency; they have to be widespread in their adoption and standardised as a medium of exchange. It is especially important that they are backed by a centralised administration and adopted as a medium for taxation and the payment of dues, including those imposed as fines in legal proceedings. This takes time, but is to some extent self-fulfilling; once coinage reaches a certain stage of development and standardisation, it tends to become incorporated into systems of governance, which in turn increases its adoption in many spheres of life, including market relations. The initial question then becomes how did a territory first encounter coinage, for that helps explain its later consolidation into a monetary system? In Crete, coinage arrived in two contexts both of which facilitated its widespread adoption. It came first in a trade context and second as a means of payment for services.

COINAGE AND EARLY TRADE

Money existed long before the invention of coinage. Forms of money have included, *inter alia*, sharks teeth, cowrie shells, camels, slaves and wives but coins as money have many obvious virtues. The Greeks did not invent coins. This honour is normally reckoned to fall to King Alyattes II of Sardis in Lydia, now part of western Turkey, but the Greeks were very quick to spot their potential first in the island of Aigina, followed swiftly by Corinth and later by Athens.[5] This fact does not resolve one very important question, which is why coins were introduced (Martin, 1996). The most obvious answer – to facilitate trade by using a standard unit of exchange – was undermined by evidence that the early Lydian 'lions' were denominated far too

---

5 Weber notes that Greeks traded well before they adopted coinage but what was particularly significant was that 'the Greeks were the first to exploit fully the invention of coinage' (1976: 163).

highly to be used for this purpose (Kraay, 1964). What made the Aiginetan coinage so useful by contrast was that it was issued in a range of values to a standard of silver content and each coin of higher value was a multiple of those below. This meant that it could be easily employed for trade and, as overseas trade grew in importance, it came to circulate in areas far distant from its point of origin.

The question of *when* the first coins were produced has been the subject of intense debate amongst numismatists and ancient historians. The view in the first part of the 20th century was almost unanimous, that the first coins were minted on electrum in Lydia in the first half of the 7th century BCE and possibly nearer to the opening years of this century.[6] This would have meant that coins from Aigina might have been as early as the first quarter of the 7th century and that this was followed some years later by mints opening in Athens and Corinth (Kagan, 1982: 359). This accorded with Greek tradition that proclaimed the first silver Aiginetan coins to have been minted by Pheidon of Argos. The alternative 'low chronology', more favoured by numismatists than by classicists, argues for a date for the introduction of coins into Greece at the beginning of the 6th century, or possibly even later. The famous French numismatist Le Rider has suggested that the Lydian coinage was not minted before 590–580, which would have meant that Aigina could not have opened a mint much before 570 BCE (cf. Kroll and Waggoner, 1984). In favour of this argument was the retention of pre-coinage units of currency in the early specimens from Aigina. Before the advent of coinage, iron bars or 'spits' had been used as units and the very earliest coins were in units of obol (from *obelos* meaning spit of iron) or drachm, meaning a 'handful' of (six) spits. All were agreed, however, that the sequence was right, first the electrum coinage of Lydia, then the silver obols of Aigina, followed by the coins of Corinth and, later still, Athens. In about 510 BCE Athens began producing a fine silver tetradrachm (four drachm) coin using silver from the large mines at Laurion. The coin, with an owl's head on it, circulated from 510 to 38 BCE. The owl was a reference to the city's goddess Athena, the goddess of wisdom. The tetradrachm was minted to a different weight, thereby introducing the 'Attic standard' that eventually became preeminent in the whole Aegean, particularly after 322 BCE.

But for Crete, the most important part of the story lies with Aigina. Aigina is a rather small and barren island within sight of Athens lying at the head of the bay of Piraeus. Seafaring was an early preoccupation of the Aiginetans, and traders from the island were among the first to open up trade with Egypt establishing the port of Naucratis on the Egyptian coast. Aigina is famous for its silver coinage featuring a sea turtle on the obverse. Although lacking its own source of silver, the Aiginetan mint imported it from the neighbouring island of Siphnos. The early standardisation of the Aiginetan coinage was one of the major reasons for its success. The weights were as follows:

6 Electrum is an alloy of gold, silver and a small amount of copper found originally in the Pactolus River near ancient Sardis.

Stater	194 grs	(12.571 gr)
Drachm	97 grs	(6.285 gr)
Triobol	48 grs	(3.110 gr)
Diobol	32 grs	(2.073 gr)
Trihemiobol	24 grs	(1.555 gr)
Obol	16 grs	(1.036 gr)
Hemiobol	8 grs	(0.518 gr)
Tetartimorion	4 grs	(0.259 gr)

From this it can be seen that the Aiginetans invented a whole series of inter-changeable coins with standardised weights ideally suited for establishing a trade-based economy. In fact, right down to the Peloponnesian War in the last quarter of the 5th century, these coins were the main international medium of exchange.

Having so little chance of establishing an indigenous agrarian economy, the Aiginetans took to trade with alacrity. Trade became the source of the island's great wealth (Herodotus, 7: 147). One of their most important routes took their merchant fleets south towards Crete and in particular towards the west where the port of Kydonia offered a safe harbour and access to a large internal market. The result was the rapid adoption of Aiginetan coinage in Crete, from the second half of the 6th century and precisely at the time that most of the Archaic laws of the island were being written (Stefanakis, 1999: 256; cf. Stefanakis 1997). As Stefanakis writes:

> During the second half of the 6th Century and especially towards its end, Kydonians and Cretans in general came into greater contact with minted coinage – indeed with the most substantial coinage in the Aegean region (1999: 256).

The largest hoard of Aiginetan coins ever found comes from Matala in southern Crete; these have been dated to 500–490 BCE (Kroll and Waggoner, 1984: 337; Holloway, 1971).

The adoption of coinage in Crete probably took a number of years, but certainly it would not have been later than the last quarter of the 6th century and possibly before. The fragmentary texts on the walls of the temple of Apollo Pythios at Gortyn, dating from the mid-6th century, make no mention of money as we understand it today (Roberts, 1888: 11). The Gortyn Great Code, however, dates from the middle of the 5th century when coinage was referred to frequently in units that replicate those used in Aigina, which allows us to be reasonably certain that coinage in Crete was exceptionally early. Perlman argues that from the beginning of the 5th century BCE, the Gortynians used money to calculate fines (2002: 203). Stefanakis concludes that 'Cretans had become accustomed to coinage as early as the second half of the 6th century', which is as early as anywhere else in Europe (1999: 249). This means that perhaps two centuries before indigenous coinage became established, a monetary economy linked to a major trading partner had already been achieved.

The Aiginetan dominance in Aegean trade towards the end of the Archaic period did not go unnoticed by others. The island of Samos, for example, never achieved the same pre-eminence, but was a rival to Aigina in the early corn trade with Egypt. As Erickson argues 'the Samians came under pressure first from Sparta and later from Aigina as commercial rivals compelled the Samians to relinquish their stake in the Laconia-Crete-Cyrenaica-Egypt trade circuit', but like the Aiginetans, the Samians also spotted the strategic value of Kydonia and the fact that at that time it possessed only a very small indigenous community with a large and protected harbour (Erickson, 2000: 256). This allowed them, apparently without a very significant struggle, to establish a colony in Kydonia in 524 BCE. They set about rebuilding temples, including that at Diktynna above the Bay of Menias near the tip of the Rodopou peninsula. But their local dominance was not to last. Given their earlier involvement and use of Kydonia's harbour, the Aiginetans could hardly let things stand and, with the support of local Cretans, they displaced the Samians in 519 BCE and this time set up their own settlement (Herodotus, *Historia* 3.59).[7] It is not clear how large the Aiginetan community was, but it was significant enough to establish the Kydonian mint, initially producing Aiginetan coins featuring the famous sea turtle on the obverse. At a later date the coinage, although on the Aiginetan standard, was made by overstriking Aiginetan specimens. The importance of this initiative was enormous for not only were 'pseudo-Aiginetan' coins from Kydonia used throughout the island, but when the first genuine Cretan coins from the mints in Gortyn and Phaistos were made (ca. 470 BCE) this was done by overstamping Aiginetan flans with local dies (Stefanakis, 2005).

Later, as Athenian influence became more powerful in trading terms, conflict with Aigina became inevitable and the importance of the small island declined. In 459 BCE Athens and Aigina went to war resulting in a shift of economic power to Athens, eventually culminating in the expulsion of the population in 431 and the repopulation of the island by Athenian *kleruchs*.[8] Cretan mints still retained the Aiginetan standard for some years but eventually bowed to the inevitable and shifted to the lighter Euboic-Attic standard (Stefanakis, 1999: 259).

MERCENARIES AND MONEY

John Davies has called the rise of the mercenary the 'most significant wage-labour market, with the widest geographical scope' (Davies, 2007a: 352) and in her study of the development of capitalist markets, Schoenberger recognises the importance

---

7 Strabo suggests that the Cretans colonised Aigina (Book 8, 6: 16) but this may just reflect the welcome relationship for a people whose involvement had brought such tangible benefits.

8 The islanders were allowed to return home after Sparta vanquished Athens in the Peloponnesian War in 404 BC, when the turtle on the coins was replaced with a tortoise.

of mercenaries in the medieval period and terms it 'perhaps one of the better-developed branches of international trade' (2008: 682). As the discussion in Chapter 5 made clear, mercenary service was a hugely important part of the Cretan experience, particularly in the Hellenistic period but undoubtedly starting much earlier. Indeed mercenary soldiers have been called the island's 'most abundant product' (Spyridakis, 1970a: 91). As Sekunda (2007: 343) writes:

> Hellenistic armies relied on mercenaries to supply specialist units to supplement the main force, such as light infantry (*euzonoi*). Cretan archers, able to fight at close quarters thanks to their bronze *peltai* (protective armour), as well as at a distance with their bow, were highly valued. Hellenistic armies sought to enlist contingents of Cretans and formed units of troops 'equipped in the Cretan manner' to supplement them, such as that fielded by Antiochus III at Magnesia.

In an important sense, therefore, Cretans did not have to engage in external wars to reap their economic benefits.

Mercenaries are a form of temporary migrant labour and they brought home or sent home a large amount of wealth that would have boosted the local economy. Migrant remittances and sums carried on return rank alongside the trade in goods and other services as an important contribution to 'export' revenue, but the existence of such regular streams of labour also had the effect of ameliorating unemployment and social unrest, and they contributed to social capital in terms of education, skills and an awareness of different cultures. To set this in a modern context, prior to joining the European Union Greece was still ranked among the countries of the world that benefited most from remittances. In that year more than 1.2m Greeks were working abroad and sending remittances home (Simeon, 1998). In the 1991–96 period, Greece ranked sixth in the world in terms of income from remittances, which totalled over $15 billion for those six years (World Bank database; cf. Glytsos, 1993; Lianos, 1997). This effect would have been compounded in the Cretan case since returning mercenaries would have been not only comparatively wealthy, but also of high social standing. They were highly skilled, and therefore well rewarded, but their successes accorded with the long-standing values of the ancient *polis* in which skills in soldiering ranked amongst the highest forms of achievement.

An important point to note is that for the most part this invisible trade was organised by the *poleis* for service to foreign powers. Contrary to what is often thought Cretan mercenaries were seldom individual adventurers offering their services to the highest bidder. That may have occurred elsewhere, but in Crete the city states themselves were deeply involved in providing professional soldiers in accordance with international treaties and contracts. In this sense success in fulfilling these agreements would have made Cretan city-states known to the outside world as places to be both respected and cultivated. In addition, the transformation of soldiering into a professional activity altered the classic model of the *polis* for ever. As Runciman has argued, when mercenaries came to replace the citizen-hoplites of the old *poleis* 'the young male citizen would no longer assume, as his father and grandfather had done, that when his city-state went to war he would himself be obliged to take part' (1998: 744). What changed was the culture that provided status to those who risked death for the community as a whole. The mode of fighting changed and the methods of achieving prestige changed with it. In economic terms the effects were just as significant, for prestige came to be measured more in terms of the *rewards* that soldiering could bring rather than from the activity itself. For the most part, those returns were in the form of coin, often that of a foreign power.

The returning mercenary, then, had three options. He could seek to exchange the coinage for one of greater use locally, he could have the coinage melted down and restruck or the coins could be simply used as flans and overstruck. The last was a very common choice:

> About 322 a great number of tetradrachms from Cyrenaica were brought to Crete by mercenaries returning home. These coins, weighing c. 12.8–13.4g, were cut down by 1–2g and then used as flans for staters of Aiginetan weight (somewhat below 12.00g) struck primarily at Gortyn and Phaestus (Mørkholm, 1991: 13).

In this way the wealth of returning mercenaries made it much more probable that a *polis* would see the virtues in establishing a local mint of its own.

It is also important to recognise that these two phenomena – an early exposure to trade in goods, alongside the currency in which it was conducted, together, largely at a later date, with the state-sponsored provision of mercenary service – interacted with each other. In other words, visible trade followed the networks of contacts generated by overseas military service. As the following examples show very clearly, this was not just a question of some items being taken from Crete overseas or a few luxury goods making the return journey. It helped to establish trading links that had a profound effect on the fortunes of some of the island's major *poleis*. The effect of the Aiginetan link with Kydonia has been discussed earlier, but it continued in later centuries as mercenaries from the city appear to have been engaged in some of the major conflicts in the region as a whole. The so-called 'Chania hoard', for example, discovered in 1922, consisted of at least 1400 silver fractions – 800 belonging to Kydonia, 11 to Tanos, three from other Cretan mints and 147 from non-Cretan mints (with 42 of uncertain origin). The non-Cretan coins came from a wide area including Macedonia as well as Aigina, Argos, Chalcis, Corinth and Rhodes (Stefanakis, 2002: 233; 234). Evidence from coinage also gives an insight in particular into the other three 'independent *poleis*' and their rise to pre-eminence as important trading hubs.

In the case of Phalasarna, Stefanakis has shown a large inflow of coins from Cyrenaica from the early years of the Hellenistic era, opening up what he terms 'a period of intense relations between Cretan cities and the Libyan coast' which grew in significance during the reign of King Magas of Cyrene (300–250 BCE) (2006b: 48). These were used as flans for overstriking coins from Phalasarna, particular drachms, while other denominations came from coins originating in Argos, thereby suggesting the importance of both North Africa and the Argolid (2006b: 47). He also documents finds from the necropolis suggesting a long-standing period of foreign contact. Items from the Archaic and Classical eras tended to be from Corinth and Attica. Western Crete was particularly significant for Athens because of its proximity, which might only take two days' sailing, and because it lay directly on the route of vessels bringing grain from North Africa and Egypt (2006b: 46). Later, in the Hellenistic era there was evidence of imports from Chios, Rhodes, Cos, Thasos and elsewhere (2006b: 45). In other words both returning mercenaries and trade helped create the prosperity of this important *polis*. Moreover the design of the harbour (two linked basins connecting to the sea by a channel or *cothon*) suggests Phoenician influence (2006b: 58). It is most likely that this came from seafaring contacts, although for many centuries before there is evidence in Crete of imports from the Syro-Palestinian coast. Stampolides and Kotsonas (2006), for example, document imports from this region from the late tenth century onwards in western and central zones. Deposits of bronze artefacts have been found at Kommos, Eleutherna and Knosos providing evidence that Phoenicians were also living in Iron Age Crete and playing a role in community life, apparent from their influence on cultic activity (Stampolides and Kotsonas, 2006: 352; Stampolidis and Karageorghis, 2003; cf. Hoffman, 1997). Genetic evidence too provides ample testimony to the Phoenician colonisation of Crete, third only to that of Sicily and Cyprus (Zalloua et al., 2008).

The same twin processes of mercenary service and trade also lay behind the presence in Crete of coins from Ptolemaic Egypt, albeit at the other end of the island. The role of Itanos in providing a major point of contact has been referred to already but Ptolemaic coins have been found more widely, though mostly in the east (Stefanakis, 1996a). More than 100 coins from the Hellenistic era were studied by Stefanakis covering a number of centuries and rulers from Ptolemy I to Ptolemy XIII. Mercenary service, he argues, produced an 'influx of silver coins from North Africa [that] occurred around the end of the fourth century earned from 320 onwards' (1996a: 198), while the second process concerned visible trade itself with Egypt (1996a: 200). A very similar story unfolds in relation to Rhodes. Again the influence of this major trading power was widespread owing to the influence of both processes. In this case, the focus of economic activity was in the south, particularly at Hierapytna and Gortyn. Of particular interest is the fact that this association led to the production of imitation Rhodian coinage. Under careful physical analysis these coins can be shown to be quite different in their composition from real Rhodian currency, but they suggest a trade influence, possibly analogous to that of Aigina on Kydonia a century or more before. As the authors of a report on this phenomenon point out, this coinage gives the lie to the reputation that Crete was isolated in the Classical and Hellenistic eras (Barrandon and Bresson, 1997: 155). Again, however, at least by the beginning of the 2nd century, mercenary service and trade were both factors in the widespread circulation of this so-called 'plinthophoric' currrency (Stefanakis and Stefanaki, 2006).[9] In other words, it is no accident that the *poleis* that were particularly well known for providing mercenaries were also those that were nodal points for emerging trade relations. It may also have been the case that competition over trading contacts and routes was one of the factors that led to conflicts between Hierapytna and Itanos, and Kydonia and Phalasarna, in the 2nd century. In the former case, the loss of Ptolemaic connections may have stimulated competition with Hierapytna over Rhodian trade, while in the latter the emerging power of Rome in North Africa may have spurred Phalasarna to compete more for the lucrative Attic routes, and thereby to incur the wrath of the Kydonians.

It is important to note that these emerging trade networks were never confined solely to the 'independent *poleis*', nor even to those located on the coast. What they do tend to show, however, is that regions were affected differently according to the external network to which they were closest. Brice Erickson, for example, has made a detailed study of pottery styles from the Archaic through to the late Classical periods. By re-examining finds from different cities, what he shows is that imports from Laconia penetrated into those *poleis* closest to the trade routes to the north and west:

> The distribution of Laconian craters on the island is confined exclusively to Central and West Crete at Kydonia, Kastello Varypetrou (Lachania), Lappa, Eleutherna and Knosos (Erickson, 2000: 245).[10]

This situation contrasts with the east of the island, where at Olous and Itanos the Archaic imports were nearly all from the Cyclades.

The importance of trade from the early Classical period is also shown by its occasional disruption. Sites, for example, that appeared to be trading before 460 and also after 400 have not provided evidence of imports between these years. Erickson considers in turn the reasons for this curious pattern, dismissing an import ban and a change in local tastes as reasons for it. Rather, he suggests, the reason was the activities of Athens, then at the height of its imperial power, in seeking to disrupt trade links involving its rival Sparta (Erickson, 2005: 636). Support for this view comes from an article by Perlman who suggests that with the fall of Athens seaborne trade was stimulated (particularly with Egypt) and that this led to the dramatic growth in cities along Crete's southern coast (Perlman, 2000).

Thus it cannot be said that Crete was isolated at this time; rather it was embedded in a growing trade networks. Another excellent example comes from the burial ground deposits at Orthi Petra, a cemetery of Eleutherna in north-central Crete:

> Contrary to the accepted picture of Cretan isolation, finds from Orthi Petra document thriving commercial relations at Eleutherna throughout the Late Archaic and Classical periods (Erickson, 2000: 229).

9 So-called 'plinthophoric' (from *plinthos* meaning a brick) coins refers to a series produced by Rhodes between 190 and 84 BCE in which the reverse features a design (usually a rose) in an incusive or recessed square.

10 A crater / krater is a large vessel, usually of pottery but sometimes of metal, typically used for mixing wine and water and from which the Greek term for wine (*krasi*) is said to have been derived.

The imported pottery at Eleutherna was successively Corinthian, Laconian and Attic, reflecting the growing importance of Athens as a trading hub (Erickson, 2000: 237). The early port of Eleutherna was at Pantomatrion, which was probably close to present-day Stavromenos to the east of Rethymno. It was here in the cemetery that many pottery samples were found including an 'Atticising' gravestone again suggesting trade links to the north (Bowsky, 1997; Erickson, 2000: 245). Martha Bowsky (1997) in what purports to be an exploration of this one 'Atticizing stele' from western Crete in fact subtly shows much more. She compares this example with all others of a similar kind and demonstrates that where they were found reflects trade and settlement patterns in the 5th–4th centuries. First they confirm the influence of Athens in the western end of the island, but equally important, they show a spread of influence from the north-west, to the south-west and eventually to the north-south corridor between Gortyn and Knosos. From the names contained on these monuments, which reflect those attested as much in Egypt and Athens as in Crete, she concluded that the island in this period 'constituted a cultural, personal, material, and economic crossroads between Athens and Egypt, and a homeland for Cretans abroad in the post-classical world' (1997: 206).

In the Hellenistic period, Eleutherna established Rhithymna as its trading port, enabling the *polis* to become what Erickson calls a 'western hub for overseas commerce' (Erickson, 2000: 246).[11] Traded goods would have included oil, wine and timber (cypress) and Peloponnesian bronze vessels, as well as pottery items (cf. Yangaki, 2004–5: 503 ff.). After the fall of Athens in 404 BCE, patterns of trade shifted to provide new opportunities in Egypt and the Middle East, which meant in turn that settlements on Crete's southern shores were better placed to assume a greater importance. As Martha Bowsky suggests, 'it may well be trade that best explains Hierapytna's growing power and prosperity in eastern Crete in the second-first centuries BME (BCE)' (1994: 15).

Trade relations were not, however, confined to the external world. The period from the 6th century onwards shows a growing intra-island trade network. This can be traced through pottery finds since petrographic and other forms of fabric identification can show clearly where pottery was made. Again Erickson uses this form of analysis to show how trade networks operated for some of the major *poleis* in the two centuries after 600 BCE. These links reveal a complex web of trade, centring on Kydonia, Itanos and Hierapytna but also including Eleutherna, Knosos, Arkades and Gortyn (Erickson, 2000, Figs 41–47). With modern transport systems and political integration, it is easy to underestimate today the significance of inter-*polis* trade in the past. In such difficult terrain even commentators on the modern world often make this point, as when Kolodny concludes that '*la Crète fait figure de continent en miniature*' (1968: 228).

---

11 The port of Rhithymna lies beneath modern Rethymno, probably beneath the Venetian Fortetza. Remains of slipways can be seen on the shore immediately to the west of the fortress.

A CONSOLIDATED CURRENCY

Unsurprisingly, these patterns of trade, together with the demands of returning mercenaries, led to pressures for individual states to strike their own coinage. Even though the bulk of Cretan *poleis* did not start minting their own coins until after 330 BCE, Gortyn and Phaistos appear to have started their own production as early as 470 BCE (Stefanakis, 1999: 258). Four other cities may have started their mints about 425 BCE (Knosos, Praisos, Itanos, Lyktos) (Le Rider, 1966; Wroth, 1886). By 300 BCE coins were being produced by 22 of the primary *poleis* discussed in Chapter 4, as well as all four of the independent *poleis*. Wroth (1886: xv; cf. Le Rider, 1966) adds Apollonia, Chersonisos, Lisos, Rhithymna and Tarrha to the list, while a few years later the Greek numismatist Svoronos (1890) estimated the total number (including some that had ceased minting or whose whereabouts was unknown) at forty-three.

Many cities show the work of fine coin engravers at a very early date and often these coins are an opportunity to reflect a Cretan memory and identity that seems to transcend the local loyalties of the *polis*. Myths and legends abound, including those of Minos, the Minotaur and Labyrinth at Knosos, Europa at Gortyna and other local deities at Phaistos, Kydonia, Aptera and many others. The work of the craftsmen creating the dies often shows evidence of external cultural contact. Some fine quality work from Chersonisos, for example, copied a coin type from Stymphalus in Arcadia, and numismatists agree that there were many artistic links between Crete and the Peloponnese (Mørkholm, 1991: 89; Stefanakis, 2002: 47; 50; Stefanakis, 2007: 310). Again, it has been argued that the 'coinage of Sybrita shows late fourth century numismatic art at its very best', and one image of Hermes appears to be based on a famous statue by Lysippus (Mørkholm, 1991: 89; Stefanakis, 2002: 47). Thus not only was coinage the means by which trade could move in an entirely different realm, it also embodied creative work of high quality and reflected a world that had already been opened up to major external cultural influences.

At first sight, what could be less common than having approximately 40 separate mints in a relatively small geographical space each producing its own coinage? In fact, all the mints on Crete produced their silver coinage in the same denominations and to a *common* standard. Thus each produced staters, drachms, hemidrachms/ triobols and obols containing the same amount of silver. This meant that, just as a German euro is fully exchangeable with a Greek euro, so a Polyrrhenian stater was worth the same as one from Hierapytna. Although in the early period there were important variations in weights, a survey of Crete's silver coinage concludes:

> The bulk of the pieces struck on the Aiginetic standard in Crete must have been looked upon as readily interchangeable, although each city continued, as a rule, to maintain at its own mint the particular norm which it had adopted when it first began to issue coins (Macdonald, 1919: 7).

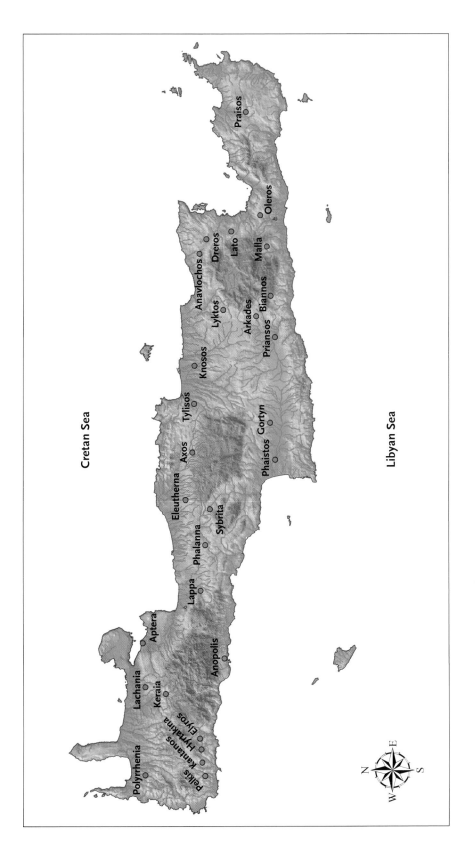

MAP 1 Primary *poleis* in relation to topography

MAP 2
Primary *polis*
locations in relation
to topography
(Dreros and Praisos)

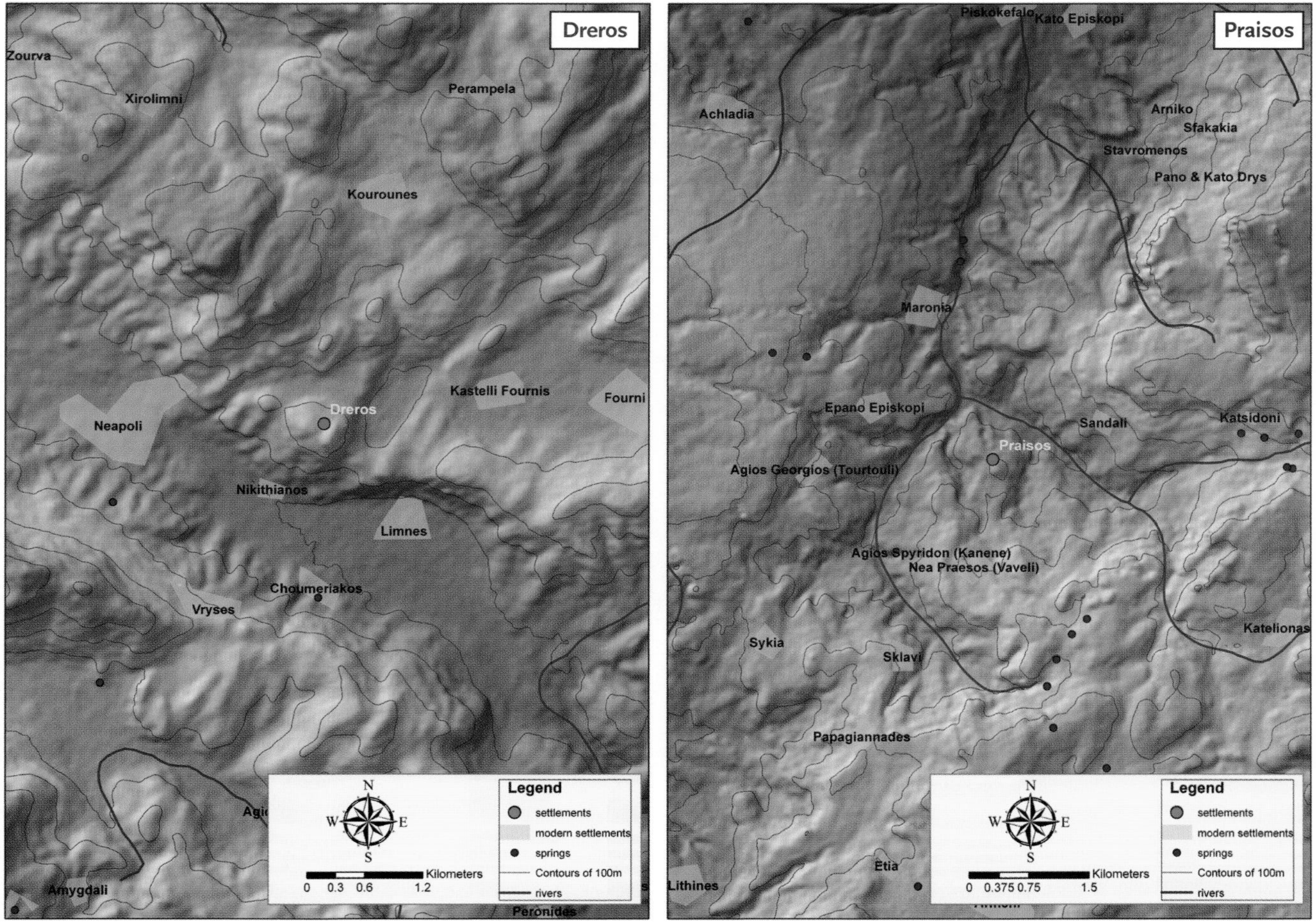

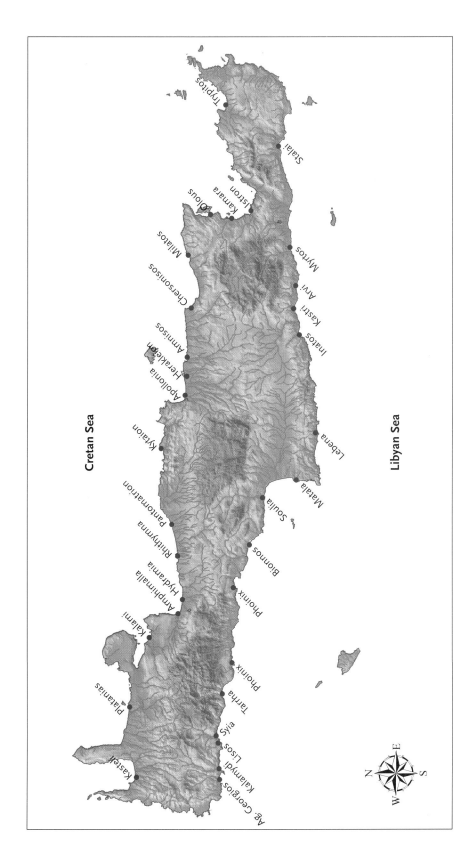

Cretan Sea

Trypitos
Stalai
Kamara
Olous
Istron
Milatos
Myrtos
Chersonisos
Arvi
Kastri
Inatos
Apollonia
Herakleion
Amnisos
Kytaion
Lebena
Pantomation
Matala
Rhithymna
Soulia
Bionnos
Amphimalla
Hydramia
Phoinix
Kalami
Phoinix
Tarrha
Platanias
Syia
Lisos
Kalamydi
Kasteli
Ag. Georgios

Libyan Sea

MAP 3 Secondary settlements in relation to topography

MAP 4 Primary *polis* urban centres and secondary settlements

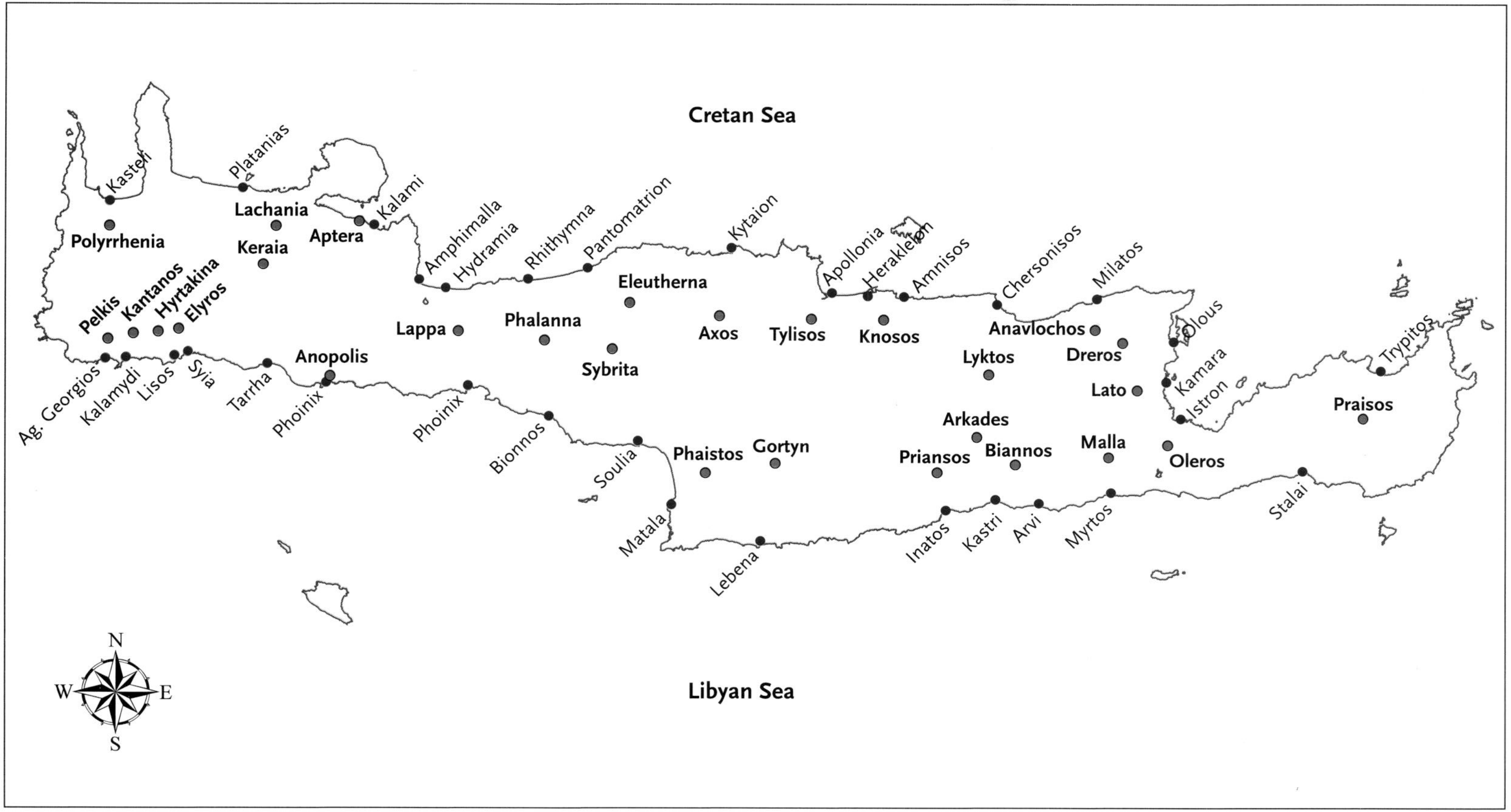

Cretan Sea

Libyan Sea

Trypitos
Praisos
Stalai
Kamara
Istron
Snous
Olous
Oleros
Milatos
Dreros
Lato
Anavlochos
Malla
Chersonisos
Lyktos
Arkades
Biannos
Amnisos
Priansos
Myrtos
Heraklelon
Anvi
Apollonia
Knosos
Kastri
Kytaion
Tylisos
Inatos
Axos
Gortyn
Eleutherna
Phaistos
Lebena
pantomation
Soulia
Matala
Rhithymna
Sybrita
Phalanna
Bionnos
Hydrania
Amphimalla
Phoinix
Kalami
Lappa
Aptera
Anopolis
Phoinix
Platanias
Lachania
Tarrha
Keraia
Syia
Elyros
Kaster
Hyrtakina
Lisos
Polyrrhenia
Kantanos
Kalamydi
Pelkis
Aig.Georgios

N E W S

MAP 5
Primary *poleis*
and ports: North
(Axos–Kytaion /
Eleutherna–
Pantomatrion)

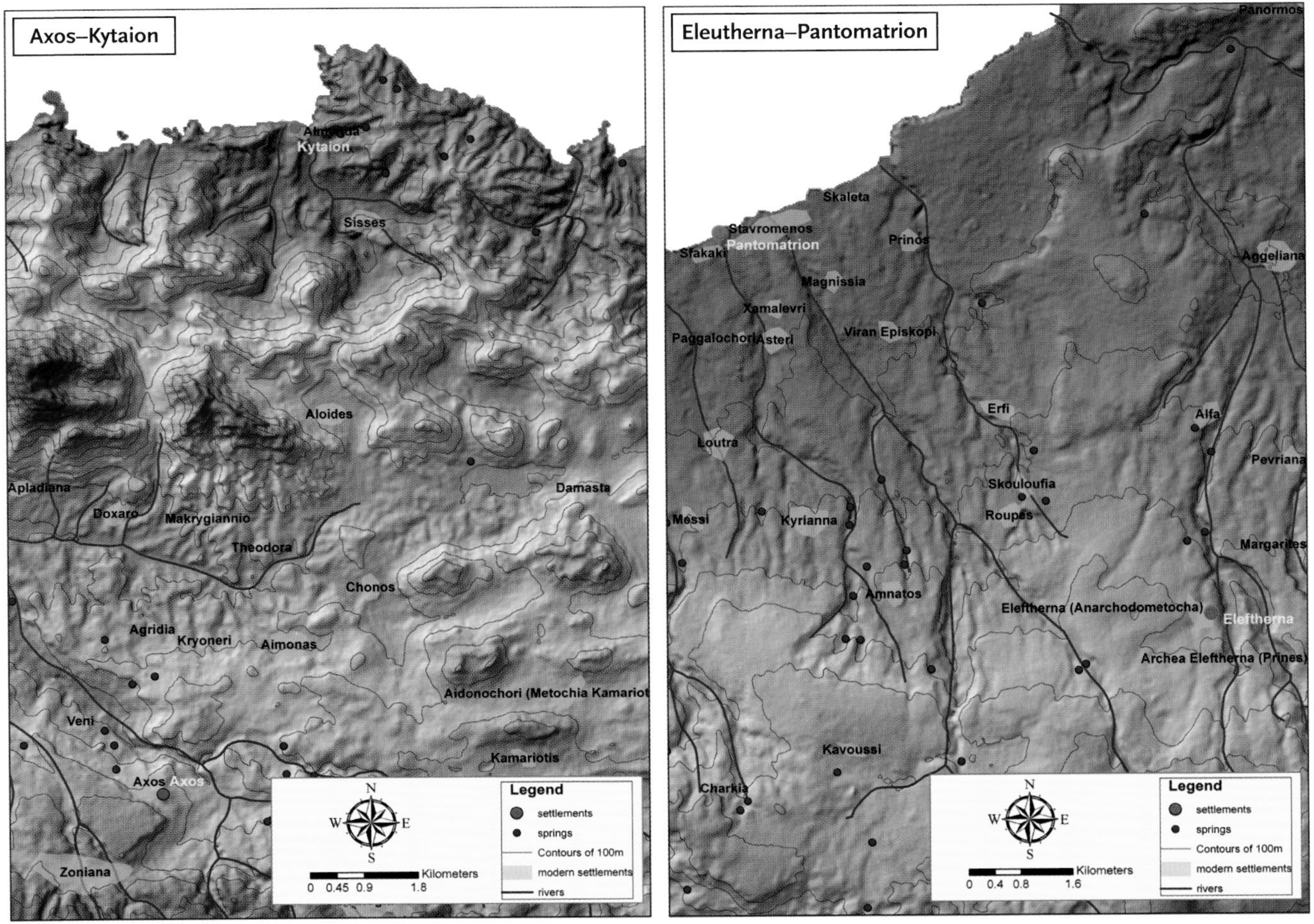

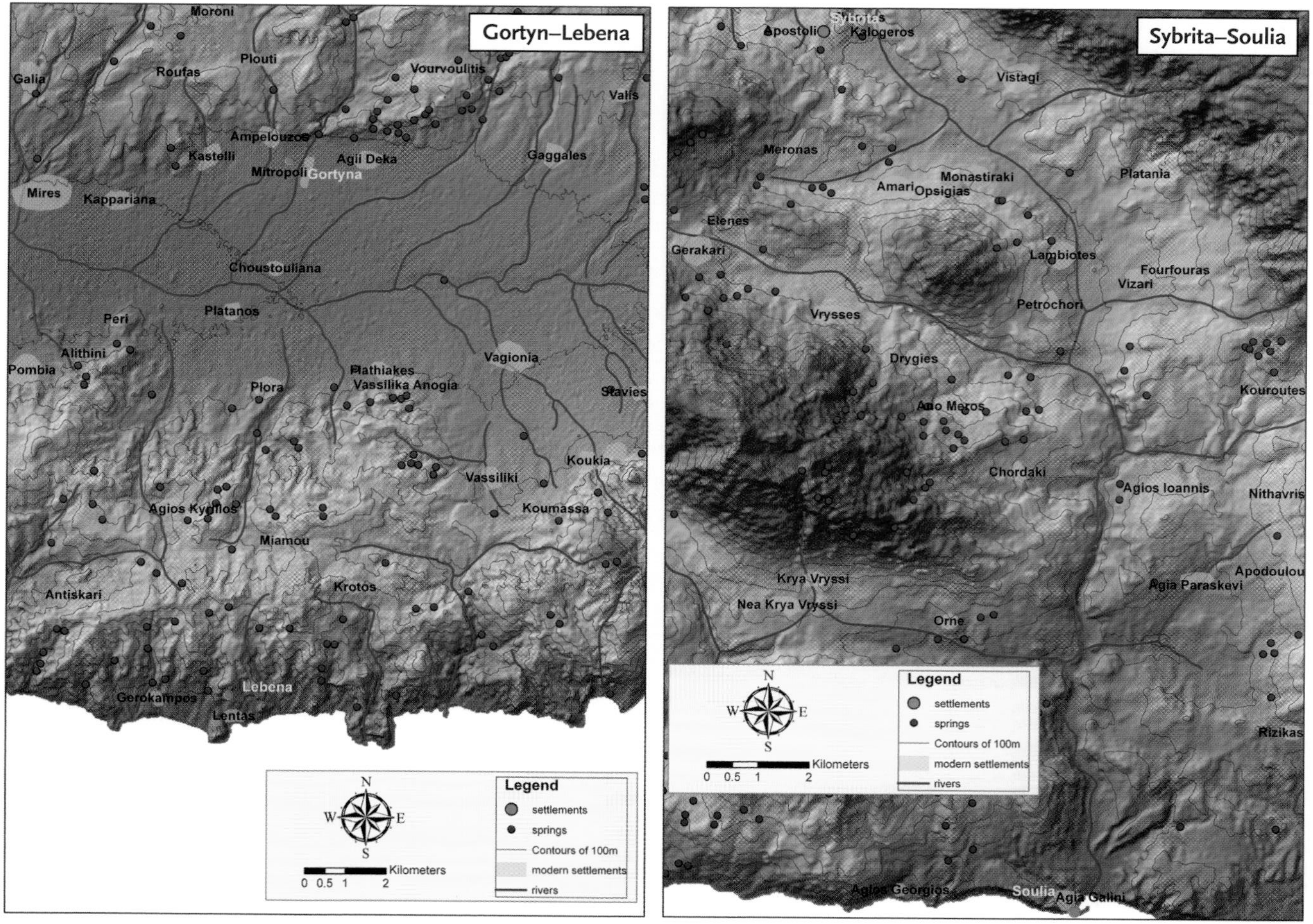

MAP 6
Primary *poleis*
and ports: South
(Gortyn–Lebena /
Sybrita–Soulia)

Sybrita–Soulia

Gortyn–Lebena

MAP 7
Primary *poleis*
and ports: East
(Priansos–Inatos /
Praisos–Trypitos)

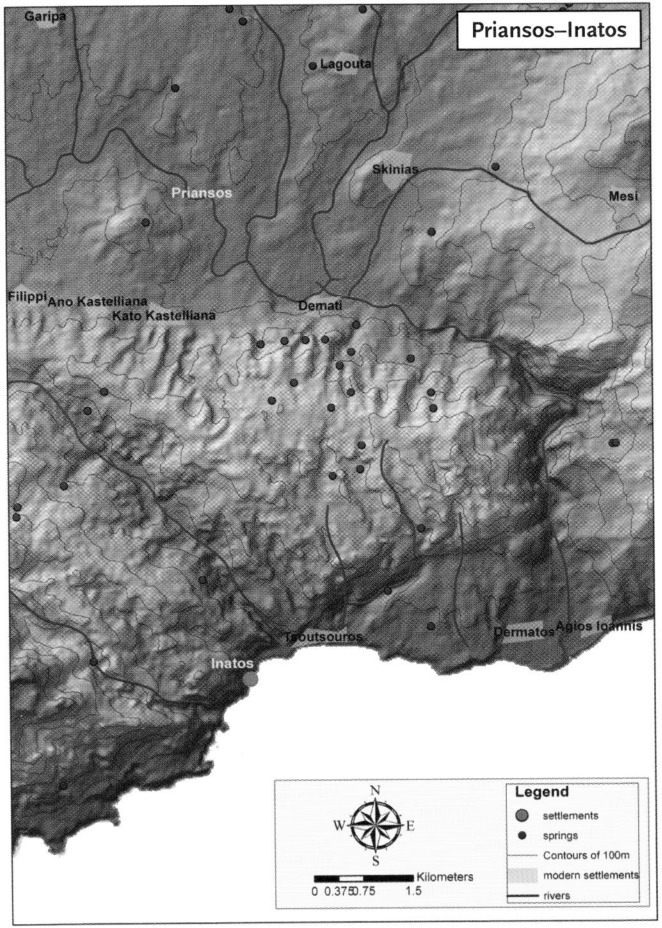

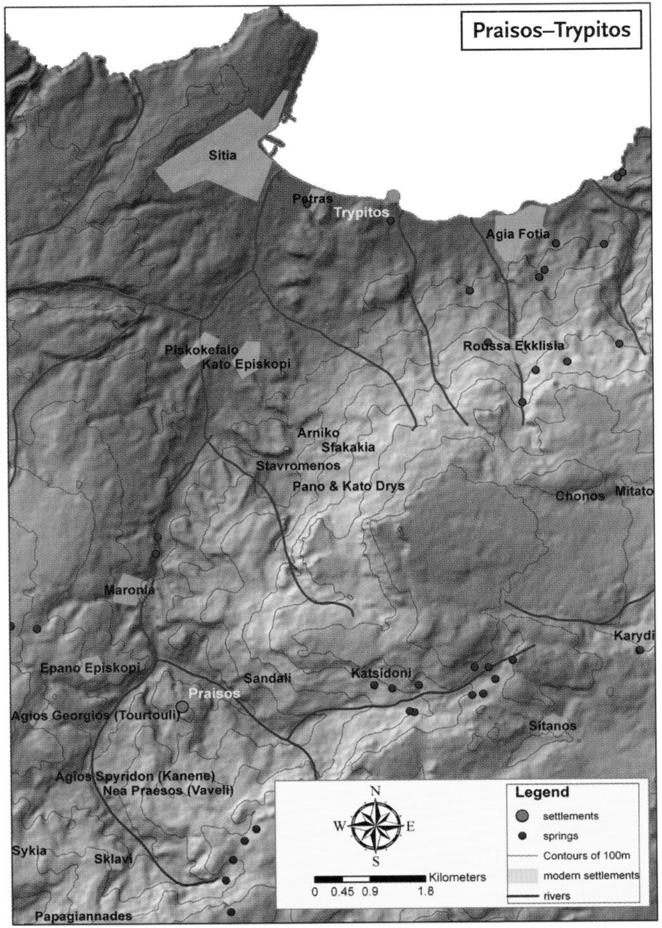

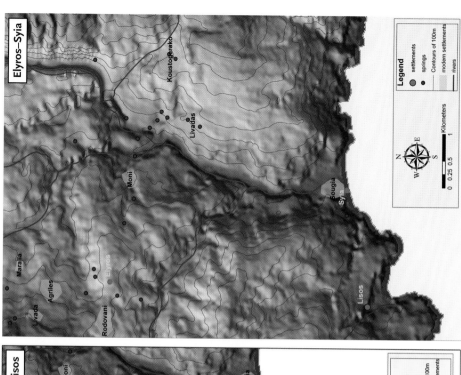

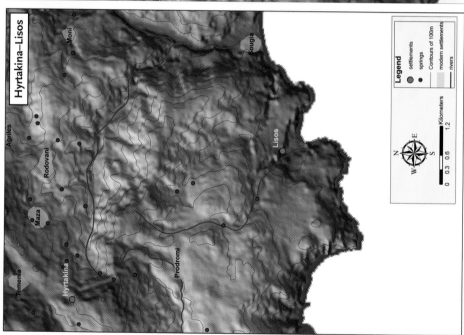

MAP 8
Primary *poleis*
and ports: West
(Hyrtakina–Lisos /
Elyros–Syia)

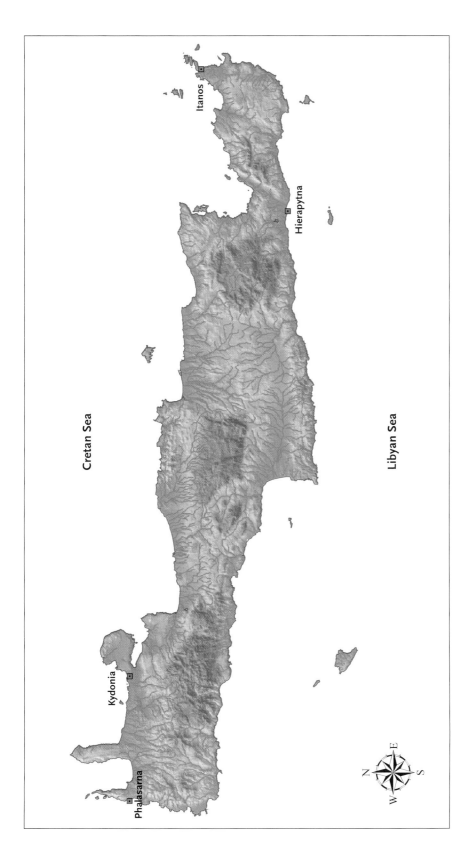

MAP 9   Independent *poleis* in relation to topography

MAP 10
Independent *polis*
urban centres
(Phalasarna and Itanos)

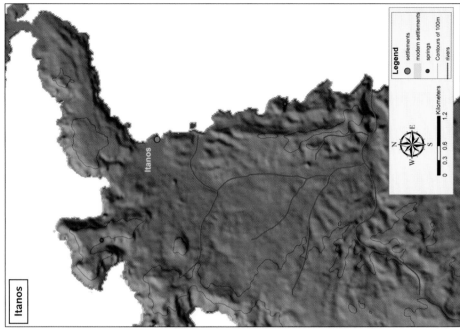

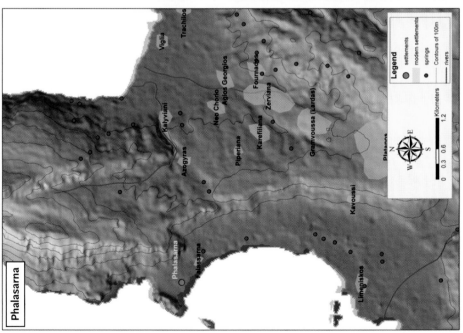

PLATE 1   Aptera – remains of defensive wall protecting urban centre.

PLATE 2   Hyrtakina – remains of defensive wall protecting urban centre.

PLATE 3 Sybrita – view from north-east of Thronos showing double acropolis.

PLATE 4 Polyrrhenia – view from east showing double acropolis and remains of Hellenistic fortification wall (top left).

PLATE 5 Lato – view north of major public buildings (*prytaneion*, *exedra* etc) on saddle between acropolises.

PLATE 6 Praisos – view of major public building (possibly an *andreion*) on north-western slope of main acropolis, facing second acropolis.

PLATE 7   Lato – view east to Gulf of Mirabello and Lato pros Kamara.

PLATE 8   Elyros – view south-east to Syia.

PLATE 9 Phalasarna – view south from Cape Koutri across Bay of Livadia showing remains of public building in foreground.

PLATE 10 Itanos – view south-west from eastern acropolis.

PLATE 11   Gortyn Law Code (part of the Great Code).

PLATE 12
Dreros
inscription.

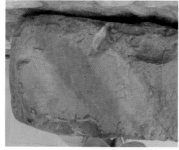

In the Hellenistic period, the Cretan mints produced to a standard that was on average 11 per cent below that of Aigina. After the age of Alexander, the Attic weight standard gradually replaced the Aiginetan, and just over a century later the mints in a number of cities (e.g. Kydonia, Gortyna, Hierapytna, Lappa, Polyrrhenia, and Priansos) issued copies of Athenian tetradrachms, but carrying their own names and symbols (Svoronos, 1890: 78 *passim*; Le Rider, 1968: 313–315). It is conceivable that this apparent debasement was to save precious silver, or it might have been a product of the frequent overstriking of other coinage that tends to reduce average weights. It is more plausible, however, to see it as a policy choice motivated by a desire to enhance trading possibilities with the rest of the Aegean and elsewhere. Stefanakis puts it succinctly:

> It may not be accidental that the weight standard employed by the Cretans already existed in nearby Asia Minor, Kilikia, Syria and Cyprus (1999: 260).

Indeed, MacDonald in 1919 had noticed that the Kydonian mint appeared to be producing silver coins which were almost identical but differed in weight. His surmise is that this was motivated by a desire to fit the coinage to what was expected in different overseas markets (1919: 10).

This research is suggestive but not conclusive. There are both necessary and sufficient conditions that have to be fulfilled before the existence of coinage can be said to be a part of a monetary system. The necessary conditions include the duration of coinage use, evidence for its adoption in market exchange and its utilisation as payment for labour, whereas wider issues are raised before money in any form can be said to exist as a separate economic sphere. In particular, it must be shown to be recognised in legal, political and cultural terms as having a legitimate place in public life. It is to those issues that we can now turn.

COINAGE IN USE

The widespread use of coins is suggestive of economic activity but flawed as a definitive criterion because of the many reasons for coin production. Where mints have existed over many years, however, and where coin has evolved to meet international standards of weight, there are perhaps more reasons for supposing it to have a strong trade-related purpose. The pioneering and classic study by the Greek numismatist J-N. Svoronos, published in 1890, lists the then known discoveries of coins for 43 mints existing at some time during the Classical and Hellenistic eras. These are listed under each mint in terms of the variations in each type of coin. Some may be no more than a slight alteration to the legend or symbolism that appears on the coinage of a *polis*, but nonetheless they do suggest how well established the coinage of a city state had become, and perhaps also may be taken as an indirect measure of its significance. Certainly the vagaries of discovery make it a more interesting measure than the number of coins that have been found, even if it is not possible to take these numbers as a direct measure of economic activity. It is also an open question whether, even where long-established usage can be shown, this means that monetary exchanges were more smoothly transacted.

Certainly as Table 7.1 suggests, however, there is a strong correlation between size and the number of coin types that have been found. This is not wholly self-evident since the data do not reflect the number of coins themselves but variations in their design or appearance. More important, the forty-three city states on this measure appear to fall into six categories.[12] At the top, with an astonishing mean average of 185 variations, are the two giants, Gortyn and Knosos, which not only were among the first to establish mints but also came clearly to depend from an early date on coinage as a means of paying their armed forces, collecting taxes and dues, and supporting their emergent tradesmen. The second category, with only half as many coin types, is a mixed bag that includes the independent trading centre of Kydonia, together with three primary *poleis* whose economic importance – at least on this measure – has not perhaps been fully appreciated. Lyktos, for example, particularly when bracketed with its port at Chersonisos and despite its varied political fortunes, appears to have evolved a well-established coinage over many years.[13] It is also very noticeable that western Crete is strongly represented mainly as a result of the unexpected evolution of Aptera's coinage. Overall, well over half the mints had produced coins passing through ten or more variations, which suggests that coinage was relied upon for something important over a lengthy period of time.

One use to which coinage was put was to facilitate market exchange. Although this is notoriously difficult to measure in the absence of written records, it does have an impact in terms of physical infrastructure. For example, in their wide-ranging field survey of the Mesara, Watrous and his colleagues (2004) revealed a distribution of farms and landholdings that they attributed to a 'powerful market-oriented cash economy' that was evident from the 4th century onwards (Watrous and Hadzi-Villianou, 2004: 334). The origins of this appeared to go back to the introduction of Aiginetan coinage in the 6th century (2004: 334). At that time they suggest that coined money must have been 'widely accessible' in the Mesara. Moreover, there seems little doubt that this was for reasons related to trade, both visible and invisible. The authors point out that in Phaistos alone, coins were found from nineteen other Cretan *poleis* together with numerous examples from overseas (Aigina, Argos, Boeotia, Carthage, Corinth, Cyprus, Cyrene, Rhodes, Sikyon, Siphnos, and Thera) (Watrous and Hadzi-Villianou, 2004: 335). This is surely a vein of research that deserves to be explored in other areas of Crete at this time.

As far as the use of coin in payment for labour other than mercenary service is concerned, the record is possibly even more meagre. If as early as the 6th century

---

12 The table includes five locations that are known by their coinage, but whose whereabouts is uncertain, and two that have been excluded from this study for other reasons (Rhaukos and Dictynna). Their names are italicised in the table.

13 It is probable that Chersonisos became the more important *polis* after the destruction of Lyktos (see Spratt, 1865, I: 99).

TABLE 7.1 City states by number of coin types found[a]

Extra large	Large *poleis*	Medium-large *poleis*	Medium *poleis*	Small *poleis* and important ports	Small *poleis*, ports and unknown
Gortyn (191)	Kydonia (93)	Polyrrhenia (51)	Rhithymna (30)[b]	Lisos (12)	*Tanos* (4)
Knosos (179)	Lyktos (87)	Praisos (50)	Priansos (28)	Tylisos (11)	Apollonia (3)
	Phaistos (79)	Eleutherna (47)	Lappa (24)	Lato (11)[c]	*Dictynna* (3)
	Aptera (73)	Hierapytna (44)	Hyrtakina (19)	Olous (11)	*Malla* (3)
		Itanos (44)	Phalasarna (18)	Arkades (7)	Pantomatrion (3)
		Chersonisos (43)	Sybrita (15)	Anopolis (6)	*Polichne* (3)
		Rhaukos (39)		Keraia (6)	Biannos (2)
		Axos (40)		Elyros (6)	Kamara (2)
				Allaria (5)	Kasteli (2)
				Dreros (5)	*Moda* (2)
					Mycenae) (2)
					Phalanna (2)
					Tarrha (2)
Mean 185	Mean 83	Mean 45	Mean 22	Mean 8	Mean 2.5

a   Based on Svoronos (1890). Excludes coins produced after 67 BCE and those whose proper attribution is in doubt. Settlements in italics are not included in the Gazetteer.
b   Includes 14 coin types from Arsinoë.
c   Includes some from Kamara.

coined money was being used in shaping land holdings, then we would expect it to affect the division of labour in relation to waged work. Evidence to this effect comes from Paula Perlman's study of the epigraphic evidence in 6th century Eleutherna (2004b). After very careful examination of the inscriptions, her conclusion is unambiguous:

> The Archaic inscriptions evince not only the traditional economy based on land, agricultural production, and animal husbandry, but also a market economy with its specialist craftsmen, wage earners, surplus production, state intervention and monetization (2004b: 131).

If replicated elsewhere, this would suggest that even at this very early date, any proposition that the Cretan *poleis* were based on a simple division between the landed and the tribute-paying landless would be very wide of the mark.

It is important to stress that the argument so far does not necessarily make Crete exceptional. On the contrary, although Rome did not introduce coinage until the end of the fourth century and Sparta did so only rather reluctantly in 280, John Davies is right to stress that 'by the late fourth century coinage was being issued by nearly all major and most minor states on the Mediterranean littoral' (Davies, 1984: 276). The fact that four out of five of the Greek coin hoards discovered by 1973 were buried in the three centuries from 330 to 31 BCE is indeed an indicator of the widespread adoption of coinage in the Hellenic world (Davies, 1984: 277). But this does not mean that coin issues lasted for many years in all places, nor that they were incorporated as the means by which payment for land or labour was made. It certainly does not imply that legally, politically and culturally money was the only measure of value and return.

Money and value

If the use of coin as money is vital to its economic role, then the integration of currency as a separate sphere in legal, political and cultural institutions is no less important for the creation of a monetary system. What we should expect to find when this has been achieved is laws that seek restitution in monetary terms rather than retribution in kind, political decisions that lead to obligations in terms of taxes, rather than service, and a culture that places a value on private property and wealth creation, rather than status generated by family connections or honour.

The argument has been made that the Great Code of Gortyn certainly established the rule of law, but it is also true that the anonymous legislators who devised the code were in no doubt about the value and importance of private property. In almost every topic considered (e.g. divorce, inheritance, rights of children etc.) property rights are central to the logic of the code. John Davies (2005: 320) has estimated that inheritance alone accounts for one fifth of the Great Code and that the clauses only make sense 'if land as well as movables could change hands'. Merriam (1885), writing soon after the discoveries by Halbherr, was clearly impressed both by the individualism and rights to own and dispose of property that the 'Gortynian lawgiver' provided:

> [V]ery much that is novel, and perhaps the greater part of that which appeals to us so forcibly for its justice, its deep-hearted humanity, its respect for the rights of the woman and the slave, the child and the orphan – so striking in their contrast with the boasted Athenian spirit, even the Platonic – must have been his. We seem to see the heart of a Homer trained to the law, evolving the deepest ponderings upon the rights of individuals and property (1885: 326).

The fact that these rights are exercised so as to deliver more into the hands of citizens rather than *woikeus*, and above all more to men than women, would not have struck Merriam as strange as it does to the modern eye. What is particularly important in the present context, however, is the fact that restitution was laid down in monetary terms, rather than that all individuals were seen as worthy of equal treatment.

The law was also used to regulate trade itself, particularly in relation to customs dues. Didier Viviers, in an important paper, has examined inscriptions to see how treaties between *poleis* dealt with this issue. He first saw mention of a 'customs-free zone' in an agreement between Knosos and its neighbour to the west, Tylisos, dating from the mid–5th century.[14] This inscription, he says, 'inaugurates a series of Cretan treaties in which the regulation of exchanges plays an important part' (1999: 221). While in some cases the agreements were not aimed at anything more ambitious than agreeing on grazing rights for peripatetic herding, the treaties 'also covered a trade in goods, which aimed at satisfying the wish of certain cities to fit into contemporary commercial networks' (1999: 222). He cites the agreement that marked the end of long-standing tensions between Lato and Olous at the end of the 2nd century as one good example. Another would have been the treaty between Hierapytna and Priansos. Francesco Guizzi has shown that the clauses in this treaty assume large flocks of animals and a surplus of animal products that could be exported and imported from one city state to another, even when they were not contiguous.[15] Moreover, this *isopoliteia* treaty allowed for freedom from taxes for private citizens of both *poleis* when these goods were shipped by land or sea between them, again confirming that such goods existed (Guizzi, 2001: 241). In the Archaic period at least, there may well have been a link between revenue raised by commerce and that gained as a product of conflict, since references to both sources of *poleis* income occur close together in the same inscriptions, but that is not the same as arguing that state revenues – let alone trade itself – was dependent on warfare.[16]

Treaties, however, were not solely concerned with free trade. More often than not the relevant sections drew a distinction between inter-*poleis* trade and overseas trade, seeing in the latter a way of raising money through customs dues. Indeed, the growing enthusiasm of inland *poleis* for sea access can be explained partly in terms of a need to import and export, but also as a way of raising revenue regardless of whether the eventual destination of products was in Crete or not. For example, when Praisos extended its borders to both the south and north coasts, it may have been partly motivated by a wish to cash in on taxation opportunities (Viviers, 1999: 226). The pattern of using customs dues as a taxation strategy does not suggest that seaborne imports and exports were uncommon; rather the opposite, since *poleis* would not have gone to so much trouble to set out regulations if they did not generate an important revenue stream. Purcell, in his examination of customs duties throughout the Mediterranean, specifically notes the Cretan examples, citing the treaty arrangements between Gortyn and Lappa and also that between the former and its dependent territory, the island of Gavdhos; he called them

---

14 This is a well known treaty between Knosos, Tylisos and Argos that is normally interpreted as suggesting that the Cretan *poleis* may have been originally populated by migrants from Argos (cf. Vollgraff, 1913).

15 In this case, the *polis* of Biannos lay between Hierapytna and Priansos.

16 Perlman (2010: 98) has suggested that 'booty and inter-state commerce were linked conceptually as sources of public and private revenue'.

'part of a carefully delineated portfolio of revenues available to the community of *katoikountes* and the city from which they come' (2005: 208; note 21).

Stefanakis has suggested that these treaty agreements, together with the common standard for coinage, might indicate a very early form of *koinon*. He notes that the idea of *synkretismos* was mentioned as a feature of Crete in the early years of minting by Plutarch (*Moralia*: 490). In Plato's *Laws* also there is a reference to a common currency. By the end of the 4th century, when external coinage generated by trade became plentiful and Cretan mints were established to produce coins to a common Cretan standard, this 'probably indicat[ed] a change in the thought and attitude of Cretans towards a monetary economy' (1999: 264). Indeed, there are a surprising number of cases in the Greek world as a whole where a greater degree of economic integration and co-operation was evident than might be anticipated from the fissiparous political structure of the city states. Mackil and van Alfen argue that this interconnectedness was common and that it is not possible to conclude from widespread political fragmentation that there was something similar in the economic sphere:

> ... the local and regional economies of the ancient Mediterranean were deeply interconnected, so that state practices such as the minting of coinage, the issuing of civic decrees regulating interstate commerce, and functional co-operation in monetary production should be seen as responses to that fact (2006: 204).

Mackil and van Alfen create the term 'co-operative coinage' to refer to this network of obligations. Notwithstanding these relationships, it is clear that maintaining a separate mint has an additional role in emphasising the authority and independence of the organisation that issued it (Snodgrass, 1980). This is why coins nearly always employ signs, symbols and lettering that underscore the traditions and power of the issuing authority. It is not insignificant that both the obverse and the reverse of most coins reflect protecting deities, collective myths or other symbols of group identity (Mitchiner, 2004).

At about this time too, money began to mean something other than coin. Dareste de la Chavannes identified Knosos as possessing a *chreophylakion* in the 3rd century (1882). A *chreophylakion* was essentially a state-run archive of contracts of sale, debts, titles of ownership and other business contracts. Not only does this suggest that the state was involved in recording and regulating land sales and business deals, it is also important to note that a *chreophylakion* provided sureties for loans and in this sense provided a form of banking service. Dareste de la Chavannes shows how it was used to avoid fraudulent claims and to settle disputes between claimants. The one at Knosos was employed in underwriting the treaty between Lato and Olous on pain of a penalty of ten talents for infringement (Homolle, 1879). In the field survey of the Mesara, the authors conclude that by the 2nd century, in Gortyn and other local *poleis* there was a *chreophylakion* that issued credits and organised contracts for sales, purchases and the provision of loans (Watrous and Hadzi-Vallianou, 2004: 335). It is true that the downside of credit is debt, and if one takes the standard negative view of Crete's economic fortunes, then the passages in the Gortyn Code dealing with debt, which involved provision to pledge one's labour to pay-off the loans, can also be cast in a negative light. For example, John Davies writes:

[E]ven the adoption of coinage need not have generated a monetary economy, still less a market oriented one, especially in those regions which coined only intermittently. Probably for much of Greece, as the Great Code of Gortyn makes brutally clear for Cretan conditions, so far from credit providing opportunities for enhancing production, its blacker downside, debt, drove men to pledge their bodies and to suffer social degradation within a static and isolated economy (2007a: 360).

The sanctions against debt were indeed harsh in the Gortyn Code, but can nearly two hundred separate issues of coin over four centuries be thought of as 'intermittent', and why go to so much trouble to maintain a monetary system if it had no productive purpose? If economic development above subsistence level is denied, then some major features of Crete's Classical and Hellenistic economy have to be explained away. Why, for example, is there evidence of significant internal and external trade? Why do workshops exist for the production of amphorae, which are the customary vessels for the transport of oil, wine and other commodities? Why, indeed, do nearly all inland *poleis* go to such lengths to construct, incorporate or create ports into the fabric of their organisation? Why do more than forty mints arise, all of them coming to be integrated around a common standard of value? Why do the *poleis* appear to focus a major part of their revenue generation on taxing traded goods?

City state support for economic institutions may indeed have had a wider purpose. Previous chapters have commented on the overriding importance of achieving social solidarity and cohesion. Helping to solve 'the problem of order' may also have been a motive for the adoption of coinage. Coinage establishes standardised values and prices. It regularises the inequalities that arise in traditional societies from divisions of social esteem. It is not that the wealthy do not have more money than the poor, but that the wealthy man's cow is worth no more than the peasant's. In this way social relations are regularised and, regardless of levels of inequality, social cohesion is enhanced. This view was first put forward by Will in the 1950s but it has also been applied and developed more recently in relation to the Greek world (Vidal-Naquet and Austin, 1977; Will, 1955). It has also been clearly stated in *The Invention of Coinage and the Monetization of Ancient Greece* by David Schaps (2004). Schaps argues that not only did the adoption of coinage lead to a transformation in Greek society, it produced something even more important:

From the Greeks onward, we find a new way of speaking and of thinking. Now a person might state the entirety of a household's possessions in terms of money, as no member of a pre-monetary society would ever do (2004: 16).

More important perhaps is the perception of the mechanisms by which a market-based economy is sustained. Polybius was in no doubt that the virtuous Spartans gained their preeminence in his eyes through their rejection of private property in favour of state ownership and 'secondly their view of money-making; for, money being esteemed of no value at all among them, the jealous contention due to the possession of more or less is utterly done away with' (Polybius 6, 45–6). The contrast he draws with Crete could hardly be starker:

> The laws allow them to possess as much land as they can get with no limitation whatever. Money is so highly valued among them, that its possession is not only thought to be necessary but in the highest degree creditable. And in fact greed and avarice are so native to the soil in Crete, that they are the only people in the world among whom no stigma attaches to any sort of gain whatever (Polybius 6, 46).

In other words, land ownership amongst citizens was potentially unlimited, private property was encouraged and personal gain was highly valued. What was greed and avarice to Polybius, at least when coupled with the will to save and invest, looks remarkably like Max Weber's Protestant ethic.

Over a period of nearly five hundred years at least some of the Cretan *poleis* made unprecedented economic strides. Values of acquisitiveness appear to have coexisted with those of loyalty to the political institutions. Cretans spotted very early on that coinage allowed internal and external markets to develop and the evidence suggests they exploited this realisation by building commercial links both with their neighbours and with trading partners overseas. The individual *poleis* offered a regulatory framework for businesses to operate and provided one avenue for credit. This new economic reality took material form in the growing importance of coastal settlements. It did not, in other words, take the advent of Roman imperial incorporation for Crete to rise above subsistence agriculture. It is much more probable that things were the other way round and that it was Crete's economic success and its strategic role in trade networks that motivated Rome's desire to ensure its eventual subjugation to imperial dominion. But none of this makes Crete *more* economically advanced than elsewhere; what differences there were may be appreciated by comparison with the two most well-researched economies, Athens and Sparta, and it is to them we now turn.

The Athenian and Spartan economies

The first point to note is that the 'substantiveness' argument, which evolved almost entirely in the Athenian context, is still not without its supporters. It will be recalled that the argument focuses upon three central points. The first concerned the *autonomy* of economic life itself. In Karl Polányi's (1957; 1963; Polányi et al. 1957) original formulation, goods and services could only circulate through one of three processes – reciprocity, redistribution and market exchange. It was only in the last that economic life became detached as a free-standing entity where individuals met and interacted in the market place solely for personal gain. Polányi suggested that in the closing years of the Classical era, Athens was near to becoming a market economy but never in fact managed to do so. In some important respects, the contribution made by Moses Finley goes a long way to explain why. City states were quintessentially the products of *homo politicus*, who made the duties of the citizen to uphold the standing and status of the *polis*, and in particular to its conservative preoccupations with order, such a priority that the messy business of personal profit and gain was beyond the pale. As Morris et al. recently put it:

> This severely limited the ability of the rich to buy the labor of their poorer fellow citizens, forcing them to alienate exploitation outside the citizen community, above all onto chattel slaves. The bonds of egalitarian male citizenship made even profitable practices like lending, trade, and financial services seem morally dubious (2007: 3).

Where state coffers had to be refilled, this duty would fall directly upon the citizenry as individuals rather than through general processes of taxation. In turn the state's contribution would be to use the power of the *polis* to engage in expansion and warfare as the means of channelling funds into the public purse. As Finley noted, the result was that urban cores were not zones of production, but rather came closer to Max Weber's ideal type of the 'consumer city' living off its lands supplemented by booty from conquest (Finley, 1999: 138–41).

THE ATHENIAN ECONOMY

On the question of values regarding accumulation, the issue is frequently polarised between the instrumental rationality of the maximising *homo economicus*, beloved of classical economists, and the man who seeks social standing through the adoption of the values of traditional authority. It was this latter *homo politicus* who was perceived by Finley to be treading the streets of the ancient *polis*. But as Paul Christesen (2003) reminds us, a third option is 'expressive rationality' or that behaviour which, while cognisant of traditional beliefs and values, *also* seeks a profitable return. The case of silver mining in 4th century Athens provides an excellent example of precisely this form of human action. In a detailed analysis of the Laurium region of southern Attica, Christesen shows that rational decisions were adopted for controlling costs of production and that these were motivated by an attempt to maximise incomes (2003: 13). He is also able to show correlations between investment risks and returns consonant with normal maximising economic behaviour. In this sense, therefore, those involved in the silver mines came quite close to the instrumental rationality of the classical economic man. The important point is that at least one in eight, and possibly as many as one in five, of the investors behind the mining operations came from the wealthiest sections of the Athenian citizenry (Shipton, 2000). This does not imply that tradition held no sway in 4th century Athens. On the contrary:

> The evidence suggests that fourth century Athenians were responsive to the sort of concerns associated with *homo economicus*, not that they were sensitive *only* to those concerns (Christesen, 2003: 54; emphasis added).

Traditional values of the responsible citizen were not abandoned; they were simply moulded to accommodate a new economic reality.

Trade too appears to have grown very considerably from the Archaic period onwards. Ian Morris has suggested a ratio of 5:1 when comparing the volume of trade between the 5th and 1st centuries (Morris, 1999: xxx). Evidence from shipwrecks also suggests a significant change. Only two have been discovered in the Aegean dating from the 8th century but 46 have been discovered from the 4th century which, when taken with the increased size of vessels, might suggest that Morris's ratio was on the low side. The evidence on the importance of trade is another indication that Finley's original argument cannot be uncritically accepted. As Robin Osborne (1996) suggests, Finley did not believe that markets in either ancient Greece or Rome behaved as modern ones do in being so interconnected that prices and the flow of goods and services were shaped by supply and demand alone. Rather, market exchange was seen as operating in unrelated zones, controlled more by state *Diktat* than by *economic* laws, with the goal not of maximising returns but merely of ensuring subsistence survival. Osborne takes the case of pottery from Athenian 'redware' workshops, arguing that there was a consistent flow of pottery goods throughout the Aegean during the Archaic period as well as later, producing a 'density of intercommunications' that could only come from a high degree of interconnectedness (1996b: 43). From as early as the 6th century, he shows that the Nikosthenic workshop in Athens, for example, was producing Etruscan pots for trading purposes. As he argues, 'a model of exchange for the 6th century must accommodate the possibility of systematic targeting of precise foreign markets by particular exporters' (1996b: 32).

Does it follow, therefore, that we can happily reject the Finley thesis and argue instead for an unfettered 'formalist' position? The answer is 'not entirely', largely because of peculiarities in the Athenian case that perhaps stand out more clearly when viewed from a less 'Athenocentric' standpoint than is adopted by much of the scholarship on the ancient Greek world. The first of these is the unusual bellicosity of the Athenian *polis*, together with the strength of its imperial ambitions, at least in the early period. While it is true that many of the wars that ancient Athens undertook were relatively minor skirmishes with neighbours, and Athens cannot be considered as militaristic as Sparta, from the beginning of the 5th century until the end of the Classical era Athens was at war for three out of every four years. The creation of *Magna Graecia*, which either directly or indirectly was the point behind so many conflicts, had a primarily economic aim – to guarantee the corn supplies upon which so many citizens and others depended. As with most empires, the purpose was to exploit the wealth of others, but the costs involved in creating this web of suppliers were not inconsiderable. These costs involved both the creation of naval power to police the empire and the flows into Athenian granaries and the severe economic hardship that war itself brought about. As the Peloponnesian War showed so clearly, set piece battles (in this case between Athenian and Spartan led leagues) were often indecisive and one or the other side resorted to attrition through blockades and sieges. As French put it in a review of the economic conditions in Athens in the century after the war:

> Her treasure was spent, her empire at an end; her losses in manpower had been terrible; the farming land which had traditionally been the economic basis of her existence, had been deliberately and extensively damaged (French, 1991: 24).

While the recovery was relatively fast, the economic hardships endured for many years and, as the same author observes, the experience 'left an indelible impression on the historical record' and led to a feeling among some commentators that Athens would never again regain its greatness. Others were more sanguine, seeing in the peace a way out of the onerous burdens that more than thirty years of conflict had wrought. As the contemporary rhetorician Isocrates, himself to experience war-related hardships, wrote:

> War has made us poorer ... If we make peace, we shall dwell in our city in security and advance in prosperity, relieved of paying war taxes, of building triremes, and carrying the burdens of war; cultivating our lands without fear, sailing the sea, and engaging in other occupations which now have been terminated by warfare. We shall see our city enjoying twice the revenue she now receives, and thronged with merchants, foreigners, and resident aliens, by whom she is now deserted' (Isocrates, *On the Peace*: 19–21 quoted in French, 1991: 40, note 27).

In addition to complaining about the 'burdens of war', Isocrates makes the point that peace will bring freedom from the *eisphora* or the property levy that was imposed on the relatively wealthy (including aliens) to finance the costs of war or overseas adventures. His wish was barely realised, however, since Athens still pursued imperial ambitions. Later in the 4th century, the tax rose to ten talents on *metics* (and probably all male citizens) to pay for the infrastructure associated with improved harbour facilities for the war fleet. In theory these 'ring-fenced' taxes were intended to be repaid from booty acquired through successful campaigns, although over time it appears that this tax was collected annually and *additional* taxes were incurred for the war effort (Christ, 2007). Similarly, those with considerable wealth could be called upon to contribute to major public works (the contributions were termed *leitourgiai*) or to underwrite the construction of a trireme (*trieres* or warship) or other military hardware (the *trierarchy*). In this event, the wealthy citizen could expect some preferment or favour in return. For example, service to the state (*choregia*) might lead to exemption from *leitourgiai* service. In 378–7, a form of delegated powers of individualised taxation was introduced and those liable to the *eisphora* were divided into one hundred *symmoriai*, each with fifteen members, and the three wealthiest from each were required together to advance the total sum required (the *proeisphora*) and recoup contributions from others named within the syndicate. Membership of the 'Three Hundred' or *proeispherontes* achieved special status, particularly at times of military success.

The central point here is that this form of individualised and targeted taxation is fundamentally pre-capitalist. It reifies the state, which by being particularistic in its strategies for raising funds, cannot adopt a commercialised standpoint. It is no surprise therefore that in the 4th century, even with the wealth generated by the export of silver coinage from the Laurium mines, Athens was unable to pay for grain imports without continuing to plunder through warfare and imperial adventures. As French observes, custom rather than impersonal rules still held sway in the distribution of goods and services, seeking profit continued to be regarded as unjust, and for the all important supplies of grain it was illegal (French, 1991: 32). Partly as a result, Classical Athens saw significant falls in population. Estimates of total population size are notoriously difficult to make but the economic demographer Walter Scheidel concludes that the total population of Athens fell from 60,000 adult male citizens and possibly 100,000 slaves (or 250–300,000 residents in total) in the 430s BCE to 20,000 adult male citizens and 50,000 slaves (150,000–250,000 residents) in the 320s (Scheidel, 2007: 44–45).

The other main reason for the decline was the paradox of warfare itself. Athens needed conquest and booty to feed its population but in the process inhibited its own development from a promising pre-capitalist start. This is far from being a new argument. The economic historian M.I. Rostovtzeff argued something similar on the first page of his study of the Roman Empire:

> Greece and especially Athens, which in the fifth and fourth centuries B.C. had developed, from the economic point of view, a flourishing state of commercial capitalism, began gradually to lose their importance. The primary cause of the steady decline of economic life in Greece proper was the constant, almost uninterrupted, succession of wars in which the cities were involved in the fourth and third centuries B.C. (1926: 1).

Whether the starting point was really one of capitalism is more debatable and Rostovtzeff himself argues that the baton was picked up elsewhere in the Hellenic world where the corrosive effects of constant warfare were less evident.

The second idiosyncratic feature of Athens when compared with many other *poleis* in the Hellenic world was its relationship with its main port, the Piraeus. The Piraeus grew up only in the 5th century and it became, after the *asty* (urban centre of the Athenian *polis*), the largest centre of population in Attica (Roy, 1998). The relationship with Athens was however fraught and it is not entirely clear whether this was simply because of the threat constituted by its relative wealth or, as is more probable, that it betrayed a profound sense on the part of the average Athenian that the Piraeus possessed a value system out of keeping with the less capitalistic instincts of the *asty*. Aristotle referred to the relationship between the two *poleis* as one of *stasis* (balance of opposing views giving rise to potential civic conflict), largely on the grounds that the port had a citizenry more committed to *demokratia* when compared with the more oligarchic Athens (*Politics*, 1962: 196). Even during the period of Athenian democracy, the relationship between the urban centre and its port was complex and difficult, and it probably says more about the former than the latter. As Edward Cohen wrote in his study of Athens:

While Attika's principal port, the magnificent Piraeus harbor, offered unparalleled access to the sea and to required commodities, many Greeks deemed involvement with maritime trade inherently inconsistent with the proper organization and functioning of a *polis*: sea commerce brought into a community foreign merchants, men reared in alien ways, resulting in an enlarged and heterogeneous population destructive of the *polis*'s orderly way of life (*eunomia*) (2000: 16).

The fact was that Athens was a particularly traditional *polis*, notwithstanding its many innovations, and this did not sit comfortably with the more trade-oriented and less hidebound coastal *polis*. As Sita von Reden put it, 'the very construction of the *polis* and definition of the citizen maintained that "ditch" between harbour and *asty* which Aristotle regarded as detrimental to political unity' (1995: 35).

It is perhaps preferable to regard this gulf as one of economic belief rather than simply one of political persuasion. In this sense, Polányi may have been right to see the Athenian *agora* as dependent upon reciprocity and redistribution, or cemented into a pre-capitalistic set of obligations and customs, whereas the Piraeus, with its large *metic* and trader population, was more capitalistic in orientation. While it is important not to overstate this case, in that citizens in the *asty* were often keen to involve themselves in supporting voyages in pursuit of both necessities and luxuries overseas, it would have been inconceivable for the Athenian citizen to consider a wholesale reorientation of *polis* life to the coast. As C.M. Reed (2003: 3–4) has argued, traders were often both foreign and poor, and Athenians thought of trade itself as a necessity rather than as *intrinsically* desirable. Both merchants (*emporoi*), who owned their goods but not the means by which they were conveyed, and the ship owners themselves (*naukliroi*), who usually owned only one vessel each, were considered outside the normal life of the *polis*. As Ian Morris commented in reviewing Reed's book 'Athenians only cared about *emporoi* and *naukliroi* because they needed imports, and did not worry where they came from' (2005b: 576).

The third issue concerns the question of whether in the Athenian case we can conclude that a 'monetary system' emerged in the structure of the economy in the period leading up to the Hellenistic era. Clearly, an answer to this question must depend upon what we take the term to mean. The orthodox view of money and its functions, often associated with the early 19th century economist Carl Menger, is that it emerged out of barter as a medium of exchange. This perspective, which might be termed 'economistic' for its sole reliance on the economic functions of money, strips it of its administrative and legal context. A fuller picture, from a position more imbued with the insights of political economy, interprets money in the context of law and the state, and includes both debt and taxation (Peacock, 2006). It can be argued that a 'monetary system' qua *system* cannot exist without this wider view. It is when a state enters the economic realm that a monetary system can come into being, because it then develops a legal basis. A state imbues money with value by declaring that it will be the means by which debt is honoured or tax paid. Civil law does something similar by denominating the price of restitution. It is therefore not surprising that the Greek work for coinage, *nomisma*, has the same root as the word for law – *nomos*. The link between law and a monetary system is reciprocal. Not only does law sustain a monetary system but the adoption of a state-backed coinage allows for punishments meted out by courts to become monetarised in the form of fines. Coinage becomes the way through which social as well as economic intercourse is regulated. In this way social stability is maintained as the old system of family-based retaliation gives way to a greater emphasis on what is more likely to be considered as equitable retribution (Seaford, 1994: 204). The state gains by taking over the role hitherto the sole domain of powerful families and clans.

This means coinage acquires a value greater than the market price of the material it contains. This concept, sometimes referred to as 'fiduciarity', produces great rewards to the state itself and in turn increases its motivation to support and entrench the official mint. A monetary system, therefore, is one in which both law and the state are intrinsically involved and from which both benefit (*seigniorage*), even before the rewards of market exchange have been accrued. Of course, trade is not dependent upon money, let alone a monetary system. It can and did take place through barter, and quantification and value are just as intrinsic to a barter system as they are to a monetary system. Coinage standardises value into units that facilitate quantification, but it is only with the role of the state that the transition from barter to a monetary system can occur (Schaps, 2004). Although the motivation of the state may not have had anything to do with monetarising the economy of the *polis*, in achieving this it unleashed a force that transformed obligation from payment in kind through tithe to payment in cash through coin. Not only did this loosen the bonds of obligation between a particular peasant and a particular landowner, it also weakened the landowning class just as it strengthened the state. Moreover, in a territory comprising many states, it promoted the concept of inter-state co-operation.

All of this makes a monetary system entirely compatible with state socialism or systems of regulation that are entirely driven by the needs of the state itself. Hence, to arrive at a more modern definition that would make the concept of a monetary system recognisable within a capitalist economy, it is important to add two further requirements. The first is a high degree of independence of monetary institutions from the state itself, even though it may retain the powers of overall regulation, and the second is the existence of a value system that accords saving and investment (alongside labour) as appropriate mechanisms for the acquisition of private wealth. In other words, a monetary system must be free to function and be supported by values and mores that define it as fulfilling the needs of the general population. The requirement is then for an independent realm of activity, not dependent upon political and social needs, that operates through a series of institutions whose sole purpose is economic in nature and which function within a culture that values private property and personal acquisition.[17]

17 In Max Weber's original formulation it was ascetic Protestantism that provided the cultural context in which capitalism could prevail (Weber, 1961: 268ff.).

With all this in mind, how does the Athenian case stand up? Purely in terms of coinage, there seems little doubt that Athens played a leading role in the monetarisation of the Aegean. Morris (2005b) argues that as early as 550 BCE Athenian goods were traded all round the Mediterranean using coinage introduced at about the same time, and this is supported by the number of Athenian 'owls' that have been found outside their territory of issue (Kraay, 1964). Osborne, however, has suggested that high levels of monetarisation were not achieved until the 4th century when Athens was no longer self-sufficient in grain and other foodstuffs. Indirect taxes did exist, particularly in the form of duty paid by *emporoi* on their traded goods. By the end of the 5th century Athens had imposed a five per cent duty on all goods traded at ports throughout her empire and by the second half of the following century new legislation was introduced to support commercial activities, particularly through making it easier to use legal means to resolve commercial disputes. As Osborne puts it:

> The measures signal an awareness of the importance of commercial activities and the existence of economically rational behaviour. Also by the fourth century, the Athenians had developed a private banking system, engaged in taking deposits and lending to private entrepreneurs (1991: 63).

During the same period, it was common for loans to be made to traders to finance voyages, often at a high rate of interest, with all the vessels owned by the borrower used as collateral (Cohen, 1992: 140).

Even in relation to land sales, there is evidence to suggest that traditional values were gradually giving way to a more 'commodified' perception. As French (1991) has suggested, the way land was viewed did undergo some changes, sometimes being traded after a brief period for profit so that 'the commercial exploitation of the soil' brought this most traditional of items into the nexus of all other commodities (1991: 27). This new commercialisation was supported by and depended upon a network of banking institutions and was set within a cultural context which, it has been claimed, supported entrepreneurship (Cohen, 1992; Bitros and Karayiannis, 2008).

Does that mean therefore that Athens evolved a monetary system in the way that it has just been defined? In some respects the answer tends towards the affirmative, but there are important provisos. While economic institutions emerged to sustain a monetary system they appear to have done so without any direct involvement from the state. Banking was, for example, a largely personal issue between those with funds and those who needed them for short-term support, for trade voyages for example. Most frequently this was an arrangement between friends, and while agreements were very likely to have been contractual, the relationship appears to have been one of *affect* or sentiment rather than one of simple economic logic.

Edward Cohen's important book on banking in ancient Athens makes it quite clear that these institutions existed on a large scale (Cohen, 1992). As Ian Morris (1994) has suggested, however, this is not the same as saying that these bodies possessed the same functions as modern banks (1994: 391). What Cohen demonstrates is that banking in ancient Athens had a more important role than is often assumed but certain peculiarities stand out. First, bankers were part of an invisible economy. Wealthy Athenians would deposit money with them secretly while overtly still adhering to the traditional concept of wealth as being located in land and household (*oikonomia*) (1992: 27–36). Second, these economic institutions could only operate effectively by bending the law to fit them, rather than because the legal system sustained them. Thus Cohen shows that women and slaves assumed a far greater economic role than has been previously assumed, precisely because they were *outside* many of the rules that governed the lives of male citizens (*politai*). Slaves frequently lived outside the household (*oikos*) where their role was anything but servile. Citizens could use the economic freedoms of the slaves to carry out functions for profit which they were unable to pursue themselves, even running profitable banking businesses for their masters (Cohen, 2000: 148). Operating outside the household was often a stepping stone to full manumission and Cohen's research suggests that many *douloi* became independently wealthy and therefore able to pay for their full freedom (Cohen, 2000: 153–54).

Similarly Bitros and Karayiannis (2008) have recently suggested that entrepreneurship was encouraged by the ancient Athenian state and that it 'applied policies that encouraged *metics* and slaves to assimilate into the Athenian society through success in business' (2008: 208). But this argument supports the view that profit-seeking was not seen as a pursuit for the male citizen. Moreover, three important conditions were applied:

> The first of them was that entrepreneurs would seek to realize 'moderate' profits. The second was that wealth would be spent according to certain ethical and social standards; and the third condition was that the distribution of wealth would not become 'too unequal' (Bitros and Karayiannis, 2008: 226).

They go on to argue in defence of a 'modernist' position that social status was only accorded to those who gained their rewards by work through ethical and fair means and who voluntarily shared it by undertaking public works or contributing to public expenses (2008: 227). This is hardly a capitalistic orientation.

A third peculiarity is the role of money itself. The expansionist capacity of money springs from its symbolic function as a token. Money in its modern sense is far more than coin; it is, as many banknotes remind us, a 'promise to pay' whose value is not intrinsic but lies within a normative framework of obligation. Credit arrangements, for example, *create* money not by producing coins or notes but by extending a promissory obligation, usually for a fee. David Schaps has written persuasively on the significance of the monetarisation of ancient Greece in general and Athens in particular, but 'after more than twenty years of looking at Greek money, I still see a coin' (2008, 48; Schaps, 2004).[18] What he means by this is that

---

18 It is notable that Athens was also very slow to adopt bronze coinage, when the small denominations in

he has not found evidence of sophisticated credit instruments:

> [T]here comes a time … when people who have been looking for something must admit that their failure to find it is not just a lack of results, but a negative result: they are not finding what they are looking for because it is not there (Schaps, 2008: 39).

This conclusion means that Moses Finley may have been right in his judgment that for Athenians in the ancient world money was coin and that in this important sense the economy could only be pre-capitalist. Even where it developed a more commercial function, von Reden argues that coinage served primarily to support civic rather than economic life (von Reden, 2002a; 2002b).

What all this means is that modern research suggests that the formalist case has been advanced over that of the early supporters of 'substantivism'. Ancient Athens was far more economically adventurous than a reading of the philosophers or early economists such as Xenophon would have us believe. From the battle of Marathon in 490 BCE through the years of direct democracy ending with the success of Philip II in 338, Athens evolved an economic strategy that in many respects looks remarkably modern. Yet, there is one critical difference that indicates the limits of this evolutionary path. Ancient Athens still possessed a culture that prized civic responsibility over individual gain, defined economic endeavour as a necessity rather than something to be intrinsically valued, and regarded waged labour as inferior to self-employment. In this sense none of the recent research would appear to overthrow entirely the 'substantivist' proposition found in Polányi that 'economic interests were sub-ordinated to or absorbed within politics, honor, and war' (Morris, 1994: 353). To this extent, therefore, and notwithstanding important revisions to Finley's rather backward-looking interpretations, there continues to be little evidence for Max Weber's famous 'spirit of capitalism'.

It is important to stress that this is far from being a negative judgement. On the contrary, there is much in ancient Athens that is almost 'postmodern' in its concern for welfare and the public good, even though it is allied at the same time with the exploitation of women, slaves and foreigners. There are similarities too with what occurred over two millennia later, in the sense that an agricultural revolution was followed by a new emphasis on trade and manufacture with concomitant economic growth. Ian Morris captures the difference precisely when he suggests that the fundamental contradiction of Athenian society was that 'economic growth was the motor of civic egalitarianism, but civic egalitarianism was a brake that slowed economic growth' (Morris, 1994: 366). One might only add that inequality between the citizen and non-citizen would have had the same effect. Capitalism commodifies labour and not those who undertake it, and in this sense, too, Finley cannot be lightly dismissed.

---

which it was struck would have made it ideal for local trading. Athens did eventually do so in the late fourth century; one possible reason for the apparent reluctance may have been a reflection of a wider lack of interest in coinage for trading purposes. Certainly, an earlier attempt to adopt bronze coins in the aftermath of the Peloponnesian War had not succeeded (Grandjean, 2006).

THE SPARTAN ECONOMY

Until very recently, the image of Sparta could not have been more different from that of ancient Athens; one embraced democracy while the other held on to monarchy; one defined equality in terms of a citizen's duties, while the other adhered to a communitarianist notion of equal desserts; one prized individualism, particularly in public displays of wealth, while the other sought austerity and duty above material possessions. More recently, a re-examination has challenged these assumptions and suggested that inequalities of property and wealth always existed in Spartan life and indeed, that extreme disparities were an important factor in the decline of Sparta after the battle of Leuctra in 371 BCE (Hodkinson, 2009). Stephen Hodkinson's revisionist interpretation also undermines the classic image of the Spartan state allocating equal land holdings to male citizens in return for military duties, which returned to the state on the death of the holder, and argues instead that both land holdings and inheritance were much more flexible and could favour daughters as well as sons. These factors, he suggests, led to a disastrous decline in households in the century or so between the Persian Wars of 480–479 and the Battle of Leuctra when the Spartan citizen body (adult male) contracted by more than eighty per cent (Cartledge and Spawforth, 2002: 5). Losses in manpower during the fifth century, opportunistic marriages to wealthy widows (helped in part by the great earthquake of ca. 464 BCE) and strongly controlled endogamous marriage patterns all contributed to the concentration of wealth in fewer and fewer hands, and to the rise in wealth itself as a symbol of status. Hodkinson argues that Spartiates skilfully used activities that accorded with the egalitarian ideology, rather than those that ran against it, to display their wealth, such as equestrian pursuits and the funding of victory monuments for both military and sporting prowess, even though before the fourth century these were likely to be sited outside Sparta itself. Although helots may have been owned, and may have paid a tithe in produce to their Spartiate masters, they stayed with the land when transferred from one landholder to another. Nonetheless, the helotry system, with its inbuilt complexity of ownership and control in the hands of both landowners and the community itself, produced a surplus that served as a conservative force militating against the emergence of a trade-related sector. Coining may have been absent throughout much of Sparta's history, when it was widely adopted elsewhere, but this did not mean that physical transfers of wealth in the form of bullion or foreign currency did not occur when market exchanges took place (Hodkinson, 2009: 180 *passim*). However:

> Sparta's foreign trade was relatively unimportant and anyway not in Spartan hands. Sparta did not employ mercenaries on any scale before the late fifth century and could in any case use the currency of other states for that purpose (Cartledge and Spawforth, 2002: 31).

While the disinclination to adopt an indigenous coinage by no means undermined all economic exchange (not least because of a reliance on Aiginetan coins), this was very different from the familiar Cretan experience of *polis* minting and mercenary remittances that served to locate coinage so centrally in the island's economic experience.

So even if we accept that earlier depictions were more of a caricature than an accurate portrayal and that, as result, ancient Sparta was much more like other city states than is commonly imagined, there are certain features that are more difficult to ignore. Sparta can never be considered a 'trading *polis*', nor one oriented to the sea as a way of building trading partners. It was still a conservative society with a landed agrarian elite, an indigenous servile labour force bound to the soil and a conscripted hoplite army. Ultimately, it was still true that private property rights were constrained by communal needs including the right of the state to share in produce and to use private land holdings for public purposes. These may have had little effect on shaping egalitarian outcomes, but economic resources could not operate in a separate and private realm under these conditions. Moreover, while there may have been great divisions between rich and poor; nonetheless, the state sought to impose an egalitarian lifestyle on all citizens including in terms of education, equipment, physical appearance and funerary practices. Egalitarianism may, therefore, have been an ideological weapon that masked a very different reality in which a concentration of wealth in ever fewer hands, and a subsequent loss of citizen numbers, contributed to Sparta's decline to a second-rank *polis* during the early fourth century, but the important point is that this decline took place when elsewhere some city states were entering a period of consolidation and positive change. So, although we can no longer accept the depiction of Classical Sparta as shaped by a form of primitive communism, in which equality between citizens was allied to and symbolised by communal dining, this does not mean that in economic terms it was much like the Cretan *poleis*. Again, the intrusion of state power in the distribution of economic rewards may not have served to generate greater egalitarianism as is sometimes claimed, but it was markedly different from the role of Cretan states in promoting new forms of economic endeavour and thereby benefiting from taxes upon them.

This is not to argue that no parallels existed. One area of marked similarity was in the salience of a culture of egalitariaism that may have derived from the *syssitia* experience. Considerable disparities of wealth were therefore allied to a disinclination to show it, leading in both locations to the absence of public benefactions that were such a feature of life in ancient Athens and elsewhere. Hodkinson's analysis suggests that aspects of sacred observance (e.g. bronze religious votives) and sporting prowess (e.g. equestrian competitions) were some of the few avenues open to more conspicuous consumption. Perhaps for this reason, in neither Crete nor Sparta can we look for signs of economic surplus in monuments and benefactions.

Positive exceptionalism or a third way?

Given the foregoing discussion it would be appropriate if it was possible to demonstrate that the economies of Cretan city states from, say, the 5th century surpassed those of Athens, Sparta and possibly others in their adoption of monetary systems and in the application of market principles to trade and exchange. Unfortunately, this is far from an easy or straightforward task. In the first place, there is the question of the comparison itself. It is one thing to compare Athens with Sparta because their respective populations are not too dissimilar in number. It is quite another to compare ancient Athens, with a total population of approximately 250,000, with, say, Knosos or Gortyn whose size may have been a tenth of that of Athens. Second, the debates about the economy of Athens and Sparta are far from over, with some authorities arguing for the abandonment of the Finley thesis, while others maintain that it is broadly correct. Finally, with some notable exceptions, the economies of the Cretan city states during the relevant years have not been the focus of research interest. There are, therefore, many comparisons that it would be fascinating to make that are simply impossible. The best that can be offered is an assessment that is suggestive rather than conclusive.

The most general conclusion is that, perhaps from a very traditional base, Crete saw economic changes that appeared to have reflected similar transformations in other comparable parts of the Mediterranean. The most compelling evidence for this is in the gradual transfer of economic life from the traditional upland *polis* to the new, or newly energised, ports. The concomitant growth of a merchant class engaging in seaborne trade made more possible by an interchangeable domestic currency and sustained by an appropriate credit and legal infrastructure points in this direction. Although we can question the 'frozen backwater' assumptions of many commentators, this is not the same as arguing that Crete was in any way *more* advanced than others. In the absence of statistical series that enable modern economic historians to disaggregate the elements from which economic change is composed, the study of the ancient economy is normally reliant on a much broader picture. One element of this is the way in which land, labour and capital appeared to be employed.

In relation to land, the main feature in the Cretan case is the way that the use of the landscape went from being 'internalised' into self-sufficient protective settlements, via the 'primary' *poleis* controlling a fertile hinterland, towards open access to the sea. If the Minoan period ended with the collapse of coastal sites and a flight to the hills, the Classical era closed with the relative decline of the upland settlements and a return to the sea. Of course not every coastal settlement achieved the same level of population growth and trade-related wealth, but as Max Weber concluded, 'sea trade was the most important source of new private wealth' (1976: 210). The result of these changes, however, was in one sense the same; all the primary *poleis* began their journey to oblivion. The architects of the Cretan *poleis* created stable, ordered communities and realised that they were a good platform for generating a larger economic surplus. Perhaps what they did not realise was that success in this latter endeavour would ultimately be at the cost of their traditional communities.

Unfortunately, we have little information to go on concerning how land itself was employed. We do know that as elsewhere there were lands owned by the *polis* itself whose product contributed to the *andreion* (men's house) or system of common meals (*syssitia*), together with one tenth of the normal product of landed estates (Strataridaki, 2009). We also know that land was traded, accumulated and passed on through inheritance, but not a great deal about the distribution of estates by size or main area of economic activity. Watrous et al. (2004) have reported from their survey in the Mesara that land holdings appeared to be based on an economic logic; that is, holdings grew in size as the fertility of the soil decreased and distance from ports increased. Immediately around the urban centre of Phaistos on the best land was a zone approximately one kilometre wide that had few farmsteads, probably because the owners lived in the *asty* itself (Watrous et al., 2004: 333–4). Beyond that was a second zone, approximately 3km wide and with many large farms, that appear to have been relatively prosperous since they possessed 'roof tiles, stone presses, walls, inscribed tombstones, cooking ware, basins, *pithoi*, amphorae, loom weights, spindle whorls, and beehives' (334). Beyond this area again were more marginal lands stretching south to the foothills of the Asterousia and, in particular, around the Phaistian port of Matala, suggesting the growth of an independent peasantry. In Athens, by contrast, the needs of the state had major effects on how land could be held. If each productive unit or share of land (*kleros*) was required to supply one fit man for military service, then it was in the interests of the state to maximise their number, regardless of whether in so doing they undermined its capacity to amalgamate and thereby to provide a surplus for trade (Davies, 2007a: 350). In Sparta, despite the fundamental change in the image of state-controlled, equal land holdings found originally in Plutarch but now rejected by modern scholarship, it remains clear that there was never an open market in land, but rather citizens used subtle methods involving marriage, inheritance and foreign ownership to build land-based wealth (Hodkinson, 2009).

As far as labour is concerned, the vast majority of those who were employed, regardless of their status, worked on the land. Indeed many of those who were employed as soldiers and mercenaries were also for some of their year engaged in agricultural production. There are clear references to social status in the Gortyn codes and other laws, and these were undoubtedly reflected in the division of labour, but exactly how is unknown. In particular, gender would have been an important distinction in labour market terms and the role of women from all but the highest social classes would then, as now, have been critical in the *oikos* (household) as well as in the fields. The whole of the economic system would also have been changing quite rapidly from the Archaic through to the Hellenistic period, and there is no reason to suppose that the progress of the Greek economy was changing everywhere at the same rate. There is also no doubt that for many individuals, seeking work in soldiering was motivated by a wish to escape poverty induced by access to inadequate land, or by pestilence or by disease. But Crete differed from many other sources of mercenaries in two important respects. First, they were not unskilled workers but tended to have specific capabilities for which they had been very well prepared by a strict training regime. Second, they tended to have been selected to fulfil interstate agreements that governed how they were treated, how they were paid and when they could return. As Chaniotis rightly observes:

> A review of the evidence concerning mercenaries shows a very particular case of a controlled movement of population: the numbers and conditions of service were usually described in detail in bilateral treaties; the formulaic language and the standard content of the relevant clauses show the existence of generally applied norms; and the very nature of this mobility (military engagement) made it necessary that lists of the soldiers were kept (personal names, ethnics, reference to status or rank). This safeguarded the control of the foreigners during their temporary stay (2004: 487).

Those selected would not have been a ragbag of the unemployed or destitute and, although in some cases their families may have joined them, they would be more likely to return than individual adventurers seeking to better their lives wherever that took them, and who were as content to be paid in land as in coin. It is the fact that most returned with greater wealth than they left with, and more often than not in coin, which made Cretan mercenaries such an important force for economic change. What we might be able to say is that ancient Crete may have been particularly adroit at using those techniques for generating an economic surplus for which it was well endowed, namely the provision of skilled manpower at home and abroad. In sum, if war was Athens's and Sparta's main business, Crete made a business out of war. This fact is most probably related to the absence of internal conflict within Cretan *poleis*, the avoidance of engagement as a combatant in external wars and the creation of a monetary system, but these are conclusions that deserve to be tested by further research.

Although we know relatively little from Crete about how capital generated through this process, or through inter-*polis* trade was employed, it is clear that one parallel development was an island-wide enthusiasm for minted coin. Part of that might have been for reasons of civic pride, but evidence of a parallel interest in private property and market relations suggests that a primary motive was economic. It is probably true that in all settings political and economic motives for monetarisation vie with each other and are often intertwined, but it is very noticeable that in research on ancient Athens, political motives are normally given primacy:

> Though coins may have had a dual use once they existed, the reason they existed was political, not economic. That is to say, commercialization and monetization of society were not per se the state project (Schoenberger, 2008: 669).

In this argument the link between the political forces emerged through the twin processes of democratisation and imperialism. As far as democratisation is concerned state payments for participation in the democratic process widened the availability and use of coinage while warfare 'was looked upon as a normal and legitimate way of expanding the resource base of the polis' (2008: 669). A market came into existence, but it was one that remained subordinate to the state's political project (Martin, 1996). The Athenian state, by monetising its own activities in order to achieve its political and geopolitical ambitions, directly created the conditions that promoted increasing commercialisation, but it was what Max Weber termed 'political capitalism' or the economic operations of the state itself, which he saw as a cul de sac in terms of the evolution of capitalism.

In ancient Crete by contrast, there is no evidence that the availability and supply of coinage were directly linked to military ambition, even if economic motives may have played a part in inter-*polis* struggles. The impulse towards order and discipline produced a plethora of contacts and interactions that were intended partly to resolve disputes, but also to cement co-operative understandings in connection with festivals, contests and the movement of peoples from one *polis* to another. Crete did not fight overseas wars and did not need to pay citizens to participate in democratic politics, because its political system was organised in another way and did not depend upon continuous mass participation. If Athens subsumed the economy to the needs of war and imperialism, Crete regulated markets to make them work better. If in Athens trade was largely ignored or indulged out of necessity to feed a population that would otherwise go hungry, then in Crete it was promoted as a means of maintaining employment, increasing public revenue and promoting economic integration. Comparisons with Sparta are equally telling. Private property and the accumulation of family wealth may have figured far more in 5th and 4th century Sparta than has previously been realised but, as in Athenian banking, this was *despite* the official ideology, not because of it.

This is not to say that the support of mercantile ambitions by Cretan states was entirely altruistic; the public coffers began to depend more and more on revenue generated by trade tariffs but, as Hopkins has argued in the Roman case, commodity trading can then become enhanced in order to cope with the burden of tax imposts (1980; 2002). It is also not to suggest the absence of a link between state actions and economic fortunes. For example, as the social anthropologist Michael Smith has argued, there is often an inverse relationship between state power and commercialisation (2004: 93). We have already noted the longstanding, but not always successful, quest for a political union (*koinon*), and in so far as this may have reduced the power of individual states, it may have boosted economic integration. Indeed, it may well have been that economic considerations lay behind its original foundation. Further support for this idea comes from Epstein's work on medieval Europe, where he notes the role of declining state power in promoting market integration and thereby reducing transaction costs and promoting trade growth through market liberalisation (Epstein, 2000). It is not therefore a contrast between one setting where the state is involved and one where it is not; rather it is *how* the state is involved that makes a difference. If coinage, for example, is introduced to pay for triremes, or the wages of rowers, then the conclusion that Hans van Wees comes to is probably correct:

> Coinage did not introduce fundamentally new attitudes towards trade, value, or wealth; it merely introduced a more convenient medium of exchange. Its only advantage over uncoined metal was that one did not need to weigh it (2009: 462).

With this passive use of coinage, there is no need for the state to be concerned with exchangeability but only with supply. By contrast, where exchangeability was paramount, there is every reason for supposing that this was because state-sponsored commercialisation was itself seen as a good.

If the sea was of little importance to Sparta, or feared as a source of influences that could undermine the classic culture of the *polis* as in Athens, then in Crete it was seen as a way of maximising the economic advantage of geographical location. In this sense, Cretan *poleis* were more Mediterranean than either of the other two since like so many other city states, customs dues were an important source of revenue. Public income was neither dependent upon individual fealty, to be repaid from waging war, nor solely derived from the land. It is true that in the late Archaic and early Classical periods the ideology of militarism may have defined booty as a just return for overrunning an enemy, and thereby helped to stimulate what came to be seen as 'piracy', but public returns from trade in the form of dues and undermining trade through support for illicit capture at sea run counter to each other so that in time, whatever logic such strategies possessed from a state point of view were replaced by one stressing order and co-operation.

Crete was different and possibly more 'modern' than either of the Aegean's two behemoths, but not perhaps exceptional. There was no equivalent in the economic realm of either the unique creation of a public law code, or the special form of democracy suited to societies divided by traditional group loyalties discussed in earlier chapters, and yet each may have played a part in the stability and predictability that led to economic progress. There is always a danger of believing that because one location is more prosperous than another it is necessarily more advanced. Ancient Athens was undoubtedly more prosperous than ancient Crete, as the great building programmes of the Classical period show so well. But saying this is rather like saying that Dubai is more advanced than the Netherlands. Athens and Dubai became wealthy because they seized 'booty' from the labour of others or from the ground. What is more significant is whether a society develops institutions that will provide self-sustaining economic growth. Aristotle (*Politics* 2: 11) believed that Crete seemed 'intended by nature for dominion in Hellas' largely because of its situation, extending 'right across the sea, around which nearly all the Hellenes are settled; and while one end is not far from the Peloponnese, the other almost reaches to the region of Asia about Triopium and Rhodes'. The way these words are expressed, together with a reference to the sea power of Minos in subduing and colonising the Aegean and beyond, makes it clear that he had in mind both political and economic dominion. Yet the Cretans kept themselves to themselves and unlike Athens, whose economic power was so clearly linked to political ambitions, they foreswore any overseas adventures, including for the most part military engagements in which many other territories in the Hellenic world became embroiled.

There is little doubt that at the outset, Cretan city states were as traditional and conservative as orthodox *poleis* anywhere in the Hellenic world. The great strength of the writings of Ronald Willetts (1965, 1976) is that he captured the main features of this semi-feudal world. Far from being innately stable the Cretan *poleis*, possibly uniquely, were riven by ethnic differences, a product both of their past and of subsequent immigration. Survival required a special politics based upon rigid adherence to a rule of law that both controlled political ambition and focused attention outward. Occasionally this took the form of territorial ambitions and inter-*poleis* wars but more commonly it led to co-operation in the use of sanctuaries, in engagement with Panhellenic festivals and various forms of treaty agreements, leading eventually to stronger moves down the road of *koinon*. Given this political settlement, often combining inward coherence with outward co-operation, it is not surprising that a merchant class should emerge, buoyed by the existence of wage labour, private property and a culture of acquisition. Above all, this was facilitated by a monetary system, embodying an exchangeable coinage but sustained by state support, credit facilities and a system of trade-related agreements. As in Athens, it could well have been that the merchant class was initially somewhat suspect, but if that was so, it did not last long, for far from there being a cultural divide between urban centre and coastal port, the Cretan model was largely one of symbiosis, leading eventually to a reversal of fortunes as the inland *poleis* gave way to their vibrant offspring.

CHAPTER EIGHT

Liberation or a lost inheritance?

It could be argued that the successful conquest of Crete by the Romans in the period from 69 to 67 BCE brought an end to Cretan independence that has never been totally regained. True, the periods of autonomy, hard won in the closing years of the 19th century after centuries of Ottoman domination, marked a turning point that culminated with the union with Greece in late 1913, but for nearly two millennia Crete knew little but rebellion, suppression and everyday accommodation to the dictates of foreign powers. How and why this occurred, like so much of what went before, is clouded by myth.[1] In the first part of this chapter the most powerful mythology is examined in the light of the preceding argument and an example is adduced that suggests some of the consequences that may flow from the orthodox position. The remaining section offers a very brief synopsis of what came after the Romans.

The Roman accession

The consolidation of territories in the eastern Mediterranean occurred in the closing years of the Roman Republic (509–27 BCE) when infighting and civil war gave way to the age of Augustus and the emergence of the Roman Empire, normally said to have lasted until AD 476. The understanding of what happened in Crete was influenced by late 19th century studies of the Roman world, which tended to identify parallels with Britain's 'civilising' mission in India, Africa and elsewhere. A rethink in recent years has emphasised that even before the dawn of the empire, Rome was far more oriented than hitherto believed with expansion and the subjection of territories with weaker military strength than its own. When applied to the eastern Mediterranean, where perhaps this tendency is most clearly expressed, the debate has focused less on the outcome and more on the specific *form* that expansionism took.[2] The question arises as to whether the massive growth

---

1 Sadly, these mythologies have been unwittingly maintained by many scholars in archaeology who refer to the 'Greco-Roman' period, which is rather like referring to French history between, say, 1930 and 1950 as the 'Franco-German' period.

2 Perhaps the most influential work on the expansionist tendency of republican Rome is William Harris's

was simply to serve Roman interests or whether the Greeks themselves played a part in inviting Roman influence, even to the point of helping to shape the patterns of intervention that evolved over the final two centuries of the millennium. A small *polis*, for example, when threatened by a larger neighbour might have much to gain from seeking an alliance with Rome. Kallet-Marx (1995), however, interprets Roman motivation as changing as a result of responses to the Roman presence in the eastern Mediterranean. In particular, the protracted conflicts with the Pontic king Mithridates appear to have focused the Roman mind on the necessity of pursuing a more concerted policy of empire building.[3] Having lost the first Mithridatic War, Rome was no longer seen as invincible, which turned a more passive presence in the region into a quest for permanent annexation owing tribute to Rome.

As far as Crete is concerned, it is probably fair to argue that the jury is still out, but what we know tends to support this interpretation. Thus in the mid-140s BCE, Hierapytna invaded and destroyed its neighbour to the north-east, Praisos, and took over its lands. This meant that it was then adjacent to the *polis* of Itanos, recently weakened by the decline of Egyptian influence following the death of Ptolemy VI. There had been a long-running feud between Itanos and Praisos concerning the ownership of the island of Leuke and the sanctuary of Zeus Diktaios that lay on the border between them, and this soon led to conflict between Hierapytna and Itanos over the same territory. The protagonists, recognising the hegemony of Rome in the whole Mediterranean, appealed to the Senate for arbitration, which in turn passed the case to the Greek territory of Magnesia on the Maeander (now part of western Turkey bordering the Aegean), stipulating that the boundary should be as it was before hostilities broke out (Kallet-Marx, 1995: 177). Skirmishes continued, however, for a number of years and once again in 115–114 BCE the protagonists appealed to the Senate for another resolution. The Senate, after receiving a report from a senatorial commissioner by the name of Quintus Fabius, again referred the dispute to the Magnesians on the same terms, with the added stipulation that buildings erected by the Hierapytnians should be removed (Kallet-Marx, 1995: 177–78). These seemingly benign acts of conciliation were a far cry from the events that led to the takeover of the whole island some forty years later – and, more important, less than twenty years after Rome's defeat at the hands of Mithridates in 88 BCE.

What was it that changed in those years? Why did Rome alter course from being a hegemonic power with by far the greatest influence in the eastern Mediterranean to being an aggressive imperialist bent on not just subduing dissent but on total domination and control? The conventional answer is to accept the interpretation given by Rome itself, and repeated by many Roman authors, that the conflict with Crete was inevitable because of the latter providing a home for some of the most

---

War and Imperialism in Republican Rome (1979), while the argument that the *form* it took was essentially Greek can be found in Erich Gruen's (1984) *The Hellenistic World and the Coming of Rome* and also in Robert Morstein Kallet-Marx (1995) *Hegemony to Empire. The Development of the Roman Imperium in the East from 148 to 62 B.C.*

3 Mithridates VI Eupator 'the Great' ruled the large, mostly Greek, kingdom of Pontus just south of the Black Sea (Pontus Euxinus). He died in 63 BCE after a reign of 57 years, more than forty of which were characterised by conflict with Rome.

predatory pirates in the Mediterranean.[4] Even today there are those who accept this mythology, arguing that the *imperium populi Romani* liberated Crete from its lawlessness and opened the door to a new age of prosperity. Angelos Chaniotis, for example, suggests that life was so dreadful in the Hellenistic era that 'the victory of Octavian at Actium came as a blessing' and that, particularly for economies like Crete's that were based on plunder and piracy, the benefits of the Roman invasion and the new era to which it gave rise were as dramatic 'as the introduction of the market economy into the communist countries after 1990' (Chaniotis, 2005a: 140). Before looking in more detail at why this interpretation is so suspect, it is worth noting the degree to which it has coloured the analysis of some of Crete's most important archaeological sites.

Perhaps the best example is in the interpretation of the city state of Phalasarna in the extreme north-west of the island. Much of the little we know of this important *polis* is derived from the work of Elpida Hadjidaki and her colleagues (Hadjidaki, 1987; 1988a; 1988b; 2001; Frost, 1989; Frost and Hadjidaki, 1990; Pirazolli et al., 1992). Focusing almost entirely on the outer and inner harbours with their remarkable fortification towers, rather than on the town itself that remains largely unexcavated to this day, the research has demonstrated very clearly that the town was sacked in the middle of the 1st century BCE and never reused. It has also confirmed Captain Spratt's judgment concerning the uplift to the western end of the island, and by careful analysis of the fill in the harbour demonstrated the consequences of what may have been a relatively minor tectonic event in AD 66 and a much larger earthquake and accompanying tsunami in AD 365 – the latter being the most likely explanation for the uplift of between six and seven metres.[5]

The researchers are almost certainly right to associate the first destruction with the Roman invasion in 69 BCE, and it may well have been true, as Frost (1989) has argued, that Phalasarna rather than Kydonia was the first port of call in the second Roman campaign that opened in that year (cf. Frost and Hadjidaki, 1990: 513). The difficulty arises with the uncritical acceptance that the Roman invasion was designed to eradicate piracy and, as a consequence, that Phalasarna was a 'pirate's nest' containing nothing but a naval port (Hadjidaki, 1988a):[6]

> Because of the impressive size and extent of the fortifications around its harbour, it is often assumed to have been one of the many Cretan cities whose revenues were primarily derived from piracy during the Hellenistic period (Frost and Hadjidaki, 1990: 513).

Moreover, despite noting the Phoenician influence in the design of the harbour and the presence of sherds of fine Hellenistic pottery, the researchers were still

---

4 For example, from the authoritative voice of the *Cambridge Ancient History* we learn that Antonius in his campaign against the 'pirate bases in Crete' was defeated not by the association of states in the Cretan *Koinon* but by the 'light flotillas of the pirates which had received support from the organized cities of Crete' which was the 'main centre of piracy in the southern Aegean' (Crook et al., 1992: 249–50).

5 This is in the harbour area but wave notches suggest a rise of up to 10 metres elsewhere.

6 For example, in the report by Pirazolli et al. (1992: 385) 'there is little doubt that the excavated harbor was a military port, probably one of the famous Cretan pirate nests terrorizing the Mediterranean'.

convinced that 'the remains of various impressive public buildings and fortifications prove the existence of financial and human resources that only piracy could have provided in such a place' (Pirazolli et al. 1992: 385).

It would be wrong to suggest that this implausible interpretation has not been challenged by others. Philip de Souza, for example, in his fine study of piracy in the Mediterranean (2000), has pointed out that '...there is little evidence to indicate that any particular place might have owed its prosperity to the ill-gotten gains of pirates' and on Phalasarna in particular 'there is no clear evidence to suggest that its wealth depended in any significant way upon piracy' (2000: 58, 59). Nonetheless, this interpretation has played its part in maintaining the myth that Crete did not contain at this time trading ports of great importance and wealth.

The making of the piracy myth

Clearly, it would be folly to deny that there were pirates operating in Cretan waters in the centuries before 69 BCE. Certainly there seems little doubt that attacks on merchant ships were not uncommon and there is equally no doubt that Cretan adventurers raided foreign shores for booty and slaves (Garlan, 1987: 9). As early as the 3rd century BCE, there are claims that pirate ships were involved in warfare at sea. In 217 BCE, for example, Philip V of Macedonia had managed to have himself declared president of the Cretan *Koinon*, possibly because of a wish to guarantee a steady supply of Cretan mercenary soldiers for his various objectives in the eastern Mediterranean (de Souza, 2000: 81–82). One of these was to open up trade routes for his ships, which at that time were dominated by fleets from neighbouring Rhodes. Although the circumstances are not entirely clear, ancient sources mention that a small number of Cretan pirate ships were involved in what was to become the First Cretan War with Rhodes (206–203 BCE). For example, the historian *Diodorus Siculus* wrote:

> With a fleet of seven ships the Cretans began to engage in piracy, and plundered a number of vessels. This had a disheartening effect upon those who were engaged in commerce by sea, whereupon the Rhodians, reflecting that this lawlessness would affect them also, declared war upon the Cretans (27. 3).

Philip de Souza (2000: 81–82) argues that Philip recruited the Aitolian Dikaiarchos to lead a fleet of twenty more ships to assist the Cretans, who nonetheless eventually succumbed to the greater maritime strength of the Rhodians (cf. Diodorus 28.1). Interestingly, the war reflected the internecine tensions within the *Koinon* itself with Gortyn, allied with Eleutherna and Hierapytna, separate from a number of other *poleis* allied to the Knosians (Chaniotis, 2005a: 9; Walbank, 2002: 120). The eventual settlement treaty with Hierapytna (ca. 200 BCE) also refers to piratical attacks, but by this time the underlying struggle actually reflected a wider engagement with the Romans supporting the victorious Rhodians against their enemy Philip V, an influence that was to grow with the second struggle between these local trading powers (the so-called 'Second Cretan War') in 155–153 BCE (Ormerod, 1997: 148). Put simply, it would appear that the term 'piracy' was readily applied to opponents in warfare that had itself been instigated to defend trade routes (de Souza, 2000: 82).[7] As Avidov (1997: 24) has pointed out the very presence of foreign powers on opposing sides makes it quite clear that even if 'piracy' was referred to as a cause of hostilities, it could not have been the only factor. Indeed the phrase 'cleansing the sea' was a time-honoured way in which recognition of political supremacy was claimed in the Hellenistic world. The Second Cretan War makes this point rather clearly, since by this time the Rhodian navy had declined in significance and the use of the pejorative label 'piracy' as applied to foreign forces also diminished. As Avidov puts it, 'it would appear to have been no mere coincidence that Cretan piracy ceases being a problem precisely after the island's victory over Rhodes, in 153 BC' (1997: 25). Later, in the years immediately before the Roman invasion, there is little evidence of Cretan piracy (Omerod, 1997: 225). There is also no evidence that whatever piratical attacks may have remained were coordinated or guided by Cretan *poleis*. On the contrary, 'in our records of early Crete we can see the first attempts of a civilised state to cope with the evils of piracy and protect its seaborne commerce' (Ormerod, 1997: 13).

The term 'pirate' is therefore intrinsically pejorative and cannot be separated from the political power or affiliation of those who use it. As Avidov, who is concerned primarily with the claim by the Romans that the Cilicians were a 'nation of pirates', argues, 'not once, as far as I know, is one of these seemingly neutral terms applied by an author to a party with whom he sympathizes' (1997: 8). The involvement of so-called 'pirate ships' in the First Cretan War may well, initially at least, have been a case of privateering or an action by a non-belligerent against the enemies of a belligerent state (1997: 15). This is not, however, to diminish the *consequences* of labels being used in this way, as can so clearly be seen in the events that led to the loss of Cretan independence. It is also not to argue that traditional piracy never occurred, only to stress its exaggeration for the purposes of justifying intervention and the oppressive treatment of those that were defined as neither friends nor allies of the Romans.[8] An additional difficulty in separating myth from reality was that the activities of some *poleis* included the right to 'violent seizure' of another's assets, even when no state of war had been declared between them. This can be seen from inscriptions that announce the suspension of this right in the case of a *polis* or *poleis* so favoured. As Gabrielsen puts it, this would include those 'with war-chests so poorly fed by conventional fiscal devices as to make "booty-seizure" (*leisteia*) a principal mode of financing their operations' (2003: 400), but there is little reason to accept Brule's thesis (1978) that growing inequalities and population increases

---

7 This connection has long been noted. For example 'War, trade, and piracy are one/An indivisible trinity', Goethe's *Mephistopheles* (Faust II, Act 5, Sc. 2, ii. 1184–8, Penguin trans).

8 The exact extent to which Cretan piracy ever existed, or continued after 153 BCE, is difficult to assess. Pro-Roman historians such as Plutarch (*Pompey* 29) argue that it was second only to Cilician piracy while the more independent-minded geographer Strabo argued that it was destroyed by the Cilicians (10.4.9).

in the early years of the Hellenistic era generated a population explosion that could only be resolved by large-scale and systematic piracy. Certainly population growth as a result of steadily rising incomes might have had a bearing on young citizens seeking employment as mercenaries, but evidence of land surveys shows that another alternative lay in developing new forms of agricultural settlement (Watrous et al. 2004).[9]

In 74 BCE the Roman Senate, on the purported grounds of controlling piracy, gave a new kind of command to Marcus Antonius, the son of the commander sent in 102 BCE to control the waters off Cilicia (the southern coast of today's Turkey) and the father of Mark Antony. Already controlling, through the policy of *imperium populi Romani*, almost the whole of the Greek-speaking world, this command was not tied to one geographical location but was what Kallet-Marx calls '*imperium infinitum*' to control the 'pirate epidemic' (1995: 305). From the Roman side, Antonius's demands on what was almost certainly the Cretan *Koinon* was for the cessation of official support for piracy and the sending of mercenaries to assist Rome's enemies. We do not know precisely how the *Koinon* responded but it is very likely that it did not see itself as officially supporting pirates and was opposed to any measures that would hinder trade either in goods or services such as mercenary soldiers. Its seeming indifference was interpreted by Antonius as insolence and in 71 BCE he declared war on Crete. The upshot was a swift defeat for Antonius when he encountered Cretan forces, numbering more than 20,000, led by a Knosian citizen, one Lasthenes, off Kydonia. Not only was Antonius's *quastor* (administrator) captured but, according to Florus (1. 42) the iron fetters the Romans had confidently brought with them were used to restrain their own men. Antonius then negotiated a truce but shortly thereafter died, producing a short lull in hostilities.

During this period the *Koinon*, aware of the upset the Cretans had caused to the hegemonic power, felt the need to try and ensure no repeat of this conflict. The Roman Senate, stung by this unusual affront to its *imperium*, may have decided by 70 BCE that nothing short of full provincial status for Crete was essential (Kallet-Marx, 1995: 309). But the Cretans very nearly managed to prevent this by sending a thirty-strong delegation drawn from a number of *poleis* to Rome to argue the case for the peace negotiated with Antonius. Even though the Senate's decision to progress with the concept of '*Creta provincia*' may have been taken in 70 BCE, and a new commander appointed, the skill of the Cretan negotiators was such that by February 69 BCE they had succeeded in that 'the Senate voted to absolve them of the allegations against them and restore to them the title of "friends and allies", presumably on the terms settled with Antonius' (Kallet-Marx, 1995: 310). At this juncture a member of the tribunate, one Cornelius Lentulus Spinther,

---

9 The idea of a linkage between mercenaries and pirates is very well established although no one has been able to adduce evidence for it. Karafotias, for example, defines the two roles as 'the backbone of the economic activities of the island' arguing that 'a mercenary of 210 could be easily a pirate in 209' (Karafotias, 1997: 351). The elision is very reminiscent of that in the modern period between migrants and criminality.

intervened to 'invalidate' this decision and, on behalf of the Roman people, voted to pursue the original policy of turning Crete into a full province of Rome. As a one-sided attempt at compromise, the Senate responded by offering the Cretans an ultimatum demanding surrender of the two Cretan commanders (Lasthenes and Panares) who had been victorious over Antonius, all ships with more than four oars, all Roman captives and a sum of 4,000 talents. The seeming impossibility of acceding to these conditions, and in particular the tribute, may be gauged from the fact that at the time all of Rome's massive eastern territories yielded only 8,500 talents (Sanders, 1982: 3).

The new commander, Quintus Caecilius Metellus, was thus dispatched to attack Crete from Roman bases in the Peloponnese. Metellus came from an extraordinary military family. His brother, father, grandfather, three uncles, great grandfather, and great great grandfather had all been consuls like himself and he was probably one of Rome's leading commanders. It is likely that he and his three legions made their base in Kasteli (Kisamos), the port of Polyrrhenia, which was known to be sympathetic to Rome, and from where in 69 BCE he laid waste Polyrrhenia's rivals, Phalasarna and eventually Kydonia itself.[10] After the siege of Kydonia, probably by land and sea, the commander Lasthenes fled back to Knosos and the city under his colleague Panares surrendered in return for the latter's personal safety. The following year, with great severity, Metellus destroyed Knosos, and moved west against Eleutherna and Lappa. But there was still to be one important twist in the tale that made it absolutely clear that Metellus was not interested in piracy but in total control. The Cretans, witnessing the advance of Metellus and the savagery of his actions, appealed in early 67 BCE to Pompey who had been charged, like Antonius before him, with a pan-Mediterranean campaign to control the seas in order to maintain grain supplies to the eternal city, particularly from Sicily, Sardinia and North Africa. Pompey had gained a reputation for greater leniency and it was probably this that motivated the Cretans' decision to surrender to Pompey in the hope that his status would enable them to be rid of Metellus's repression. Pompey, through his legate Octavius, accepted this surrender and ordered Metellus out of the island, but in a foretaste of the civil wars that were to bring the Republic finally to a close, Metellus refused and went on in 67 BCE to move against Hierapytna, making it the last city to fall to Roman control. As Kallet-Marx puts it:

> Metellus imposed terms on the Cretans that signified the end of their long-lived independence, doubtless including the payment of *vectigalia* (tribute) to Rome. Crete was 'ours,' said Cicero in 63 (1995: 319).

Crete and Cyrenaica were assigned to a single *quaestor* with his base in Gortyn and the defeat was complete. Metellus, like the ill-fated Antonius, was awarded

---

10 It is, however, perfectly possible that the rich trading port of Phalasarna,which in 174 BCE is reputed to have sent 3,000 mercenaries together with Knosos to assist Perseus in his fight against the Romans, may have been the first port of engagement, particularly after the failure of Metellus's predecessor off neighbouring Kydonia (cf Frost, 1989; Hadjidaki, 1988a: 140; Karafotias, 1997: 331).

the cognomen 'Creticus' and a triumph through Rome, although the latter was somewhat delayed by Pompey's efforts to challenge the legitimacy of his actions.

But if 'cleansing the seas' of piracy was not the real motive for Rome's actions, what was? The answer is probably threefold. First, there is little doubt that Crete's fighting men posed a real threat to Rome's hegemony. Well before the first invasion of the island, Crete had allied itself with those alarmed by the change in Rome's involvement in the eastern Mediterranean from a more or less benign presence to that of an open aggressor. There is evidence, for example, that the Pontic king, Mithridates, had emerged as the leader of an anti-Roman bloc that included Crete, as well as other disgruntled peoples fearful of the rise of Roman domination. Once Mithridates had assumed the mantle of leadership against Rome, the contacts between those who wished to resist greatly increased. As Avidov writes, they existed between:

> [T]he Cilicians and Mithridates; the Cilicians and Sertorius; Mithridates and Sertorius; Mithridates and the Cretans, who are also said to have supported the Cilicians in 102 BC; Mithridates and the kings of Egypt and Syria; Mithridates and Sertorius; and the Cilicians and Spartacus (Avidov, 1997: 39).

This did not amount to an integrated campaign, but nonetheless an understanding emerged that greatly helped Mithridates drive the Romans out of Asia Minor and Macedonia in 88 BCE. The Cretan classicist Spyridakis put it succinctly when he wrote, 'it is natural that the Romans, as a rising world power, would become interested in Crete, for Roman dominance over the island would, inter alia, affect the flow of mercenaries to the various states that opposed her eastern expansion' (1992: 131).

The second factor was economic. The expansion of Roman activity in the Hellenistic era had generated, as it had for the Athenians some centuries before, a massive dependency upon overseas grain supplies. Indeed the initial activities of both M. Antonius and Pompey had been to maintain Rome's domination of trade routes in the western Mediterranean. But even the grain supplies from well-established suppliers in Sicily and Sardinia were insufficient and grain scarcity, and subsequent malnourishment, were a source of popular disquiet that frequently alarmed the Roman Senate. This led to a revival of interest in Cyrenaica (North Africa). Cyrenaica (or Cyrene) had been a Roman possession since being ceded by its former king, Apion, in 96 BCE, but thereafter had been neglected until pressing grain deficiencies stimulated the belief that here could be another source of supply (Kallet-Marx, 1995: 308). The attentions of neighbouring Ptolemaic Egypt may have also played a part in prompting the Senate to establish Cyrene as a *provincia* in 75 BCE. Whichever route was taken, Crete – with by then well-established trading links north, south, east and west – represented a competing presence in the area. Ormerod noted for the western Mediterranean the intimate connection between claims of 'piracy' and rival commercial interests when he wrote that 'commercial rivalries constantly prevented peaceful intercourse by sea, and gave rise to a form of buccaneering in the truest sense of the term' (1997: 99). Crete represented another commercial gain and it was this that led eventually, after the island's subjugation, to Rome bracketing the two provinces together for administrative purposes.

But there was also a wider economic purpose. As earlier chapters have argued, contrary to the *communis opinio* Crete was not poor. One way of interpreting the Senate's massive demands on the island after the failure of the *Koinon's* mission is to see it as merely a ploy for military action by setting impossible terms. While these were extraordinary demands, the fact that they were given serious consideration by the Cretans before being rejected, suggests that Rome considered the island to have been singularly prosperous and thus capable in principle of meeting this demand.[11] De Souza (1998: 113) notes that L. Cornelius Sulla in 84 BCE had imposed 'fines' on Roman holdings in Asia that amounted to five years of taxation or 20,000 talents, so that Crete was being asked to contribute the same revenue as the whole of Roman Asia for one year (1998: 113). As de Souza has written, 'if it is assumed that the Cretans were expected to be able to pay this sum, then it is testament both to the desires of the Roman policy-makers and the wealth of the Cretans' (1998: 113).[12] It is very probable, therefore, that a quest for Crete's riches was a major factor in the island's subjugation. After all, as Keith Hopkins has argued for the two centuries after 250 BCE:

> Repeated successes in war enabled the Romans to bring back to Italy huge quantities of booty in the form of treasure, money and slaves. The accumulated treasure of the eastern Mediterranean was transferred to Rome. Booty delivered to the state treasury was soon supplemented by provincial taxes which then gradually became the chief source of state revenue (1981: 113).

Particularly after Sulla's reforms, the amount of money extracted by tribute from possessions in Asia and elsewhere increased dramatically and the link between *imperium* and economic exploitation became even clearer. This continued well after Sulla's death when the 'powerful military presence not only protected current revenues but increased the demand for further revenues for its maintenance' (Kallet-Marx, 1995: 341).

The third reason could loosely be termed 'ideological'. The Romans' reaction to the Cretan victory over them not only cemented their conviction that total control, rather than the previous policy of indirect influence sustained by a minimal military presence, was called for; it also underpinned an emerging depiction of Rome's enemies as tyrants, brigands and pirates in a constant state of internecine violence. It was, as Avidov suggests, a world view 'that Roman conquest was beneficial to the conquered in that it put an end to the state of constant war which characterized

11 There is some reason for believing that the debate that took place at this time was between the younger citizens (many of whom may have been among the 20,000 who saw off the first Roman invasion), and the older generation who wanted a settlement on these terms (*Dio.* 40.1.1; cf. Chaniotis, 2005a: 44).

12 De Souza is possibly the only other commentator to advance this economic argument. Thus 'the invasion of Crete was a deliberate act of imperialism, motivated principally by the desire to plunder the island and exploit its economy for the benefit of the Roman people' (1998: 112).

their prior existence' (1997: 43). Roman laws themselves often incorporated this 'them–us' dichotomy as in the *lex de provinciis* which was intended to impose on the eastern Mediterranean the consequences of being, on the one hand, 'Roman citizens, allies of the Romans and "friends", or on the other, barbarians deserving of little mercy and no rights to autonomous self-rule' (Avidov, 1997: 54). The link between supremacy at sea and Roman domination is quite clear in Cicero's speech in support of the Manilian Law (65 BCE) when he declares that only when this is achieved will the Romans 'at last seem truly to command all peoples and races on land and sea' (quoted in Kallet-Marx, 1995: 317). The savagery of Metellus's repression in Crete has to be interpreted in this light.[13]

The real consequences of myth

At its simplest, the attack on Crete, which admittedly might have turned out in numerous other ways, was largely motivated by political pride and economic necessity, buttressed by a cultural myth of innate superiority. When the Roman historian Lucius Annaeus Florus wrote in his famous *Epitome of Roman History* that 'the Cretan war, if the truth is to be told, was due solely to our desire to conquer that famous island' (1. 42), he appears to accept this reason. Notably, he is careful not to propagate the piracy myth, and goes on in the following sentence to accept the threat of Cretan mercenary forces, but fails to consider the underlying economic pressures that generated both the reasons for Roman expansionism and the form of appropriation that it took. The central point, however, is that the common failure to appreciate the real motives behind Roman aggression has important consequences for the way independent Crete is understood. This is not just a question of wealth, it has implications also for the appreciation of where Crete should be placed in terms of its sophistication and progress in education and scientific understanding. A fascinating example of what can happen when all that is accepted is the negative image of Crete at this time is provided by the curious story of the so-called 'Antikythera Mechanism', whose discovery and investigation deserves a brief diversion.

This instrument was found between north-western Crete and the small island of Antikythera in 1900 in what became one of the first ever nautical archaeology investigations. The wreck was that of a three hundred ton Roman merchant ship probably bound for home laden with plunder, which included bronze and marble statues, coins, filled amphorae and many other items together with the encrusted remains of what has turned out to be one of the most remarkable scientific instruments ever discovered. The mechanism, which predates medieval clockwork machines of similar capability by more than a millennium, is an extraordinarily sophisticated lunar-solar calendar using the Metonic cycle (the 235 months it takes

13 The Roman historian Florus, recording these events, wrote, 'So severe were the measures which he took against the prisoners that most of them put an end to themselves with poison, while others sent an offer of surrender to Pompeius across the sea' (1.42).

for the full moon to appear in the night sky in the same position) and the Callippic cycle (four times the Metonic cycle or a 76-year period) together with an eclipse predictor using the more precise Saros (18 year 11.33 day) and Exeligmos or 'triple Saros' (54 year 33 day) cycles. One of the machine's 30 dials has been shown by X-ray tomography to be able to establish the precise dates of the main Panhellenic games held every two or four years. The dial identifies games held at Isthmia, Olympia, Nemea and Pythia, along with two other lesser events at Naa (held at Dodona) and another that awaits deciphering (*Nature* 454, Issue 7204, 31 July 2008).

In addition to exploring how this machine functioned, the other questions that have been asked concern when and where it was made, by whom and from where its passage commenced. Initial investigations suggested a date of manufacture in the first quarter of the 1st century BCE. This was the date of the badly eroded marble statues that turned out to be copies of earlier works. Some of the bronzes, however, dated back to the 4th century BCE, including the famous 'Youth of Antikythera' now on display along with the mechanism itself at the National Archaeological Museum in Athens. The amphorae suggested a date of 80–70 BCE while the Hellenistic pottery was dated to 75–50 BCE. The formation of the lettering on the dials of the mechanism, however, pointed to an earlier date and it is now more usual to accept that it was constructed between 150 and 100 BCE.

The machine is clearly of Greek manufacture and three main theories have been advanced concerning its origins. The first is that it was built by a craftsman from the Hipparchos school in Rhodes. It has been shown that the mechanism incorporates an ingenious way of coping with one of the anomalies in the Moon's motions and Hipparchos (ca. 190–120 BCE) was the first to develop geometric models for the movement of both the Sun and the Moon, including an understanding of these irregularities. Moreover, he spent the last twenty years of his life in Rhodes. The astronomer Poseidonios developed this thinking and according to Cicero, who studied in Rhodes in the 1st century BCE, managed to build a mechanism 'which at each revolution reproduces the same motions of the Sun, Moon and the five planets that take place in the heavens, each day and night'. If, as seems rather clear, the ship was laden with war booty, it is improbable that she could have set sail from Rhodes since that island had resisted a siege by Mithridates and remained an ally of Rome at this time.

The second theory is that the mechanism was plundered by the Romans as they reasserted control of Anatolia and the Black Sea regions following their initial defeat by Mithridates in 88 BCE. All of the contents of the ship could have come from Sulla's successes against Mithridatic forces in the 80s, particularly at Chaeronea. Alternatively they could have come from the penalties imposed on the cities of Adramyttium, Clazomenae, Ephesus, Miletus, Mytilene, Pergamum, Tralles and perhaps Phocaea as part of the reparations imposed on those cities that had supported Mithridates. But this says nothing about where the mechanism was made or who made it. The only thread of reasoning from this part of the world that might answer this question occurred later with the advances of the Roman General

Lucullus (Mastrocinque, 2009). Lucullus laid siege to the Greek cities of Sinope and Amisus on the Black Sea in 71 BCE and Strabo writes that 'Lucullus took away the sphere of Billarus and the Autolycus, the workmanship of Sthenis' (12.3.11). The 'Autolycus' was a famous statue but it has never been identified from the contents of the wreck and the mechanism was not strictly speaking a 'sphere'. Moreover, the astronomer Billarus is not known from other references, although astronomical or astrological spheres are mentioned in Strabo as having been constructed by Crates (2.5.10) while Cicero mentions the sphere of Archimedes and that created by Poseidonios in Rhodes.

The link with Archimedes (3rd century BCE) is also adduced in the third theory that was advanced following the results of the latest computed tomography and X-ray imaging which revealed the names of twelve months engraved on one of the inner dials.[14] These appear to be from a calendar from one of the Dorian-influenced regions. The suggestion in the 2008 article in *Nature* is that the names and sequence of the calendar from Tauromenion in Sicily come closest with seven of the named months being found in this Corinthian colony. Tauromenion had received settlers from another Corinthian city, Syracuse, and there is a connection therefore with the earlier studies of Archimedes, but it is very tenuous indeed.

On the question of the mechanism's last home before it was plundered, the picture is even less clear. Clearly it need not have been taken from where it was constructed and it is very striking that no one has suggested that it may have come from Crete, even though it sank so close to the island. Later dives on the wreck site by Jacques Cousteau brought up coins from Pergamon and Ephesus which, in the case of the former, were from before 67 BCE, the exact date that Cretan mercenaries would have ceased returning from these regions following the Roman conquest of the island. There is no reason to think that the celestial mapping that may have formed part of the world view of the Minoans was necessarily lost.[15] It is known that maps of the heavens circulating at that time must have been perceived by someone on or near the 36th parallel leading some to ask whether Crete was the 'ancestral home of the heavenly circles' (Kuzmin, 2001). If wealth, rather than piracy, was the main reason behind the early conquest of, say, Phalasarna, then some of what was on the doomed vessel could have come from here or from Knosos, which was also systematically sacked. At least three of the months engraved on the Metonic dial are Cretan (*Kraneios* at Knosos; *Agriamios* and *Appellaios* at Lato) and somewhere like Phalasarna had a very good reason to know when the Panhellenic games were due to take place since this *polis* was (or had earlier been) the first port of call of the Delphic *theoroi* on their passage from Kythera to western Crete and onwards further south and east for the purpose of arranging participation by major Cretan *poleis* in the games (Plassart, 1921: 59–60). Perhaps the most interesting possibility, however, is that the instrument was taken from Itanos. The Italian epigraphist Federico

---

14 The months are *Phoinikaios, Kraneios, Lanotropios, Machaneis, Dodekateis, Eikleios, Artemisios, Psidreis, Gameilios, Agriarnios, Panamos* and *Appellaios*.

15 The Lion and Bull symbols that are integral to Minoan cults are thought to be derived from celestial maps.

Halbherr reports walking to the very end of the promontory in the far north-east of Crete, which would have marked the northern extremity of the territory of Itanos, where once stood the temple of Athena Salmonia. When he visited (around 1890) there was a lighthouse at this point just beneath the chapel of Ag. Isidoros (from whom Cape Sidero gets its name). Halbherr describes an inscription now 'fixed in the wall above the door of a construction adjoining the lighthouse', which, he was informed, had come from the ruins of Itanos. Although the inscription appeared small and insignificant, he interprets it as furnishing 'an important contribution to the history of astronomy amongst the Greeks' (1891: 245). He continues:

> It contains, in characters which are not later than the fourth century B.C., the dedication made by a certain patron to Zeus Epopsios of a *heliotropion* or of some instrument made to determine the winter solstice, that period of the year in which, amongst the ancients, all navigation used to be interrupted [*sic*]. The words referring to the use of the instrument show that it was like the apparatus placed by the celebrated astronomer, Meton, on the Pnyx at Athens (1891: 245; emphasis in original).

This is not a sufficient proof, but the point is that when a Roman vessel carrying the treasures of war goes down off a major island that has just been conquered, it is not unreasonable to ask whether these two events might conceivably be linked.

Continuities of colonialism

Crete's extraordinary history over five millennia can be characterised in many ways but at its simplest it can be seen as having passed from a powerful, independent civilisation of non-Greeks, through a gradual process of Hellenisation to a more fissiparous but nonetheless creative era of Greek independence, then to a period of 2,000 years of dependency and subservience, not ending until the closing years of the 19th century. The vicissitudes of this final phase reflect the fortunes of three of the most powerful empires ever to have existed – Roman, Venetian and Ottoman Turkish.

More than a thousand years were to pass, however, before the impress of the Roman Empire faded entirely from the lives of most Cretans. As the Empire fell apart in the west, so too the eastern territories gained greater independence. By the fifth century AD diminishing resources and overstretched supply lines, together with mounting pressure from new or newly invigorated enemies, ensured that the Latin west and the Greek east would to all intents and purposes go their own ways. It was the combination of a Greek heritage, Christianity and Roman Law that were the building blocks of the Byzantine Empire that lasted from 331 to 1453, centred on its capital city, Constantinople. In the case of Crete, however, this period was foreshortened by the arrival of the next imperial power in AD 1212 and interrupted by an unwelcome interlude of Arab rule.

Attacks on Crete from the Arab world were becoming increasingly common in the centuries after the Roman conquest and the Christianisation of what remained of the empire. In AD 654, Rhodes was sacked and Cyprus and Crete also came under attack. The same happened in 675. In the spring of 828 a band of some 12,000 Arabs, coming from Andalusia via Alexandria, landed on Crete, which was then almost undefended (Treadgold, 1997: 436). Christos Makrypoulias refers to this conquest, and the creation of the Emirate of Crete, as 'a turning point in the struggle between the Byzantine Empire and the Arabs in the Eastern Mediterranean' (2000: 347). It created a Muslim state which tipped the scales in favour of the Islamic navies in the Aegean Sea (2000: 347). Mythologies surrounding the issue of piracy again became central since in 866 the Byzantines planned a campaign to retake Crete, which on some accounts had become a base for Arab piracy (Treadgold, 1997: 453; cf. Makrypoulias, 2000: 347). Another failed attempt to retake Crete occurred in 911 when the Byzantines mustered a fleet of 119 ships and 43,000 men, only to be defeated by the Saracen Arabs off Chios. In 949 another Byzantine expedition was mounted that was again unsuccessful. After this the Byzantines appeared to step up the level of attack and under the new Emperor, Romanus II, divided the *Scholae* (division of imperial guards) into an eastern and a western section. The former, under the command of Nicephorus Phocas (or Nikephoros Phokas), in the winter of AD 961 mounted a massive attack on Crete involving 77,000 oarsmen and soldiers. By killing 40,000 Arabs and placing their capital Chandax (Iraklio) under seige, they at last succeeded, but only because they had the good fortune to receive new supplies from Constantinople in the spring of 961 when starvation was facing both the Arabs holed up in the 'City of the Moat' and the Byzantine army just outside its walls (Makrypoulias, 2000: 361). The Byzantines were to retain this control for a further 243 years.

In the centuries after the reconquest, the major conflicts were between the Byzantines and the Latins, culminating – as far as Crete was concerned – in the former selling all Cretan holdings for 1,000 marks to the arbitrators of these disputes, the Republic of Venice, at the close of the Fourth Crusade. After a struggle with the rival city state of Genoa, which had first seized Crete, the Venetians eventually established their rule in AD 1212. The Venetian Senate was unusually involved in the day-to-day running of colonial Crete and McKee argues that the ethnic basis of Venice's rule over Crete laid the groundwork for a type of control found in later colonial models. She calls it 'a harbinger of modern colonization' (2000: 57). Initially, the two main groups (Greeks and Latins) were clearly separated with the colonial group dominant in all major regards. During these early years, Latin ancestry was all that was required to maintain the status of a free citizen, while Greek heritage made it possible for a person to be enslaved (McKee, 2000: 124). The colonisers controlled Crete's rural areas, often in large estates, but each Venetian landowner had to maintain a residence in Candia (Iraklio). Perhaps partly because of this, as well as through intermarriage, the spread of the Greek language to the colonial settlers, and a blurring of the boundaries between the two wings of Christianity, over time the distinctiveness between the ruled and the rulers tended to become less clear-cut. So although in these centuries frequent tensions existed between the Greek Orthodox Christians and the Roman Catholic Venetians, over time the boundaries softened. The most famous example is that of the 'revolt of St Titus' when adherents to the two branches of the church came together to oppose debilitating taxes imposed by the metropolis.[16] The Latin elite joined with wealthier Cretans in opposing an order by the Venetian Senate in August 1363 requiring them to pay a levy ostensibly to go towards the cleaning and maintenance of Candia's port (McKee, 2000: 133). It should not be thought, however, that the Cretans were passive bearers of this continuation of foreign rule. Many uprisings occurred, some of the most famous initiated by the residents of Sphakia in Crete's mountainous and inaccessible south-western region. The Sphakians saw themselves as direct descendants of the island's pre-Roman population and they have always played a vital role in fomenting opposition to foreign occupation, usually with the result that they have enjoyed a greater degrees of independence than elsewhere.

Eventually the expanding aspirations of the Ottoman Empire focused on Crete, culminating in the Cretan War of 1645–69 that brought most of the island under Ottoman control. Outposts of Venetian resistance included Candia, which eventually fell in 1669 after a siege of more than 20 years, and outposts on the islands of Spinalonga and Gramvousa and in Souda Bay that held out until 1715. Muslims, some of them Ottoman Turks and other converts from Christianity, eventually comprised approximately 60 per cent of the populations of Candia (Iraklio), Canea (Chania) and Rhethymnon, while a clear majority of small towns and rural areas remained Christian. There followed more than two centuries of suppression in which Cretans were again subjected to the violence and indignities of occupation. The frequency and intensity of uprisings against Turkish rule intensified in the 18th century. Again the Sphakians played a leading role, particularly in 1770 when the legendary Sphakian leader Daskaloyiannis (Ioannis Vlachos) from Anopolis led the uprising. Claiming to support Russian Orthodox ambitions against the Ottomans, Daskaloyiannis, having been promised Russian aid that never materialised, found himself arrayed against overwhelming Turkish forces from the cities of the North Coast, with the result that he and many other Cretan rebels were put to death with the utmost savagery.

It was hardly surprising, therefore, that as what came to be called the 'Greek War of Independence' gained momentum in the first two decades of the 19th century, Cretan uprisings also became more numerous and intense. Weakened by fighting on many fronts, the Turks drew in Egyptian assistance and, once it became clear that Crete would not be permitted to merge with newly independent Greece, the Egyptians played an increasing role in maintaining Islamic domination of the island. Indeed the governor of the island, an Albanian sent from Egypt and known locally as Mustafa Pasha, stayed on after Britain, fearing a weakening of influence in Turkey, forced Egypt to return Crete to Ottoman rule in 1840 (Stavrinos, 1992).

---

16 This revolt led to a change in the administration of the colony from a 'kingdom' to a republic. St Titus, the patron saint of Crete, is credited with bringing Christianity to the island in the first century AD.

More revolts followed in 1841 and 1858 that managed to secure a small measure of recognition for the Orthodox population, but by this time the goal of union with the newly independent Greek state was well established. This was the central plank of the demands that fuelled the major revolt of 1866, again leading to some concessions but not shaking Ottoman control. The bravery of the Cretan Christians in the tragedy at the monastery of Arkadi in November of that year, when more than 900 rebels and their families, faced with an overwhelming force of Turkish troops, blew themselves and their opponents up rather than surrender, brought renewed sympathy for the anti-Turkish cause. Yet another rebellion in 1878 led to a greater measure of autonomy, and the concession that the Ottoman governor had to be Christian, but again unrest broke out in 1889, on this occasion leading to the imposition of martial law and the hardening of Turkish policy towards the island as a whole and its Christian population in particular. Inevitably, the result of this was a more entrenched Cretan opposition to continued Ottoman rule, leading by the summer of 1896 to Turkey losing control of the island. Greek forces from the mainland attempted to intervene and this, when civil war looked likely, resulted in intervention by the so called 'Great Powers' (Britain, France and Russia) and the eventual declaration of autonomy under the authority of Prince George, son of King George of Greece, as High Commissioner.

Given the history of oppression, it is extraordinary that the northern European powers should have dallied so long in excluding the collapsing Ottoman Empire from Cretan affairs. Their motives were quite evidently concerned with appeasing the Turks to protect colonial interests further afield, but in so doing they created so great a confusion that, as Theodore Ion suggested at the time, diplomats might again need 'the clue or thread of Ariadne to find their way out of this Cretan labyrinth of modern times' (1910: 276). As he saw clearly, it was also a question of failed diplomacy, naked self interest and a disinclination to learn the lessons of the past:

> [O]ppressed both by the disciples of Christ and those of Mohammed, compelled to abjure their religion, at one time for the sake of the one, at another for that of the other faith, the Cretans are, what they were three thousand years ago, a branch of the Hellenic nation, and their island, the pearl of the Mediterranean, purely a Greek island, having never divested itself of its Hellenic soul (1910: 276).

Perhaps the greatest responsibility for this state of affairs lay with Britain, for it was only after the infamous 'massacre of Heraklion' in August 1898, when a contingent of British soldiers and officials were attacked and mostly killed by angry Turkish mobs bent on the destruction of Christians and their property, that Britain appeared to wake up to the realities on the ground. By November of that year the last Turkish soldier was ordered out of Crete by the British navy, something that could have been achieved decades before. As any student of recent Cretan history knows, even this did not bring an end to the 'Cretan Question'; it took the emergence of Eleftherios Venizelos, and his self-proclaimed declaration of unity with Greece from his base in Theriso in 1905, before actual unification seem likely. In the event, it was not until Greece, Serbia and Bulgaria declared war on the Ottoman Empire over Macedonia in 1912 that Cretan deputies were finally allowed to sit in the Greek Parliament. And it was only with the cessation of hostilities in 1913 and the Treaty of Bucharest that formal recognition of Crete as part of the Greek state was achieved.

What can be concluded from this brief summary of an extraordinary history? Above all else, one cannot help but be impressed by the dogged determination of Cretans to free themselves from the shackles imposed by others. The resistance shown by colonising powers also signifies how desirable the control of Crete was, both strategically and because of its native wealth. Sadly, as the centuries passed, the costs to the average Cretan rose from the relatively benign years of the Christianised Roman Empire, through the colonial repressions of the Venetians, to the alien presence of the hated Turks. The incidence of uprisings faithfully charts this worsening scenario. What memories must have been stirred in the minds of the elderly when, yet again, the Cretans were called on to defend their island after the German invasion of May 1941? But that is another story (see, among much else, MacDonald, 1995).

CHAPTER NINE

Implications for
the modern world

The Cretan *poleis* were pre-industrial societies and today, arguably, many of us live in a post-industrial world. Interdependency and predictability have reached levels unknown in the ancient world and with them has come a completely different approach to technological creativity. As Lyn Foxall recently reminded us in the conclusions to her fine study of olive production in ancient Greece, there was little incentive for adopting new technology or diversifying production when markets were unpredictable and where specialization could lead so easily to disaster (2007: 257). Moreover, it is not just on the production side that these differences exist. We take for granted the presence of institutions whose sole purpose is to commodify objects as valuable for consumption. In Foxall's words:

> The key issues for spotting the differences between us and them then become why the social locations where value is conferred on objects have expanded and how the range of institutions through which desire is fulfilled via consumption have come into being (2007: 259).

For those living in vast swathes of the world today, however, the worries of the post-industrial world are nearly as foreign as they were unknowable to the ancients. Thus the relevance of the lessons from the extreme past is perhaps clearer for today's 'developing' world than it is for those struggling to maintain their preeminence in the G8, the G20 or the other clubs to which the richer nations belong.

But this is not the only reason why the past is important. At its simplest, it is valuable to get it right. This study has argued against conventional wisdom but some of the conclusions need to be examined by further enquiry. This is especially true for the claims made concerning the evolution of an early form of capitalist economy. At another level, one might hope that the comparative element in this story would spur others to offer additional or better comparisons. That said, this chapter will conclude by focusing on three further issues. The first is the salience of the conclusion concerning the rule of written law for today's world. The second issue is why the promulgation of a new form of democracy might be considered an important innovation. Finally, the chapter will conclude by considering the significance of the *relationship* between the rule of law, forms of democratic accountability and the development of a market economy, because arguably that is what ancient Crete reveals.

Regulation and the rule of law

It is clear that the issue of whether the laws of Gortyn or other Cretan *poleis* meet modern criteria for the 'rule of law' turns partly on the evidence from Crete and partly on the definition that is applied to the concept itself. Brian Tamanaha (2004) offers some definitional guidelines, but more recently still an eminent British judge has attempted both a definition and a guide as to what the concept means in practice (Bingham, 2006, 2010).[1] The central principle of the rule of law on this interpretation is 'that all persons and authorities within the state, whether public or private, should be bound by and entitled to the benefit of laws publicly and prospectively promulgated and publicly administered in the courts' (2006: 5). He does not say so but there is no doubt that the reference here is to *written* law.

Tom Bingham then suggests eight sub-rules that follow as implications of this principle. On examination, these eight sub-rules fall into three categories that we may call for the sake of convenience 'substantive' (four), 'procedural' (two) and 'supplementary' (two). Two of Bingham's substantive sub-rules cover much of the ground outlined by Gagarin (2008); first, that questions of legal rights and liability should be resolved by the law and not by personal discretion, and second, that the laws of the land should apply equally to all 'save to the extent that objective differences justify differentiation'. When applied to ancient Crete, this second sub-rule may seem problematic unless one accepts that the divide between citizen and non-citizen or slave constitutes an 'objective difference'. This is clearly not what Bingham meant, but he does say elsewhere that 'a legal system may uphold slavery without violating the rule of law'. It cannot be concluded therefore that rigid social divisions negate the possibility of the rule of law.

Bingham's other two substantive sub-rules were not mentioned by Gagarin but had they been, the case for accepting that the rule of law obtained in Gortyn, and possibly elsewhere in Crete, would have been strengthened. The first is that 'the law must be accessible and so far as possible intelligible, clear and predictable', and Bingham quotes the European Court of Human Rights making the same point.[2] The main reason why we know something, albeit tantalisingly little, about the laws of the Cretan *poleis* is precisely that they went to great trouble to display them in a public setting. Earlier, we have sided with Gagarin in the literacy debate in believing that the Gortyn laws were meant to be read and, even if literacy rates were

---

1 The sections that follow were drafted before Bingham's book *The Rule of Law* (2010) was published but the book is largely based on the Sir David Williams Lecture given in 2006 that is used here (chapters 3–10; pp. 37–129).

2 '... the law must be adequately accessible: the citizen must be able to have an indication that is adequate in the circumstances of the legal rules applicable to a given case ... a norm cannot be regarded as a 'law' unless it is formulated with sufficient precision to enable the citizen to regulate his conduct' (quoted in Bingham, 2006: 6).

low by modern standards, that a significant proportion of the population could read them.

The final substantive sub-rule identified by Bingham is that 'public officers at all levels must exercise the powers conferred on them reasonably, in good faith, for the purpose for which the powers were conferred and without exceeding the limits of such powers'. It is usual to consider the evidence from Gortyn relating to the regulation of public officials as part of procedural or administrative law. Bingham's rule, however, opens up a different appraisal in which the same regulations can be viewed as helping to sustain the rule of law. The Gortyn regulations on public officials provide one general principle and two that relate to the exercise of legal decision-making. The general rule, found famously also at Dreros but probably evident in slightly different form elsewhere, is the one specifying the period of tenure of public office holders and the equally important exclusion clause governing the period before which public office can be held again. Corruption, and the potential for tyrannical rule, would have been severely constrained by a regulation accompanied by powerful sanctions that allowed for an official to serve for only one year in eleven (Dreros) or for one year in four (Gortyn).

The inscriptions from Gortyn suggest that the *kosmoi* served as both political leaders and as judges, but as Perlman (2002) reminds us, by the early 5th century the office of judge (*dikastes*) was added, possibly because of a need to keep legislative and executive powers separate. This was combined with enactments that guaranteed immunity from prosecution while in office, presumably in relation to both roles. While it might be possible to construe this as simply an enhancement of their powers, it is more likely that it was intended to meet the point made by Tom Bingham that the rule of law requires that office holders should be free to exercise their powers without let or hindrance. Finally, the Gortyn inscriptions include some fragments from the early 5th century appearing to make a provision that would force officials themselves to pay twice the fines they imposed in the course of their duties if a defendant did not pay up (Perlman, 2002: 204). In Bingham's terms this can be construed as constraining the temptation for officials to 'exceed their powers' by exercising favouritism in the collection of fines.

The two procedural sub-rules proposed by Bingham for the existence of the rule of law are, first, that access to the law must be straightforward and without undue delay or cost to the parties, and second, that court proceedings should be open and fair. There is no way by which we can be sure that legal restitution and remedy were freely available to the citizens of Gortyn or other Cretan cities, or that proceedings were sufficiently open for justice to be seen to be done. We do know that in some cases (e.g. adoption) both accepting an undertaking and rescinding an undertaking 'shall be made in the market-place, when the citizens are gathered, from the stone from which proclamations are made', which certainly suggests that part of the legal process took place under the public's gaze and, given the oral tradition and the openness of the architecture, it is highly probable that all or nearly all of the administration of justice was accessible (Merriam, 1886: 33).

Tom Bingham's modern interpretation of the rule of law includes two supplementary conditions that he observes are not necessary for the maintenance of the rule of law. The first is the need to protect human rights and the second is the need for compliance with the obligations of international law. It is fair to say that even a generation or so before the present, these points would not have been included, so it is perhaps reasonable to argue that requiring compliance with them in an entirely different cultural context operating twenty-five centuries ago is a step too far. The contention here, however, is that even when held up against a yardstick provided by a respected practitioner of Western law in today's world, the Gortyn Code, and perhaps other similar bodies of Cretan law, fare rather well, or at least well enough to argue that Gortyn and probably other *poleis* really did achieve the rule of written law, even as understood in a modern context. Other codes of law were certainly much earlier but none would have met the conditions that Bingham proposes. There is a great deal of difference between a body of laws and the *rule* of law.

Ethnic divisions and consociational democracy

Plato was among the first to spot the dilemma that lies at the heart of polities that are formed through migration from populations of diverse ethnic origins. Through the mouth of the 'Athenian philosopher' in the *Laws* he contrasts the situation where one ethnic group has been forced to migrate and settle elsewhere with the opposite, and more common, scenario in which new settlements are formed with peoples of diverse loyalties and cultures. The former suffer from an innate conservatism that leads them

> to kick against any laws or any form of constitution differing from that which they had at home; and although the badness of their own laws may have been the cause of the factions which prevailed among them, yet from the force of habit they would fain preserve the very customs which were their ruin ... (*Laws*, 4: l. 53–56).

The second pattern is much more dynamic and creative because no one perspective can be easily imposed, but this itself represents a major political challenge: namely, how to 'make them combine and pull together, as they say of horses'. It is, says Plato, 'a most difficult task, and the work of years'. This prescient observation, which from the context of the whole discussion was focused on Classical Crete, has a remarkably modern ring to it. From Northern Ireland to Iraq, from Burundi to Chechnya and from Canada to the Balkans we can observe the challenges that multi-ethnicity presents to a modern political system. It seems clear that 'one person-one vote' procedures are often divisive and, as such, undermine markets just as much as they do civil order. As Amy Chua has argued in a series of publications (1998, 2002, 2003) democratisation in its simple form deriving from Ancient Athens can generate powerful ethnonationalist tendencies that can lead to anti-market pressure or, even more extreme, attempts at exclusion (Chua, 1998: 6). The central point is that democracy based upon the principle of 'one citizen-one vote' tends to make things worse. Except in very special circumstances, it can have the effect of excluding minorities and thereby stultifying political change and undermining the institutions of the state. Political discourse in settings such as these all too easily descends into a struggle over resources, and violence is often exacerbated by the perception that the central institutions of the state are being used to sustain majorities in power and to repress the claims of those who do not believe they are being allowed to share in the social and cultural capital available to the majority.

The history of Western political thought draws a distinction between the role of popular participation and the practice of governance itself. Ancient Athens is usually credited with the initial impetus for the former but the emergence of larger nation states required another principle in which practising governance became the responsibility of *representatives* of the people. Even as late as the 18th century, Rousseau could argue in the *Social Contract* (Book 3, Chapter 15) that 'sovereignty cannot be represented for the same reason that it cannot be alienated', so that the British electorate, for example, was only truly free in a democratic sense when it voted and not at other times; but this was not an argument that eventually triumphed. According to the political scientist Robert Dahl (1989), democratic theory went through two major stages of evolution – the acceptance first of the Athenian principle of popular participation, and second, of the principle of representation – so that modern democratic theory is now firmly based upon the fusion of these two ideas.

In ancient Crete, however, the principle of representation was also clearly established, together with rules to ensure that no one representative could gather to himself a right to rule in perpetuity. This is not to argue that such a system was indistinguishable from modern forms; liberal democracy also entails a free press and a far wider definition of citizenship rights. In other words, the Cretan model does not come close to what Robert Dahl has termed 'polyarchy' (1989). The principles underlying 'polyarchy' include a franchise encompassing all adults, the equal right among all citizens to hold office, and freedom of expression and association. We know that the first of these was never applied in ancient Crete, but we have no idea concerning the others.

The tension, first noticed by James Madison (1996), one of the architects of the U.S. Constitution, between the principle of democracy and that of group loyalty was seen by him to be one of the main benefits of representative governance. With a large electorate and a strong constitutional system for regular voting, the possibility of a tyrannical majority would be lessened; indeed he felt that the 'public good' would be more probably safeguarded in a properly constituted representative system than the muddle that would emerge from a direct democracy. In many ways, John Stuart Mill (1951), often regarded as the father of modern liberal democracy, added to this notion because for him governance required professional competence, and systems of representation enable this to be incorporated through the selection of appropriate candidates for the legislature (cf. Held, 1996).

While one tradition of political thought on the concept of democracy traces its progress from an origin in ancient Athens, through the incorporation of the principle of representation, to what has been termed the 'Westminster model', another strand has emerged very strongly over the last four decades. Although the term had been used before, it was Arend Lijphart in 1969 who first set out what he termed 'consociational democracy' (Lijphart, 1969). What he had observed was that nation states with deeply divided populations could achieve political stability through a compromise among their elites while still maintaining forms of political accountability that were no less democratic than the more individualistic model derived from the Athenian precedent. As he defined it:

> Consociational democracy means government by elite cartel designed to turn a democracy with a fragmented political culture into a stable democracy (Lijphart 1969: 216).

Under this system, governance does not depend upon majoritarianism, but rather a forum is provided in which compromise through coalition can be achieved. The problem is that majoritarian democracy is based upon the assumption that individuals vote on the basis of a preference for policies set out by political parties. In fact in many parts of the world, particularly where individual preferences are subordinate to group loyalties, political appeals will be made to those identities rather than to ideologies of the familiar left-right form, and the result of democratic elections will simply be the continuance of one group's domination over all others. Empirical studies have charted the evolution of 'consociational' political systems in societies as diverse as South Africa, Belgium, Northern Ireland and Israel. All these are nation states with racial, linguistic or religious segments where without some form of compromise structure they would descend (or in fact have descended) into fractious political conflict. Ethnic segmentation is inherently unstable, but where political leaders are either wise enough or fearful enough, threats to political stability can be 'neutralized at the elite level by the use of various non-majoritarian mechanisms for conflict resolution, institutionally anchored by inclusive coalitions and proportionality in appointments' (Anderweg, 2000: 512).

Over time, as more empirical investigations were completed, four criteria emerged that have come to be taken as indicative of the presence of a consociational democracy – the existence of grand coalitions, segmental autonomy, proportionality and mutual veto. The term 'grand coalition' refers to a council or political structure that contains representatives from each of the constituent segments. They may take many forms in different settings but they include the principle of rotation or 'diachronic coalitions' (Anderweg, 2000: 520). It is not the mechanism itself that is crucial but rather the commitment and skill of political leaders who realise the consequences of not pursuing a self-denying strategy. As Lijphart makes clear:

> [T]he essential characteristic of consociational democracy is not so much any particular institutional arrangement as the deliberate joint efforts by the elites to stabilize the system (1969: 213).

At various times since the original formulation, Lijphart has mentioned conditions that make consociationalism particularly appropriate or likely to succeed (Lijphart, 1977, 1999). They normally include small size, a light administrative load, external threats, strong segmental identities but an overarching loyalty to the whole (Anderweg, 2000: 522). They also appear to operate most successfully where the segments are cross-cut by class loyalties or, in other words, where one ethnic group is not overly represented amongst the poor or the wealthy, but where each has class diversity within it. Other features that appear to be conducive to this strategy for achieving political stability include segments that are of roughly equal size and segments numbering between three and five (Anderweg, 2000: 524).

Almost all commentators have noted in addition the importance of organisations or associations that reflect membership from each social segment, possibly to articulate issues of concern for their members. In turn these organisations are often seen as one reason why consociational democracies sometimes retain their segmented structure when the original reasons for their existence have passed into obscurity. Consociationalism has short-term problems, such as building consensus among elites and negotiating with rather than dominating others, but it has clear long-term benefits in terms of societal survival (Anderweg, 2000: 529).

The central point of this excursus is clear. Ancient Crete pioneered this form of democratic accountability more than two and a half thousand years before political theorists identified it in Western Europe. The boards of *kosmoi* comprised grand coalitions. The constituent *phylai* with their representative institutions had segmental autonomy as their frequent identification in inscriptions testifies. The *kosmoi* were elected by their *phyle* for a limited period of office; the role of *protokosmos* was rotated (or the whole board was moved from one *phyle* to the next) and the outcome was a remarkable period of stability, in terms of both long-term survival and an absence of internal conflict in the *poleis* as a whole. We do not know if proportionality and a mutual veto existed but it is not unreasonable to expect, given this history of success, that they did. Certainly, there are many cases where the number of *phylai* listed in inscriptions is less than the number of *kosmoi* thought to have existed, which might suggest proportionality, and references at Gortyn and elsewhere to the '*polis*' as a whole could indicate the importance of consensus.

While there are some who would regard these forms of power sharing as inherently less democratic, that is not a view shared by most commentators. They point out that the issue turns on what one considers the main purpose of democracy to be. If it is simply accountability then competitive ('Westminster') systems have an important place, but 'if democracy is perceived as the avoidance of tyranny, inclusiveness is vital. Neither perspective is inherently more democratic than the other' (Anderweg, 2000: 531).

Power-sharing along these lines can be criticised in a number of ways. It has been argued that all forms of coalition governance slow down decision-making and that they reify ethnic differences that might otherwise decline in political salience (Barry, 1975a; 1975b). Lijphart would contest these assertions, showing through empirical analysis that 'consensus' democracies are not in fact so stagnant. They may show fewer fluctuations when compared with majoritarian forms but that does not necessarily mean inflexibility. Undoubtedly there is a tendency for segmentation to become reified, but many would consider that a price worth paying for the avoidance of ethnic conflict or even civil war. Moreover, Lijphart himself has come round to the view that a modified form of consociationalism, which he terms 'consensus democracy', is actually preferable to majoritarian rule, even where the original conditions of societal segmentation do not occur (Lijphart, 1999). Moreover, political leaders who have to depend on large coalitions to stay in office generally take actions that foster economic growth and political debate. The length of time political leaders stay in power is inversely related to the production of relative prosperity, so that systems that prevent longevity in power aid economic development (Bueno de Mesquita and Root, 2000). In other words, the general thrust of modern empirical research is to suggest that the Hobbesian solution to the problem of order – a powerful monarch – is far less desirable than a more republican set of institutions. For tyrannies what appears to be bad policy, such as rewarding cronies and elites, is actually good politics in the sense that it prolongs survival (Bueno de Mesquita et al. 2003: 19). On the other hand, more open systems promote *better* policy not because leaders are necessarily morally superior but because strategies designed to promote general welfare are the ones that aid political longevity. Inevitably systems based on representation, however variously democratic they may be, lead to greater turnover of political elites, even where this is not written into constitutions as it was in the Cretan case.

Regulated markets and trade networks

It has not been argued that ancient Crete achieved an economic system closely resembling what today would be called a 'capitalist economy'. What has been shown is that stable, regulated polities associated with a culture of acquisition prompted a major departure from the archaic notion of the inland city state, with its preoccupation with landed wealth and status honour, towards a more open, market-driven world coming to depend more and more on trade networks. This could be termed 'protocapitalism' to suggest what might have occurred if Crete had been able finally to resist the might of Rome. Clearly what is implied is a link between the rule of law, a form of democratic accountability and a market-driven economy.

In modern-day terms, that link has been shown to be rather more complex than this unilinear path suggests. Perhaps the most interesting empirical study is that by the Harvard economist Robert Barro (1997) which examines in detail the factors leading to economic growth, together with a later report that focuses specifically on the possible links between the rule of law (measured through property and commercial rights), democracy (measured through access to electoral representation) and economic performance (measured in terms of GDP growth) (Barro, 2000). The results are unambiguous and can be summarised as follows. First, there is no direct relationship between the rule of law and democratic institutions. The two may be found together in the Western world, but there are many countries that strongly sustain the rule of law without allowing democratic rights, and many with democratic rights that are not very firm on the rule of law. In the empirical study, thirteen out of nineteen countries in the former category came from the Islamic world, while in the latter five out of eight came from Central and South America. Perhaps of greater significance for the present study is that there is a definite relationship between the rule of law and economic growth and this, possibly through better schooling, may be linked to the promotion of democracy. The statistical effect of democracy itself on economic fortunes is weaker overall and where it can be seen it appears to operate through the mechanism of controlling the excesses of governments. Where democracy survives in wealthier settings it has a tendency to lead to greater claims for social welfare and this in turn impedes further economic growth (Barro, 2000: 41). Finally, the empirical analysis provides support for the thesis first advanced by Aristotle that democracy (by which he meant the Athenian variant) could only work in a setting where wealth was sufficient to allow the time for popular participation. Barro argues that:

> [I]ncreases in various measures of the standard of living forecast a gradual rise in democracy. In contrast, democracies that arise without prior economic development— sometimes because they are imposed by former colonial powers or by international agencies—tend not to last (2000: 42).

Moreover, although this result is predictive, so that at every level of democratic rights greater wealth will predict higher levels of democracy, this is only true if the wealth leads to greater investment in physical and human capital. If riches are extracted from the ground, or from those whose resources are plundered, then this effect does not occur (Barro, 2000: 43).

Barro's main conclusion is that anyone interested in economic development should focus on the rule of law, particularly in relation to property rights and free markets, rather than the electoral system. As he argues, 'if the legal system does not enforce the repayment of loans, then loans will be scarce and many productive investments therefore will not occur' (2000: 32). As a recent empirical study also concluded 'democracy enhances growth by establishing and enforcing rules that protect property rights, promote general education, allow accumulation of private capital, reduce income inequality, and facilitate demographic transitions' (Feng, 2003: 295). Political repression, political instability and political uncertainty all inhibit economic development. It is not democracy itself that is significant but political stability, security and property rights. Elections, for example, may be an effective method of gauging popular will; they could be regarded as necessary for a democratic polity, but they are clearly not sufficient. Indeed modern evidence suggests that without the rule of law, particularly that which relates to the conduct of public office and traditions of probity, elections can become intimately associated with the promotion of ethnic conflict, civil war and corruption (Collier, 2009). In other words, democratic principles are more likely to develop deep roots where the rule of law obtains, and where both exist, economic development itself becomes more likely.

The central argument, therefore, is that property rights and the predictability and integrity of contracts support trade by providing greater incentives for investment, which in turn raise the efficiency of resource allocation and therefore produce economic growth. This process also contains an informal nexus as well as that embodied in legal codes (Haggard et al. 2008). Unfortunately we know as yet almost nothing about these informal processes in the ancient world as a whole, and for this reason it is not possible to deduce quite how successful a favourable institutional context was in practice. For example, ancient Crete may have promulgated laws permitting high levels of social stability, and even pursued policies that were trade friendly, but we know very little about the effectiveness of enforcement or how these mechanisms were perceived by those subject to them. It is almost certainly true that 'credible third-party enforcement of property rights and contracts increases private returns, extends time horizons, and deters opportunistic behavior' but at best we can only know the *outcomes* of the economic calculus resting upon these perceptions (Haggard et al. 2008: 207).

Where the problem of social order has not been resolved, or there is what the Ancient Greeks would have termed a condition of *stasis*, the consequences are not just social, they are also profoundly economic. Resources are diverted into the mechanics of war and are likely to be consumed by the ensuing conflict. Crime and corruption are more likely and human capital is inevitably expended, not just through the losses of military manpower but also through disruption to civilian life. Even without civil war, corruption is a cost since it lowers returns on investment and thereby acts to deter it. Haggard et al. (2008) note that rule of law measures are now central to the World Bank's attempts to implant institutional reform as part of a development package. Democracy may represent one way of generating checks on governmental power but it is not the only way. It may depend on the type of democracy and whether it is accompanied by other rules regarding the length of tenure and return to office. Moreover, 'the stability and duration of political systems and the associated time horizons of leaders may be as significant as formal checks on government' (Haggard et al.: 215).

Perhaps partly because of a lack of precision about what 'democracy' actually is, modern econometric analysis tends to show that while both 'democracy' and the rule of law have measurably positive effects on economic performance, the latter has a much stronger impact on incomes (Rodrik and Rigobon, 2005: 538). The relationship between law and markets is both direct and indirect. In a direct sense laws exist that govern market exchanges but, perhaps of even greater importance, the stability and consistency of expectations generated by the rule of law allow markets to function at their most efficient level (Fried, 2000: 13). Butkiewicz and Yanikkaya

(2004) argue that both the rule of law and democratic institutions aid economic growth, but this appears to be through the effects of democracy on maintaining the rule of law. Adherence to the rule of law is manifested by maintenance of property rights and absence of corruption. These characteristics can serve as alternative measures of the establishment and practice of the rule of law. In the theoretical literature, the maintenance of property rights is considered one of the most important pillars of a free market economy. Well-defined property rights are an important determinant of economic growth through their effects on the level of investment (2004: 2). Particularly in rather undeveloped economies, measures of democracy are statistically linked to faster economic growth but possibly through these intervening factors (Butkiewicz and Yanikkaya, 2004: 11–12).

This is not irrelevant for the argument in the previous chapters. Arguably, ancient Athens started with a form of democracy, whereas ancient Crete started with the rule of written law. Those laws provided for a form of stable governance, less overtly democratic than that of Athens but tailored to peculiar local needs. They came to sustain property rights and, later still, more or less free markets. Above all, while economic progress may have been modest by comparison it was endogenously derived and not dependent, as in the Athenian case, on the costly vicissitudes of plunder.

Thus, far from being a place that was languishing in the Classical and Hellenistic periods, Crete was actively involved in reinventing its past. There is no way to be sure how much of this can be attributed to the 'Minoan heritage' but these are strands that deserve further exploration. In north-west Europe, cities emerged from a web of villages for religious, administrative or trade related reasons; they were in a sense created by the countryside. In Classical Crete the two were created as a unity, so that the city was the nucleus of an organic whole. Similarly, cities in the early medieval world tended to be located at the interstices of economic endeavour; they did not predate it. In Archaic and Classical Crete, the urban centre was the *political* force from which administration and trade emerged. These features were certainly shared by other city states that did not possess the heritage of the Minoan palace societies, but if it is true that Cretans invented the city state concept then ancient precepts could have played a part in shaping how this was achieved. It is not possible to determine with any certainty the continuities of culture that may have extended beyond a millennium from the Minoan times to the Classical era. In the opening chapter, the point was made that Cretan archaeology has been 'Minoanised' in the sense that the emergence of the communities of the Late Bronze Age became the prism through which all later developments were viewed, but this is a very different argument from suggesting a link between institutional progress and another civilisation a thousand years before. Rather, Classical Crete was a multicultural world in which the distribution of ethnic groups, while almost certainly reflected in settlement patterns, never gave rise to homogenous blocs. While some families and clans were clearly more important than others, the existence of rules governing the rights and duties of foreigners and the roles they played, together with the epigraphic evidence, suggest that each *polis* was culturally mixed. The evidence from much later periods suggests that multi-ethnic societies tend to be more vibrant and creative, provided there is mixing at the local level, even though 'otherness' may well play a significant role in inducing conflict. In other words, far from being a 'Dorian outpost' Crete from the Archaic period onwards was a multi-ethnic world whose inventiveness benefited from this cultural complexity. In terms of Colin Renfrew's (2001) approach, in which a contrast is drawn between 'individualizing' and group-oriented approaches to state formation and development, ancient Athens was towards one end of the continuum and ancient Crete towards the other. Sometimes in the latter these vertical divisions were territorial, as with the 'Eteocretans' possibly descended from the original population and found notably in the east, but more often they were not.

Subscribers to the view that innovation spreads by a process of cultural diffusion would see in Classical Crete an inward looking world unlikely to incorporate new ways of thinking. This judgment only makes sense if change is exogenous. If it springs from within, then isolation – or at least a disinclination to engage in external campaigns, colonial conquests and other foreign adventures – might be regarded as a positive force. Far from being negatively affected by being relatively cut off from what was going on elsewhere, the case for the opposite appears to be more plausible. The disinclination to tolerate monarchies, with their tendency to place tradition before reason, and the centrality of the rule of law both reflect a preoccupation with social integration and not simply with order induced by force of arms. The almost total absence of popular uprisings, especially when compared with Sparta, is not a reflection of greater levels of equality but it does suggest a superior system of administration and leadership.

Under these conditions, the solution to the Hobbesian problem of order, which all ancient Greek communities felt was critical, could not have been one of individual participation since that would simply cement the dominance of the group that was numerically superior. Cretan polities could share in the wish to demand of their officials compliance with the rules, but given the way the *phylai* were incorporated this had to be on the basis of rotation in office between the most appropriate representatives of constituent social groups, together with lengthy periods outside the body politic. Unfortunately, while we know the ethnic groupings identified in inscriptions, we have no clear idea of their numerical strength or whether those identified were *all* those that existed, so it is not easy to make connections between periods of exclusion from office and the number of groups that had to find a voice in the affairs of the *polis*. For example, Gortyn had only a three-year minimal period between assuming public office as a *kosmos* but there were at least six *phylai*, suggesting that in practice the period was longer unless it was common practice to recruit from more than one *phyle* at a time (Jones, 1987: 226).

Pillars of the modern world?

Many commentators have observed that being 'modern' is normally defined by a yardstick that encompasses multi-party democracy, an independent judiciary and a complex of economic institutions regulating free markets in industrial products or post-industrial services. By these standards only nations of the so-called 'developed' world fit the definition, and all others – whether in today's world or that of the past – can only be seen as 'developing' towards this ideal. On the other hand, if 'modernism' is a state of mind then both Ancient Athens *and* Ancient Crete might have fulfilled the criteria of being led by those bent upon doing things differently than before (Runciman, 2009: 188–189). But if modernism is defined in a different way as possessing the elements that would be needed to overcome the problems facing the majority of today's population, then the precepts from *some* societies in the past have greater salience. How many countries of the world would value a political system that adopted the compromise necessary to give representation in turn to the ethnic groups that comprised it? How many would aspire to a tightly controlled limitation on corruption and the abuse of power? How many would wish for all to be subject to law and due process? How many would appreciate the freedom to operate in almost free markets where material rewards, whether gained by trade or labour at home or abroad, could accrue to those who had earned them without interference from the state? Above all, how much enthusiasm would there be among city planners if it was possible to establish cities with an organic link with their surrounding lands, rather than the chaotic urbanisation that imperils progress in so many countries of the 'developing' world?

To establish validity for the claims made in the previous chapters is only part of the story. Does any of this have significance for the modern world? The answer is both 'yes' and 'no'. City states were absorbed into the structure of the Roman administration and whatever potential they may have had was largely dissipated in subservience to this external power. Creativity in the realm of ideas and institutions, even when successfully applied, does not necessarily have the influence it deserves if events unfold that constrain the adoption of these ideas elsewhere. But there is significance nonetheless. It can be argued that the three pillars that evolved to sustain the Cretan city states in the four centuries before the Roman imperial succession are essentially the same as those that came to support the Western world to this day.

The previous chapters have argued that Cretan city states were involved in the evolution of democracy, in establishing the rule of law and in the founding of a monetary system. We have seen that in each case, there are other contenders for these honours, but that none has quite such a compelling case for developing all three. It is this *linkage* that is perhaps of greatest significance. There is a contrast here between this argument in the Cretan case and the way others have approached the Athenian example. In the latter case many commentators have been impressed by the emergence of direct democracy out of tyranny; rather fewer have been persuaded that Athenian law constituted a precedent for the rule of law and fewer again have been prepared to argue that the ancient Athenian economy really did possess the seeds of the spirit of capitalism. In other words, there is a connectedness in the Cretan case that is arguably missing in the massively researched and documented Athenian literature.

The connectedness of the rule of law, forms of government accountability and the growth of free markets is not apparent when approached from the vantage point of neoclassical economics. *Homo economicus* maximises his returns through the rational pursuit of accumulation, without regard for the wider social and political context in which he lives. More modern approaches to market behaviour take a very different view. The 'new institutional economics', associated with the doyen of the movement, Douglass North (co-winner of the 1993 Nobel Prize in economics), argues that institutions are not exogenous; they rather mediate economic behaviour so that rationality is a cultural achievement, or in other words a critical part in any economic explanation (1973, 1981, 1990). Thus, if we wish to understand the direction and ultimately success of economic change then human organisational rules embodied in legal, social and political institutions matter.

This perspective goes beyond both neoclassical approaches (in, for example, price theory) and also beyond technological determinism. The latter point is palpable. Many poor countries have access to technologies imported from the richer world that have not made them any wealthier (North, 2005). This does not deny the role of the neoclassical concern with the maximisation of returns, but what it says is that the operation of neoclassical economic rules is mediated by both formal and informal rules. In the Cretan case, these would have been the formal rules governing property rights and contract law and the informal constraints arising, if Polybius is to be believed, from a culture of private acquisition. The Cretan institutions changed but slowly, and this itself can be considered an economic strength. Political instability is bad for economic growth and it can arise in part from a disjuncture between formal and informal institutional rules. As North concludes:

> When there is a radical change in the formal rules that makes them inconsistent with the existing informal constraints, there is an unresolved tension between them that will lead to long-run political instability (1990: 140).

Far from making an *assumption* of rationality, North urges us to understand it as a cultural product (2005: 25). When this is translated into the case of ancient Crete, we are confronted with a puzzle. On the one hand, communal dining and the strength of the communal ethos in general might not be conducive to wealth accumulation, notwithstanding favourable institutional arrangements. On the other, there is testimony to the high regard for *private* property and a culture of personal acquisition. Without further research, therefore, we cannot finally say whether the economic development that institutional arrangements suggest might have been seen was actually delivered in practice. Moreover, we are dealing with slow but sure change over time. The communal and egalitarian institutions that grew up alongside the early political and legal structures may not have survived the increased division of labour. If they did not, then further economic change would have become more likely.

In other words, it is important to stress that in the Cretan case, there appears to have been a temporal sequence in which the evolution of constitutions and the emergence of the rule of law preceded the development of ports and the major strengthening of trade links. For many years in the Western world, the assumption was that things were the other way round. Economic development was thought to be good for representative political institutions and the rule of law. The democratic revolution in Eastern Europe and the former Soviet Union demonstrated the opposite, and it is this that has now been shown in a large number of empirical studies from more than a hundred modern states. This 'new' thinking in the West has not only pushed the agenda for development towards the promotion of democratic institutions, it has also led to the emergence of the so-called 'rule of law' programmes that have as their objective the introduction of unbiased judicial procedures and non-arbitrary decision making (Jensen and Heller, 2003). It is extraordinary to note that Cretan and other city states more than two thousand years ago exhibited precisely this characteristic. It is important, however, not to overstate this case. While the Cretan experience, particularly the Gortyn Code, focused on civil law, as do most advocates of the role of law in development, it did not embody very clearly the separation of powers between the judiciary and executive that maximises a sense of political security.

There is an important distinction to be made between Athenian law and Cretan law, because the concept of the rule of law in ancient Greece is normally equated with the former. Athenian law was intimately linked with the popular concept of democracy in which all citizens made the law and played a part in its implementation. In other words, there were no court or state officials separate from the body of citizenry. To avoid a tyranny of democracy itself, the law was revered and tended to be set apart and be very difficult to change. Both Plato and Aristotle, who saw the rule of law as a way of ensuring that tyrannies of the people or of unjust autocrats did not prevail, supported this concept of the law as being unchanging and above the citizenry. Clearly Crete was not this kind of democracy and law in this setting may have been more amenable to change. Of course, there were similarities. Equality before the law, for example, did not mean that all were treated the same; rather it meant that all who were in the same category of the population (citizen, slave etc.) were treated in a similar way (Tamanaha 2004: 8). Unfortunately, however, in our present state of knowledge we simply do not know whether specifically Cretan legal traditions were more able to adapt to, say, economic pressures. The tone and tenor of the Gortyn Code suggest they were, but this remains an area for further inquiry. The argument herein has tended towards the proposition that Crete possessed commutarianism in politics and individualism in law and economics, and that Athens by contrast was more individualistic in politics but showed a more commutarian ethos in law and in economic life.

In recent years, governments of every political persuasion have battled with finding the balance between an overweening state on the one hand and uncontrolled markets on the other. The answer has been seen to lie in regulation, limiting the realm of the state and providing order and coherence to market and exchange relations. It can therefore be argued that the source of modernity lies in regulated institutions that work together. These were certainly inchoate in the Cretan case, but to a degree not found elsewhere at that time, they did exist.

GAZETTEER

The argument in the foregoing chapters depends mainly on the analysis of material provided by others. The aim was to put what is known together in new ways, rather than to uncover new material. This depended upon a selection of appropriate sites and the drawing together of what is known about them from pre-existing research on the periods under consideration. In turn, this was supplemented by site visits, including photographic records and the collection of mapping data. The Gazetteer is the result of that process.

There is no descriptive overview of all the Cretan city-states that places them in an economic and social context. There are, of course, detailed archaeological reports on individual sites, many of which are an essential source for a synoptic perspective such as this. Famously, there are the historical accounts, ranging from Homer's elaborations on his estimates of the number of city-states (100 in the *Iliad* [2.649]: 90 in the *Odyssey* [19.174]) to the ancient geographers who, with varying degrees of certainty, tried to describe where these were located and how they related to each other. In some cases, they are the only sources available, even though they occasionally disagree.

In the modern period four sources stand out as worthy of special mention because they list or map Cretan settlements in periods that are relevant to this book. The first of these is Ian Sanders's (1982) study of *Roman Crete* that includes an extremely helpful gazetteer of the locations of all the sites of Roman settlement. His focus is on a later period than herein, but many of the towns and villages that he mentions were also inhabited in the Hellenistic period, if not well before. The second source is the *Barrington Atlas of the Greek and Roman World* (Talbert, 2000). The map on Crete, compiled by John Bennett of Sheffield University in 1994, lists more than two hundred places or settlements of importance on Crete from the Archaic through the Roman era (Map 60 in the Atlas). These include geographical features (e.g. mountains, caves, promontories, islands/islets etc.) mentioned in ancient sources as well as outlying sanctuaries. The list is particularly helpful in that it provides close modern locations, as well as the sources that led to the inclusion of the ancient settlements.

The third source, appearing after the *Barrington Atlas* (*Barr*) and to some extent guided by it, is the inventory of *poleis* of the Archaic and Classical era compiled by Paula Perlman (2004a) that was published as part of a longer work from the Danish Polis Centre (Hansen and Nielsen, 2004). In a study of extraordinary scholarship, Perlman provides a summary of forty-nine *poleis* from the Archaic and Classical periods giving toponyms, together with a summary of epigraphic and some of the archaeological evidence for each. She even summarises the evidence for another fifty-one locations that are unattested as *poleis*, or whose whereabouts are unknown, thereby demonstrating the apparent accuracy of Homer's first declaration on the total number of 'cities' on the island.

The fourth listing is contained in a doctoral thesis by Lena Sjögren (2003). This work printed in book form as *Cretan Locations: Discerning Site Variations in Iron Age and Archaic Crete (800–500 B.C.)* is a detailed descriptive study of the archaeological evidence relating to 307 archaeological sites dating from these three centuries. Although the focus of the work is described as the 'early polis', in fact under half the sites are dwelling places and the descriptions of all but a small number of these are very brief. Nonetheless for nine *poleis* that existed before 500 BCE, the descriptions are valuable.

These sources were used to provide an initial list.[1] The criterion for selection was that either each settlement was known as a *polis* or there was some reason for believing that it had served as a port for a *polis*. From this list were removed those whose whereabouts were not just contested but unknown and those that were subsumed within a larger *polis* following a period of takeover and consolidation in the late Classical period. Therefore an additional criterion was that they had to have been functioning independently during the periods under discussion. This gave a total of 65 settlements (28 inland *poleis* and 37 coastal settlements, only some of which attained *polis* status).[2]

There is no doubt that a case can be made for other entries in the list that follows and in some instances those that are included may be controversial. The Gazetteer follows the logic of the preceding argument in listing the 'primary *poleis*' separately from the secondary (coastal) settlements of which fourteen may have achieved *polis* status in the period under review. In addition, four locations, all of them *poleis*, are identified as 'independent' cities in the sense that they were or became unattached to any other Cretan city. This raises the issue of why the other nineteen have been included, particularly since there are literally hundreds of other settlements from the same period that could have been chosen. The answer is that a coastal location is included if it appears to have been a dwelling place that had a role in providing access to the sea for an inland *polis* or was independent of any other Cretan city-state.

It is also important to enter a word of caution about the existence of toponyms and their attribution to a particular archaeological site. There are only three ways by which these tentative conclusions may be drawn. First, there are the toponyms found not only in Homer but in Polybius, Thucydides, Xenion and other ancient authors, some of whom were writing centuries after the foundation of the settlements they describe. Second, there are the ancient geographers such as Strabo and Skylax, and more modern authors who have specialised in identifying archaeological sites, ranging from Pashley and Spratt in the 19th century to Paul

---

1 Except Sjögren, which was not consulted until after the first draft was written.
2 In only two cases (Lachania and Pelkis) do we not have epigraphic information or coinage that would confirm *polis* status for these settlements.

Faure in the 20th century. Finally, there are cases (e.g. Aptera, Dreros, Gortyn) where inscriptions found on the site can be used to infer which it is, or where references in treaty inscriptions happen to mention physical features (rivers etc) as boundaries. Inevitably, some attributions are false, some sites have not been found and some are contested. This is in addition to the obvious problem that not all sites mentioned existed in 600 BCE and a number, including some that probably did, had disappeared by 67 BCE.

Strabo and Skylax (and to a limited extent Pliny) are useful in including cities and settlements in order from east to west or west to east. However, there is only one source published before the modern studies identified above that sets out settlements in order on each of Crete's four coasts, and then in a separate listing from west to east all those cities and settlements that lay in the interior. This is W. Smith's *Dictionary of Greek and Roman Geography* published in 1854. Smith identifies thirty-two settlements on the north coast, two on the east coast, sixteen on the south coast, five on the west coast and forty-two in the interior, a total of ninety-seven in all. Smith's ordering is reproduced below with his original spellings. These are compared with those of the modern authors cited above, particularly the *Barrington Atlas (Barr)*. There is considerable agreement as to where settlements existed, with some important differences of view. Where one of Smith's entries is contained in the Gazetteer, the name is listed in bold and the reader is referred to that longer entry. In general those settlements that are identified by Smith, but not included in the Gazetteer, are of Roman (R) date, although there are some cases where the location is unknown or contested, one or two that were satellites of larger centres and a few that were too small for inclusion.[3]

ON THE NORTH COAST IN THE DIRECTION FROM WEST TO EAST:

Agneum On eastern side of modern-day Gramvousa Peninsula (ancient Korykos Pr) (Gondicas, 1988: 145).

Cisamus **Kasteli** (q.v.).

Methymna (port of Rocca) Listed in *Barr* as HR Nopigeia (Gondicas, 1988: 275–76).

Dictynna Listed in *Barr* HRL Diktynnaion / Menies Bay (Gondicas, 1988: 287–96).

Pergamum Listed in Barr as Pergamos or Pergamia ACHR Grimbiliana: Ag. Eirini (Hood, 1965: 105–106; Gondicas, 1988: 280–85; Plutarch, *Lycurgus* 31) but cf. **Polyrrhenia** (q.v.).

Cydonia **Kydonia** (q.v.).

Minoa Listed in *Barr* as HR Marathi; PECS Marathi.

Marathusa Listed in *Barr* as unlocated toponym (Marathousa / Moratousa) of Roman era in the region of Kydonia? (Mela 2.113; Pliny, *NH* 4.59; Faure, 1993, 73).

Aptera **Aptera** (q.v.).

Cisamus port of Aptera included as **Kalami** (q.v.).

Amphimatrium included in *Barr* as false toponym for **Amphimalla** (q.v.).

Hydramum **Hydramia** (q.v.).

Amphimalla **Amphimalla** (q.v.).

---

3 Abbreviations are used for periods in this listing (e.g. H = Hellenistic; C = Classical; A = Archaic; R = Roman). PECS refers to the *Princeton Encyclopedia of Classical Sites*.

Rhithymna Rhithymna (q.v.).

Pantomatrium Pantomatrion (q.v.).

Astale Listed in *Barr* as a Roman settlement at Bali (Sanders, 1982: 13/4).

Panormus Listed in *Barr* as 'Panormus/Aulopotamos? To the west of Astale and Roman or later (Mylopotamou/Panormos IC II: 142; Faure, 1960, 240, no. 17; Sanders, 1982, 13/3).

Dium Listed in *Barr* as 'Dion' promontory close to Astale (ancient Korakias Pr). (IC II: 43; van Effenterre, 1991: 18–19).

Cytaeum included here as **Kytaion** (q.v.)

Apollonia this is probably the site listed as Apellonia or Apollonia in *Barr* as ACH near Ag. Pelagia but see **Apollonia** (Sanders 1982, 9/1; Alexiou 1984).

Matium This may be a false toponym (Faure, 1960: 248).

Heracleum Herakleion (q.v.).

Amnisus Amnisos (q.v.).

Chersonesus Chersonisos (q.v.).

Olus Olous (q.v.).

Miletus Milatos (q.v.).

Camara Kamara (q.v.).

Naxus whereabouts uncertain but Naxos (Νάξος) sometimes believed to be identified with remains south-east of Elounda near the modern village of Kalos Lakos.

Minoa included in *Barr* to the east of Istron as HR at Pakheia Ammos (PECS Pachia Ammos).

Istron Istron (q.v.).

Etea almost certainly at modern Siteia listed in *Barr* as 'Setaea/Etis' (H and later) (Sanders, 1982: 1/12). This is possibly the same site that is identified today as **Trypitos** (q.v.). *Barr* includes another settlement labelled 'Polichna' at approximately this location just to the east of Siteia.

Grammium listed in *Barr* as unlocated (Faure, 1960: 236). Pliny, however, says that 'Granos is the promontory of Crete towards the rising sun' (4.20).

ON THE EAST COAST:

Itanus Itanos (q.v.).

Ampelos listed in *Barr* as HR Farmakokefalo/Kastri (Sanders, 1982: 1/30; Schlager, 1991: 23–25).

ON THE SOUTH COAST, IN THE DIRECTION FROM EAST TO WEST:

Erythraea not positively identified but *Barr* lists promontory called Erythraion close to the possible location of Syrinthos an ACH settlement and it could be the same place (Schachermeyr, 1938: 479; Faure, 1959: 192; 1960: 238, no. 86).

Hierapytna Hierapytna (q.v.).

Hippocronium *Barr* does not identify this location as a settlement but lists 'Hippokoronion' as the possible ancient name for Mt Drapanokephala (Faure, 1988: 88). This is not, however, in the right location for the listing in the Smith dictionary (i.e. the first coastal settlement west of Hierapytna which would have been at **Myrtos** q.v.).

Histoë not identified. A mountain range at Hieron/Arbion or modern-day Mt. Keraton is a possible location (Hood et al., 1964: 84; Sanders, 1982: 7/15; Kitchell, 1983). The coastal settlement at **Arvi** (q.v.) is also very close.

Priansus Priansos (q.v.) Early commentators, including Smith, located this *polis* on the coast at Tsoutsouros but this is now believed to be the site of **Inatos** (q.v.), the port of Priansos.

Leben **Lebena** (q.v.).

Matalia **Matala** (q.v.).

Sulia **Soulia** (q.v.).

Pyschium identified in *Barr* as HR at east of Psycheion promontory (Cape Melissa) (Hood and Warren, 1966: 170).

Apollonias *Barr* includes Apollonia just to the south of **Phoinix (Sellia)** (q.v.) and these are probably the same place (cf. Hood and Warren, 1966: 184; Sanders, 1982, 15/2).

Phoenix **Phoinix (Loutro)** (q.v.).

Tarrha **Tarrha** (q.v.).

Poecilasium Poikilasos – a small settlement listed in *Barr* as CHR (Trypiti PECS) that was probably a member of the Confederation of the Oreioi.

Syia **Syia** (q.v.).

Lissus **Lisos** (q.v.).

Calamyda **Kalamydi** (q.v.).

ON THE WEST COAST:

Inachorium the exact location is unknown. *Barr* follows Gondicas (1988: 77–78) in locating Ina Chorion as a CHR settlement at Vathi (formerly Kouneni) some distance inland.

Rhamnus location unknown. *Barr* identifies 'Rhamnous Limen' at the modern-day Stomiou Bay.

Chersonesus *Barr* follows Gondicas (1988: 80) in locating ancient 'Chersonesos' as a R settlement at Cape Karavoutas or Koutoulos.

Phalasarna **Phalasarna** (q.v.).

Corycus not listed in *Barr* but was probably on the Gramvousa (ancient Korykos). Modern-day islets Gramvousa and Agria Gramvousa used to be known as the Korykiai Islands and the settlement may have been on one of these (Gondicas, 1988: 146–50).

IN THE INTERIOR OF THE ISLAND FROM WEST TO EAST:

Eleaea the whereabouts of this settlement is unknown but Gondicas (1988: 163) suggests that the town of Elaia was on the Selli promontory very close to Kasteli (Kissamos). Pliny identifies Etæa after Phalasarna in a list going west to east (Pliny 4.20).

Polyrrhenia **Polyrrhenia** (q.v.).

Rocca Listed in *Barr* as *Rokka* and located on the flanks of the Trouli hill just above the modern village. This is definitely a CHR site but may have been a dependency of Polyrrhenia (cf. Sanders, 1982: 20/18; Gondicas, 1988: 265–69).

Achaea *Barr* lists Achaia as being unlocated but in the region of Polyrrhenia (Kitchell, 1977: 43–50; Gondicas, 1988: 258–60). Thenon (1867: 115), however, believed that it was located at Temenia (Hyrtakina).

Dulopolis According to *Barr* 'Douloupolis' is probably a false toponym and may therefore never have existed, but if it did it may have been a mining settlement near Sklavopoula dependent, as its name suggests, on slave labour (Faure, 1960: 236; Gondicas, 1988: 67–69).

Cantanus **Kantanos** (q.v.).

Hyrtacina **Hyrtakina** (q.v.).

Elyrus **Elyros** (q.v.).

Caeno The location of this settlement or city is not certain. Its position in this inland listing, might suggest somewhere near Kydonia. Modern-day Kaina (Apokorona) is a possibility but the absence of remains argues against this.

Cerea This position supports Faure's (1963: 18) view that **Keraia** (q.v.) was an HR *polis* at

Meskla. This location is supported in *Barr* and also in Perlman (2004a) who regards it as a probable *polis* in Archaic times.

Arden or Anopolis **Anopolis/Araden** (q.v.)

Polichnia *Barr* (Polichna) and Perlman (2004a) (Polichne) both follow Faure (1963: 21–22) in placing this settlement near to Vryses at Ag. Georgios. See entry for **Polyrrhenia** below for why this is not very likely.

Mycenae The location of this settlement is not clear. *Barr* cites Sanders (1982, 20/9) and (Gondicas, 1988: 156) in locating Mykenai near to Kasteli which is far to the west of the location suggested in this listing.

Lappa or Lampa **Lappa** (q.v.).

Corium or Korion *Barr* identifies this as a CH settlement at Melambes, Voulgari Armokastella following Hood and Warren (1966: 169–70).

Aulon *Barr* follows Kitchell (1977: 316–18) in placing Aulon/Alonion at Agioi Deka where it would have been a suburb or dependency of Gortyn. The suggestion here, however, is that it was further to the west.

Osmida *Barr* suggests that Osmida is a H settlement of unknown location but possibly at Monopari (Scylax 47; IC II: 141). However, it has also been identified by others at what is now thought to be **Phalanna** (q.v.).

Sybritia **Sybrita** (q.v.).

Eleutherna **Eleutherna** (q.v.).

Axus **Axos** (q.v.).

Gortyn or Gortyna **Gortyn** (q.v.).

Phaestus **Phaistos** (q.v.).

Pylorus *Barr* follows Sanders (1982: 10/15) in suggesting Pyloros was the Roman town Plora in the Mesara.

Boebe *Barr* puts this close to Pyloros as another Roman settlement (Pompia) (Kitchell, 1977: 382–87).

Bene *Barr* agrees this ACH settlement was to the east of Boebe and just north of the Asterousia range at Panagia, Kastelos (Kitchell, 1977: 325–30).

Asterusia *Barr* follows Kitchell (1977: 301–304) in locating this H settlement in the Asterousia range.

Rhytium Rhytion/Rhytiassos ACHR settlement at Rotasi in the eastern Mesara. Perlman (2004a: 1186) argues that it was a *polis* in its own right but also a dependency of Gortyn.

Stelae **Stalai** (q.v.).

Inatus **Inatos** (q.v.).

Biennus **Biannos** (q.v.).

Pyranthus *Barr* follows Sanders (1982: 7/26) in identifying this as a Roman settlement (Pyranthos) at Pyrathi, Trokhales in the northern Mesara but to the west of Biannos.

Rhaucus *Barr* places Rhaukos to the south of Tylisos at Ag. Myronas. Perlman (2004a: 1185) agrees on this location and argues that this was an important *polis* town at least in the early Hellenistic period and probably before. There are references in inscriptions to its borders with Knosos and Gortyn but it was destroyed by these city states and its land divided.

Tylissus **Tylisos** (q.v.).

Cnossus **Knosos** (q.v.).

Thenae Listed in *Barr* as a toponym (Thenai) of H date at an unknown location SW of Irakleion (Faure, 1960: 233; 237). Note also the sanctuary of Zeus Thenatas ACHR at Palaiochora/Amnisos (PECS Karteros; Schäfer, 1992).

Omphalium Listed in *Barr as* 'Omphalion' of H date at lower Platyperama/Giophyros valley (IC I: 45).

Pannona identified by *Barr* as to the east of the Ida mountains in the central area at Ag. Thomas. A Roman site. (Sanders, 1982: 7/2; Faure, 1993: 70).

Lyctus **Lyktos** (q.v.).

Arcadia **Arkades** (q.v.).

Olerus **Oleros** (q.v.).

Allaria It is interesting that Allaria should be identified as being so far to the east since both *Barr* and Perlman place it at Chamalevri many kilometres to the west and just east of Rhithymna. This location is not very plausible (see **Pantomatrion** below) but in this case the site of Allaria is unknown. Belli in the 16th century located the *polis* in the east, 7 miles south of Praisos at 'Monteforte' (cf. Falkener, 1854: 270).

Praesus **Praisos** (q.v.).

As far as the inland (Primary) sites are concerned, Smith's dictionary only omits four that are contained in the Gazetteer (Dreros, Lato, Anavlochos and Pelkis). Of these, Anavlochos is not surprising since it may have gone out of existence in the 3rd century and in any case its toponym has never been established. The omission of Dreros and Lato is puzzling since they are of major importance. It is possible that they were known at one time by other names, but this is unlikely since the epigraphic evidence for their location is in both cases very strong. Although they are not all in the position suggested herein, Smith's dictionary included all of the coastal sites in the Gazetteer if we can accept that in some cases other names may have had more common currency at the time of its composition. The absence of the isolated settlement of Pelkis is not surprising. Our knowledge of this settlement is very limited and it could have been a sanctuary rather than a fully-fledged *polis* (but see following entry under **Pelkis**).

The *Barrington Atlas* entailed professional cartography of a high order but does not provide location co-ordinates. The Perlman listing provides co-ordinates, but it is unclear how they were obtained and they only record Longitude and Latitude data to two decimal places. Geographical Information Systems (GIS) estimates from these data proved too imprecise to be very helpful for mapping purposes. More accurate data were obtained from the database of archaeological sites on Crete run by the Institute of Mediterranean Studies (FORTH) in Rethymno. These data were in the Greek Projection System (EGSA'87 or HGRS'87) but were only available for some of the sites included here. They were supplemented in more than forty cases with co-ordinates obtained from a handheld GPS instrument which is accurate to within 3m (5 decimal places). The co-ordinates were taken from a central location (often a temple site on an acropolis). The Gazetteer provides decimal co-ordinates for all included entries in Lat/Long (WGS84/World Geodetic System 1984) but EGSA'87 projections, together with WGS84 in conventional format (degrees, minutes etc), are contained in a table at the end of the Gazetteer.

I – The Primary Poleis [4]

Anavlochos (Ἀνάβλοχος)

Location: 35.28060°N; 25.56114°E

This site is located on the Anavlochos hill at an elevation that reaches 625m above the modern village of Vrachasi. Sherds and extensive remains of walls suggest occupation from as early as 900 BCE through at least to the Classical era (Demargne, 1931: 365–407; Mariani, 1895: 244–246, Taramelli, 1899: 393; Sjögren, 2003: 160). The remains of a massive wall running north-south on the west of the settlement suggest that the whole site may have been fortified at one time although Sjögren (2003: 27) disputes this (cf. Driessen and Farnoux, 1991: 749–50; Nowicki, 2000: 171–173).

North of the settlement site, there are remains of what was interpreted when excavated as a cult site, largely because of finds that included a number of anthropomorphic terracotta figurines and plaques dating from the 7th–6th centuries (Demargne, 1931: 379–407; Sjögren, 2003: 160). Slightly further north are two excavated rock-cut *tholos* tombs dating from the 8th century. A city state may have been established here in the Archaic period and if so, its remains are to be found on a saddle of land at 462m between two acropolises to the north-west and south-east on whose flanks are the remains of extensive structures. The remains of further buildings can be seen at the valley head to the north-east of the saddle. [5]

The topography suggests that Anavlochos would have access to the sea at Milatos, 5–6km to the north and visible from the north-west acropolis. The latter is thought to have been destroyed by Lyktos ca. 220 BCE and it is very likely that the same fate befell this probable *polis*. The toponym for this site is unknown. Paul Faure identifies the toponym *Prepsida/Prepsidai* as an Archaic site lying between Dreros and Milatos, but it is unclear whether he is referring to these remains (Faure, 1960; 233, 238). *Barr* and Perlman (2004a) list this toponym as at an unknown locality.

Anopolis/Araden (Ἀνώπολις/Ἀραδήν)

Location: 35.21213°N; 24.08585°E (Anopolis)
35.22301°N; 24.06190°E (Araden)

The urban centre of Anopolis was located at 675m on the Riza ridge above the modern village of Loutro in southern Crete (Sphakia). There are remains of cyclopean walls showing evidence of fortifications with towers (Nixon et al., 1989). There are also some remains of cisterns and a water supply from the same date. The port for the city was on the coast below at ancient Phoinix on the eastern side of Cape Moures.

Anopolis signed the alliance treaty with Eumenes II and also a decree with Lappa in the 2nd century (Sanders, 1982: 165). In Pashley's judgement, the city state was Hellenistic, although it was also occupied during Roman and later periods (Pashley, 1837, II: 241–243). Bronze coins from Anopolis have been found dating from the 3rd century (Svoronos, 1890: 5–6).

Some confusion exists between this site and that of Araden, three kilometres to the west above an eponymous gorge. The latter is of Hellenistic date and it may represent a refounding of Anopolis. The site of Anopolis is exposed and unforgiving, suggesting that defence was a major issue in its founding. Araden is a little lower (587m), more sheltered and has slightly easier access to the sea via an ancient pathway down the Aradena Gorge. It may therefore have been preferred as trading opportunites replaced defensiveness as a major priority. Certainly Perlman (2004a) suggests the refounding theory and Stephanus Byzantius (*Ethnica* – 6th century AD) also thought they were the same place. On the other hand the list of *poleis* produced as a result of the Delphic *theorodokoi* identifies both places separately and both appear to have had their own mints. If they were separate then they were not completely so for they appear to have shared the all weather harbour at Phoinix (Loutro).

Aptera (Ἀπτέρα/Ἄπτερα)

Location: 35.46268°N; 24.14101°E

The urban centre of Aptera/Aptara is located on a plateau, some 230m above Souda Bay 12km to the east of Chania. The walls of the

---

4 The listing is in alphabetical order.
5 The topography of this site and its land use patterns are discussed in Wallace (1997–2000) but not the question of whether it ever achieved *polis* status.

city, built in various styles and far more elaborate to the north and west, extend to 4km and enclose an area of more than 60 hectares. The general view is that this area was administrative and sacred rather than residential. There are indications of up to eight residential areas on the sides of the Stylos valley to the south.

References to the city extend as far back as the Minoan period, but they probably refer to the Stylos site 2km away. References to a *polis* can be found in *proxenia* decrees of the 2nd century when there are also mentions of harbours at Kisamos (not Kasteli Kisamos), probably near Kalami (q.v.) (cf. Perlman, 2004a: 1151; Spratt, 1865).

Many of the buildings that are visible today date from the Roman period or later, but temples and (unusually) a theatre are Classical and Hellenistic. The small temple to the south-west of the monastery of St John of Patmos (which occupies the centre of the site) is from the 5th century and is notable for its heavy bronze clamped ashlar masonry. Near to the theatre (recently restored in part) is another small temple in the Dorian style. West of Aptera is Mt Malaxa (ancient Berekynthos) which, according to Diodorus Siculus (Greek historian writing in the 1st century BCE), in Cretan legend was the home of the Idaean Dactyls who discovered both the use of fire and the working of copper and iron. Diodorus writes (Dio 5.64.5) that, contrary to later legend, it was one of their number, Herakles, who established the Olympic Games (cf. PECS; Pashley, 1837, I: 58).

For reports on the results of recent archaeological investigations see Andreadaki-Vlasaki, 1989–90 and Niniou-Kindeli (1993; 1994; 1995; 1999). The cemeteries are on the southern periphery and on the ridge to the west near the village of Megala Chorafia where there are numerous rock-cut tombs. These have produced many finds of Classical and Hellenistic date (Niniou-Kindeli, 1990). Recent work has provided information on an extensive road network that appears to be Roman, but may have had earlier origins (Baldwin Bowsky and Niniou-Kindeli, 2006). Certainly the evidence suggests that the *polis* had a major trading role, both internally and externally (Svoronos, 1890: 13).

The coins of Aptera are often early, possibly starting to appear from the middle of the 4th century. These coins are on the Aiginetan standard, showing the head of Artemis of Aptara and the legend ΑΠΤΑΡΑΙΩΝ (or ΑΠΤΕΡΑΙΩΝ) on the obverse with an armed bearded warrior standing with hand raised to salute a sacred tree on the reverse. Later coins tend to have a head of Apollo on the obverse. Some examples mention the artist's name ΠΥΘΟΔΩΡΟΥ (Pythodoros) who also sometimes appears on coins of Polyrrhenia.

Arkades *(Αρκάδες)*

Location: 35.10276°N; 25.34056°E

Both the list of Archaic and Classical *poleis* in Perlman (2004a) and the *Barrington Atlas* suggest that the site of Arkades is on the side of a low rise south-east of the village of Ini, 5km to the north-west of modern Skinias. In this they are following the view of Svoronos expressed in 1896. However, in the same year, the Italian epigraphist Federico Halbherr, the excavator of the Gortyn Law Code, doubted the attribution of Arkades to the site at Ini, preferring instead the hill at Prophitis Ilias west of Aphrati which he says 'corresponds far better to the importance which this city is known to have had in ancient times' (Halbherr, 1896: 564).

There is indeed nothing about the site at Ini which supports its attribution as Arkades. The site is too low and accessible (260m at the summit) and the area is simply too small at under 10ha. There is also no evidence of building stones outside an area that was excavated in 1924. There are ample sherd scatters on the hill itself but these are mostly early, suggesting pre-Classical use. The excavated site is a mixture of Geometric walls and foundations with Roman material.

On the other hand, the site at Prophitis Elias, west of Aphrati and a few kilometres to the east of Ini, which Halbherr preferred, is a large (50+ha) very imposing site at 672m with commanding views over the eastern end of the Mesara. Below the church at the acropolis there is evidence of a larger temple structure made from ashlar blocks. The heavy sherd scatter is of Archaic through Hellenistic periods (cf. Erickson, 2002).[6]

References to Arkades as a *polis* occur in the agreement of Miletos in the middle of the third century (Perlman, 2004a: 1152). Arkades struck silver and bronze coins on the

---

6 Perlman (2004a) and the *Barrington Atlas* list the site at Aphrati as Datala. In rejecting this, the implication is that the site of ancient Datala remains unknown (but cf. Viviers, 1994).

Aiginetan standard during the period ca. 330–200. These have images of Zeus on the obverse and Athena standing armed and, in later coins, laurel wreathed on the reverse.

It is not known where Arkades had an outlet to the sea. One possibility is at the mouth of the Anapodaris River at Ag. Ioannis. Just south-east of Aphrati is the source of a tributary of the Anapodaris (Parissia) and footpaths are marked that link the village of Demati, lying in the valley of the river, and the low land at the mouth of the Anapodaris. However, other ancient tracks and and plentiful Minoan remains around the village of Chondros suggest that Kastri / Keratokambos was the more likely port since signs of earlier occupancy often appear significant in determining the track of ancient pathways (cf. Sjögren, 2003: 45).

Axos (Αξός)

Location: 35.30798°N; 24.84420°E

Axos (Oaxos) may have had a very long history from the Early Iron Age to the Venetian era. The urban centre of ancient Axos was located on a substantial flat-topped hill (587m) above an eponymous modern village 11 km west of Tylisos and just north of Mt Psiloritis. The acropolis has 360 degree visibility particularly along a north-west corridor to the coast 11km distant. It would have been relatively easy to defend. The town centre extended towards Livada to the north-east and occupied an area of at least 40ha. A 2nd century inscription describing the borders of Gortyn and Knosos also mentions Axos as having adjacent territories. It is probable that the *polis* territory bordered Eleutherna to the west, Tylisos to the east and Gortyn to the south-east.

It is not entirely clear where the *polis* had sea access and some have suggested a site at the western side of the Almyrida Bay at Bali, but the topography and ancient footpaths suggest a more probable location at the eastern side of the bay near Sises (Kytaion q.v.).

It has been claimed that Axos in the Geometric era was ruled by the only post-Minoan king known on the island (Perlman, 2004a: 1153). Later administration was entrusted to a board of three or four magistrates whose members were elected by the citizenry of the *polis*. They reserved the right to fine their leaders for poor performance. Most coins that have been found feature the head of Apollo and date from 380–270 BCE.

The site contains the remains of two temples from the Archaic era, one on the acropolis and the other below the summit to the east (Levi, 1930–31). The protecting deity was probably Apollo and Perlman suggests that the former may have been dedicated to him (2000: 73). Levi's excavation in 1899 found votive fragments of female forms in the lower temple that suggested to him that Aphrodite was worshipped there (1930–31: 50). Perlman argues that she was Astarte-Aphrodite, Artemis, or Athena and suggests that the worshippers may also have been women (2010: 105).

There is a large cistern to the north-west of the summit together with what may have been the *andreion* referred to in inscriptions (Perlman, 2004a: 1154). Paula Perlman, following Guarducci, also suggests that some of the Archaic laws of the *polis*, partly visible on slabs near the site of the first temple, were originally inscribed on the walls of the two temples (Perlman, 2004a: 1154; 2010).

Biannos (Βιάννος)

Location: 35.05589°N; 25.41569°E

The *polis* town is thought to have been located on a hill called 'Chorakia' above and to the north-west of the modern village of Ano Viannos, south of the Dikti mountain range (Perlman, 2004a: 1154; Hood et al., 1964: 83). At the summit of this hill there is evidence of an extensive and fortified building complex and the foundations of domestic buildings on the slopes to the south and west below. There is no direct evidence of a port for the town but the topography would suggest either Kastri / Keratokambos as one possible site, since it lies 6km to the south at the mouth of the Portala River, or Arvi slightly to the east. Ancient paths run north from Arvi through the Arvi Gorge towards Amiras where there are extensive Minoan remains (cf. Hood et al., 1964: 89–91), but then branch north-west towards Biannos, suggesting that Arvi may be the more probable port. This hypothesis gains some credence from the fact that the 'landmark' site at the top of the Arvi gorge at 'Fortetsa' (a unique 'U' shape) is clearly visible from the summit of the 'Chorakia' hill (for an excellent description of the 'Fortetsa' site see Nowicki, 1996). This 'visible link' is a common feature of urban centres and their associated outlets to the sea.

Perlman reports on a Hellenistic inscription referring to a *prytaneion* at Biannos, and she also suggests that the sanctuary of Hermes and

Aphrodite at Kato Symi would probably have been in the lands of the *polis* (2004a: 1154). The site at Ano Viannos reveals surface sherds from a period up to the Roman era from at least 500 years before.

Biannos struck coins in the Hellenistic period with a female head (possibly Artemis) on the obverse and the word BIANI or BI in a circle on the reverse (Le Rider, 1966: 233).

Dreros (Δρῆρος)

Location: 35.25650°N; 25.62677°E

The urban area was located on one of the southern spurs of Mt Kadiston east of modern Neapolis and dominated the inland plain of Mirabello to the south and to the west of Olous. The centre of the ancient city lies on the north side of a saddle of land between two peaks running east-west, on the former of which is the church of Agios Antonios at 488m. Thirty-five metres from the church to the west is a small cistern with plastered walls of uncertain date. Ancient walls surrounded the whole city area (ca. 40ha) with a second wall protecting the acropolis. Many of the remains are early in date, mostly from the Geometric period.

There are a number of textual references in treaties and agreements, relating to conflicts either with neighbouring Milatos to the north-west or between Knosos and Milatos, that Dreros co-signed. Perhaps the most famous written sources, however, are the Archaic inscriptions that include the earliest known full constitutional law found in Greece. Perlman (2004a) suggests that during the Hellenistic period the inscriptions identify four types of public officials – citizen landowners, the twenty members of the city's council qualified to serve as magistrates, the judges and those entitled to call out an assembly or possibly marshall the troops for action (2004a: 1158). In a well known civic oath of the late 3rd century the one hundred and eighty *epheboi* were identified as representatives of the citizen (male) population. The stele bearing the Drerian Oath was found on this hill in 1854 and thus allowed the identity of the site to be known.

The western summit shows the remains of a large temple and the main public space (*agora*) lies to the north of the saddle at 442m (Marinatos, 1936). The remains there are of different dates with stone steps or seats of an early date and a large cistern (approximately 250m³) also with stone steps from the Hellenistic period, containing an inscription

recording the protection of Apollo Delphinios (Demargne and Effenterre, 1937a; 1937b). Numerous important finds, including bronze figures and animal remains, were found in the temple area, most dating from the 8th century (Willetts, 1955; 1965). When excavated this temple was found to contain a central hearth and a stone bench for offerings on which were terracotta figurines, vases and bronze items (PECS).

The only known cemetery is of Geometric date and is located at the base of the eastern summit on the north side. In the 2nd century Dreros appears to have been conquered by either Knosos or Lyktos and thereby to have lost its independent status.

Svoronos (1890: 126) reports that Dreros struck four types of coin, identifiable by the letters ΔP that they show on the reverse. This view has been contested by Paul Faure (1959: 181–83) and, given the fact that by the end of the 3rd century Dreros may have lain in ruins, it is now considered more likely that the coinage was that of Dragmos. On the other hand, the coins that might have come from Dreros show the goddess Athena Poliouchos who, with Apollo Delphinios, was a major protecting deity. It is not known for certain which port Dreros used but Olous is the most probable candidate, although Milatos to the northwest is another possibility. This is unlikely since tensions existed for many years with the latter. The conquest of Dreros may have meant that it did not figure much in the relative prosperity of the Hellenistic era and for this reason may have had undeveloped port connections.

Eleutherna (Ελεύθερνα)

Location: 35.32833°N; 24.67642°E

The important and wealthy *polis* of Eleutherna was founded in the Geometric period or possibly earlier. By the Archaic period its territory had grown so as to border Axos to the east and it extended to the north coast to include its port town of Pantomatrion. It continued as an important Roman and Byzantine settlement and excavations into two large basilicas are ongoing, one on the lower levels of the Pyrgi ridge and another in the valley to the east. Eleutherna has been the focus of considerable archaeological interest from about 1900 with the British and Italian schools involved (Katsonas, 2008). For the last twenty years, however, the main work has been carried out by the University of Crete at Rethymno (Stampolides, 2004).

The *polis* town was located on a highly defensible spur (*Pyrgi*) at 372m immediately to the north of the modern village of Archaia Eleutherna where there is evidence of a temple. It has clear sight lines to the west and east and an excellent view of the coast 8km to the north. The town evolved from an early settlement on the Pyrgi ridge to another called Nisi to the west, thereby creating a double-acropolis layout (Stampolidis, 1993; 1994; 1996). Both ridges contain evidence of residential districts dating from the Hellenistic period (Kalpaxis, 1994). Many finds have come from the Geometric-Classical cemetery at the western end of the Pyrgi ridge (Stampolidis, 1990; 1993; 1994; 2004).

The settlement was identified as a *polis* in an agreement with Miletos in ca. 259–50 (Perlman, 2004a: 1159). Van Effenterre (1991) suggests that a large sanctuary building (*peribolos*) on Nisi was also used as the meeting place of the Cretan *Koinon*. Perlman (2004a: 1159) cites an Archaic law from Eleutherna controlling wine consumption and others that regulated the position of resident aliens. Other epigraphic evidence reveals laws relating to witness statements, oath taking and the conditions under which freedom from prosecution could be granted.

Erickson has shown evidence that imported pottery at Eleutherna was successively Corinthian, Laconian and Attic (2000: 237). He argues that Eleutherna was a western centre for Mediterranean trade as early as the 6th century. The port for the *polis* was at Pantomatrion near modern-day Stavromenos where an 'Atticising' gravestone also suggests overseas involvement. In the Hellenistic period, the Eleuthernians established Rhithymna as a larger and more sheltered port (Erickson, 2000: 246).

Eleutherna struck its own coinage (staters) on the Aiginetan standard from ca. 350 BC and many examples are on display in the museum in Rethymno. The early coins feature Apollo holding a sphere and bow on the obverse and Artemis as huntress with bow, quiver and dog on the reverse. Later coins have the head of Apollo or Zeus on the obverse and the full figure of Apollo on the reverse (Stampolidis, 1998).

Stephanus of Byzantium suggests that an early name for the *polis* was 'Apollonia' and this god was important, although Zeus Poliouchos may have been the protecting deity. The *polis*

is famous for the 'Lady of Eleutherna', which is a small statue of a woman dressed in Cretan robes. Its similarity to another Cretan statue, once exhibited at Auxerre in southern France and now in the Louvre, has suggested to some archaeologists that this limestone figure also came from Eleutherna.

Elyros (Ἔλυρος)
Location: 35.28720°N; 23.79406°E
Reputed to be the largest Hellenistic city of south-west Crete, the urban centre was located on the Kephala hill near the village of Rodovani. The acropolis is at approximately 560m elevation with fine views to the Libyan Sea at Syia, which served as the port of the *polis*. There are some indications of an ancient roadway to the coast and the urban centre was surrounded by a wall of approximately 3km in length.

Pashley (1837, II: 107) claimed credit for rediscovering the site and the remains of a substantial temple near the church of Panagia. The cavea of the theatre is still visible and some excavations by the Archaeological Service (25th Ephorate) have recently been completed. Very little else is known of the urban centre, although it continued to be occupied in Roman times and later still it was the seat of an archbishopric. The remains of a sixth century AD basilica can still be seen below the acropolis.

Mythology indicates a link between Elyros and Delphi, and Pausanias (10.16.5) refers to the dedication to Apollo of a bronze goat at the sanctuary sent by the Elyrioi (Perlman, 2004: 1161). A goat features on the obverse of most coins from the city (drachm) which date from as early as 400 BCE. The reverse usually features a bee that may refer to a legend connected with the infancy of Zeus. This coinage is very similar to that from Tarrha (q.v.) which shared with Elyros membership of the Confederation of the Oreioi. Other than collaboration within this federal structure, the link between Hyrtakina and Elyros is unclear. The two urban centres are very close to each other and Elyros is both lower and later in date. Together with the similarity of coinage, it is possible that Elyros may have had a more formal association with Hyrtakina in the Hellenistic period as inaccessible defensive sites became seen as less desirable or necessary.

Gortyn (Γόρτυν)
Location: 35.06329°N; 24.94791°E
References to the city in the *Iliad* (2.646) and

Odyssey (3.294) suggest that there was probably a Late Bronze Age settlement somewhere in the vicinity of the Greco-Roman city of Gortyn. The foundation of the city is unclear but is thought by some to be the work of Laconians (Konon, *History* 36), by others to originate with Tegeans (Paus. 8.53) and by others again to be the responsibility of Minos (Strabo 10.4. 76–7). It is likely that the city was founded in the early Archaic period (PECS). The earliest inscriptions from the site date from the late 7th century, and the oldest of the temples was of either Geometric or Archaic foundation. Gortyn was one of the most important Cretan cities in the Classical and Hellenistic periods (with Knosos) and became the capital following the Roman occupation. Ptolemaic influence appears to have been considerable and it is claimed by Strabo (10.4.11) that Ptolemy Philopator paid for a circuit wall for the urban centre, although it ran for less than a kilometre and was never completed.

Gortyn lies on the northern edge of the Mesara Plain, some 15km east of Phaistos. The Roman remains are so extensive that it is not entirely clear how the earlier *polis* was arranged. Perlman thinks that the original ca. 7th century establishment of the urban centre lay at the base of the hills, but this would have been very unusual (Perlman 2004a 1162). More probably the original settlement occupied a double-acropolis either side of the river valley of the Metropolianos (Lethaios) River just above where it enters the Mesara Plain, in which case it is likely that the domestic area lay on the slopes below Ag. Ioannis. On the western side (275m) were a temple to Athena Poliouchos at Ag. Ioannis, a number of unexplored public buildings and a fine theatre facing to the south (Johannowsky, 2002). On the eastern side (ca. 170m) there are traces of another temple (ca. 170m) and plentiful sherds of the 5th–3rd centuries (Rizza and Scrinari, 1968). In support of Perlman is the fact that the temple of Apollo Pythios, possibly built in the second half of the 7th century, now lies in the plain 700m south-east of the base of the hill containing this acropolis. It was on the walls of this temple that some time later the Gortynians first began to inscribe their famous laws.

At the beginning of the Classical period, the Great Law Code was written on the curved inner surface of a building, possibly a law court, twelve blocks of which were later used by the Romans for the foundations of their Odeion.

This was located below the ancient acropolis at Ag. Ioannis on the banks of the Metropolianos River. Other similar blocks, containing part of what is sometimes referred to as the 'Second Code', were also used in a building of Hellenistic date (that may have been a *bouleuterion*), while still more can be seen reused in the nearby early Byzantine church of Agios Titus (Halbherr, 1897; Perlman, 2000: 61–62; 2004a: 1162).

There are a number of textual references to Gortyn in the Archaic period, and the Great Code also makes reference to the city as a *polis*. By the 3rd century BCE Gortyn had conquered Phaistos (with which Gortyn had earlier been bound by a *sympoliteia* treaty) and added its harbour at Matala to the relatively inaccessible one it already possessed at Lebena. In 221 BCE civil war broke out in the city between those favouring an alliance with Knosos and those preferring links with Lyktos. For a century and a half, until the Roman conquest, intermittent squabbles characterised the relationship between Knosos and Gortyn. The latter had a number of dependent areas, possibly also *poleis* in their own right (see 'Aulon' and 'Latosian' in Perlman, 2004a). The size and power of Gortyn meant that other communities in the whole Mesara tended to become dependencies. Eventually these included Phaistos and Amyklaion to the west and Rhytion to the east. To the north lay Rhaukos which was destroyed by Gortyn and Knosos in the 2nd century, its territories being divided between the victors.

Coins were minted at Gortyn from a very early date (ca. 470 BCE). Early examples reveal the *sympoliteia* or political alliance with Phaistos. Later examples (4th century) of staters show Europa in a tree on the obverse and the bull with which she is said to have consorted on the reverse, with the legend ΓΟΡΤΥΝΙΟΝ (Svoronos, 1890: 153–181).

Hyrtakina (Ὑρτακίνα)

Location: 35.27800°N; 23.75167°E

The twin peaks between which Hyrtakina was located lie less than 5km to the west of Elyros and 5km in a direct line from its port at Lisos. Hyrtakina has been subjected to minimal archaeological investigation. It is normally regarded as having been founded in the Classical period but the extensive fortifications and defensive site of the urban centre would suggest an earlier date.

The urban centre occupied a saddle of land

between twin acropolises, which also extends to a considerable extent to the west. Directly between the southern (885m) and northern acropolis (907m) there are the remains of a substantial public building measuring 40m by 9m whose size and central position suggest that it may have been a *prytaneion*. The urban centre is said to have contained a *prytaneion* where hospitality was offered to visiting *theoroi* from the sanctuary at Delphi. Perlman (2004a: 1167) notes that this building was called 'the Delphinian' in inscriptions.

The southern acropolis, where there are the remains of a temple to Pan dating from the Classical-Hellenistic period, is in a highly defensive position with extensive views to the sea and to the smaller hill above the *polis's* port of Lisos. On the slightly lower plateau west of the southern acropolis there is another public building complex, constructed of fine ashlar masonry, the largest part of which measures 20m by 7m. The door jams, still standing in part, originally supported a massive pedimented lintel. Slightly to the north-east, there is evidence of at least one other major public building and what was possibly a large cistern close to the remains of the polygonal defensive wall, which may have been double in parts. The remains of the fortification wall extend east-west for just under half a mile (Pashley, 1837, II: 112; Savignoni and de Sanctis, 1901: 408–24). The urban centre was walled in those parts of the plateaux that were not naturally defensive (Sanders, 1982: 171).

The whole area of the urban centre extended to 30–40ha and is surrounded on all sides by evidence of ancient terraces. Numerous tombs can be seen on the southern and northern slopes of the acropolis and there are rock cut tombs on the hill Ag. Ioannis to the north-east.

Hyrtakina was a member along with Elyros, Lisos, Tarrha and Poikilasos of the league of small states in the south-west (Oreioi) that came together in the 4th century and lasted until the beginning of the 2nd century (van Effenterre, 1948). Coins were minted at Hyrtakina after 330 BCE which, apart from the inscription, were very similar to those of its neighbour Elyros (Perlman, 2004a: 1167). It also produced an alliance coinage with its port at Lisos (Svoronos, 1890: 198).

Kantanos *(Κάντανος)*

Location: 35.27917°N; 23.70194°E

Hierocles mentions 'Cantania' in his listing of Cretan cities as being next to 'Elyrus' and 'Lissus' (Falkener, 1852: 308). The *Peutingeria Tabula* places the city of 'Cantano' sixteen miles west of 'Liso', and Pashley in 1837 located a quadruple defensive wall and other remains that he too identifies with Kantanos. The Smith directory also places 'Cantanus' west of Hyrtakina and there is a reference in Stephanus Byzantius to the city. The exact location of the ancient urban centre is contested, but Pashley and these earlier writers were referring to a site on the eastern side of the valley of the Kakodikianos or Vlithias River above the tiny modern village of Kadros, six kilometres north and slightly east of modern-day Palaiochora in the Selino district of southwest Crete. More than a century ago, however, Savignoni and de Sanctis argued that ancient Kantanos was nearer to modern-day Kantanos which lies 8km to the north-east of this site (1901: 395). Daphne Gondicas (1988: 49–51) follows Paul Faure in believing that the site at Kadros is that of 'Katre' and others, including the *Barrington Atlas*, follow that lead (Faure, 1959: 195). Sanders identifies the site at the modern village of Kantanos as largely Roman with mineworking and smelting installations for iron, copper and possibly gold, as well as a basilica of the 5th and 6th centuries AD (Sanders, 1982, 19/10: 171). Faure's suggestion of 'Katre' follows the use of the term by Herodianos in the second century and he bases his argument partly on the similarity of the name with that of 'Kadros' together with a rather tenuous link with Cretan mythology. Although Gondicas confirms that no remains of the Hellenistic period or before have been found north of the village of Kakodiki just north of Kadros, she is reluctant to accept that the site at Kadros is that of ancient Kantanos (1988: 45). Her reason for doubting this is that the Romans would not have settled in modern-day Kantanos unless it had been occupied before. Moreover they, unlike the Greeks before them, were not averse to settling on the shore since they had nothing to fear from the sea. But this disregards the wealth to be generated by the mines at modern-day Kantanos. Moreover, she also doubts whether the site at Kadros could have been ancient Kantanos because of the lack of very fertile land at Kadros when compared with the high valley. But this will not do either, since we know that a substantial settlement existed at Kadros and the inhabitants must have found land enough for their subsistence. It is impossible to imagine two urban centres within the confines of one river valley. Since we know that there was an urban centre at Kadros, there cannot have been one at modern-day Kantanos during the same period, unless it had another route for access to the sea. Moreover, the whole district is known as 'Kantanos', probably named after the ancient city, and it is not at all uncommon for a newer village to take the district's name and to become its modern capital. In the absence of epigraphic evidence from the site itself, it is impossible to be certain what the settlement was called or whether indeed that it had *polis* status. Recently, however, this attribution has become more secure with the first reports of coinage from Kantanos (Stefanakis, 2000b). Its inclusion is therefore based on the balance of probabilities, given the size of the site, its conformity with the ideal type of a primary polis and the numerous references in ancient sources.

The site at Kadros, which is at a height of over 500m, is extensive (exceeding 20 hectares) with numerous springs that flow year-round. Ancient terraces are evident on the 'Pyrgos' hill that extends south towards modern-day Spaniakos. The sacred areas of the urban centre were at the summit of the conical hill now occupied by the tiny church of Prophitis Ilias, with a second lower acropolis two hundred metres to the south. Willets (1976: 198) cites epigraphic evidence from the 2nd century that refers to the main deity being Zeus *Agoraios*, which suggests that the flat area immediately to the east would have contained a market place and meeting area.[7] The domestic areas lay on the western-facing flanks of the 'Glimata' hill that rises to 773m on the eastern side of the site. There is extensive evidence of house walls of polygonal masonry and the remains of a *tholos* tomb, partially above ground level, suggesting an early date for the foundation of the city.[8] On gently sloping ground that lies slightly to the east of the double acropolis there is an extensive cemetery area with numerous rock-cut tombs that can also be seen carved in the rock face north-east of the main acropolis. Sanders refers to Classical and Hellenistic material at

Kadros, but also to Roman sherds and tombs with fine glass of the 1st–3rd centuries AD (1982: 19/20: 172). The sherd scatter at Kadros does indeed appear to contain Roman wares, but also those of an earlier date. The rock-cut tombs, however, are just as likely to be Hellenistic as they are to be Roman, although if glasswares were found within them that might confirm a later date. On the flat ground below Prophitis Ilias there is evidence of at least one large public building whose walls were comprised of massive ashlar masonry while other buildings of substance can be seen on the north-eastern slopes of the main acropolis. The sight lines north and south down the river valley are clear and the view to the sea would suggest that ancient Kalamydi, which is thought to have been just to the east of modern-day Palaiochora, would have served as the port for the city state (Hood, 1967: 48–49; Gondicas, 1988: 53–55). To the south of ancient Kantanos, there are the remains of four fortresses of the Hellenistic era at Anydri, Loutra, Spaniakos and Vlithias which appear to have been built to protect the vulnerable southern opening of the valley to the sea (Thenon, 1867).

One important question that arises in relation to this fortified valley, which is the major north-south route to the west of the Lefka Ori, is how the settlements here related to those immediately to the east. Thenon (1867) is one of the few to have considered this question and to believe that some form of unity existed with Hytakina and Elyros.[9] On the other hand he notes that access to the Vlithias valley was through a double defensive wall near to modern-day Anydri, which might suggest that settlements west of Anydri were independent of those to the east.

Keraia *(Κεραία)*

Location: 35.39457°N; 23.95511°E

There is no doubt that a *polis* with the name 'Keraia' existed since the mint produced coins from ca. 330 and the city state was a member of the Cretan *Koinon* when the alliance was made with Eumenes II in about 183 BCE. As Perlman notes, in addition a *proxenia* decree was issued in Gortyn to someone identified as coming from Keraia (Keraïtas) (2004a: 1168). In the absence of significant archaeological research, what is not so clear is where the *polis* town was

---

7 *Inscriptiones Creticae opera et consilio Friderici Halbheer collectae* (Vol 2; Titula Cretae Occidentalis) VI. 1, (Rome, 1939)

8 This is presumably the 'tholos or vaulted apartment six or seven feet high' to the south-east of the city that is referred to by Pashley (1837, II: 119).

9 'C'est la même peuple que l'on trouve à peu de distance à l'est, aux ruines de Téménia' (1867: 107).

located. Paul Faure identified a site near Meskla in Western Crete as the most likely candidate and both the *Barr* and Perlman (2004a) accept this designation, but the *evidence* for so doing is rather thin and at one time this site was thought to be ancient Rhizenia.

The site lies to the south of the village of Meskla and close to the hamlet of Zourva in a steep valley running north-south at a straight line distance of ca. 13km from the sea on the north coast. The land to the south forms the northern sector of the Lefka Ori and steep-sided mountains rise to well over a thousand metres at this point. The valley is the source of a stream which joins the Kalabouki River, itself tracking north past the town of Fournes and flowing into the Keritis (ancient Iardanus) River whose outfall, after a further confluence, lies just west of modern-day Platanias. The remains of fortification walls and ramparts are evident, together with a ruined watchtower at Ellinika, south of Meskla but north of the settlement. This guarded against intrusion from the north, and another similar fortified tower was found overlooking a path of possible invasion from the south. Surface remains include pottery, dating from the Archaic period onwards, and there is no doubt that the area was the location of Roman villas (Faure, 1962: 49–54). Above the remains on the western and eastern valley flanks are the remnants of ancient terracing extending to a height of over 500m.

The port of Keraia is unknown but from the site at ca. 380m it is possible to see the coast and the island of *Koite/Akoitos* (modern-day *Ag. Theodoroi*) just offshore from modern Platanias. The common practice of siting *polis* urban centres so that they had oversight of the sea and their ports suggests that the port at Platanias may have belonged to Keraia. Access to the sea would have been down the wide and fertile valley of the Iardanus (Xekollimenos-Keritis); this is only speculation, but it may resolve an additional puzzle. The population of Keraia may have comprised people uprooted from Kydonia by invasion, because this would account for the reference in Homer (*Odyssey* iii 292) to the River Iardanus 'near the banks of which the Cydonians dwelt' but this would also be true for the settlement at Vryses (see Polyr-rhenia below). The coins of Keraia featured a crowned head of Artemis on the obverse and an arrow and spear with the word KERAITAN on the reverse.

Knosos (Κνωσός)

Location: 35.29639°N; 23.95511°E

Surprisingly little is known about the *polis* centre of Knosos, approximately 5km south of modern Iraklio, given its illustrious earlier status, although apart from the century after 630 BCE, it appears to have been in continuous occupation from prehistoric times through to the Roman conquest (Coldstream and Huxley, 1999; Perlman, 2004a: 1170).

The *polis* town was located to the north of the Minoan palace and to the west of the Kairatos River in an area of about 100ha. Temples of the Archaic and Classical periods were located on the Old Palace site but some material was destroyed by Evans in his search for Minoan Knosos (Hood and Smyth, 1981). A fortification tower on the Kephala ridge and dating from the 3rd–4th centuries was excavated by Sinclair Hood in the 1950s. Given the fact that this was at a corner where two curtain walls met, it may have been part of a longer defensive wall for the Classical *polis*, although this is not the view of the excavators (Hood and Boardman, 1957: 224). On the other hand, the tower looked over the Classical and Hellenistic town to the south, and had a sight line to Herakleion to the north, making it very similar to the layout of other primary *polis* urban centres.

Excavations in the 1950s by the British School revealed a great deal about the pottery, particularly during the Hellenistic period (Hood and Boardman, 1957; Coldstream, 1973; Coldstream and MacDonald, 1997; Coldstream, 1999; 2001). The *agora* in the centre of the urban area dates from the 5th century. Apart from a lack of excavation, the interpretation of the site is made more difficult by the remains of large Roman buildings to the west and south of the *agora*.

The territory of Knosos bordered that of Tylisos at the Platyperama River in the west and reached the lands of Lyktos in the east. To the south it would originally have reached to modern Ano Archanes and substantially further after Knosos, in a rare alliance with Gortyn in the middle of the 2nd century, conquered Rhaukos, which lay between them and divided her lands. It is widely recognised that the original Minoan port at Amnisos to the east of Herakleion proved inadequate and Knosos is usually credited with the founding of Herakleion to serve as its new port (Strabo 10.4.7).

There are many examples of Knosian coins. The earlier forms from the beginning of the 5th century feature the Minotaur holding a stone on the obverse and a labyrinth on the reverse. Later coins from the 4th century show a head of Demeter with either Zeus or Minos seated on the reverse. All of these normally carry the label ΚΝΩΣΙΟΝ. Later still the head of Hera or Apollo features on the obverse and in the Hellenistic period the reverse on some coins (e.g. Attic tetradrachms) shows an owl standing on an amphora next to a reduced labyrinth, all surrounded by an olive wreath. During periods of peace with Gortyn some issues also feature Europa (Jackson, 1971).

Lachania *(Λαχανία)*

Location: 35.45780°N; 23.97992°E

Paul Faure (1988) identified the site at Kastelos, seven km south-south-west of modern-day Chania as that of Lachania. This designation is followed by Perlman (2004a) but she does not find evidence of *polis* status for the site, at least during the Archaic and Classical periods. Sanders and others have also commented on the size of the remains and Richard Pococke, writing in the first half of the eighteenth century, thought the remains were those of ancient Kydonia (cf. Sanders, 1982: 168).[10]

The site occupies two adjoining plateaux, each with a small peak, at an elevation of 321m with commanding views over the plain of Chania below. The site has never been properly excavated and controversy continues as to its significance. This has not been aided by evidence of occupation at three other periods. At the summit of the hill behind the two plateaux, at the location known as Dembla, there is evidence of an Early Minoan settlement excavated in the early 1970s by Warren and Tzedhakis (1974: 299–342). Early Minoan sherds and obsidian flakes can still be seen at this site near the trig point. At the southern extremity of the second plateau, there is a Venetian watchtower or fortress of the 13th century AD utilising building materials of a much earlier date. Confusion is further added by the re-use of the site again by the German army in World War II.

It must be stressed that this site is very similar to those of other known *poleis* in the Classical and Hellenistic periods. There is

much evidence of buildings of the Hellenistic period and a sherd scatter that is largely of this period or before, including Hellenistic black-glazed wares. Moody (1987: ref VPT2) reports artefacts found as 'scored ware, black burnish and incised ware, grey ware, and other lightly burnished sherds. Later pottery includes amphorae handles and Hellenistic ring bases some with traces of black lustrous paint'.

The total area of Classical and Hellenistic remains may be greater than 20ha and there is evidence of monumental public buildings of this period comprised of ashlar blocks, as well as later remains. Given the move of the main *poleis* to their ports in the Hellenistic period, and the subsequent rise to prominence of these, it is not fanciful to speculate that this is what occurred in this case. Captain Spratt may have been right to suggest that there were 'two Cydonias', the one referred to by Homer (*Odyssey* 19: 176) which 'may have stood upon some inland eminence' and another directly on the sea (Spratt, 1865: 140). Spratt may have been wrong, however, to believe that the inland city was at Vryses. The toponymic connection between *Λαχανία* and *Χανιά* is perhaps another clue (see Kydonia below), although it is clear from Hellenistic inscriptions that Lachania was a *kome* or dependency of Kydonia by this time as by the 2nd century may have been true of a number of small settlements in the region (Faure, 1988: 90–91).

Lappa *(Λάππα)*

Location: 35.28563°N; 24.33537°E

Lappa is at an elevation of 274m on a raised plateau between the Rivers Petres and Mouselas. Some of the original urban centre is now under the village of Argyroupoli about 6km south of the coast and 17km to the west of modern Rethymno. The name of the modern village suggests the presence of silver and mines have been attested, but it is also possible that the name is a reference to the copious springs that feed the Mouselas river and were much favoured by the Romans in later periods for supplying bath houses.

According to the *Periplous* of Pseudo-Skylax the territory of Lappa originally 'extended to both sides' which is normally taken to mean that it covered the 18km of this very narrow part of the island. If this is so then the *polis* could have had harbour outlets at Hydramia and Amphimalla (just to the west and south of modern-day Georgioupoli) on the north coast

---

10 Pococke describes the site which he visited in 1739 in some detail and suggests that it must be Kydonia 'as there are no signs of antiquity about Canea, and what remains here shows it to be no inconsiderable place' (1745: 603).

and Phoinix (q.v.) west of modern-day Sellia to the south.

There are reputed to be more than thirty coin types from Lappa. Coins from the early Hellenistic period show a female head on the obverse and a bull's head with one horn turned down on the reverse. These were struck on the Aiginetan standard. Later coins on the Attic standard show the head of Poseidon or Artemis on the obverse and a trident with two dolphins or the earlier bull's head on the reverse with the word ΛΑΠΠΑΙΩΝ.

Lato *(Λατώ)*

Location: 35.17859°N; 25.65560°E

The well-visited and well-excavated site of Lato lies 4km north from the village of Kritsa and 12km by road to the west and slightly to the south of Ag. Nikolaos. The site occupies a saddle of land (357m) between twin peaks ranged north-south with imposing views over the Bay of Mirabello 5km directly to the east and a steep-sided valley to the west.

There is evidence of occupation from the 7th century but most of the buildings are late Classical and Hellenistic. The *prytaneion* complex, which occupies the north side of the saddle, has been dated to the 4th century (Picard and Ducrey, 1972). It contains a steep flight of steps that would take about 80 sitting or about 180 standing, and features a central hearth and side benches. At the centre of the public buildings on the lowest point of the saddle there is a large cistern, previously roofed, with steps to the water below. Behind that there is a small temple and behind that again an *exedra*. To the east of the central area there is a monumental building sometimes suggested as a theatrical area but more probably a building for public assemblies (*ekklesiasterion*) (Demargne, 1929). The main temple area lies above the 'theatral' area on a small plateau to the south (Ducrey and Picard, 1970). A very fine examination of the domestic properties, showing their layout, construction methods and contents can be found in a research report by Vanna Hadjimichali (1971). The French School at Athens also carried out detailed excavations of pottery kilns found on the site, which revealed votive figures and fragmentary images of a female deity, possibly Eileithyia (the goddess of labour and childbirth) (Picard and Ducrey, 1969).

Perlman (2004a: 1173) lists late 2nd century treaties that define the borders of Lato and indicate that these extended to approximately 66km in total length. By the end of this century, however, the citizens of Lato appear to have left their city in favour of their port at Lato pros Kamara. Coins from Lato date mostly to the middle Hellenistic period and have a head of Artemis or possibly the protecting deity Eileithyia on the obverse and Hermes either walking or as a bust on the reverse.

Lyktos *(Λύκτος)*

Location: 35.20798°N; 25.36773°E

The urban centre of Lyktos, sometimes known as Lyttos *(Λύττος)*, is situated on a ridge to the north-west of the Aigaion (Dikti) mountain range, overlooking the plain to the south-west. It is approximately 600m to the north-east of the modern village of Lyttos (Xida). The *polis* town has been estimated to have covered 100ha and the site at 623m commands extensive views to the west and south with good visibility all round. The sea is visible to the north.

There are numerous references to the *polis* of Lyktos in the Archaic and Classical periods, but the city was destroyed by Knosos in the 4th century and later rebuilt. Perlman (2004a) cites an interesting inscription linking the *polis* with the island of Lindos in the 5th century. Another important connection is that between Lyktos and Sparta, and according to Pausanias (4.19.4) archers from the city state fought alongside Sparta in the Second Messenian War. The laws of the *polis* are regarded as the earliest in Crete and are said to have been Minoan in inspiration. Lykourgos (Lycurgus), the architect of Spartan laws, is said to have borrowed many features of his code from Lyktos (van Effenterre and van Effenterre, 1985). In the late 3rd century the *polis* was again destroyed by Knosos at the end of the Lyktian war, when the menfolk of the *polis* were away fighting the Hierapytnians.

Lyktos, after being rebuilt for a second time with the support of Polyrrhenia and Philip V of Macedonia, was joined with Chersonisos in a *sympoliteia* agreement after 183 BCE. At that time the connection with the seaport at Chersonisos appears to have been very close since the latter was referred to officially as 'Lyktos by the sea'.

Lyktos struck its own coinage from the late 5th century with an eagle on the obverse and a boar's head within a square frame on the reverse. This general pattern is observed in coins of many different periods (Svoronos documents 89 types of coins). The contacts with the Laconians and others, together with the fine road that is said to have existed linking Lyktos with Chersonisos, suggest important trade links both within Crete and overseas.

The site occupies an extensive ridge running east-west and has wide and apparently early terraces. A temple, probably of Athena, stood at the highest point on the ridge (628m). This structure, unexcavated and in poor condition, may have had a floor area of approximately 150sqm. Very few other buildings are now apparent except for a series of small rectangular buildings with semi-circular north-facing walls. These are the remains of windmills, probably from the 19th century, since others of a newer date still lie a short distance to the west. The remains of Roman buildings are evident in the construction of the two churches on the ridge (Timios Stavros and Agios Georgios). A cemetery has been located at the foot of the acropolis, probably dating to the Archaic period.

Given its importance, it is surprising that Lyktos has never been the subject of sustained archaeological investigation. Indeed, some of its monuments appear to have disappeared in the relatively recent past. In 1586, the Italian traveller Onorio Belli drew a sketch of the theatre at Lyktos, probably at the foot of the acropolis. He describes the seats made from soft stone called locally *'lepida'* (blade) which was still in use to provide roofing material (Falkener, 1854: 16-19). Writing to his father, Belli observed 'were you to see these ruins you would be filled with amazement at the extraordinary character of the people who could originate such works' (Falkener, 1854: 18-19). Other remains at that time were Roman and statues of Marcus Aurelius and Trajan are now exhibited at the museum in Iraklio. None of the other remains survive.

Erickson argues that the change in pottery at the sanctuary at Kato Symi from 400-390 BCE, when Lyktian material replaces that from Aphrati (Arkades), might be explained by the expansion of Lyktos – possibly associated with its attempt to control a port on the south coast (Erickson, 2000: 360). Certainly after the fall of Athens and the rise of Sparta, there was a change in trade routes.

Malla (Μάλλα)

Location: 35.06861°N; 25.59778°E
The precise location of Malla is uncertain. Pendlebury (1965: 376) reports seeing sherds

and walls at 'Khlia' but Sanders (1982: 2/2, 138) was unable to find this location. It is normally assumed that the urban centre of what was undoubtedly a *polis* in the Hellenistic period lies beneath the lower village of modern-day Malles at the head of the Myrtos river valley to the south-east of the Dikti mountain range. Sanders reports that the church of Ag. Georgios, on the track between Malles and Christos, appears to be on earlier foundations and Nowicki (2000: 134-35) found remains from the Archaic and Classical eras near the spring of Ag. Paraskevi. In fact the church, dating from 1865, is not the only building on earlier foundations and the layout of the ancient urban centre does not appear to depart very much from common practice elsewhere. The urban centre is on a saddle of land between two low rises and the *agora* may have been on the flat land to the east of Ag. Giorgios, now planted as an olive grove. Building remains can be seen on the land that rises to modern-day Malles and from the *agora* an ancient track leads past a spring with fine ashlar masonry of the Classical or Hellenistic periods towards Myrtos, which can almost be seen in the distance. There is a thin but evident scatter of sherds of the same period in the olive groves to the north and west of the abandoned village.

Ducrey (1970) has reported on a treaty between the king of Pergamon and the citizens of Malla at end of the 3rd century BCE, as recorded on a stele found at Christos. The agreement allows for the provision of men from Malla to assist the king, Attale 1st, and for reciprocal military aid should it be necessary in relations between Malla and neighbouring *poleis* (Hierapytna, Arkades and Priansos). There is provision for 300 men and their officers from the king to the people of Malla and, on at least one interpretation, more were to be made available if necessary (Ducrey, 1970: 647). Perlman (2004a: 1177) documents Hellenistic inscriptions concerning treaties between Malla and Lyktos, and others that refer to a citizen as Μαλλαίος. Although the urban centre was probably small it is reported in inscriptions to have possessed both an *agora* and a *prytaneion*. The protecting divinity was probably Zeus Monnitios (Μοννίτιος or Μονη-ίτιος) although the whereabouts of his temple is unknown. Coins dating from the 3rd or 2nd century BCE show the head of Zeus on the obverse and the letters ΜΑΛ with a standing eagle on the reverse (Stefanaki, 2009).

Oleros (Ὤλερος)

Location: 35.08431°N; 25.71098°E

The remains of Oleros are located at the village of Meseleri at an altitude of 358m. The ruins of the polis town are largely buried beneath the modern village, but the village of Meseleri used to be two villages and was merged. It is possible that the ancient settlement was on the saddle between the plateau to the east and that to the west, over which the modern road now passes.

The likely ports for this polis were Istron in the north and Hierapytna in the south. The latter, which is the only port attested, eventually took over the *polis* lands entirely as it grew in size and importance. The detailed survey by Hayden et al. (2004) of the whole Vrokastro valley focuses mainly on the LMI-III and Geometric periods but makes some reference to the urban centre of Oleros and its likely boundaries.

Pelkis (Πέλκις)

Location: 35.27139°N; 23.65333°E

A political entity referred to as 'Pelkis' is known to have existed in Hellenistic times because of its inclusion in the list of Delphic *theorodokoi* where it is placed between Polyrrhenia and Lisos. The procedure was that the *theoroi* from Delphi (or Athens or other centres) issued an invitation to participate in Panhellenic games and festivals and the responding community or *polis* appointed a *theorodokos* to manage affairs and handle hospitality for visiting officials (Perlman, 1995: 139; 2004a: 1148). The route of the Delphic *theoroi*, periodically between 260 and 200 BCE, went from Kythera to western Crete, making landfall at Phalasarna. They then went on to Polyrrhenia, then south to Pelkis and the south coast. From there they headed eastwards visiting Lisos, Elyros, Tarrha, Araden and Anopolis before heading north again towards Kydonia (Plassart, 1921: 59–60). There is good reason for believing therefore that Pelkis lay south of Polyrrhenia and west of Lisos and, since all inland urban centres were within reach of the sea, it is not unreasonable to suppose that it was closer to the south than to the north coast.

The exact site of Pelkis is not known for certain, but through the toponymic connection it is tempting to place it in the vicinity of the Pelekaniotikos River. Gondicas reports that from 1577 until 1890 there was a village called 'Pelekanos' in this vicinity and that the

whole area is today referred to by the same name (Gondicas, 1988: 63). The north-south route would have passed through the Typhlos gorge between the mountains of Apopigadio and Plakosellia and then south through the valley of the Vlithias. This might then suggest that Kantanos, in the Vlithias valley, was actually ancient Pelkis, and there are those who have maintained this argument (e.g. Guarducci, 1939; ii, VI: 84). As Gondicas points out, however, the *theoroi* may have travelled by sea, heading westwards from Polyrrhenia and making landfall at the nearest harbour on the south coast, which could have been at the mouth of the Pelekaniotikos River (Agios Georgios). The urban centre of Pelkis would then lie close to this river, rather than further eastward in the Vlithias valley.

The most useful identification of an actual site in this area comes from Robert Pashley (1837). After visiting the site at Kadros, and two of the forts in the Vlithias valley, Pashley reports that he was told of other remains 'between Pelekanas and Kastel-Selinou' (1837, II: 124). He describes how he walked from Vlithias, where one of the forts is located, down to the river and steeply up the other side onto the ridge that separates the Vlithias from the Pelekaniotikos River valleys. From there he descended to the village of Kontokynigi and then to the church of Ag. Antonios. He then went south on the ridge that rises east of the Pelekaniotikos River but west of another small valley that today contains the road between Palaiochora and Kontokynigi. Pashley found rock-cut tombs on the way on this track, which still exists today, joining Agios Antonios and the mouth of the river. When he reached the church of Ag. Georgios (not to be confused with the eponymous sanctuary on the sea) he found walls extending to 'three or four hundred paces' following the contours at the summit of the ridge (1837, II: 124). Pashley believed this site, just above the hamlet of Tsaliana, to be that of Kalamydi, but it is more probable that it is the remains of ancient Pelkis. Savignoni and de Sanctis also report on an ancient city near to Kontokynigi and include a picture of the site (1901: 459–460). They record seeing the rock tombs found by Pashley but doubt whether the site could be that of Kalamydi. The *Barrington Atlas* identifies this site as a Classical, Hellenistic, and later settlement that may have been ancient Pelkis, citing Sanders (1982, 19/7) and Gondicas (1988: 63–66) in support.

South of Ag. Georgios there are two further peaks where the possible remains of temples comprised of ashlar blocks are still visible, but few remains can be seen of other buildings. In all other respects, however, the site appears similar in layout to other inland *poleis*.

In addition to the problem of identifying the site correctly in the absence of inscriptions or coinage, there is also the difficulty of establishing its political status. Perlman (1995) argues convincingly that the appointment of a *theorodokos* does not necessarily imply that the community concerned was a *polis*, and even if it was, it may well have been one that was dependent upon another larger settlement. Rather, she says, 'the presence of a *theorodokos* reflects the political history of the community and the role of the panhellenic ideology in the self-definition of the *polis*' (1995: 135). Given its apparent small size, it is thus quite possible that Pelkis was a satellite of Kantanos, or in some kind of league with its larger neighbour four kilometres to the east. Imported vases from Attica (*lekythoi*, possibly dating from the 5th century, that would have held oil for anointing during religious ceremonies and burials) have been found in the area and it is also possible that the site to the south of Kontokynigi was a regional sanctuary attracting visitors from overseas (Savignoni and de Sanctis, 1901: 463–466). As Gondicas says, '*c'est un problème qui reste ouvert pour le moment*' (1988: 66).

Phaistos *(Φαιστός)*

Location: 35.04833°N; 24.81306°E

The site of Phaistos at the western end of the Mesara Plain is well known. In addition to its Minoan importance, Phaistos is attested as a *polis* from the Archaic period (Perlman, 2004a: 1180). It shared a border with Gortyn to the east and the port was at Matala, but possibly another was at Amyklaion whose whereabouts is uncertain, although the *Barrington Atlas* locates it near or at Kommos. In the middle of the 5th century, Phaistos and Gortyn shared a *sympoliteia* treaty but a little over two centuries later the *polis* had been taken over by its powerful neighbour.

The archaeological remains of the *polis* town of Phaistos are unclear. There are reports that it may lie on the lower ground to the west of the Minoan site, but this is rather unlikely given the preference for high ground by all primary *poleis*. More probably, it lay above the Minoan remains or possibly on the higher ground

above them to the north-west (middle hill). There are, however, traces of a temple to the west of the Minoan palace site and Hellenistic remains extend to the west of the palace either side of a well-built ancient road. On the southeast slope of the main (middle) hill there are remains of Hellenistic houses destroyed either by earthquake or by the Gortynian invasion (PECS, 1976).

A legal inscription from the end of the 6th century mentions an *agora* or market place and around this, if it is ever located, would have been the public buildings (La Rosa, 1992: 235; Sjögren, 2003: 16–17). In the Hellenistic period, the town area was large and surrounded by a defensive wall (La Rosa, 1992: 238).

Phaistos struck coins from very early on (ca. 470 BCE). They normally feature Europa riding a bull or, later, seated with a bull. Others show Herakles the father or grandfather of Phaestus, sometimes with bow and club and a lion skin over his arm with a bull's head on the reverse (stater).

Phalanna *(Φάλαννα)*

Location: 35.27011°N; 24.50250°E

The remains of this *polis* are situated 11–12km south and slightly east of Rethymno on a north-facing plateau south of the modern village of Goulediana. Remains on the hill at Onithe north-west of Geni belong to the same site from where it is possible to see the coast at Rethymno (cf. Sjögren, 2003: 147). It is impossible to be certain whether the designation of this site as 'Phalanna' is correct. The *Periplous* of Pseudo-Skylax, written in the 4th century BCE, identifies a number of Cretan *poleis* commencing in the west with Phalasarna, and the one he places between Lappa and Eleutherna is 'Osmidas' (Ch. 47). Captain Spratt (1865: 2/105) agrees and both Pendlebury (1939: 340) and Paul Faure (1959: 196; cf. 1960: 233, 238; 1988: 86) follow this lead and identify the site at Onithe Goulediana as 'Osmida'. Nicolas Platon (1954: 377–382; 1955: 298–303; 1956: 226–228) however prefers the Phalanna attribution, which is also supported by Guarducci (1935–50: ii; 216–217) and the *Barrington Atlas* follows this latter designation, which is also the view of Sanders (1982: 14/7). The site is thought to date from the second half of the 7th century and in the *Barrington Atlas* it is listed as being inhabited in the Archaic, Classical and Hellenistic periods.

Phalanna is included by Perlman as a

settlement predating the Hellenistic era but not attested as a *polis*. However, Phalanna is referred to as a *polis* by Stephanus Byzantius (655.20–22). Its *polis* status is made more probable by the fact that the toponym was cited as a location for the visiting *theorodokoi* from Delphi. Svoronos identifies silver coins with the head of Hera on the obverse and two fish on the reverse as coming from Phalanna. Its port is unknown but the site lies 14km due north of Bionnos on the Libyan Sea, south of Kerames. This would not have been easy to reach as a port, but some support for this possibility comes from the fact that an ancient track leads from the highest acropolis south through the modern village of Geni in the direction of Kerames.

Sjögren describes the site at Onithe Goulediana as a 'possible village or hamlet' (2003: 47). The main building complex still visible dates from the end of the 7th century (2003: 18). The building consists of two 'houses' separated by a dividing wall, each with an entrance on the long side of its rectangular shape. The first 'house' had three large rooms (ca. 40m²) with evidence of column supports for the roof. A corridor ran in front of these rooms from which they were entered. Two rooms had stone benches on which were found pottery, bronze and iron objects. Each house had a storage room and in one this contained 20 *pithoi*. Other storage vessels and *pithoi* were found in the other unit and sherds of *pithoi* were also evident. A limestone statue of a seated woman from the middle of the 7th century was found in a nearby well. The site is, however, far more extensive than this excavated area suggests and more remains cover the whole plateau (10–12 hectares) beneath the high point at Onithe (601m).

Polyrrhenia (Πολυρρήνια)

Location: 35.45737°N; 23.65503°E

The remains of the urban centre of Polyrrhenia dominate the hilltop (381m) to the east of the modern village of Polyrinia, seven kilometres from the north coast and the town of Kasteli (Kisamos). Near the summit are the remains of a Venetian watchtower and other walling of uncertain date. The old names for the upper and lower parts of the modern village were Ano and Kato Palaiokastro, suggesting that the Venetian remains may be of a more substantial structure. The hill itself, which is sandwiched between the Pyrgianos River to the west and

the Kamarianos River to the east, is honeycombed on its western and northen flanks with the remains of rock-cut houses, cisterns and tombs, most of which date from the Classical and Hellenistic period, or perhaps earlier. Not visible from the north, but clearly from the east, is a much smaller hillock that gives the whole complex a double acropolis layout. To the north-west of the main acropolis, there are remains of a temple or sanctuary, possibly of Roman construction, although much of the superb masonry from this structure found its way into the adjacent 19th century AD church (Ag. Pateres), where a number of inscriptions are now to be found embedded in the walls. The main cemetery lay on the western slopes of the acropolis hill, below the modern village, where fine rock-cut tombs can be seen, dating from the Classical and Hellenistic periods. Further rock-cut tombs can be seen on the western flanks of a neighbouring hill to the east (Korfi) a little south of the modern-day village of Tsikalaria.

Perlman (2004a: 1182) notes that Polyrrhenia is identified as a *polis* by the end of the Classical period. According to Strabo (4.13) the settlement was originally a series of villages that became synoecised (united) by Achaean and Laconian settlers when the acropolis was also fortified (the name itself means 'many sheep' which may be a reference to this federal structure). Dedications exist that suggest an early link with Sparta and later, in the Hellenistic period, the *polis* took the side of the Roman invaders and was thus saved from destruction.

Despite the lack of excavations, most commentators accept the view of early sources that suggests that Polyrrhenia was one of the most powerful *poleis* in the west of Crete. Its territories bordered Phalasarna in the west and Kydonia to the east and some claim that they extended from the north to the south coast (Skylax, 47; Sekunda 2000: 328ff). Polyrrhenia may have had a number of dependencies such as Rokka on the Trouli hill to the east and the sanctuary to Diktynna at the northern end of the Rodopou peninsula. While there is no conclusive evidence to support this proposition, the Plain of Chania appears to have supported a number of small towns in the Classical and Hellenistic eras (e.g. Keraia at Meskla, Pergamon, probably at Vryses but possibly south of Kolymbari, and

Modaia).[11] Some of these may have had their own access to the sea but they may have all been dependencies of either Kydonia or Polyrrhenia.

In relation to Pergamon, Faure (1958: 496) argues that ancient authors make it clear that this city was located in a high place, near the coast between Diktynna and Kydonia, and that its history must have run from LMIII to the Geometric period and beyond.[12] He points out that 20 minutes to the north-west of the village of Vryses, Nicolas Platon found eight tombs of the Geometric period in December 1952, and that alongside the church of Timios Stavros in Vryses itself, other tombs had subsequently come to light. He also points to a necropolis of the Classical era at the junction of the road between Vryses and Patelari (Faure, 1958: 499). Mainly, however, the focus is on the double summits of Kastelos and Ag. Georgios, just south of Vryses. Faure maintains that the summit of Kastellos, which is only accessible from the south, has a surface area of at least 125m × 40m with traces of occupation that were difficult to date, but what for him clinched evidence for the occupation of this site was the discovery of the large cave called *Kera Spilaiotissa* that lay on the north-western flank of the hill of Ag. Georgios (1988: 500).

The entrance to the cave is hidden by olive trees and large fallen rocks but it is located at an altitude of 135m halfway between the church in Vryses and that of Ag. Georgios. The inside of the first chamber is approximately 7m × 3.5m with a height of 3m, but this is

followed by a much larger chamber with many sherds, animal bones and obsidian flakes. He argues that the cave had been used from Neolithic times onwards, through the Bronze Age to that of the Geometric period (Faure, 1958: 500). Further in, he found the remains of vases and pithoi. There were also the calcified remains of a large animal (possibly a pig) that villagers told him was known locally as 'the lady of the cave'. He argues that the settlement was probably destroyed by Kydonia in the 3rd century because at that time there was a shared boundary between Kydonia and Polyrrhenia lying to the west of the Rodopou Peninsula.

The settlement at Vryses utilises a double acropolis layout with remains of a large cistern and possibly a temple area alongside the church of Ag. Georgios (270m) to the west, and a sanctuary on the southern slopes of Kastelos to the east. Faure (1988) remarks on the remains of a fortification wall between the two peaks protecting ingress from the south as well as to the main residential area on the saddle. All of this would be enough to guarantee the inclusion of Pergamon at Vryses an entry as a primary polis were it not for the competing claim that this site is that of Polichne and not Pergamon.[13] Faure himself in later years was unsure and both *Barr* and Perlman (2004a: 1182) cite Faure (1963 and 1988 respectively) as supporting this claim, which is also supported by Gondicas (1988: 284). Thucydides (2.85.5) states that Kydonia and Polichne were neighbours. Perlman notes that in 429 BCE the Gortynian *proxenos* at Athens, persuaded the Athenians to attack Kydonia, then primarily an Aiginetan stronghold, in order to please the *Polichnitai*, thereby suggesting the maintenance of old enmities (Figueira, 1988). On the other hand, at a later period Polichne issued bronze fractions that bore a striking resemblance to the Kydonian coinage which may have meant that by then the two were allied or, more probably, that Polichne was a dependency of Kydonia. Unfortunately, the coins were found at Kasteli (Kisamos) so do not help with the identification of the site at Vryses. Polichne's currency appeared in the early years of the 2nd century with the head of Diktynna wearing an earring, necklace and quiver on the obverse, and a hound with the legend ΠΟ on the reverse. Stefanakis too argues that earlier

---

11 As far as Modaia is concerned, coins and burial wares have been recovered from Hellenistic tombs near the modern village of Modi. Some 800m to the south-east is the double acropolis near the village of Vryses, where some commentators have located the site of ancient Pergamon (Hood and Warren, 1967) and others Polichne (Perlman, 2004a: 1181–2; *Barr*, Map 60). The proximity of one location to the other suggests that they are likely to be the same urban centre. Paul Faure, for example, warns against basing a location argument on toponymic similarity and suggests that Modaia was actually close to Nokhia (1962: 56). *The Barrington Atlas* reserves the name 'Modaioi' for a small league of settlements in west Crete (Rokka at Trouli, Phalelliana and Mithymna), citing Gondicas (1988: 272) and Faure (1993: 72–73) in support. Modaia is known to have minted coinage on its own behalf featuring the head of Zeus on the obverse and a bull's head with the word ΜΩΔΑΙΩΝ on the reverse and it was Svoronas (1890: 244) who first suggested that they may have come from Modi.

12 For example, Pliny places Pergamon between Kisamos and Kydonia in a list of coastal settlements running west to east (Pliny 4.12).

13 In earlier contributions Faure argues that Polichne may have been on the Trouli Hill at Rokka (1962: 56).

hostilities were forgotten and that Kydonia drew in neighbours such as Polichne, Tanos (that lay at an unknown site near Kydonia) and even Polyrrhenia in order to focus her fire on Phalasarna, which she eventually overran after a five year campaign in 184 BCE (Stefanakis, 1996b: 154).

Another intriguing theory is that the name itself (derived from *polichnitai* – those who dwell in small cities) is significant and that a *polis* of Polichne never existed (Sekunda 2000: 328 *passim*). Rather, it was the name for a federation of northwestern settlements comprising the original ethnic group (the Kydones) who fled Kydonia after its colonisation first by Samians and later by Aiginetans at the end of the 6th century. Neil Sekunda also suggests that all these small towns may have formed a federal association analogous to the Confederation of the Oreioi but in which case they may have been dominated by Polyrrhenia. Some support for this argument comes from the fact that the once fortified site at modern Polyrinia is not large enough to support a community of the importance of Polyrrhenia, although some would disagree with this assertion (Sjögren, 2003: 37). The topography of the whole area features many small but impressive hillocks with evidence of occupation in antiquity (e.g. the Trouli hill at Rokka). When taken together these would certainly have provided the space for a large *polis* which Polyrrhenia undoubtedly was.

After a period of alliance with Phalasarna, which may have served as Polyrrhenia's original port (Spratt, 1865, II: 213; Pashley, 1837, I: 54; Hadjidaki, 1988a), there was a major conflict between the two some time between 304–294 BCE, probably because of Phalasarna's growing economic power. From this time, Polyrrhenia avoided contacts further west and built its port at Kasteli (Kisamos). There is also considerable evidence of Roman remains, including aquaducts and a watchtower with a cistern at its base. Polyrrhenia struck coins from ca. 330 BCE. These were originally on the Aiginetan standard and showed Diktynna (obv.) and a bull's head (rev.). Later coins (after 100) included copies of Athenian tetradrachms and also showed Diktynna or Athena (Le Rider, 1966).

Praisos (Πραισός)

Location: 35.12300°N; 26.09091°E

The important *polis* of Praisos was located on two hills to the west of the village of Kalamafki in eastern Crete and near to the village of Nea Praisos. The lands of the polis extended from Siteia in the north to Stalai on the Libyan Sea. The Classical and Hellenistic *polis* town lay behind defensive walls enclosing the two hills. On the higher of the two are the remains of a temple building, but there is also evidence of walling from the Minoan period (Whitley et al., 1995). The site commands a fine view on all four sides and is especially well placed for sight lines down the valley to the north.

The *polis* town is reputed to have been an 'Eteocretan' stronghold and Spyridakis (1970: 23) claims that the non-Greek language of the native population survived here until the 3rd century BCE. James Whitley also argues that Praisos was the political centre of the 'Eteocretans' or the native Cretans, distinct ethnically from the Greek-speaking, Doric-descended population elsewhere (Whitley, 1998; 1992–93). He argues that the material culture reveals these differences (Whitley, 2006). The Praisians were also credited with having a powerful fleet venturing as far north as Olympia and Delphi (Spyridakis, 1970: 27). The urban centre was destroyed in 145–140 BCE by Hierapytna and never reoccupied.

The city's *agora* lay on the saddle between the two acropolises, and on the lower slopes of the higher hill a large building of ashlar blocks was excavated by Bosanquet in 1902 (292m). Largely because of the contents of this building, it is sometimes regarded as having served either a residential or an agricultural function, but its size and method of construction would suggest a public role.[14] Perlman (2004a: 1184) follows Bosanquet (1901–2) in supporting the idea that this building was for public use as an *andreion*, and its location near the *agora* and its position on the saddle between two hills certainly supports this proposition, although it is equally likely to have been a *prytaneion*. An ancient path appears to lead from the saddle north through the valley to the sea. Residential areas may be found on the slopes of both the first and second hills.

A third hill to the south, but outside the city walls, contains the remains of buildings

---

14 On excavation the building, sometimes referred to as the 'Almond Tree House' was found to contain evidence of olive oil pressing and other more domestic activities but these are now thought to have come from later re-use.

of an earlier date (mainly from the Geometric period). This southern acropolis had originally been enclosed by its own wall, except where the rock is almost vertical. The only part of the temple to be seen now is a levelled area of rock (nearly 120sq.m), but many pieces of masonry and columns have been found in the field below. Archaeological research at this location revealed a sanctuary with votive figurines, bronze and terracotta vessels and jewellery. There are a number of other local sanctuaries and a source of conflict with neighbouring Itanos to the north-east was the control of the sanctuary of Zeus Diktaios at Palaikastro. South again from 'Altar Hill' there are remains of *tholos* tombs from LMIII and possibly later (Whitley et al., 1999). There are reasons to believe that a Minoan settlement may have been located south of these tombs on lower land. Other cemeteries were situated on the east and possibly west of the city, while some 400m north-west of the lower acropolis there are quarries used during the building of the city. Also in that direction is the Skales Cave where finds from an earlier era have been located (Papadakis and Rutkowski, 1985). The city was supplied with water from a spring more than 3km to the south, where the remains of a small temple can still be seen.

Praisos struck coins on the Aiginetan standard from the 4th century BCE. Several coins refer to the worship of Zeus Diktaios on the obverse, usually with Herakles standing wielding a club and holding a bow on the reverse. Others feature a head of Apollo with various designs on the reverse.

Priansos (Πριανσός)

Location: 35.04499°N; 25.26027°E

The urban centre of this *polis* was on a large flat-topped hill at 396m near the village of Kasteliana in the province of Monofatsi. The summit area could have been approximately 50ha and there is evidence of four cisterns, a large temple building (the goddess Athena Polias was the protecting deity), and other public buildings. The site has a 360 degree visibility with particularly good views to the west and north-west. The hill-top also contains the remains of a Venetian fortress that appears to have reused many of the stones from the temple area. There are the remains of other substantial buildings (also probably Venetian) 30m to the west of the trig point.

An inscription dating from the late 3rd or the early 2nd century refers to an *andreion* at Priansos, and this may be identified with the remains of what must have been substantial public buildings to be seen at the hill-top site today, where also there is a scatter of Hellenistic sherds.

The city state of Priansos was a *polis* in the political sense of an independent state by the late Classical period, and in the Hellenistic period its borders extended to the south coast to include the sanctuary of Eileithyia at Inatos (Tsoutsouros) (Perlman, 2004a: 1184). The port for the city state was also at Inatos.

Priansos struck coins on the Aiginetan standard from the beginning of the Hellenistic period. Staters show a seated goddess (Athena?) on the obverse with Poseidon or sometimes a goat or palm tree. Later, around 200 BCE, the mint at Priansos struck tetradrachms on the Attic standard inscribed ΠΡΙΑΝΣΙ. A number of coins have marine themes leading some (e.g. Pashley, 1837) to conclude that Priansos was on the sea. It is more probable that this simply reflects a link to its port as in other inland *poleis*.

Sybrita (Σύβριτα)

Location: 35.25940°N; 24.63999°E

Sybrita has an exceptionally long history going back at least to Late Minoan times. The earliest evidence of settlement is LMIIIC but other material has been found from Protogeometric, Geometric as well as the Classical and Hellenistic eras. The name means 'town of the wild boar', although in the pre-Greek era the name may have meant 'sweet-water'. Perlman (2004: 1187) argues that an *asylia* decree of the 3rd century provides the earliest reference to the city as a *polis*. In the Hellenistic period, Sybrita formed an alliance with Gortyn in a *sympoliteia*.

Sybrita lies to the west and above the villages of Thronos/Klisidi in the Amari valley. The city was on the main route linking Eleutherna with the Mesara Plain. It is on a substantial hill (Kephala) from which there is a commanding view of the Amari valley and Mt Psiloritis. As Captain Spratt wrote after his visit 'a finer site for a city I have not as yet seen in Crete' (1865, II: 104). The top of the hill together with terraces covers an area of at least 50ha. The hill rises to over 620m and has many springs and clear sight lines on all sides. There is evidence of defensive walls and associated gates. A massive fortification wall, mostly of isodomic construction, links Kephala with a lower rise to the east (Keratidi), thereby creating a double acropolis layout (cf. Spratt, 1865: 104). The flat grassy area at the summit of Keratidi may have contained a sanctuary and there is evidence of another on the top of Kephala, surrounding the trig point. If *polis* layout elsewhere can be used as a guide, then it is probable that the unexcavated saddle of land between the two hills once served as an *agora*. The residential districts appear to have been on the southern and south-western slopes of the acropolis. Three cemeteries have been found, two to the south-west of Kephala and a third some distance to the north-east.

An Italian-Greek excavation in the 1990s discovered a fine public building of ashlar blocks (ca. 11m × 6m), built partly over an earlier structure, that may have served as a *prytaneion*. It is important to note that this building, facing south near the summit of Kephala, is described by the recent archaeological team as dating from the 1st to the 3rd centuries AD, and that there is in fact no evidence of Kephala having been occupied during the Archaic, Classical and Hellenistic periods (Rocchetti and D'Agata, 1999). While it is true that remains of the Roman period were found in this building, its position, construction and apparent function all suggest that it performed a major public role during the Classical and Hellenistic periods. Both Kephala and Keratidi have abundant surface sherds, some earlier than the Archaic period and some clearly Roman, but also many that could indicate extensive use during the intervening centuries (cf. D'Agata, 1999). The remains of Roman occupation occur at lower levels beneath both the modern village of Thronos and its neighbour Ag. Fotini.

The same team also investigated a group of buildings on the northern sector of Kephala dating from the 12th to the 9th centuries, including one that was found to contain ceramic material, votive offerings and animal bones (Rochetti and D'Agata 1999; Rochetti, 1994). During excavations in 2002 on the north plateau of the Kephala hill, a terracotta bell-krater was discovered, showing scenes of warriors on all faces, which dated from the end of the 11th century or the early 10th century BCE. Recent petrographic work on other Early Iron Age artefacts has demonstrated links between the settlement on Kephala at this time and other early communities in west-central Crete (D'Agata and Boileau, 2009).

Perlman (2004a: 1187) reports on a sanctuary of Hermes Kranaios at a site 0.5km to the south-west.

While it is not possible to be entirely certain, the most probable location for the port of the city was at Soulia (modern Ag. Galini) at the southern end of the Amari valley. Sybrita was one of the earliest city states to mint its own currency (ca. 380 BCE). Hellenistic examples show Hermes on the obverse and Dionysos with the word ΣΥΒΡΙΤΙΩΝ, ΣΥΒΡΙ or ΣΥ on the reverse. Svoronos cites 15 coin types, including some that follow the Gortynian pattern and suggest close collaboration with that city. The numismatist Mørkholm (1991: 89) argues that 'the coinage and trade of Sybrita shows late fourth century numismatic art at its very best'. One of the coins showing Hermes is, he suggests, evidence of contact with the mainland, being based on a famous statue by Lysippos.

Tylisos (*Τύλισος*)

Location: 35.29972°N; 25.02948°E

Tylisos lies between Knosos to the east and Axos to the west above the western end of the fertile plain of north-central Crete. The exact location of the *polis* town remains rather unclear, partly because of the Minoan site that is adjacent to the village of the same name. There are reports of a monumental altar and *temenos* wall (a wall surrounding a sanctuary) north-west of the Minoan buildings but little else (Perlman, 2004a: 1189). Spratt refers to the finding of ancient tombs on this site which lay 'a few hundred yards to the north-east of and below the modern village' (Spratt, 1865, II: 65).

It is possible that the Classical and Hellenistic *polis* town has not yet been located. The normal inland *poleis* location would suggest a site at a higher level, possibly on the hill to the north-west ('Pyrgos'; 685m at the peak) but no exploration of this site has been made, other than in connection with a Minoan peak sanctuary near the summit where it is known that rituals were also held in Classical and Hellenistic times (Kyriakidis, 2005). Some of the buildings from this period would have been destroyed in the excavation of the Minoan site near the modern village, but this area is simply too small to have accommodated a medium-size *polis*. It is much more probable that this was the western edge of the urban centre which extended eastward for more than a kilometre at approximately 170m overlooking the fertile valley below and the sea at Gazi. Spratt writes that he arrived at the modern village of 'Tylisso, or Dylisso, occupying the upper portions of the site of the old Cretan town of Tylisso, which, from its advantageous situation, must have been of some size and importance, as is shown by its coins and by the remains of the town itself' (Spratt, 1865, II: 65). What is particularly important is that he goes on to say, 'but the name of this old town is applied also to the more evident site of the city, lower down, at some ruins nearly a mile from the present village' at what he refers to as 'Kato Tylisso'. There are indeed signs of earlier habitation at this site, including a thin scatter of sherds from the Classical and Hellenistic periods, which lies on a tongue of land to the east and slightly to the north of the modern village. Satellite images (e.g. Google Earth) show many outlines of buildings but, aside from large piles of building stone, very little evidence of them can be seen on the surface today. At the furthest point of this site, just before it drops away into a steep valley below, there are traces of a significant public building, possibly the remains of a temple.

In the Classical era, Tylisos and Knosos formed an alliance which regulated borders and inter-*polis* trade relations and provided for a tax-free zone between the two. Knosos, however, was always the larger partner and it is probable that Tylisos was a dependent city state. Its port was probably at Apollonia (modern-day Gazi, a suburb of Iraklio) (Sanders, 1982: 154). This part of the coast is directly over-looked from the highest point at 'Kato Tyliso'. From this position, the *polis* would have controlled the route west through the mountains towards Axos.

Tylisos struck staters on the Aiginetan standard at the beginning of the Hellenistic period. They normally show the head of Hera with floral decoration on the obverse with Apollo holding a goat's head and bow on the reverse. The coins contain the legend ΤΥΛΙΣΙΟΝ or ΤΥΛΙΣΙΩΝ sometimes retrograde.

II – Secondary Settlements

Secondary settlements are defined as having served as ports for inland city states. Sometimes that connection is very clear, on other occasions much less so. The port towns are generally far smaller than the urban centres of primary city states, in some cases so small that almost no physical remains exist. Sea erosion, possibly exacerbated by the tipping of the island up in the west and down in the east in the 4th century AD, has made matters worse, and as population centres have grown in coastal areas in later years they all but obliterated many earlier settlements. On top of this, the relative paucity of archaeological evidence on Cretan city states as a whole is far more evident on the coast, partly because in many areas only 'rescue digs' are possible without destroying existing buildings.

Agios Georgios (Αγ. Γεώργιος)
Location: 35.23667°N; 23.65037°E

The Grammenos peninsula (now called Akrotiri Trachili) lies three kilometres to the west of Kasteli Selinou and modern Palaiochora. Just to the north-east and near the hamlet of Gialos is the outfall of the Pelekaniotikos River, and it is here that Sinclair Hood reported finding the remains of a settlement dating from the Hellenistic and Roman eras just to the east of the river mouth but now some way back from the coast at the point where the old coastline would have been (Hood, 1967: 49). He found numerous sherds, which included fragments of Classical and Hellenistic vases with traces of red glaze. Recent disturbance has revealed many more of the same period. Just to the west of the river at the same point there are remains of a landing stage of the Roman period where Savignoni and de Sanctis found a number of tombs on higher ground containing some important Roman vases (Savignoni and de Sanctis, 1901: 467). Given its position, this small settlement would probably have served as the access to the sea for the small city of Pelkis that was located on a ridge two kilometres to the north-east and visibly connected with this site.

Amnisos (Αμνισός)
Location: 35.33115°N; 25.20597°E

Amnisos was located at the outfall of the Karteros River just to the east of modern Iraklio on a low hill (32m) right above the beach where surface sherds are evident from Minoan until Roman times. It is best known as the port of Minoan Knosos. Excavations there by Arthur Evans and others revealed very beautiful wall paintings from the 'Villa of the Lillies' which is almost at sea level (Kitchell, 1977: 138–64). On the slope below the hill on which the Classical town was located is the cave where according to legend the goddess Hera gave birth to Eileithyia, herself the goddess of mothers and motherhood (Schäfer, 1992: 73–75). Amnisos continued as a port of Knosos through to the Hellenistic period when its importance was superseded by Herakleion.

Amphimalla (Αμφίμαλλα)
Location: 35.35845°N; 24.25344°E

The site of this settlement, sometimes referred to as Amphimallion, is on a hillock known as Venou or Kephala approximately 1,200m south and west of modern Georgioupoli where sherds of the Classical and Hellenistic eras are evident. Amphimalla, whose name probably means 'surrounded by mountains', was not a city state in the political and economic sense and no coins have been located. It served as one of two ports for Lappa on the north coast, the other being Hydramia (Barr, Map 60; Sanders, 1982: 17/13). The site overlooks the harbour at Georgioupoli that may have been built over the ancient installations.

Apollonia (Απολλωνία)
Location: 35.34229°N; 25.05236°E

The Barrington Atlas follows Sanders (1982: 9/8) in placing the port of Apollonia at Gazi just to the west of Herakleion where the most probable site for the harbour itself is near to the outfall of the Almyros River. Pashley, however, locates Apollonia, which is obviously a common name, towards Megalo Kastron on the Giophyros River (1837, I: 261). The topography suggests that the former location would have enabled the town to serve as a port for Tylisos less than a day's march south-west up the valley of the Almyros River. It must be said, however, that there is no archaeological or epigraphic evidence that makes this connection.

Further difficulties arise with the excavation by Alexiou (1975) at a site further west near the village of Agia Pelagia. This showed evidence of a *prytaneion* which tallies with inscription evidence offering state hospitality to visiting ambassadors (Perlman 2004: 1151). Apollonia signed the decree with Eumenes II and there is another between the *polis* and Milatos and externally with Ionia in 193 BCE (Polybius, 28.14; 27.16). The town was probably destroyed by Kydonia in 173 BCE. Some coins that may be from Apollonia show Herakles and a deer on one side while others show a garlanded Artemis.

Arvi (Ἄρβη)

Location: 35.98611°N; 25.46056°E

The modern village of Arvi lies on the south coast and dominates a small plain to the north. More important, it benefits from a year-round stream which issues through a spectacular gorge leading up to two settlements on the southern slopes of the Dikti range (modern Amiras to the west and Ag. Vasilios to the east).[15] On either side of the gorge are significant heights, a ridge leading eventually to Mt Keraton (621m) to the west and Viglais (685m) to the east. On the eastern summit of the limestone cliff cut by the gorge, there is a significant 'refuge site' dating from the LMIIIC period, and possibly a little earlier (Nowicki, 1996). The absence of any visible remains at the promising location just back from the sea below, together with some uncertainty concerning the spelling of the ancient name, has led to doubt about the exact location of the old city. Stephanus Byzantius writes of Mount Arbios in Crete where Zeus Arbios was worshipped, noting that the inhabitants of the mountain were known as Arbian. Pashley describes the discovery of a marble

---

15 The extraction of water for the cultivation of horticultural crops under plastic now means that this important source runs dry in the summer months.

sarcophagus found on the shore at Arvi, and also that residents of Ag. Vasilios had seen the remains of ancient walls before the stones were incorporated into the village church (1837, I: 275–6). It is now normally assumed that Mt Arbion is Mt Keraton and that the ancient city lay somewhere on its flanks with the port itself beneath the modern village. In 1962, the British archaeologists Sinclair Hood, Peter Warren and Gerald Cadogan (1964: 84–91) found evidence of 'Greco-Roman' habitation at the site of the present village and on a low rise on the western side of the river valley (an area known as 'Komitas'), but aside from some reused limestone blocks there is no evidence of this today, although the site is very similar to others where the presence of such towns is unambiguous. A 'Greco-Roman' cemetery was also found south of the hill called 'Kamini' on the eastern side of the river valley.

The only relevant epigraphic evidence is a treaty between Gortyn and Miletos, probably dated to 252–250 BCE, which has Lyktos, Arkades, the Hyrtaioi and the Ariaioi as co-signatories, suggesting that these were all in central southern Crete. Kitchell (1983) has convincingly argued that coins of the 'Ariaioi', mostly featuring a beardless head and the abbreviation API on the obverse and ΑΙΩΝ and a herm (square pillar surmounted by the head of a deity) on the reverse, can be identified with a city called 'Aria'. The beardless head is, he suggests, that of Zeus. Moreover, both the names 'Aria' and 'Arbion' emerged from a word stem containing the digamma, an archaic letter of the Greek alphabet phonetically similar to 'w' which survives in some Greek dialects as 'v' (Kitchell 1983: 220). On this basis the location of the city near or possibly beneath modern Arvi is highly probable.

Bionnos (Βιώννος)

Location: 35.14465°N; 24.51306°E

The site of the small coastal *polis* of Bionnos is not completely certain. The most probable location is south of Kerames on a rather eroded coastline between Cape Melissa and Preveli above an area now known as Ag. Fotini. Hood and Warren (1966: 173) visited the site in 1965 and describe 'well-preserved' stretches of what appears to be a defensive wall on the eastern edge of the site at a place known as 'Kionia' (possibly from kiones [columns]). On the northern side of the city, these archaeologists also describe the remains of a curtain wall running east-west with two semi-circular towers between 6–7m in diameter. On the western edge this wall abuts a much larger circular tower (12m diameter) made from rough polygonal masonry, and the remains of another smaller rectangular tower were observed at the eastern end overlooking the small valley below. Naturally enough the hill itself is known locally as 'Pyrgos' and part of the site is also known as 'Visala'. Pendlebury reports finding Late Minoan sherds at 'Visala' near Kerames as well as sherds and walls from the Archaic period at the same location (1965: 293; 340).

Perlman (2004a: 1154) notes that Bionnos is listed between Psycheion and Matala in the late 3rd century catalogue of *theorodokoi* from Delphi. Although no ancient source lists Bionnos as a *polis*, an inscription from the site dated to the late 4th – early 3rd century dealing with actions to recover debts, together with the appointment of a *theorodokos* to greet and accommodate the Delphic *theoroi* in the Hellenistic period, persuades Perlman to accept Bionnos as having been a possible *polis*.

There is no evidence confirming whether Bionnos served as a port for an inland city state but the beach at Ag. Fotini is just capable of offering sufficient shelter, at least during the summer months. If a link was ever established, the most plausible candidate is Phalanna / Osmida at Onithe. Although the site of this relatively important city state faces north, an ancient track leads south towards Kerames.

Chersonisos (Χερσόνησος)
Location: 35.32335°N; 25.39249°E
The *polis* town of Chersonisos is thought to have been located south of the peninsula Akrotiri Chersonisos and just north-west of the modern village of Limenas Chersonisou, 26 km east of Iraklio. Although an independent *polis* in the Hellenistic period and before, the town served as the port to Lyktos, 12 km to the south (Strabo 10.4.14).

Trading links are suggested by a treaty between Chersonisos and Rhodes in the late 3rd century. The city signed a *sympoliteia* treaty with Lyktos towards the end of the 2nd century and the two signed treaties with other *poleis* acting together. Strabo mentions a temple of Artemis Britomartis and this is reflected in coinage and trade. A grave stele near the town referred to a decree between Knosos and Gortyn.

The city struck coins as early as 330 BCE.

These feature either the goddess Artemis Britomartis or Apollo and Herakles. Noting the varied quality of Cretan coinage, Mørkholm (1991: 89) also comments on some fine quality workmanship from Chersonisos which shows evidence of a coin type similar to one from Stymphalos in Arcadia.

Very little systematic archaeological investigation has taken place at this site, but there is evidence of a large-scale aqueduct (dating from the Roman period) to the south-east in the foothills of the Dikti range. The site of a temple to Britomartis dating to the 2nd century is suggested by the find of an inscription to her on a small headland to the east of the town beneath an early Christian basilica (Spratt, 1865, I: 104–7). To the north there is a peninsula that contained the city's acropolis. Roman remains were extensive and included a theatre and amphitheatre visible through to the 1980s. There is little to be seen today because of the burden of tourism development (Sanders, 1982: 144–6).

Herakleion (Ηράκλειον)
Location: 35.335°N; 25.13472°E
Ancient Herakleion lies beneath modern Iraklio, once called Candia. The size of the present city is not indicative of its former size and importance in the ancient period when it was a small and not very significant port. It was a signatory to the mid–3rd century agreement between Knosos and Milatos and is also referred to in an Apterian decree of the 2nd century. Early geographers referred to it as a city-state that was the second, and eventually more important, port of Knosos, which is 5km to the south (Strabo, 10.4.7; 10.5.1; cf. Ptol. 3.15.3; Stad. 348–49).

Only scattered remains, mainly from rescue excavations, have come to light. These include tombs from the Geometric period (cf. Pashley, 1837, I: 189–90; Spratt, 1865, I: 27). Given the difficulties of excavation in the city, it is not known whether it had its own coinage.

Hydramia (Υδραμία)
Location: 35.34663°N; 24.34392°E
Hydramia was a small port for Lappa, some 5km to the east of Georgioupoli near the modern-day village of Dramia (*Barr*). Almost nothing is known of this harbour town except its toponym and location. There is almost no indication of its size and structure, but what few physical remains exist suggest a small town on a slightly

raised piece of land, which may have continued in existence into the Roman era.

Inatos (Ἴνατος)

Location: 34.98310°N; 25.27902°E

Inatos is thought to have lain at the western end of the bay of Tsoutsouros and to have served as the port of Priansos (Sanders, 1982: 7/31). Today there is fragmentary evidence of a settlement to the right of the path leaving Tsoutsouros for Maridaki at the western end of the village at a height of 32m above sea level. As well as traces of house foundations there is also evidence of an *aloni*, or threshing floor, but the date of this is unclear. As at Amnisos there is a cave where the goddess Eileithyia was worshipped and it is here that the only archaeological investigations have been undertaken. These showed evidence of use in the Geometric period but it was in the Hellenistic era that Inatos developed as a port. At that time, it has been assumed that the goddess was worshipped at a temple near the church of Agia Eleni.

Istron (Ἰστρών)

Location: 35.12758°N; 25.73640°E

Istron lay on the Bay of Mirabello near the village of Kalo Chorio and on the promontory of Nisi Pandeleimon at the northern end of the Vrokastro valley at the point where the Istron River empties into the sea (Hayden et al. 1992: 298; 330–32). Very little archaeological investigation has taken place but Perlman suggests that the existing remains are Archaic and later (2004a: 1167). The *Barrington Atlas* identifies them as Hellenistic and later. On the promontory, which is 100m east of the Istron River and at the eastern end of the bay, surface sherds can be seen from the Archaic through to the Hellenistic period. Immediately to the west, in the middle of the bay, lies the Priniatikos Pyrgos promontory which, prior to a rise in sea levels, used to be a raised hillock just back from the sea. The remains of walls, probably from the western edge of the Classical and Hellenistic *polis*, can be seen under the present sea level. Recent finds have included a large deposit of fine wares from the Classical period that also show trade links with Gortyn and other Cretan cities (Erickson, 2010).[16]

---

16 An archaeological project on Priniatikos Pyrgos carried out by the Irish Institute of Hellenic Studies at Athens in collaboration with Mediterranean Section of the University of Pennsylvania Museum is due to conclude in 2011.

Although the evidence is not entirely clear, it is probable that this small *polis* served as a northern port for Oleros, only six kilometres to the south-west. After the absorption of Oleros into the territory of Hierapytna, and the clear shift of the former's economic centre of gravity to the south, Istron appears to have been merged with the large inland city state of Lato, a day's march to the north-west.

Kalami (Καλάμι)

Location: 35.45278°N; 24.16889°E

It is not known for certain whether the port of Aptera was at Kalami on the tiny headland of Akrotiri Souda or a little further to the south-east at Kalyves. It is possible that both were used as harbours at different periods by the great city state on Palaiokastro above. The topography, however, suggests that the former may have been more important. Spratt, following Strabo, identifies the remains he saw as 'Kisamos' (distinct from Kasteli / Kisamos further west) just west of the headland and the present hamlet of Kalami. Even today the possible remains of harbour installations are visible beneath a massive concrete covering. The route of an ancient track rises slightly west again and follows a steep valley to emerge between the village of Megala Chorafia and the main gate to Aptera. Just back from the beach there are traces of unexcavated buildings of Classical or Hellenistic date.

Kalamydi (Καλαμύδη)

Location: 35.23556°N; 23.68611°E

Ancient Kalamydi was probably located to the east of the modern town of Palaiochora, near the mouth of the Vlithias River. The *Stadiasmus* identifies the name with a settlement 50 stadia (ca. 9km) west of Lisos and 30 stadia (ca. 5.5km) east of Kriou Metopon (modern-day Cape Krios) which is approximately the same as the site above. Modern Palaiochora on the Tigani promontory was probably an island prior to the volcanic uplift of the western end of Crete in 365 AD (Hood, 1967: 48–49; Gondicas, 1988: 53–55). Gondicas (1988: 146) identifies this island as ancient Iousagora. In 1966, Hood found what he calls an 'extensive settlement' on the eastern bank of the Vlithias River. The site is above the present shore line on a flat area just north of the road towards Anydri. Although he found only Roman pottery sherds, Hood regarded the settlement as 'Greco-Roman' and it is not unreasonable, therefore, to assume that it served as the port for ancient Kantanos at Kadros (Hood, 1967: 48). As Gondicas (1988: 54–55) suggests, when considering the topography of the area and its isolation in earlier times, it is not difficult to imagine the existence of a political union within the valley. Modern developments and extensive undergrowth now impede the sight line up the valley, but at one time the double acropolises at Kadros to the north would almost certainly have been in view. It would also have been possible to see one or more of the protecting forts on the eastern bank of the Vlithias, and there are remains of what could have been the ancient track on the east of the river and opposite the modern road.

Kamara (Καμάρα)

Location: 35.19128°N; 25.71760°E

Ancient Kamara, or Lato pros Kamara, lies beneath Agios Nikolaos on the western shores of the Gulf of Mirabello. It is less than a day's march to the east of Lato whose port it became. Although the city was established in the Archaic period, its main period of prosperity was in the Hellenistic era. Gradually, the population of Lato relocated to the port and eventually they merged as one administrative unit. The intricacies of the family connections between the two locations have been expertly catalogued by Baldwin-Bowsky (1989b) who also shows how the highest political positions in both settings were rotated amongst a small group of families.

Unfortunately almost no excavations have taken place at Kamara, with the exception of one cemetery. Paula Perlman does not consider it to have had separate status from Lato as a *polis*, but Baldwin-Bowsky (1989a) does. It appears to have shared a currency with Lato which suggests that Perlman may be correct.

Kastri (Καστρί)

Location: 34.99881°N; 25.37855°E

The toponym for this town in ancient times is unknown and the reference here is to its modern-day name (Perlman, 2004a: 1147). Remains of Hellenistic moles and harbour installations can be seen on the border between Kastri and Keratokambos (*Barr.*; Hood et al., 1964: 82–83). There is also a thin scattering of ca. 4th–3rd century sherds on a low hill (18m) behind the harbour. Hood et al. noted a 'tower-like' fragment of rough isodomic masonry (ashlar blocks of equal height) standing up to

3m high on this saddle-shaped hill running west-east (1964: 82). On the north side of the road by the beach and about 50m east of the stream bed they also found a thick layer of amphora fragments and suggested that this may have been the site of a warehouse. There is no evidence today of the building. This was probably the same site identified later as one of three major amphora workshops showing clear evidence of external trading from the Hellenistic period onwards (Empereur, 1991; 1989).[17] A rescue excavation reported in *Kritiki Estia* (2002: 331–2) also showed evidence of settlement from the Classical and Hellenistic periods (Whitley, 2002–2003: 81).

It is not known for certain which primary *polis*, if any, was associated with Kastri. However, old roads tended to pass even more ancient sites wherever possible and 4km due north of Kastri there are important Minoan sites at Kephali near modern-day Chondros. In the light of these, it is not unreasonable to suggest that Kastri may have been the port of Arkades, which was 12km north and slightly to the west at Aphrati.

Kasteli (Kisamos) (Καστέλι [Κίσαμος])

Location: 35.50015°N; 23.65036°E

The ancient port of Kasteli lies some way back from the sea because of the uplift of western Crete. The most likely location for the harbour is at Mavros Molos to the west of the modern town (Stefanakis, 2010: 75). D.J. Blackman, author of the PECS entry, records that in the mid-18th century AD, Pococke identified the foundations of large buildings to the west of the harbour. In that position today, in an area of rising ground just to the north of the remains of the Turkish fortification wall, there are industrial buildings that have reused much older limestone ashlar blocks. These are also found, as in Chania, in the massive Turkish fortifications. The actual location of the main settlement from the Classical and Hellenistic periods is not entirely clear and there is a suggestion that it was a short distance to the west again on the Selli hill above Cape Kavonisi where remains of the Classical period are visible (PECS).

Most famous for its remains of the Roman period (especially mosaics), Kasteli was the

---

17 Others nearby were found at Inatos (Tsoutsouros) and at Dermatos, a small hamlet lying between Tsoutsouros and Keratokambos.

port of Polyrrhenia but grew to considerable importance in its own right in the late Hellenistic era. It gradually superseded Polyrrhenia, but probably not until after the Roman occupation (Stefanakis, 2010: 75).

Kytaion (Κύταιον)

Location: 35.40921°N; 24.86924°E

The small *polis* of Kytaion was mentioned by Stephanus Byzantius and is usually considered to have been located in the Bay of Almyrida (not to be confused with the village to the east of Kalyves), just north of the modern village of Sises where the remains of a harbour are still visible (Stefanakis, 1998; *Barr*; Perlman, 2004a: 1172). Others, less plausibly, have suggested a site to the west at Astali near the village of Bali, while Pashley follows Pliny in placing the *polis* at Palaiokastro, Rogdia to the west of modern Iraklio where there is a Venetian fort but no other reported remains (1837, I: 259).

The city state had its own mint, albeit for a brief period (ca. 350–325 BCE) producing silver staters with the legend KY. The important point to note is that these coins shared the design on both the obverse and reverse with Axos, the large inland *polis* located a day's march to the south, suggesting that Kytaion served as a port for Axos (Stefanakis, 1998). Perlman (2004a: 1172) argues that the short period of independence for Kytaion was because it was annexed by Axos. This supports the argument for the site at Almyrida since the remains further west at Bali would not have been anywhere near as accessible to the citizens of Axos. Unfortunately this site cannot be unambiguously identified with that of Kytaion, since an inscription on a Hellenistic boundary stone found in the vicinity of where Kytaion is assumed to have been refers to a settlement (*polis?*) called 'Sisai', which is rather close to the modern toponym 'Sises', but it is possible that this was another name for the same place.

Lebena (Λεβήνα)

Location: 34.9375°N; 24.92222°E

A more or less straight line route through the Asterousia Range underlines the role of Lebena as a port of Gortyn to the north, although the actual journey must have been tortuous and may be one reason why the latter sought to conquer Phaistos, thereby to enjoy access to the sea at the western end of the Mesara (Matala). The site for the harbour town of Lebena is the Bay of Lendas between the headlands of Leontas (thus called because it resembles a lion) to the west and Psamidomouri to the east. The town was established in the Classical era and became well known for its Temple of Asklepios. It reached its heyday in the Hellenistic era but much earlier settlements may have existed in adjacent areas (Hadzi-Vallianou, 1989). The layout of the site today is not clear, despite some conservation efforts. Nearly all that is visible dates from the Roman era.

The relationship with Gortyn was established in an Archaic agreement (Perlman, 2004: 1174). Although difficult to access from the north, Lebena enjoyed a straightforward sea crossing to Egypt and was thus an important trading post. Perlman (2004: 1174) notes the existence of the *theorodokos* appointed by Lebena to entertain the Delphic *theoroi* in the late 3rd century, but most likely the town was a dependency of Gortyn and unable to determine its own political fortunes. Svoronos believed that the city had its own coins, but they have not yet been found. Apart from epigraphic evidence of agreements with Gortyn, the most important inscriptions arise from the healing properties of the spring and the associated *Asklepieion* (Perlman, 2004: 1174; cf. Hadzi-Vallianou, 1989). The vast majority of the extant remains today date from the Roman era.

Lisos (Λισός)

Location: 35.24372°N; 23.78556°E

Lisos was one of a series of small ports linked to inland *poleis* in south-western Crete and probably served as the port of Hyrtakina with which it had a specific alliance, and to which signs of a linking road are still visible. It was a member of the Confederation of Oreioi (mountain peoples) and at one time may have served as its capital and religious centre (Perlman, 1995). Svoronos argues that Hyrtakina and Lisos were the first to establish a close connection, followed by the other states of the league (1890: 222). He also suggests that the league was essentially a monetary union, although others also believe it existed to control the complex pattern of pasture areas in the *Lefka Ori* (Sekunda, 2000: 346). Support for the former view comes from the alliance with Magas, King of Cyrene, between 280 and 250 BCE (Perlman, 1995) although it is probable that the league had numerous functions.

Lisos occupied the bottom and sides of a

valley facing the Bay of Agios Kyrkos three kilometers to the west of Syia (modern Sougia). The urban centre was quite extensive and was probably established in the Classical period. The harbour area was originally somewhat inland of the present seafront but the remains of an extensive residential area of Hellenistic date are located on the eastern side of the valley with barrel vaulted tombs of the Roman period well preserved on the western valley walls (Perlman, 2004a: 1175). An *Asklepieion* and sanctuary near to a spring in the north-eastern corner of the site was excavated by Platon in the late 1950s (Platon, 1992). In this area were found many statues of Roman and Hellenistic date, mostly representing Asklepios (god of medicine and healing) or Hygieia (daughter of Asklepios and the goddess of health and cleanliness – i.e. *hygiene*).

Lisos struck its own coinage sometimes with a head of Artemis on the obverse and the legend ΛΙΣΙΩΝ and a dolphin on the reverse. Other issues included the abbreviation ΛΙ with a goat's head on the obverse and a bee on the reverse. Importantly for trading purposes, Lisos also struck an alliance coinage with Hyrtakina.

Matala (Μάταλα)

Location: 34.99583°N; 24.74583°E
The port of Matala probably lies mostly beneath the sea and the eponymous modern village at the western end of the Mesara Plain. The list from Delphi of the *theorodokoi*, or those appointed to welcome visiting dignitaries from the home of the oracle, includes Matala which, by the time the list was inscribed (ca. 230–220 BCE) was a dependency of Phaistos. This suggests that earlier Matala may have had a greater degree of independence (Perlman, 1995: 132).

The town served as the port for Phaistos (q.v.) in the 3rd century and was sufficiently independent as a small *polis* to be a signatory, along with twenty-four others, to the agreements made by Knosos, Gortyn and Phaistos with Miletos (not to be confused with Milatos q.v.) on what is now the Turkish coast. These agreements date from either ca. 293–2 or ca. 259–250 BCE (Perlman, 2004a: 1149).

There are no remains of public buildings of either the Classical or Hellenistic periods to be seen above the water level but traces are evident below the surface of the sea. Later use as a port in Roman times is also evident, particularly from rock-cut tombs. The acropolis

was on the Kastri promontory to the south of the modern village where at least one kiln was producing trade amphorae. When Phaistos fell to Gortyn in ca. 220 BCE, Matala became the second port of the latter and remained in use for this purpose for some centuries thereafter.

Milatos (Μίλατος)

Location: 35.30954°N; 25.57249°E
The foundation of Milatos dates from at least Archaic times. The Milatioi are known to have fought with the Drerians in the bordering *polis* to the south-east in the 6th century. It is also claimed that the Lyktians destroyed the city in 220 BCE (although this was when they were involved in the Lyktian War with Knosos). If this claim is correct then it may have been in defence of Chersonisos that bordered the lands of Milatos to the west. Milatos is perhaps most famous for having founded the city of Miletos in Asia Minor and is a co-signatory to the agreements with that city in ca. 259–250 BCE. Given its relatively early demise, it is not known whether Milatos served as a port. If it did, then from a topographical point of view the site at Anavlochos (q.v.) would have been the obvious 'primary polis' (Nowicki, 2000: 170). Unfortunately, we do not have a toponym that identifies this site with any certainty, nor any inscription evidence that might link it to Milatos.

The town was located on the terraced western-facing slopes of the Kastelos hill, 1.5km north-east of the modern village of Milatos at an elevation of 55m (and higher). There is not a great deal remaining today but house walls and ancient terracing can be made out just above the river bed. An ancient track between walls runs from this site north towards the sea.

Myrtos (Μύρτος)

Location: 34.99861°N; 25.59889°E
Myrtos lies on the south coast approximately 10km west of Hierapytna at the point where streams emerging near Malla empty into the sea after passing through the Sarakinas Gorge 3km to the north. This is an area rich in Minoan remains, particularly at Pyrgos, a conical hill a short distance east of the centre of the modern village. Hood et al. (1964: 93–96) describe this area in detail; they found ample sherds dating from Early Minoan (EM-I) through to Late Minoan (LM-I) periods and this site, and another close by at Fournou Korifi, were excavated by Peter Warren in 1967 and found

to date from EMII (Warren, 1972). Of particular interest were the remains of stone vases, made either from white limestone or from local steatite. Hood et al. also noted 'stray Greco-Roman' sherds, but for the most part the assumption has always been that beneath modern Myrtos lie the remains of a small harbour town of the Roman era. Certainly, Sanders (1982, 2/4: 138) saw on the west of the village north of the coastal road, the remains of a brick-faced concrete building with hypocausts (underfloor heating by warm air) and some fragments of mosaic that must have been Roman.

Arthur Evans is reported to have found graves here of the Hellenistic era (Pendlebury, 1965: 364). It is highly likely that the harbour at Myrtos was in use at this time and possibly earlier. It is very probable, and in keeping with the position at neighbouring Arvi, that a small town would have been located at some elevation but close to the sea. Hood et al. assume that the remains of a tower at Pyrgos, from which the site presumably gets its name, was Turkish but it could have been much earlier. It is true that the sherd scatter at Pyrgos is predominantly Minoan and that very little remains today of the eponymous 'tower', but there are much later and probably pre-Roman sherds and the site, overlooking the river and harbour, is very similar to that at other nearby coastal settlements (e.g. Kastri). It is probable, therefore, that the port provided an outlet to the sea for the small *polis* of Malla to the north.

Olous *(Ολούς)*
Location: 35.25556°N; 25.73333°E
Olous lay on the isthmus of land near modern-day Elounda in north-east Crete that separates the Spinalonga Bay from that of Poros. Some parts of the remains are only visible beneath the sea. Very little archaeological evidence is available to date the foundation of the *polis* but it is probably very early Classical or late Archaic. The temple of Britomartis in Olous contained a statue of the goddess by Daidalos (Paus. ix. 40. 3). It also had a temple of Zeus Tallaios. A rectangular building of the Geometric period was found at Ellinika which may have been a temple of Ares and Aphrodite with Hellenistic building above.

The city state's mint began issuing coins from ca. 330 and initially these were on the Aiginetan standard and featured the head of Artemis Britomartis wearing a laurel-wreath

with a quiver at her neck. The reverse contained the legend ΟΛΟΝΤΙΩΝ and showed Zeus seated holding an eagle. Later coins on the Attic standard were of similar design. Svoronos (1890) cites eleven different types of coins.

Olous is known to have had both positive and negative relations with its southern neighbour, Lato, and epigraphic evidence records both agreements of friendship and those following hostilities. There is also considerable reason for supposing that Olous was deeply engaged in trade, particularly with Rhodes and from there possibly with Egypt, and that it was open to the settlement of foreigners. What is unclear is the strength of its relation with its neighbour Dreros to its immediate west. The topography suggests that Olous could have served as a port of Dreros but there is no epigraphic or literary evidence to support this possibility, save that it would be an obvious connection for a trade-oriented *polis*. The absence of significant coin finds from Dreros makes it difficult to know whether an alliance or co-operative coinage existed between the two. In any event, by the time trading became an important feature of *polis* life, Dreros was either completely or almost deserted.

Pantomatrion *(Παντομάτριον)*
Location: 35.38250°N; 24.59033°E
Although the foundation date for Pantomatrion is unknown it appears to have served as the port for Eleutherna during the Classical and Hellenistic periods until it was eventually supplanted by Rhithymna (Erickson, 2000: 246). The most likely location for the port itself is on the north coast 12km to the east of modern Rethymno near the resort at Stavromenos. Remains from the same periods can be found on higher ground between this location and the modern village of Chamalevri. In and around Stavromenos, Hood et al. (1964) found extensive evidence of habitation from Middle-Minoan to the Roman era. In particular they found tombs of many periods including Late Minoan chamber tombs (1964: 64–66).

There is some controversy over toponyms, however, since Perlman (2004a: 1150) prefers to see the remains at Chamalevri, which are literally only a few hundred metres from the others, as the site for the *polis* town of Allaria. This is rather implausible since there is no other case where urban centres have been this close, although the *Barrington Atlas* also seems to prefer this site. The *polis* of Allaria undoubtedly existed (Polybius 5.63.12) but probably much further to the east. According to Falkener it lay 15 miles south of Siteia at 'Monteforte' where, following Belli's report from the sixteenth century AD, he says there are the remains of ancient buildings and cisterns in a high and inaccessible site (Falkener, 1854: 270).

Investigations in the early 1990s show evidence of late Classical and early Hellenistic buildings at the Chamalevri site (Gavrilaki and Tzifopoulos, 1998). Finds from the site suggest an original habitation in MMII but most of the recovered material is Hellenistic or later. The Classical and Hellenistic city appears to have been east of the stream and close to the shore line where the remains of house walls are visible. Rock-cut graves and chamber tombs are also visible and an LM sanctuary with continued use through the Classical era and possibly later can be seen on the hill of Kakavella 400m SW of the city (Hood, Warren and Cadogan, 1964: 62–66).

It seems probable that Pantomatrion had extensive trade links during the Classical and Hellenistic periods with mainland Greece. The discovery of an 'Atticising' gravestone at the cemetery in Stavromenos supports this view, as do a number of other coins and finds from the same location exhibited in the Rethymno Archaeological Museum. Pantomatrion struck its own bronze coinage during the Hellenistic period with the legend ΠΑ on the reverse.

Phoinix (Loutro) *(Φοίνιξ [Λουτρό])*

Location: 35.20611°N; 24.07°E

Phoinix, which was located on the eastern side of Cape Moures on the south coast of the island, served as the port for Anopolis at the Riza site 700 metres above. The two were linked by an ancient path that is still used today. It is very probable that the same port facility was used by the linked settlement of Araden and, again, a way is still evident from the western side of the Cape up the Aradena Gorge to the Hellenistic settlement on the plateau above.

There has been no archaeological investigation of this port. Even its name is unclear. It is sometimes referred to as 'Phoinikous', indicating a possible trade link with the Near East; at other times it is referred to as simply 'Kato Poli', suggesting its connection to Anopolis (Vasilikis, 2000). What remains today are foundation walls of harbour buildings and possibly residences, together with chamber tombs that are probably of later date.

Phoinix (Sellia) *(Φοίνιξ [Σελλιά])*

Location: 35.19490°N; 24.36038°E

Ancient Phoinix at Sellia lay at an elevation of 75 metres and one kilometre from the sea at the base of cliffs below the monastery and village of Phoinikas with its church of Ag. Efstratios, and towards the head of a steep valley notably containing the wild palms from which the town took its name (Hood and Warren, 1966: 184). The foundations for house walls and ancient terraces are visible today, as is a length of defensive wall running south-north for 200 metres. The settlement appears to have been occupied during the Classical and Hellenistic periods and probably later (Perlman, 2004a: 1172).

This Phoinix, as distinct from the eponymous settlement at Loutro further west, served as the southern outlet to the sea for Lappa (Pseudo-Skylax, 47). Strabo refers to the remains as *Phoinikias Lambaion* or Phoinix of Lappa (10.4.3), but the town is sometimes confused with the port of the same name at Loutro. Pendlebury (1965: 13), who is normally very reliable, follows Strabo by mentioning Phoinix as belonging to Lappa but wrongly locates it as being below Anopolis. Although the settlement was a little way from the sea on elevated land in a sheltered valley, it appears to have possessed harbour installations and associated buildings (warehouses etc.) right on the sea at the very western edge of the bay of Souda.[18] Very little remains to be seen of these installations but Hood and Warren (1966: 184) follow Kirsten (cf. Matz, 1951: 126ff.) in identifying the remains of a building 200 metres from the sea on the east bank of the stream and just north of a modern taverna as of Hellenistic date. Very worn sherds are evident on the surface but some of these appear to be Roman.

Platanias *(Πλατανιάς)*

Location: 35.51378°N; 23.91599°E

Beneath the blanket tourism that typifies Platanias today, there probably lies the remains of a small port town of the ancient world. The twin coastal peaks are a landmark in the more or less flat Plain of Chania and lie only 0.5km from the outfall of the Xekollimenos River

---

18　Guarducci, ii: 192 and end map identifies this settlement as 'Apollonia' but this is unlikely since it is so near Phoinix. This coast is very exposed with no natural harbours and it is much more probable that the port facilities would have been rather minimal and possibly occupied for only part of the year.

(ancient Iardanus) whose valley is still lined with the plane trees from which the modern village takes its name. The higher of the two (Pano Platanias; 108m) today contains a core from the 19th century AD overlain with modern tourist developments. There are some traces of much earlier habitation in the form of walling and some large dressed stone foundations. The smaller rise (Kephalas 77m slightly to the east) has again some traces of earlier use, although it is difficult to be sure of the dates. The modern village possesses a harbour which may have been built over earlier foundations. In the absence of archaeological or other evidence it is impossible to be certain, and the inclusion of this entry is only justified by the position of the town, its topography and a scatter of sherds of the Classical, Hellenistic and possibly Roman periods. Pashley, however, also believed that Platanias was an ancient site, suggesting that it was the urban centre of Pergamon. He argued that this explained the ancient belief that the *polis* town of Pergamon lay near Kydonia, and also Skylax's view that the sanctuary at Dictynna lay directly to the north of its territory. It is worth noting that others have placed Pergamon south of Nochia (Pendlebury, 1965: 14), to the west of the village of Rodopou (Gondicas, 1998), at the Grimbiliana hill (just south of Kolymbari) (Hood, 1964), and on the slopes below Ag. Georgios at Vryses (Faure, 1958: 499).

Rhithymna *(Ρίθυμνα)*

Location: 35.37074°N; 24.46919°E

Sometimes written as Rhithymna (*Ρίθυμνα*) and sometimes Rhithymnia (*Ριθυμνία*), the city state was probably established in the 5th century. The town is only referred to as a *polis* by Stephanus Byzantius but other references in decrees support this attribution (Perlman, 2004a: 1185). It also entered into *proxenia* alliances with other *poleis*. It was, however, a dependent port of Eleutherna and at some time in the Hellenistic period may have been renamed Arsinoë, suggesting a trade link with Ptolemaic Egypt.

The ancient site lies beneath modern Rethymno and for this reason archaeological knowledge has largely been derived in fragmented form from rescue excavations. The acropolis was probably on the high ground under the Venetian fort (*Fortetsa*). The town and harbour were to the east of the promontory on which the fort is located, while slipways and fish tanks are still visible today on the western side.

Rhithymna minted its own coins, usually reflecting maritime scenes, from ca. 330 BCE (Pashley 1837, I: 101). The mint did not survive for many years but appears to have first struck coins on the Aiginetan standard. The staters featured a head of Apollo on the obverse with the legend PI and Apollo holding a stone and bow on the reverse. Drachms showed a head of Athena on the obverse and the same legend and a trident between two dolphins on the reverse. Essentially the same pattern existed with later coins when the name of the city state appears to have changed to Arsinoë (legend ΑΡΣΙ) (Svoronos, 1890: 29). The coinage suggests Apollo and Athena were protecting deities.

Soulia *(Σουλία)*

Location: 35.1°N; 24.68472°E

Soulia is reputed to have served as the port of Sybritos (q.v.) but relatively little is known of its physical structure or role. What remains there are lie buried beneath modern Agia Galini at the mouth of the Platys River. It is thought to have had a temple of Artemis located on the right bank of the river where some remains are still visible.

Stalai *(Στάλαι)*

Location: 35.03516°N; 25.97274°E

Stalai was a significant port town that may later have become a dependent *polis* of Praisos with which it was linked by agreements. The latter provided guarantees to Stalai and to its northern outlet near Siteia in return for shipping and trade relations (Perlman, 1995).

It is probable that the urban centre of Stalai lay on the Dasonari promontory near Makrygialos on the southern coast in the Siteia district. The physical remains at this location have not been systematically explored. It is improbable that the port had its own mint but it certainly raised revenues from trade in fishing and in Tyrian purple, the dye made from the Murex sea snail, and this might suggest Phoenician influence. The fortunes of the town would probably have declined markedly with the destruction of Praisos by Hierapytna in the 2nd century.

Syia *(Συϊα)*

Location: 35.24862°N; 23.80879°E

Syia lies just to the east of Lisos next to the modern village of Sougia in the province of

Chania. It is normally considered to have been the port of the important *polis* of Elyros located a few kilometres north-west up the valley of the Kamariano River and near the modern-day village of Rodovani. On most accounts Syia was a member of the Confederation of the Oreioi and would therefore have played an important role in the trade links that were one of the main reasons for this Hellenistic league of small states.

The remains of the town are almost unknown archaeologically but the river estuary appears to divide them into two, although many of those to the east date from the Roman period. The port area probably lay to the west of the river bed in a low lying area that is now above sea level, but no excavations have been undertaken in this vicinity.

Tarrha *(Τάρρα)*

Location: 35.22694°N; 23.96389°E

Although a small settlement, Tarrha was a city state in the Hellenistic period and probably much earlier (Perlman, 2004a: 1188). It was located near Agia Roumeli at the point where the River Tarrhaios spills from the Samaria gorge into the Libyan Sea (Nixon et al., 1990: 217).

The *polis* was a signatory to the early 2nd century alliance with Eumenes II and was a member of the Confederation of the Oreioi. It would have been an important port for trans-shipment of goods from the upland areas of the Lefka Ori. The White Mountains may have exported cheeses to Alexandria, Byzantium and Antioch in antiquity, as they did to Alexandria, Constantinople (Istanbul), and northern Syria in the early modern period (Sekunda, 2000: 346). Tarrha may have served as an additional port for the two inland members of Hyrtakina and Elyros, although the topography suggests that if this was the case they must have been linked by sea from their respective ports at Lisos and Syia. In this regard, Tarrha is a most unusual *polis* since quite clearly it lacks a *chora*, or agricultural hinterland, except for the high lands to the north. Possessing a *chora* is sometimes referred to as a defining characteristic of a *polis* (Rackham, 1990: 108–9).

Perlman (2004a: 1188) follows Guarducci (1939) in concluding that a temple, possibly of the protecting deity of Apollo, stood on the site west of the river where the church of Panagia now stands. Guarducci suggests that the traveller Buondelmonti in 1415 detected the ruins

of the Temple of Apollo at this location and it is plausible that the goat's head on the coinage may be a reference to Apollo Tarrhaios, since legend has it that the twin offspring of the god's liaison with the nymph Akakallidi were fed by a wild goat. Following the finding of glasswares from the Classical era at nearby Elyros, a cemetery at Tarrha was excavated in 1959 where large quantities of surface glass sherds had also been found (Weinberg, 1959; 1960). The site, on the east slope of the hill east of the river, did not reveal a glass factory as had been hoped, but the grave offerings showed the presence of a fairly wealthy population in the Classical and Hellenistic eras and evidence of habitation up to the end of the fourth century AD. If a glass factory is ever located, it raises the possibility that the *polis* owed its existence to manufacturing glasswares.

The mint at Tarrha struck its own coinage from ca. 330–280/70 originally on the Aiginetan standard and later on the Attic. The obverse featured the legend TAP and a wild goat's head with an arrowhead and a bee on the reverse. Later issues retained a similar design but with the legend abbreviated to TA.

Trypitos *(Τρυπητός)*

Location: 35.19915 °N; 26.12988°E

It is known that Praisos had a harbour on the north coast near to Siteia and this is sometimes thought to be at Petra. Perlman (2004a: 1179) identifies 'Petra' to the west of Siteia at Liopetra, but this is implausible if it is thought of as a port of Praisos. Petra is also a Minoan site just to the east of Siteia, but within a few hundred metres of it can be found the Hellenistic port of Trypitos, which is a much more probable location for the northern outlet of Praisos to the sea. Perlman (2004a) lists Trypitos as at an unidentified location and the *Barrington Atlas* suggests the site at Trypitos is called 'Polichna'. Westgate (2007), however, follows more recently published research in placing it at the site east of Siteia.

The Hellenistic site has been excavated by the Greek Archaeological Service and was clearly an important port complex. It consists of harbour installations on the eastern side of the promontory including a remarkably well preserved slipway. Above on the eastern slope is evidence of a customs house and storage facilities. Above that again are a series of terraces with well-preserved remains of domestic dwellings.

III – Independent poleis

These city states are unusual in combining the main features of the two preceding categories. Although Minoan remains have been found at each of the urban centres of the four *poleis* concerned, the latter tend to be of later foundation than the primary *poleis*, normally in the early Classical era (early 5th century). Hence their origins are not dissimilar to many of the secondary settlements listed earlier. What is different, however, is that their rise to prominence did not depend on other Cretan *poleis* but on economic and political links to *external* powers. Geography and pre-existing trade routes helped determine how these network relations evolved, but they clearly served to embed Crete in the main zones of neighbouring economic importance (Rhodes, Ptolemaic Egypt, Phoenicia and the Greek mainland). In this sense, it is not surprising that they are four in number; nor, perhaps, given their unequal distribution on the four coasts of Crete, that conflict arose from time to time between the pair in the west and the pair in the east.

Hierapytna (Ιεράπυτνα)

Location: 35.00111°N; 25.73306°E

Ancient Hierapytna almost certainly lay beneath modern Ierapetra on the south coast at that point in the east where the island is at its narrowest. Falkener's (1860) translation of the 16th century manuscript on the 'antiquities of Candia' records both the prosperity of Hierapytna and the extent to which its riches were being carried off by the Venetian authorities (and later the Turks). As the author writes, 'if only from the numerous sculptures removed and those still existing, we might feel assured that some great and famous city had stood in this situation' (1860: 272–3). Even a pilaster containing part of an oath by the Carthaginians to the inhabitants of Hierapytna, found in 1565, was reported as having been moved a decade later to Venice where, presumably, it is still located. The ancient harbour, while partly submerged by that time, is described as a 'magnificent work' comprising three basins, although it is not entirely clear how much of this structure predated the Roman succession.

Very little is known about the *polis* of Hierapytna during the Classical and Hellenistic periods, but what there is has recently been reviewed (Guizzi, 2001). The *polis* was clearly an emerging power to be reckoned with and by the first century BCE had a dominant role in the economic and political life of eastern Crete. As Halbherr notes, the *polis* 'must have been from the beginning both powerful and rich by reason of its commerce by sea' (1893: 11). In addition to Zeus, the protecting deity was probably Athena Polias (and later Athena Oleria), but Apollo and Egyptian cults were also followed (Perlman, 2004a: 1166; PECS). Hierapytna struck its own coinage from ca. 330 BCE onwards and these showed a head of Zeus with a palm tree and eagle on the reverse (Stefanaki, 2005). Much of what is known about this important city state comes from inscriptions including a decree of *isopoliteia* with Arkades in the late 3rd century (Perlman, 2004a: 1166).

Inscriptions, mostly found elsewhere, point to both external and internal struggles with economic competitors, particularly in the middle and late Hellenistic era. Commentators on these events, however, tend to downplay the powerful role that Hierapytna came to adopt as a trading port, tending to see its role in conflicts as simply a reflection of a wider culture of inter-*poleis* feuding. Two examples, drawing on the best known epigraphic evidence, can illustrate the point that what appears at first sight to be rather mindless bellicosity was in fact an attempt to sustain continuing economic fortune. The first is the so-called 'Cretan War' of 205–201 BCE when a number of Cretan cities, led by Hierapytna and Olous, were said to have cooperated with Philip V of Macedonia's ambitions to control the eastern Aegean and, in particular, to defeat its most powerful member, Rhodes. This story undoubtedly occurs in ancient sources, usually coupled with the claim that Philip's motive in soliciting Cretan assistance was based on the latter's skills in the arts of piracy. The main evidence adduced in support of this theory is the treaty (*Inscriptiones Creticae* III, 3A: 31–6) signed at the close of hostilities, probably around 200 BCE. This is said to be a truce document reluctantly signed by Hierapytna (and similarly by Olous) as the losers, in which 'Hierapytna was compelled to revoke all its alliances with other powers and to place all its harbours and bases at Rhodes' disposal' (Detorakis, 1994: 77). In fact the treaty, found at Olous, was one of alliance between two *poleis* with many points of shared history and much to gain by cooperation in building trading networks. A Minoan settlement has been shown to have existed at Kamiros, one of the original city states of Rhodes, and the name was also used earlier for Hierapytna. In mythological terms Kyrbas, a grandson of King Minos, is understood to have been the founder of both cities, and his name too was another early one for Hierapytna (Svoronos, 1890: 183). The treaty of ca. 200 specifically calls for provisions in which both parties benefit, even though it is clear that Rhodes was the more powerful partner. Each party was to provide military assistance were the other to be threatened and Hierapytna was to assist Rhodes in raising a mercenary army from Crete should the need arise. Critically, however, Hierapytna's trading role was also protected.[19] It is hard to interpret this document as simply one signed by a defeated party.

Hierapytna undoubtedly used economic and military power in enlarging its territories in eastern Crete. Strabo (9.5.78) records that the peoples of the small settlement called Larisa were moved to Hierapytna.[20] Some time in the 2nd century Hierapytna also subsumed its former 'primary *polis*' of Oleros and the neighbouring *polis* of Priansos may have become a dependent (Spyridakis, 1970: 36). The most significant expansion, however,

was to the east when, between 145 and 140 BCE, Hierapytna overran Praisos from which the latter never recovered. It is not clear why these events occurred, but it is possible that the true target lay further east at Itanos whose own economic fortunes also depended on establishing very significant trading networks. The pretext for conflict, however, was the territory adjoining the Temple of Diktaian Zeus close to Palaikastro on the east coast, and formerly in Praisos's territory, and the island of Leuke (modern Kouphonisi) that may have played a significant role in facilitating trading networks. Conflict lasted for nearly 30 years and in 122 BCE Itanos, at that time without Ptolemaic protection, declared war on Hierapytna. On two occasions the conflicts were subjected to mediation from Magnesia at the request of Rome. The inscription evidence on each occasion supports the defensive claims of Itanos, partly because of Rome's practice of supporting the *status quo ante* in territorial disputes. As Ager (1996: 445) has pointed out, the final treaty (112–111 BCE) provides important evidence on land claims in general, since the Hierapytnians were unable to prove any of the salient criteria: that 'they had not received the land from any of their ancestors nor bought it with money nor conquered it by force nor been granted it by a more powerful state or dynast'. In fact, force was the one element in the dispute that could have been proven, so it may have been that Magnesia was being mindful of Rome's perceived wish not to promote over-mighty economic rivals in the region. In this it may have been prescient for Hierapytna was the last city state to fall to Roman domination a half century later (Spyridakis, 1970: 59; cf. 1977).

Itanos (Ἴτανος)

Location: 35.26314°N; 26.26476°E

Itanos occupied substantial territories in the far north-east of the island. The lands of the *polis* extended from the border with Praisos (and eventually in the Hellenistic period with Hierapytna) near to the sanctuary of Zeus Diktaios at Palaikastro, all the way to the far north-easterly reaches of Cape Sidero (Kalpaxis et al., 1995). Itanos is referred to as a *polis* in inscriptions from the Hellenistic period, although there are epigraphic references to hostilities with Lyktos as early as the 6th century (Perlman, 2004a: 1167). There are clear indications of even earlier occupation and an

---

19 The 12th provision states, 'and if anyone deprives the Hierapytnians of their lawful revenues from the sea, or subverts the established democracy of the Hierapytnians, and the Hierapytnians ask for an auxiliary force, the Rhodians shall send two triremes to the Hierapytnians'.

20 The site of Larisa is unknown but was probably NW of Hierapytna.

LMIII building has been excavated at nearby Vai. The remains of the town are still visible on the sides of two low hills with what was probably an *agora* on the low saddle between them. In a series of papers, Didier Viviers and his co-workers on behalf of the French school have documented important archaeological discoveries at Itanos showing, among other things, a detailed chronology of habitation for different sectors of the region surrounding the original urban area (Greco et al., 1996; 1997; 1999; 2001). These show regions inhabited in the late Neolithic, and most subdivisions of the Bronze Age through to the Roman succession, after which the area was abandoned.

Buildings of the Hellenistic era, found most obviously at the site of the urban centre itself, were built utilizing the foundations from Minoan buildings (Greco et al., 2001: 642). A particular feature of these studies has been the use of 3D-imaging to aid in the understanding of both buildings and the necropolis, situated on the north side of the second bay at Itanos (Ercek, et al., 2010). A previously unknown public building, dating from the Archaic era, was discovered alongside the necropolis. It contained a hearth and may therefore have served as a *prytaneion*, although the authors suggest other uses for this building. The remains of a substantial harbour are also visible partly submerged to the south. Another hill to the south was probably originally fortified and protected the city from incursions from the plain of Itanos (Perlman, 2004a: 1168). There is evidence of a circuit wall with towers on this southern hill that Halbherr described as 'a marvellous work of cyclopean fortification' (1891: 243).

Itanos is famous as a possible protectorate of Ptolemaic Egypt and an Egyptian garrison was stationed there until the end of the 3rd century. Although on some interpretations the Ptolemaic presence at Itanos was merely a marriage of convenience between an independent *polis* and a protective foreign power, leading to no more than a small military presence, on others the relationship was stronger and more akin to the beneficial ownership of a colonial outpost. Certainly, some of the inscription evidence can be read in the latter way. In the middle of the 3rd century a decree by the city state in honour of Ptolemy III opens with the sentence 'since King Ptolemy (III) having received the city of Itanos and its citizens from his father Ptolemy (II) and his ancestors ...' (*Inscriptiones Creticae*

III, 4: 83–5; Austin 2006, no. 265). On the other hand, the Egyptian presence is only recorded from two decades earlier, whereas the decree suggests a far longer relationship. There is no doubt, however, that the location of Itanos made it ideal as a trading city. Rich finds of pottery from Attica, Corinth and elsewhere attest to the importance of Itanos as a trading port (Greco et al., 1997; 1999). As Spyridakis has observed, 'by journeying along the coast of southern Anatolia eastward, Cyprus, Phoenicia, and Egypt may be reached without venturing out into the open sea' (Spyridakis, 1970: 3). Svoronos makes the point that Itanos is the Phalasarna of the east in the sense that each dominated its respective coasts and was similarly dependent upon a monetary economy and productive trading routes (1890: 200).

There is considerable interest in a 3rd century inscription found at Itanos, but relating to an agreement between Hierapytna and Praisos, because it opened up the possibility of a citizen of either becoming a citizen of the other after disposing of his property and renouncing his original citizenship (Spyridakis, 1970: 45). This may have indicated a wish to collaborate against powerful Itanos and obviously it predates the takeover of Praisos by the Hierapytnians in ca. 140 BCE. On the other side, it is perhaps indicative of the hostilities that Itanos suffered as a result of Hierapytnian ambitions, that the *polis* from as early as the 3rd century insisted upon new citizens swearing an oath of loyalty to the city in the names of Zeus Diktaios, Hera and Athena Polias and 'all the gods to whom sacrifices are offered in the sanctuary of Athena, Zeus Agoraios and Pythian Apollo'. As a final flourish the oath carried the threat 'for those who break the oath may their land be infertile, and may they be denied children and flourishing flocks, and may they perish miserably in their wickedness together with their [descendants]' (*Inscriptiones Creticae* III, no. 8: 89–91).

Itanos struck its own coinage on the Aiginetan standard from the end of the 4th century. The coins, for which at least 44 variations have been identified, normally contained the legend ITANION, with a marine deity in early issues on the obverse but later with the head of Athena.

Kydonia (Κυδωνία)

Location: 35.51278°N; 24.02778°E

Ancient sources identify the foundation of Kydonia with Minos or Kydas but Stephanus Byzantius suggests that Kydonia was formerly called 'Apollonia' (390.17). There is no doubt about the substantial Minoan settlement on the Kasteli hill above the harbour in Chania. The most extensively excavated Minoan sites are very close together at the Aikaterini Square on the north side of Kanevaro Street, on Katre Street and the Mathioudakis site 100m east, also on Kanevaro Street (Hallager et al., 1997; Andreadaki-Vlasaki, 1997).

Herodotus (3.59) was the first to suggest that Kydonia was founded in 524 BCE by exiles from Samos who built a number of temples, including the famous Diktynna at the northern end of the Rodopou peninsula. The Samians' presence lasted only five years before they were ousted by settlers from Aigina, possibly acting together with other Cretans (Perlman, 2004a: 1171). Given the colonists' importance as traders and their early use of coinage, this settlement was highly significant in bringing to Crete the beginnings of a monetary system.

The location of Kydonia is not entirely clear. It is generally assumed that Kydonia from the Archaic period onwards was located near the harbour of modern-day Chania, possibly above the remains of the Minoan settlement. This may be true, but it would be a mistake to assume that a centre that was very significant in Minoan times, and again later, must have been a major power in between.

There are three reasons why it is right to question the normal assumption about the location of Kydonia, at least for the whole of the period under discussion. First, from the point of view of this study it would be *sui generis* since, with the one exception of Itanos, no *polis* of an early date and importance was founded on the sea. To some extent, Kydonia *is* probably an exception, in the sense that, like Itanos, it was an early trading centre. Unlike Itanos, however, the city was encircled by a series of settlements in precisely the protected settings characteristic of 'primary *poleis*'. These included Aptera in the east, Lachania in the south and Polyrrhenia and others to the west.

Second, despite evidence of occupation from the Geometric period on the Kasteli hill in Chania, there are no remains yet discovered of substantial public buildings. The marked lack of evidence for settlement here from the Archaic through to the Hellenistic period, at least for settlement of any size, is normally attributed to the disruption occasioned by the building of the Venetian fortified walls and Turkish developments thereafter (PECS). In all locations, however, LMIIIB/C levels are found directly under Venetian structures and most of the re-used material seen today in the remains of the Venetian fortifications would appear to be from the Roman period.

Third, the literature from ancient sources and from the 18th and 19th centuries expresses some doubts about the normal assumption that Kydonia was on the Kasteli hill. Strabo, for example, places Kydonia 40 stadia from the sea, which is just over 7km (using the Ptolemaic measure of 185m). This is exactly the distance of Lachania (q.v.) from the sea (10.4.13). Moreover, Strabo places Aptera, whose site is well attested, at 80 stadia from Kydonia whereas on the Kasteli hill it would be approximately 60 stadia. On the other hand, Lachania is almost exactly 80 stadia (just under 15km) from Aptera.

In the 18th century, the travel writer Richard Pococke in his *Description of the East* (1743) supports Strabo in locating the city of Kydonia at Mt Tityros, which in turn, he thought, was five miles to the south-south-west of the modern city (i.e. at Lachania). Pashley considers but dismisses this proposition on the grounds that Mt Tityros was on the Rodopou near to the sanctuary at Diktynna (Pashley, 1837, I: 16). Captain Spratt, rather more imaginatively, suggests that there were in fact two Kydonias, the first a harbour town at the Kasteli site, the second inland in the same district (Spratt, 1865, II: 140–141). He opts for the site at Vryses but it is more probable that this was the site for Pergamon.

If we consider the cases of Lato and Lato pros Kamara, and Lyktos and Chersonisos ('Lyktos by the sea'), then it is not implausible that there were 'two Kydonias'. The first might have been at the inland *poleis* site at Kastelos (Lachania) which would have been substantially larger than the dependent village (κώμη) assumed by Perlman (2004a: 1171). In time, as in the other examples above, the economic centre of gravity would have shifted to the coastal harbour settlement. What is different, however, is that this coastal settlement was not *created* at the time of this shift but existed from the end of the Archaic period as a colonial enclave. This implies a temporal sequence with a breakpoint at some stage when the 'colonial Kydonia' was repopulated by Cretans seeking to benefit from the trade-related wealth of the Hellenistic period. The question then becomes, is there any evidence for this disjuncture?

The first piece of evidence is the dramatic shift in relations between Kydonia and Athens from the early to the later period. It is probable that the reason Aiginetans colonised the harbour site in 519 BCE was attacks by Athens on Aigina leading to their total expulsion in 431 when more arrivals in Crete may have occurred. Thucydides (2.85.5) describes the Athenians' expedition to Crete in 429 BCE in which they came to the aid of the small inland *poleis* against the Aiginetan colonists, possibly because of the latter's pro-Spartan sympathies. In any event, this was a period of conflict between 'coastal Kydonia' and Phalasarna, Aptera, Elyros and above all Polyrrhenia. In this regard, the important find of 'warrior graves' in the city's eastern cemetery dating fom the Classical period may be significant (Whitley, 2002–2003: 87).

As the seaport grew to become a major economic centre, its early opposition to Athens declined and trading links with Attica became very important. Indeed, a recently published Hellenistic inscription from the Athenian Agora (Agora I 7602) concerns a *syngeneia* between Athens and Kydonia that appears to claim a mythological kinship between the two cities (Papazarkadas and Thonemann, 2008). Agora I 7602 is the earliest *syngeneia* between Athens and a non-Ionian city and the first known inscription recording kinship between Athens and another city on grounds other than the latter's status as a colony. In this scenario, the early and late Kydonia, while both founded upon Attic trade, had totally opposite relations with the most powerful regional *polis*.

The second piece of evidence for a major disjuncture concerns the coinage, which falls into two clear periods, corresponding with the Aiginetan ascendancy and its aftermath. In the first period, from ca. 475 to 300, the coins have a number of forms such as a female head wreathed with vine-leaves and grapes on the obverse with the legend ΚΥΔΩΝ on the reverse and a naked archer stringing his bow and sometimes a dog (stater and drachm). Others have the same legend but the dog is suckling an infant (Kydon?) and the head on the obverse is variously Athena, Demeter or a young male. There is then a considerable gap of

nearly a hundred years. In the middle and late Hellenistic period (after 200) coins change to the Athenian standard and feature the legend ΚΥΔΩΝΙΑΤΑΝ with variously the head of Artemis (Diktynna) with bow and quiver (tetradrachm), the head of Apollo (drachm) or the head of a young Dionysos on the obverse.

Finally, there is the argument made by Sekunda (2000) who suggests that the Kydones were an ethnic group (*phyle*?) whose descendants can now only be seen in Sphakia. According to this argument Polichne, often considered a separate city state, did not exist but references to it are really to a League of *Polichnitai* or people from small *poleis* based on the Kydones ethnic group, which would almost certainly have included the Lachanians (q.v.). This may have been a factor in the attack by Athens on Kydonia as an Aiginetan stronghold in 429 BCE with the support of the *polichnitai* or those of Kydone ethnicity. They did not call themselves 'Kydones' because of the confusion with the *polis*; 'thus we may have a curious example of conquerors gradually adopting a variant form of the name of the conquered, forcing the conquered to adopt a new name in order to distinguish themselves from their conquerors' (2000: 335). Sekunda goes on to argue that from 429 to ca. 350 the *polichnitai* broke up into more conventional city states, particularly Polyrrhenia, but in some areas the 'Kydones' continued an earlier alliance as in the Confederation of the Oreioi dating from ca. 265 BCE.

It is not implausible therefore to argue that Kydonia has a great deal in common with other Cretan city states. Where it differs, perhaps, is in the presence of a colonial enclave in the harbour settlement and a consequent confusion of nomenclature. In order to avoid this, the designation 'Kydonia' will be used to refer to the coastal settlement, but Lachania will be considered as of much greater importance (as the 'other Kydonia') than conventionally assumed.

Phalasarna (Φαλάσαρνα)

Location: 35.51206°N; 23.56775°E

The earliest reference to Phalasarna as a city state with an urban centre is in the *Periplous* of Pseudo-Skylax (47) in the 4th century, where the reference is to the nearest point to Laconia. He also makes specific reference to an 'enclosed harbour' at Phalasarna. The slopes of the hills to the east, half a kilometre from the sea today but once closer, show evidence of MM occupation, but no building remains have been found from this period. A cemetery to the south-east of the harbour contained *pithos* burials of the 6th–5th century and Hellenistic cist graves.

Phalasarna achieved very considerable wealth on the basis of its protected position on major trade routes. This can be seen in the quality of the remains that are visible above ground today and from recent excavations. Although the full story of Phalasarna has yet to be told, enough is already clear to show that it had far greater importance than is usually recognised, and this may have been the reason why it could have been the first point of attack for the Roman invaders in 69 BCE (Sanders, 1982). The territory of Phalasarna included the whole of the Gramvousa peninsula in the far north-west of Crete as well as the coastal plain to the south. The fortified acropolis was on the high ground at Cape Koutri, where there is evidence of at least two temple buildings, one probably dedicated to the protecting deity of Artemis Diktynna (Perlman, 2004a: 1181; Gondiccas, 1988). The double acropolises, each with a temple, are separated by the L-shaped remains of a public building complex (10m × 9m), the most likely purpose for which was as a *prytaneion*. The quantity and size of the superb masonry blocks, together with its commanding position overlooking the western sea lanes and the Bay of Livadia (68m elevation, rising to 87m at the trig point), suggest an imposing building before its destruction either by the Roman invaders or, more probably, by the great earthquakes that wrought such havoc in AD 66 and AD 365.[21] The quantity and quality of ashlar masonry is impressive, particularly since worked stones of high quality are also used in domestic properties on the southern slopes of Cape Koutri, as well as on the temples and public buildings on the summit. The worked limestone was taken from a large quarry still visible to the south that was once linked by a channel to the harbour area.

The remains of public buildings near the northern edge of the harbour are such as to suggest that it was once a thriving port of very considerable significance. The harbour and fortifications date from the 4th century and settlement at this time may have been boosted by serving as the original port for Polyrrhenia (22km distant) and being linked by an old road, parts of which are still visible on the west-facing hillside to the south (Pashley, 1837, I: 54). Owing to tectonic uplift at the western end of the island following the earthquake of AD 365, it is not that easy to determine how the original harbour at Phalasarna looked, although it was clearly very impressive.[22] A natural basin, probably originally a little way inland and now much more so, was enlarged and a channel cut for access. The basin was then fortified with massive watch towers at each corner and a complex of quays and storage buildings added (Hadjidaki, 1988a; 1988b; Frost and Hadjidaki, 1990). The harbour, filled by 2–3m of silt from the tsunami that followed the great earthquake and from wash from the slopes above, has been partially excavated. The harbour installation, which is guarded by a curtain wall and defensive towers, is possibly the most ambitious and best planned in Crete. The town itself was also set mostly within an equally massive protective wall of ashlar masonry. Perlman suggests that a rather well known rock-cut 'throne' to the south of the harbour area (and two others less well known) may be Phoenician, thereby indicating the importance of Phalasarna in east–west trade links (Perlman, 2004a: 1181). The harbour design itself, a double basin with a *cothon*, or channel to the sea, may also have been inspired by Phoenician precedents (Stefanakis, 2006b: 58).

After conflict with Polyrrhenia sometime between 304 and 294 BCE, Phalasarna became allied with Knosos but evolved as unusually independent because of trade links, particularly with Ptolemaic Egypt and the Peloponnese. Phalasarna is unusual in being an important city state by the sea and, after its break with Polyrrhenia, in not having a protecting inland city state. In this regard it

---

21 The earthquake and tsunami of 21 July 365 drowned thousands of people from North Africa to the Adriatic. Recent research (Shaw et al. 2008) argues that the rise of western Crete by 10m occurred at the same time. Others have suggested that the earthquake of AD 66 may have been even more destructive (Stefanakis, 2006a).

22 The uplift of the western end of Crete impacted upon many coastal settlements but perhaps none more so than at Phalasarna. Stefanakis cites data suggesting 8m uplift at Ormos Stomiou, Mavros Bay and at Kalamydi near modern-day Palaiochora, 6–7m at Suia (Sougia) and Lisos but declining to 2m at Kydonia (2010: 73; cf. Stiros, 2009; Stiros and Papageorgiou, 2001).

is similar to Itanos in the far north-east and Hierapytna after its swallowing of Olous. Trade made the critical differences in all three cases, enabling a coastal location to become a viable settlement in its own right. The rise of this *polis* during the Hellenistic era is indicated by the fact that in 174 BCE, it was strong enough to send 3,000 mercenaries in partnership with Knosos to assist Perseus in his battles against Rome (Hadjidaki, 1988a: 140).[23]

Commencing in the 4th century, Phalasarna struck coins, initially on the Aiginetan standard normally showing the head of Diktynna, her hair bound with cord or rolled, on the obverse and with a trident on the reverse. The coinage also reveals the strong overseas links created by mercenaries and visible trade. There was, for example, a large influx of Cyrenean coins in 300–280/290 BCE as well as evidence of the continuing presence of coins from Phoenicia and Ptolemaic Egypt, often restruck as flans for local coinage (Stefanakis, 2006b: 48).

---

23 This is possibly another reason why the urban centre of Phalasarna may have been the first target of Roman aggression.

Gazetteer: Location of primary, secondary and independent urban centres

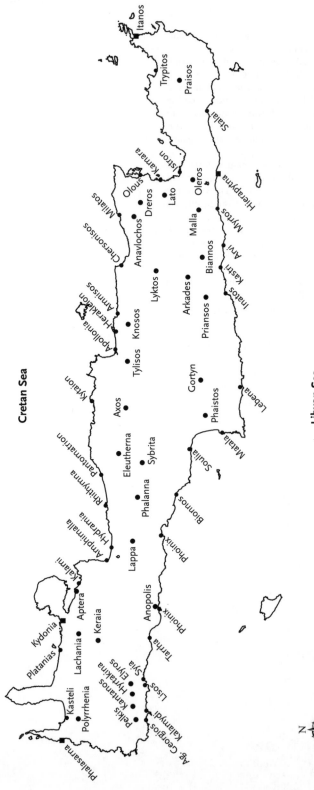

Cretan Sea

Libyan Sea

Itanos
Trypitos
Praisos
Stalai
Kamara
Istron
Olous
Dreros
Lato
Oleros
Miletos
Anavlochos
Malla
Hierapytna
Myrtos
Chersonisos
Lyktos
Biannos
Arvi
Heraklion
Amnisos
Arkades
Kastri
Apollonia
Priansos
Inatos
Knosos
Tylisos
Gortyn
Lebena
Axos
Phaistos
Matala
Eleutherna
Sybrita
Soulia
Rhithymna
Phalanna
Bionnos
Pantomatrion
Kytaion
Phoinix
Amphimalla
Hydramia
Lappa
Kalami
Anopolis
Phoinix
Kydonia
Aptera
Tarrha
Platanias
Lachania
Keraia
Syia
Elyros
Kasteli
Kantanos
Hyrtakina
Lisos
Polyrrhenia
Pelkis
Kalamydi
Phalasarna
Aŷ. Geŏrgĭos

N
W — E
S

Site Locations

Primary *Poleis*

	Latitude	Longitude	EGSA'87		WGS84	
			X	Y	Latitude	Longitude
Anavlochos	35.28060°N	25.56114°E	643051.91	3904673.05	35° 16' 50"	25° 33' 40"
Anopolis	35.21213°N	24.08585°E	500002.89	3896279.16	35° 12' 44"	24° 5' 9"
Aptera	35.46268°N	24.14101°E	512828.91	3924374.51	35° 27' 46"	24° 8' 29"
Araden	35.22301°N	24.06190°E	505488.36	3897492.56	35° 13' 23"	24° 3' 43"
Arkades	35.10276°N	25.34056°E	622178.57	3885262.83	35° 6' 10"	25° 20' 26"
Axos	35.30798°N	24.84420°E	576634.86	3907163.59	35° 18' 29"	24° 50' 39"
Biannos	35.05589°N	25.41569°E	629088.49	3880150.83	35° 3' 21"	25° 24' 56"
Dreros	35.25650°N	25.62677°E	648011.00	3902423.32	35° 15' 23"	25° 37' 26"
Eleutherna	35.32833°N	24.67642°E	560751.83	3909571.41	35° 19' 42"	24° 40' 35"
Elyros	35.28720°N	23.79406°E	480808.51	3904780.64	35° 17' 14"	23° 47' 39"
Gortyn	35.06329°N	24.94791°E	586420.95	3880477.18	35° 3' 48"	24° 56' 52"
Hyrtakina	35.27800°N	23.75167°E	477232.80	3904259.13	35° 16' 41"	23° 45' 6"
Kantanos	35.27917°N	23.70194°E	472900.54	3904050.26	35° 16' 45"	23° 42' 7"
Keraia	35.39457°N	23.95511°E	495764.67	3916499.14	35° 23' 40"	23° 57' 18"
Knosos	35.29639°N	23.95511°E	605662.31	3906524.24	35° 17' 47"	25° 9' 44"
Lachania	35.45780°N	25.16222°E	498029.11	3923524.78	35° 27' 28"	23° 58' 48"
Lappa	35.28563°N	24.33537°E	530345.66	3904478.98	35° 17' 8"	24° 20' 7"
Lato	35.17859°N	25.65560°E	650601.81	3893790.88	35° 10' 43"	25° 29' 20"
Lyktos	35.20798°N	25.36773°E	624324.00	3896687.00	35° 12' 29"	25° 21' 28"
Malla	35.06861°N	25.59778°E	645536.11	3881530.26	35° 4' 7"	25° 35' 52"
Oleros	35.08431°N	25.71098°E	655989.07	3883746.76	35° 5' 4"	25° 42' 40"
Pelkis	35.27139°N	23.65333°E	468321.94	3902906.10	35° 16' 17"	23° 39' 12"
Phaistos	35.04833°N	24.81306°E	574139.18	3878691.56	35° 2' 54"	24° 48' 47"
Phalanna	35.27011°N	24.50250°E	545554.28	3902824.91	35° 16' 12"	24° 30' 9"
Polyrrhenia	35.45737°N	23.65503°E	468548.12	3923531.57	35° 27' 27"	23° 39' 18"
Praisos	35.12300°N	26.09091°E	690520.34	3888690.11	35° 7' 23"	26° 5' 27"
Priansos	35.04499°N	25.26027°E	615195.98	3878762.58	35° 2' 42"	25° 15' 47"
Sybrita	35.25940°N	24.63999°E	557623.19	3901217.02	35° 15' 34"	24° 38' 24"
Tylisos	35.29903°N	25.02043°E	592789.12	3906667.07	35° 17' 56"	25° 1' 14"

Secondary Settlements

	Latitude	Longitude	EGSA'87		WGS84	
			X	Y	Latitude	Longitude
Ag. Georgios	35.23667°N	23.65037°E	468188.14	3899345.25	35° 14' 12"	23° 39' 1"
Amnisos	35.33115°N	25.20597°E	609382.69	3910217.89	35° 19' 52"	25° 12' 21"
Amphimalla	35.35845°N	24.25344°E	523626.40	3913588.27	35° 21' 30"	24° 15' 12"
Apollonia	35.34229°N	25.05236°E	596935.24	3911014.49	35° 20' 32"	25° 3' 8"
Arvi	34.98611°N	25.46056°E	633305.61	3872477.18	34° 59' 10"	25° 27' 38"
Bionnos	35.14465°N	24.51306°E	546586.55	3888916.07	35° 8' 41"	24° 30' 47"
Chersonisos	35.32335°N	25.39249°E	626152.49	3909011.65	35° 18' 59"	25° 23' 16"
Herakleion	35.335°N	25.13472°E	603128.19	3910792.06	35° 20' 6"	25° 8' 5"
Hydramia	35.34663°N	24.34392°E	528118.34	3911921.64	35° 21' 40"	24° 18' 40"
Inatos	34.98310°N	25.27902°E	616591.51	3871627.21	34° 58' 59"	25° 16' 44"
Istron	35.12758°N	25.73640°E	658671.78	3888376.28	35° 7' 05"	25° 44' 26"
Kalami	35.45278°N	24.16889°E	515335.83	3923261.51	35° 27' 10"	24° 10' 8"
Kalamydi	35.23556°N	23.68611°E	471435.27	3899220.72	35° 14' 8"	23° 41' 10"
Kamara	35.19128°N	25.71760°E	655890.20	3895293.29	35° 11' 28"	25° 42' 50"
Kastri	34.99881°N	25.37855°E	625652.50	3873490.36	34° 59' 56"	25° 22' 43"
Kasteli (Kisamos)	35.50015°N	23.65036°E	468862.10	3927642.32	35° 29' 40"	23° 39' 30"
Kytaion	35.40921°N	24.86924°E	578912.49	3919310.92	35° 25' 05"	24° 52' 15"
Lebena	34.9375°N	24.92222°E	584070.91	3866211.43	34° 56' 15"	24° 55' 20"
Lisos	35.24372°N	23.78556°E	480341.32	3899803.58	35° 14' 37"	23° 47' 08"
Matala	34.99583°N	24.74583°E	568167.51	3872548.16	34° 59' 45"	24° 44' 45"
Milatos	35.30954°N	25.57249°E	643290.34	3908089.81	35° 18' 30"	25° 34' 40"
Myrtos	34.99861°N	25.59889°E	646005.26	3874737.77	34° 59' 55"	25° 35' 56"
Olous	35.25556°N	25.73333°E	657535.93	3902472.02	35° 15' 20"	25° 44' 0"
Pantomatrion	35.38250°N	24.59033°E	553360.33	3915733.32	35° 23' 30"	24° 35' 21"
Phoinix (Loutro)	35.20611°N	24.07°E	506878.25	3894794.26	35° 12' 22"	24° 4' 12"
Phoinix (Sellia)	35.19490°N	24.36038°E	532371.17	3894376.25	35° 11' 40"	24° 21' 26"
Platanias	35.51378°N	23.91599°E	492393.17	3930037.05	35° 30' 50"	23° 54' 58"
Rhithymna	35.37074°N	24.46919°E	542601.64	3914091.07	35° 22' 15"	24° 28' 9"
Soulia	35.1°N	24.68472°E	562406.43	3884347.20	35° 6' 0"	24° 41' 5"
Stalai	35.03516°N	25.97274°E	679954.16	3878734.19	35° 2' 7"	25° 58' 22"
Syia	35.24862°N	23.80879°E	482455.83	3900342.68	35° 14' 55"	23° 48' 32"
Tarrha	35.22694°N	23.96389°E	496715.56	3898211.41	35° 13' 37"	23° 57' 50"
Trypitos	35.19915°N	26.12988°E	693909.00	3897208.43	35° 11' 57"	26° 7' 48"

Independent *Poleis*

	Latitude	Longitude	EGSA'87		WGS84	
			X	Y	Latitude	Longitude
Hierapytna	35.00111°N	25.73306°E	658147.29	3874550.36	35° 0' 4"	25° 43' 59"
Itanos	35.26314°N	26.26476°E	705802.15	3904271.79	35° 15' 47"	26° 15' 53"
Kydonia	35.51278°N	24.02778°E	502526.15	3929922.52	35° 30' 46"	24° 1' 40"
Phalasarna	35.51206°N	23.56775°E	460657.19	3929615.39	35° 30' 43"	23° 34' 4"

Glossary

Achaean – the term used by Mycenaeans to describe themselves but also sometimes used by others.

agora – initially a term used to indicate a public space or place of assembly but later coming to mean a marketplace.

amphoreus (s) / amphoreis (pl) – a slim ceramic vessel with two handles and a long neck used in ancient Greece and elsewhere to transport wine, oil, olives, grain or grapes. Because of its widespread use by the Romans tends to be translated in its Latin form (*amphora / amphorae*).

andreion (s) / andreia (pl) – building or rooms in which common meals (*syssitia*) were taken.

apetairos (s) / apetairoi (pl) – a class of free men who were nonetheless not accorded the status of citizen.

Archaic – the period, sometimes widely defined from 800 BCE to 480 BCE and sometimes more narrowly from 650 BCE to 500 BCE, that is perceived as exhibiting the elements in art and design that led to the Classical era.

archon (s) / archontes (pl) – the chief magistrate(s) of ancient Athens.

Areopagus – originally the council of pre-democratic Athens named after its location on the 'Ares Rock' (Ἄρειος Πάγος), a low hill north-west of the Acropolis, and composed of former *archontes* with lifetime tenure. It served as a court of appeal in both civil and criminal cases, and was made more democratic in 594 BCE under the reforms of Solon, before its powers were greatly reduced in the Classical period.

Aristotle (384–322 BCE) – Greek philosopher famous for the range and quality of his writings that included *Politics* and *Nicomachean Ethics* among much else.

ashlar – rectangular-finished stone laid in regular courses, as in a brick wall.

astos (s) / astoi – individual(s) living in the *asty*.

asty (s) – urban centre of the Athenian state.

Attica – the peninsula containing Athens, bounded on the north by the Plain of Boeotia and on the west by Corinth.

boule – a council of citizens. Membership was sometimes elective and sometimes hereditary, with functions ranging from sanctioning decisions made by others to debating and deciding on alternative policies.

bouleuterion – the building in which the *boule* met.

choregia – services given to the state by Athenian citizens during the Classical period.

chreophylakion – state-run archive of property titles, contracts of sale and debt agreements.

cist grave – a stone-lined rectangular grave ranging from a very simple hollow, usually with a stone capping piece, to an elaborate structure in which multiple *cists* occur.

Classical era – variously defined but in the context of ancient Greece normally taken as encompassing the 5th and 4th centuries BCE. The end of the period is sometimes taken as approximately 330 BCE and sometimes more precisely as 323 BCE with the death of Alexander the Great of Macedonia and the break-up of his empire.

collective consciousness – literal translation of the French term '*conscience collective*' used by the sociologist, Emile Durkheim (1858–1917), to refer to the beliefs held in common that served to maintain social order.

crater / krater – large vessel, usually pottery but occasionally metal, used for mixing wine with water.

cyclopean – a type of masonry comprised of large, irregular stones set without mortar.

demarchos – elected magistrate for each deme in Classical Athens.

deme – a transliteration of δῆμος but used specifically to refer to a subdivision of land that gained political significance in Attica as the unit of local membership for citizens under the reforms of Kleisthenes in 508 BCE.

demokratia – sometimes used as a synonym for 'democracy' but more correctly that form of direct accountability to the people found in Classical Athens.

demos – the people or population of a city state in a political sense (i.e. as citizens).

dikasterion (s)/dikasteria (pl) – building housing magistrates when deciding cases (i.e. a court).

dikastes (s)/dikastai (pl) – magistrate serving as a judge.

dike (s)/dikai (pl) – cases brought before Athenian courts in which the parties concerned had an interest (private suit).

Diodorus Siculus (Διόδωρος Σικελιώτης) – 1st century BCE Greek author of a forty-book history of Greece and the Near East that he termed an 'Historical Library'.

doulos (s)/douloi (pl) – literally a slave but may have included indentured servants.

eisphora – a tax imposed from time to time in ancient Athens, usually to meet the costs of waging war.

ekklesia or *ecclesia* – the assembly of the whole citizen body that was empowered to adopt or reject decisions by the *boule* (in Athens and possibly more generally).

ekklesiasterion – building in which the assembly (*ekklesia*) met.

ephoros – one of the five magistrates (*ephoroi*) of Sparta elected by and from the citizenry for a one year non-renewable term. Usually transliterated into English as 'ephor' (s)/ 'ephors' (pl).

epigamia – the legal right to contract a marriage across social or legal divisions, particularly between those from different *poleis* where the term could include a right to citizenship for a foreign-born spouse.

Eteocretans – those speaking the language thought to have been derived from that spoken in Minoan times, therefore a reference to the 'true' or original Cretans. A small number of inscriptions, written in the Archaic Greek alphabet, appear to be written in the Eteocretan language, two from Dreros and three from Praisos.

ethnos (s)/ethne (pl) – a nation in the sense of a people rather than in the political sense (i.e. nation state).

exedra – an uncovered, external seating area.

genos (s)/gene (pl) – a clan deriving from a family lineage.

geron (s)/gerontes (pl) – member (s) of the *gerousia* usually drawn from past magistrates over a certain age (often 50).

gerousia – a senate comprised of *gerontes* usually with an advisory function.

gnomon (s)/gnomones (pl) – magistrate (s) of lower status than *kosmos* but usually with a longer tenure in office, part of whose job was to ensure consistency in decision-making.

graphe (s)/graphai (pl) – a category of cases in an Athenian court that could be prosecuted by any male citizen.

Hellenistic – the period from 330 BCE to the invasion of Greece by the Roman Republic that occurred in most Greek states in 146 BCE but not until 67 BCE in Crete.

helots (eilotes) – the original inhabitants of Laconia and Messenia enslaved by the Spartans after their conquest of these territories.

Herodotus (ca. 484 BCE – ca. 430 BCE) – author of *The Histories* and sometimes regarded as the founder of Western history.

hetaireia – association of landowners from elite families.

hippeis – the second division under Solon's reforms in ancient Athens, comprising horsemen with a crop from their lands of 300 bushels or more.

Homer – epic poet and possible author of the *Iliad* and the *Odyssey* that are believed to date from approximately 800 BCE. It is unclear whether he was an actual individual or whether the name refers to the whole tradition of epic verse.

hoplite – an infantry soldier, usually armed with spear, helmet and shield .

isopoliteia – an *isopoliteia* agreement between *poleis* allowed the citizen of one to enjoy the citizen rights of the other.

kleros (s)/kleroi (pl) – a productive unit or share of land in ancient Athens designed to support one fit man for military service.

kleruchs – military settlers on lands conquered by warfare and allocated by lot. The term comes from the Greek word κληρούχος (*klerouchos*) meaning a 'lot-holder'.

koinon (s)/koina (pl) – from the Greek for 'common' as in 'held in common'/commonwealth. Specific *koina* were leagues or associations of city-states that occurred in a number of places in ancient Greece, including Crete.

kosmos (s)/kosmoi (pl) – the chief magistrates of a Cretan *polis*, usually ten in number serving a one-year term with variable restrictions on return to office.

leitourgia (s)/leitourgiai (pl) – usually rendered into English as 'liturgy/liturgies' – services (including funding) made by wealthy Athenian citizens to the state for public works.

mesogeion (s)/mesogeia (pl) – inland areas identified as administrative units under the reforms of Kleisthenes in ancient Athens.

metic – frequently used alternative to *metoikos* possibly derived from Latin *metycus*.

metoikos (s)/metoikoi (pl) – person or persons coming from elsewhere and lacking full citizen rights in their *polis* of residence and who comprised an identified class paying a specific tax (*metoikio*).

mnemon (s)/mnemones (pl) – legal official in Cretan court charged with responsibility for 'remembering' past decisions (i.e. case law).

nomothetes (s)/nomothetai (pl) – a body selected from citizen lists in 4th century Athens whose role was to decide upon legislative changes.

obe (s)/obai (pl) – village(s)

paralia (pl) – the coastal regions of Attica comprising, with subdivisions of the urban and inland areas, the *phylai* of Classical Athens.

Pausanias (143–176 AD) – a Greek geographer whose *Description of Greece* is said to have been the product of personal observations.

pentakosiomedimnoi – the individuals in the top class in the Athenian administrative reorganisation under Solon (literally, 500 bushels and above men).

perioikos (s)/perioikoi (pl) – a Spartan term for *apetairos* but in the Cretan case sometimes used to refer to free citizens of a dependent *polis* but at other times as a synonym for *apetairos*.

Phoenicians – peoples from the Middle East (that part which is now Lebanon and Syria) famed for their seafaring, navigation skills and trading. Phoenicians are credited by some with the first alphabetic script in ca. 1500 BCE.

phratria (s)/phratriai (pl) – 'brotherhood' or male association based on real or imagined kin relations.

phylarchos (s)/phylarchoi (pl) – a leader (civil, military or religious) of one of the ten *phylai* in ancient Athens.

phyle (s)/phylai (pl) – a descent grouping sometimes translated as 'tribe' but more correctly seen as an ethnic group, except in Attica where *phylai* were administrative categories of the population (see *trittyes* below).

pithos (s)/pithoi (pl) – large storage vessel for grain, oil or wine, sometimes used for containing the body in burials.

Plato (428 BCE–348 BCE) – ancient Greek philosopher and mathematician, student of *Socrates* and teacher of *Aristotle*, who together are usually regarded as the founders of the Western philosophical tradition.

Pliny – sometimes referred to as 'Pliny the Elder' to distinguish him from his nephew (the 'Younger'), was the author of the *Natural History* produced in approximately 77–79 AD which describes, among much else, the geography and topography of all territories in the Roman Empire.

politeia – a term used frequently by the ancient philosophers but sometimes to refer to the rules of governance or constitution and sometimes to a specific form (e.g. different from 'monarchy' or 'aristocracy').

politis (s)/politai (pl) – citizen(s)

Polybius (ca. 200–118 BCE) Greek historian and author of the *Histories* that covers the rise of the Roman Republic from a sympathetic viewpoint.

proxenia decree – a decree issued by one state to another establishing the role of *proxenos* in the second state whose job was to look after the interests of citizens of the first state residing in the second, and generally to promote good relations between the two states (i.e. a form of honorary consul).

prytaneion – the building that housed the governing magistrates of the *polis*, normally located near the centre of the urban area adjacent to the *agora*. The building typically contained a hearth with an eternal flame to the goddess *Hestia*, taken as a symbol of the city's longevity.

Pseudo-Skylax – Greek geographer writing in the 4th century (or possibly the 3rd) and author of the *Periplous* (a description of ports of call and landmarks, in this case of the Mediterranean).

stasis – a crisis of inaction created by the balance of opposing forces.

stele – a standing stone with carved inscriptions, including treaties, laws and agreements.

Stephanus Byzantius (Stephen of Byzantium) probably lived in the first half of the sixth century AD. He was the author of a geographical dictionary entitled *Ethnica* (Εθνικά) that described the peoples and cities of the ancient world. Only very small fragments of the original survive and most references are to a summary (*Epitome*) compiled later.

Strabo – early geographer (born ca. 64 BCE) famed for his description of the Mediterranean lands.

symmoria (s)/symmoriai (pl) – the one hundred contribution groups into which the citizens of 4th century Athens were divided.

sympoliteia (s)/sympoliteiai (pl) – federal agreement(s) of co-operation between city states.

symposion (s)/symposia (pl) – male debating and drinking session(s), usually following a meal, sometimes on the occasion of sporting or military achievements.

syssitia – common meals served in public to male citizens and youths for the education of the latter and to promote social and political bonds.

thetes(s)/thetai (pl) – the lowest of the four Solonic wealth categories into which the Athenian citizen population was divided – those with minimal citizen rights.

tholos tomb – beehive-shaped tomb made by corbelling stone slabs to form the roof and entered by a long passageway (*dromos*). Usually taken as an indication of Mycenaean influence.

Thucydides (ca. 460 – ca. 400 BCE) Greek author of the *History of the Peloponnesian War* and usually regarded as the originator of a modern approach to gathering historical material.

trittys (s) / trittyes (pl) – under the reforms of Kleisthenes the population of Attica was divided into *trittyes*, a third of which were from the coast, the city and the inland areas. Each *phyle* was comprised of three *trittyes*, one from each region.

xenos(s) / xenoi (pl) – foreigner(s) used in the sense of stranger (i.e. not local to the *polis* and possessing no citizen rights).

zeugites (s) / zeugitai (pl) – the third category of citizens under Solonic reforms; those with a team of oxen and 200 or more bushels of production.

Sources

Printed books are available through conventional channels, although only universities with a special interest in the ancient Aegean are likely to have libraries containing a reasonable collection of material on Crete. More importantly, they will provide online access to collections of relevant journals. Off-campus access is, however, normally restricted to members of the individual university and sometimes, even then, the subscriptions are often very limited in range. Unfortunately, the cost of books in, say, archaeology is often prohibitive owing to the high costs of production and the very limited print runs. For many people, therefore, the real issue for those with a wish to read more intensively will often turn on what is available online without charge. Here the picture is very mixed; there is far more than one might imagine, but far less than one would wish. For the sake of simplicity, what is there can be divided into the works of ancient authors, electronic journals and other material, including relevant databases.

The works of ancient authors are generally available online, either in English or the language of their original composition. For example, the 'Classics Archive' at MIT (http://classics.mit.edu/index.html) contains translations of 441 works of classical literature by 59 authors, including Aristotle, Diodorus, Plato, Strabo and Thucydides. This list can be supplemented by Bill Thayer's website (http://penelope.uchicago.edu/Thayer/E/home.html) that focuses mostly on the world of ancient Rome but includes translations of Pliny (*Natural History*), Plutarch (*Lives*), Polybius and much of Smith's *Dictionary of Greek and Roman Antiquities*. The Perseus Digital Library at Tufts University (www.perseus.tufts.edu/hopper/collections) is another excellent source of original material in translation. Where more modern books are out of copyright, there is usually no difficulty in finding them on the web. For example, both Pashley's *Travels in Crete* and Captain Spratt's *Travels and Researches in Crete* have been reprinted, but they are both available at www.archive.org. Those interested in epigraphy will find a very rich online source of Cretan material at http://epigraphy.packhum.org/inscriptions//main?url=oi%3Fikey%3D201282%26bookid%3D287%26region%3D7.

As noted above, access to electronic versions of journals is normally restricted to members of subscribing institutions, although it is possible to buy an electronic copy of individual articles. In some cases, however, back issues of journals are freely available. For example, French readers will find a wealth of material from some very important journals available freely online at the Persee site (www.persee.fr/web/revues/home). In other cases, journals in English are available freely. The Ancient World Online blogspot, for example, provides links to over 800 open access journal titles, but most are either not on the ancient Greek world or are rather peripheral (http://ancientworldonline.blogspot.com/2009/10/alphabetical-list-of-open-access.html). There are exceptions, however, including the recent issues of *Greek, Roman and Byzantine Studies* and book reviews from the *American Journal of Archaeology* and the *Bryn Mawr Classical Review*.

There are a number of databases providing useful information on some Cretan sites of the Classical era. The most useful is *The Princeton Encyclopedia of Classical Sites (PECS)* now also available as part of the Perseus Project (www.perseus.tufts.edu/hopper/text?doc=Perseus%3atext%3a1999.04.0006). Blogs, newsletters and other information sources on the ancient Aegean abound on the internet but most of them focus on *prehistory* and, in particular, the Aegean Bronze Age. The Ancient World Bloggers Group (http://ancientworldbloggers.

blogspot.com/) sometimes carries material of interest to those wanting to read further on the material covered by this book, as does 'The Digital Classicist' (http://digitalclassicist. org/) and 'The Stoa Consortium' (http://www.stoa.org/). Occasionally Nestor (Bibliography of Aegean and Related Areas) run by the Department of Classics at the University of Cincinnati also strays into the Archaic period and beyond (http://classics.uc.edu/nestor/).

Finally, the use of a search engine will usually reveal other material on specific topics or authors. Aside from obvious sources, such as Wikipedia, a hunt for relevant authors will sometimes provide access to pdf files of articles, particularly from an individual's website or from one run by her or his university department. Finally, if all else fails, legitimate access to parts of copyright material can be found through open sources such as 'Google Books' or through Amazon's 'Look Inside' facility.

References

Adams, E. (2006) 'Social Strategies and Spatial Dynamics in Neopalatial Crete: An Analysis of the North-Central Area', *American Journal of Archaeology* 110: 1–36.

Ager, S.L. (1994) 'Hellenistic Crete and Koinodikion', *Journal of Hellenic Studies* 114: 1–18.

—— (1996) *Interstate Arbitrations in the Greek World, 337–90 BC*, Berkeley and Los Angeles, University of California Press.

Alcock, S.E. (1991) 'Tomb Cult and the Post-Classical Polis', *American Journal of Archaeology* 95: 447–67.

—— (2002) *Archaeologies of the Greek Past: Landscape, Monuments, and Memories*, Cambridge, Cambridge University Press.

Alexiou, S. (n.d.) *Minoan Civilization*, Heraklion, Kouvidis.

—— (1984) 'Une nouvelle inscription de Panormos-Apollonia en Crète' in *Aux origines de l'hellénisme. La Crète et la Grèce. Hommage à Henri van Effenterre*, Paris, Publications de la Sorbonne: 323–7.

Anderweg, R.B. (2000) 'Consociational Democracy', *Annual Review of Political Science* 3: 509–36.

Andreadaki-Vlasaki, M. (1989–90) Ἀχαιολογικές Ειδήσεις 1988, 1. Προϊστορικές και Κλασσικές Αρχαιότητες, Νομός Χανίων, Επαρχία Αποκορώνου, Απτέρα (Απτάρα)', *Κρητική Εστία*, ΠΕΡΙΟΔΟΣ Δ'-ΤΟΜΟΣ 3: 249–51.

—— (1997) 'The Geometric Period: The Pottery' in E. Hallager and B.P. Hallager (eds) *The Greek-Swedish Excavation at the Agia Aikateri Square Kastelli, Khania 1970–87*, Stockholm, Svenska Instituet i Athen/Paul Astoms Forlag: 229–40.

Apostolakou, V. (2003) 'ΚΑΙ ΛΑΤΟΣ ΓΑΡ ΕΝΕΓΚΑΤΟ ΤΟΝΔΕ – or the Prosopography of the Latians', *Eulimene* 4: 81–133.

Appian *Bellum Civile*.

Aristotle *Nicomachean Ethics*.

—— *Politics*.

Arnaiz-Villena, A., P. Iliakis, M. Gonzalez-Hevilla, J. Longas, E. Gomez-Casado, K. Sfyridaki, J. Trapaga, C. Silvera-Redondo, C. Matsouka, J. Martinez-Laso (1999), 'The Origin of Cretan Populations as Determined by Characterization of HLA Alleles', *Tissue Antigens* 53 (3): 213–26.

Arnaoutoglou. I. (1998) *Ancient Greek Laws: A Sourcebook*, London, Routledge.

Austin, M. (2006) *The Hellenistic World from Alexander to the Roman Conquest: A Selection of Ancient Sources in Translation*, Cambridge, Cambridge University Press.

Avidov, A. (1997) 'Were the Cilicians a Nation of Pirates?', *Mediterranean Historical Review* 12 (1): 5–55.

Bagnall, R. (ed.) (1976) *The Administration of the Ptolemaic Possessions Outside Egypt*, New York, Columbia Studies in the Classical Tradition.

Baldwin-Bowsky, M.W. (1989a) 'Epigrams to an Elder Statesman and a Young Noble from Lato Pros Kamara (Crete)', *Hesperia* 58: 115–29.

—— (1989b) 'Portrait of a Polis: Lato Pros Kamara (Crete) in the Late Second Century B.C.', *Hesperia* 58: 331–47.

Baldwin-Bowsky, M.W. and V. Niniou-Kindeli (2006) 'On the Road Again: a Trajanic Milestone and the Road Connections of Aptera, Crete', *Hesperia* 75: 405–33.

Banou, E. (2008) 'Minoan "Horns of Consecration" Revisitied: A Symbol of Sun Worship in Palatial and Post-Palatial Crete', *Mediterranean Archaeology and Archaeometry* 8 (1): 27–47.

Barrandon, J-N. and A.Bresson (1997) 'Imitations crétoises et monnaies rhodiennes: analyse physique', *Revue Numismatique*, 6e série, Num. 152: 137–155.

Barro, R.J. (1997) *Determinants of Economic Growth: A Cross-Country Empirical Study*, Cambridge, Mass., MIT Press.

—— (2000) 'Rule of Law, Democracy and Economic Performance', *Index of Economic Freedom Report*, Washington, D.C., Heritage Foundation: 31–49.

Barry, B. (1975a) 'The Consociational Model and its Dangers', *European Journal of Political Research* 3: 393–413.

—— (1975b) 'Review Article: Political Accommodation and Consociational Democracy', *British Journal of Political Science* 5: 477–505.

Beaton, R. (2006) 'Minoans in Modern Greek Literature' in Y. Hamilakis and N. Momigliano (eds) *Archaeology and European Modernity: Producing and Consuming the 'Minoans.' Creta Antica (Rivista annuale di studi archeologici, storici ed epigrafici, Centro di Archaeologica Cretese, Università di Catania), 7*, Padua: Bottega d'Erasmo.

Beattie, A.J. (1975) 'Some Notes on the Spensithios Decree', *Kadmos* 14 (1): 8–47.

Bender, B. (ed.) (1993) *Landscape: Politics and Perspectives*, Oxford, Berg.

Bernal, M. 1987 *Black Athena*, London, Vintage.

Bietak, M., N. Marinatos and C. Palyvou (2007) *Taureador Scenes in Tell El-Dab'a (Avaris) and Knossos*, Vienna, Austrian Academy of Sciences.

Bingham, T. (2006) (The Rt. Hon Lord Bingham of Cornhill KG) 'The Rule of Law', Sixth Sir David Williams Lecture (16th November), London, Centre for Public Law.

—— (2010) *The Rule of Law*, London, Allen Lane.

Bintliff, J (1997) 'Regional Survey, Demography, and the Rise of Complex Societies in the Ancient Aegean: Core-periphery, Neo-Malthusian, and Other Interpretive Models', *Journal of Field Archaeology* 24: 1–38.

Bitros, G.C. and A.D. Karayiannis (2008) 'Values and Institutions as Determinants of Entrepreneurship in Ancient Athens', *Journal of Institutional Economics* 4 (2): 205–30.

Boardman, J. (1962) 'Archaic Finds at Knossos', *Annual of the British School at Athens*, 57: 28–34.

Boardman, J., J. Griffin and O. Murray (eds) (1993) *Oxford History of the Classical World* Oxford, Oxford University Press.

Books LLC (2010a) *Geography of Ancient Crete: Cretan City States, Port Settlements in Ancient Crete, Knossos, Gortyn, Phaistos, Amnisos, Tylissos, Phalasarna* Memphis, Tennessee, Books LLC.

—— (2010b) *Port Settlements in Ancient Crete: Amnisos, Kommos, Lentas, Lissos, Arsinoe, Matala, Crete, Chersonesos, Lato pros Kamara, Priniatikos Pyrgos* Memphis, Tennessee, Books LLC.

Borgna, E. (2003) 'Regional Settlement Patterns, Exchange Systems and Sources of Power in Crete at the End of the Late Bronze Age: Establishing a Connection' *Studii Micenei ed Egeo-Anatolici* XLV (2): 153–83.

Bosanquet, R.C. (1901–2) 'Excavations at Praisos I', *Annual of the British School at Athens* 8: 231–70.

Bowsky, M.W.B. (1994) 'Cretan Connections: The Transformation of Hierapytna', *Cretan Studies* 4: 1–44.

—— (1997) 'An Atticizing Stele from Western Crete', *Zeitschrift für Papyrologie und Epigraphik* 118: 197–206.

Braudel, F. (1949) *La Méditerranée et le Monde Méditerranéen à l'époque de Philippe II* (*The Mediterranean and the Mediterranean World in the Age of Phillip II*, translated by Siân Reynolds, London and California, University of California Press, 1995, two vols).

Bresson, A. (1993) 'Les Cités grecques et leurs emporia', in A. Bresson & P. Rouillard, (eds) *L'Emporion* Paris, De Boccard: 163–226.

—— (2005a) 'Coinage and Money Supply in the Hellenistic World', in Z. Archibald, J. K. Davies and V. Gabrielsen, *Making, Moving, Managing: The New World of Ancient Economies (323–31 BCE)*, Oxbow Books: 44–72.

—— (2005b) 'Ecology and Beyond: The Mediterranean Paradigm' in W.V. Harris (ed.) *Rethinking the Mediterranean* Oxford, Oxford University Press: 94–116.

Brock, J.K. (1957) *Fortetsa: Early Greek Tombs near Knossos*, Oxford, Oxford University Press.

Broodbank, C. (2000) *An Island Archaeology of the Early Cyclades*, Cambridge, Cambridge University Press.

Browning, R. (1983) 'Review of "The Class Struggle in Ancient Greece"', *Past and Present* 100: 147–56.

Brugmans, T. (2010) 'Connecting the Dots: Towards Archaeological Network Analysis', *Oxford Journal of Archaeology* 29 (3): 277–303.

Brulé, P. (1978) *La piraterie crétoise hellénistique*, Annales littéraires de l'Université de Besançon 223, Centre de Recherche d'Histoire Ancienne 27 Paris, Les Belles Lettres.

Bueno de Mesquita, B. and H.L. Root (2000) *Governing for Prosperity*, New Haven, Yale University Press.

Bueno de Mesquita, B., A. Smith, R.M. Siverson and J.D. Morrow (2003) *The Logic of Political Survival* Cambridge, Mass., MIT Press.

Burns, P. (1985) 'The Dorians in Crete: A Survey of the Evolution of Cretan Society circa 900–350 B.C.', unpublished DPhil thesis, University of Oxford.

Butkiewicz, J.L. and H. Yanikkaya (2004) 'Institutional Quality and Economic Growth: Maintenance of the Rule of Law or Democratic Institutions, or Both?' Working Paper No. 2004-03, Department of Economics, University of Delaware.

Cadogan, G. (1991) *Palaces of Minoan Crete*, London, Routledge.

—— (1992) 'Ancient and Modern Crete' in J.W. Myers, E.M. Myers, and G. Cadogan (eds) *The Aerial Atlas of Ancient Crete*, Berkeley and Los Angeles, University of California Press: 31–43.

Campbell-Dunn, G.J.K. (2006) *Who were the Minoans: An African Answer*, Milton Keynes, Author House.

Capdeville, G. (1997) 'Le droit international dans la Crète antique (VIIe-VIe-IIe/Ier s. av. J.-C.)', *Comptes-rendus des Séances de l'Académie des Inscriptions et Belles-lettres*, 141, Numéro 1: 273–308.

Carington Smith, J. and S. Wall (1994) 'A Late Hellenistic Wine Press at Knossos', *Annual of the British School at Athens* 89: 359–76.

Cartledge, P. (1998) 'The Economy (Economies) of Ancient Greece', *Dialogos* 5: 4–24.

Cartledge, P. and Spawforth, A. (2002) *Hellenistic and Roman Sparta: A Tale of Two Cities*, London and New York, Routledge.

Cass, L. (1839) *An Historical, Geographical and Statistical Account of the Island of Candia, Or Ancient Crete*, Richmond, Va., T.W. White.

Castells, M. (1983) *The City and the Grassroots: A Cross-Cultural Theory of Urban Social Movements*, London, Edward Arnold.

Chaniotis, A. (1995) 'Problems of "Pastoralism" and "Transhumance" in Classical and Hellenistic Crete', *Orbis Terrarum* 1: 62–89.

—— (1996a) *Die Verträge zwischen kretischen Städten in der hellenistischen Zeit*, HABES 24, Stuttgart, Franz Steiner Verlag.

—— (1996b) 'Bemerkungen zum Kalender kretischer Städte in Hellenistischer Zeit', *Tekmeria* 2: 16–43.

—— (1999) 'Milking the Mountains: Economic Activities on the Cretan Uplands in the Classical and Hellenistic Period' in A. Chaniotis (ed.) *From Minoan Farmers to Roman Traders: Sidelights on the Economy of Ancient Crete*, Heidelberger Althistorische Beiträge und Episraphische Studien 29, Stuttgart, Franz Steiner: 181–220.

—— (2004) 'The Mobility of Persons during the Hellenistic Wars: State Control and Personal Relations' in C. Moatti (ed.) *La mobilité des personnes en Méditerranée, de l'Antiquité à l'époque moderne: Procédures de contrôle et documents d'identification*, Rome, Ecole Française de Rome: 481–500.

—— (2005a) *War in the Hellenistic World*, Oxford, Blackwell.

—— (2005b) 'Inscribed Instrumentata Domestica and the Economy of Hellenistic and Roman Crete' in Z.H. Archibald, J.K.Davies and V. Gabrielsen (eds), *Making, Moving, and Managing: The New World of Ancient Economies*, Oxford: 92–116.

Chase-Dunn, C. and T.D. Hall (1997) *Rise and Demise: Comparing World-Systems*, Boulder, Westview Press.

Cherry, J.F. (1987) 'Power in Space: Archaeological and Geographical Studies of the State', in J.M. Wagstaff (ed.), *Landscape and Culture: Geographical and Archaeological Perspectives*, Oxford, Blackwell: 146–72.

Cherry, J.F., D. Margomenou and L. Talalay (eds) (2005) *Prehistorians Round the Pond: Reflections on Aegean Prehistory as a Discipline*, Ann Arbor, Kelsey Museum of Archaeology.

Christ, M. (2007) 'The Evolution of the *Eisphora* in Classical Athens', *The Classical Quarterly* 57 (1): 53–69.

Christaller, W. (1935) *Die Zentrallen Orte in Sueddeutschland*, Jena, J. Fischer Verlag.

Christesen, P. (2003) 'Economic Rationalism in Fourth Century BCE Athens', *Greece & Rome* 50: 31–56.

Chua, A.L. (1998) 'Markets, Democracy, and Ethnicity: Toward a New Paradigm for Law and Development', *Yale Law Journal* 108: 1–108.

—— (2002) *World On Fire: How Exporting Free Market Democracy Breeds Ethnic Hatred and Global Instability*, New York, Doubleday.

—— (2003) 'Markets, Democracy and Ethnicity' in S. Ramaswamy and J.W. Cason (eds) *Development and democracy: New Perspectives on an Old Debate*, Lebanon, NH, Middlebury College Press: 145–67.

Clarke, D.L. (1968) *Analytical Archaeology*, London, Methuen.

—— (1977) 'Spatial Information in Archaeology' in D.L. Clarke (ed.) *Spatial Archaeology*, London, Academic Press: 1–32.

Cohen, D. (1995) *Law, Violence and Community in Classical Athens*, Cambridge, Cambridge University Press.

—— (2005) 'Introduction' in M. Gagarin and D. Cohen (eds.) *Cambridge Companion to Ancient Greek Law*, Cambridge, Cambridge University Press: 1–26.

Cohen, E.E. (1992) *Athenian Economy & Society: A Banking Perspective*, Princeton, Princeton University Press.

—— (2000) *The Athenian Nation*, Princeton, Princeton University Press.

Coldstream, J.N. (1973) *Knossos: The Sanctuary of Demeter*, Supplement 8, London, British School at Athens.

—— (1984) 'Dorian Knossos and Aristotle's Villages', in C. Nicolet (ed.), *Aux Origines del'Hellénisme: La Crète et la Grèce: Hommage à Henri Van Effenterre*, Paris, Publications de la Sorbonne: 311–22.

—— (1999) 'Knossos 1951–61: Classical and Hellenistic Pottery from the Town', *Annual of the British School at Athens* 94: 321–51.

—— (2001) 'The Early Greek Period' in J.N. Coldstream and L.J. Eiring (eds), *Knossos Pottery Handbook: Greek and Roman*, London, British School at Athens Studies 7: 23–76.

Coldstream, J.N., P. Callaghan and J.H. Musgrave (1981) 'Knossos: an Early Greek Tomb on Lower Gypsadhes Hill', *Annual of the British School at Athens* 76: 141–66.

Coldstream, J.N. and H.W. Catling (eds) (1996) *Knossos North Cemetery: Early Greek Tombs*. British School at Athens Supplement 28 London, British School of Archaeology at Athens.

Coldstream, J.N., C.F. Macdonald and H.W. Catling (1997) 'Knossos: Area of South-West Houses, Early Hellenic Occupation', *Annual of the British School at Athens*, 92: 191–245.

Coldstream, J.N., G.L. Huxley and V.E.S. Webb (1999) 'Knossos: The Archaic Gap', *Annual of the British School at Athens* 94: 289–307.

Coldstream, J.N. and E.M. Hatzaki (2003) 'Knossos: Early Greek Occupation under the Roman Villa Dionysos', *Annual of the British School at Athens* 98: 279–306.

Cole, S.G. (1984) 'Greek Sanctions against Sexual Assault', *Classical Philology* 79: 97–113.

Collier, P. (2009) *War, Guns and Votes: Democracy in Dangerous Places*, New York, Harper Collins.

Cook, R.M. (1958) 'Speculations on the Origins of Coinage', *Historia: Zeitschrift für Alte Geschichte* 7 (3): 257–262.

Cook, R.M. and A.G. Woodhead (1959) 'The Diffusion of the Greek Alphabet', *American Journal of Archaeology* 63 (2): 175–78.

Coutsinas, N. (2008) 'Défenses crétoises. Fortifications urbaines et défense du territoire en Crète aux époques classique et hellénistique', Unpublished PhD dissertation, Université Libre de Bruxelles.

Craik, E.M. (1980) *The Dorian Aegean*, London, Routledge and Kegan Paul.

Croley, S.P. (1998) 'Theories of Regulation: Incorporating the Administrative Process', *Columbia Law Review* 98 (1): 1–168.

Crook, J.A., A. Lintott and E. Rawson (eds) (1992) *Cambridge Ancient History* Vol. 9 *The Last Age of the Roman Republic, 146–43 B.C.*, Cambridge, Cambridge University Press.

Csapo, E. (1991) 'An International Community of Traders in Late 8th–7th c. B.C. in Southern Crete', *Zeitschrift für Papyrologie und Epigraphik* 88: 211–16.

—— (1993) 'A Postscript' to 'An International Community of Traders in Late 8th–7th century B.C. Kommos', *Zeitschrift für Papyrologie und Epigraphik* 96: 235–6.

D'Agata, A.L. and M-C. Boileau (2009) 'Pottery Production and Consumption in Early Iron Age Crete: the Case of Thronos Kephala (Ancient Sybrita)', *Studi Micenei ed Egeo-Anatolici* 51: 165–222.

Dahl, R.A. (1989) *Democracy and Its Critiques*, New Haven, Yale University Press.

Darcque, P., M. Fotiadis and O. Polychronopoulou (eds) (2006) *Mythos: La Préhistoire Égéenne du XIXe au XXIe siècle après J.-C.*, Table Ronde International, Athènes, 21–23 Novembre 2002 (*Bulletin de Correspondance Hellénique* Suppl. 46), Paris.

Dareste de la Chavannes, R. (1882) 'Le chreophylakion dans les villes grecques', *Bulletin de Correspondance Hellénique* 6 (1): 241–45.

Davaras, C. (1976) *Guide to Cretan Antiquities*, Athens, Eptalofos.

Davies, J.K. (1984) 'Cultural, Social and Economic Features of the Hellenistic World' in *Cambridge Ancient History* Volume 7, Part I *The Hellenistic World*: 257–320.

—— (1996) 'Deconstructing Gortyn: When is a Code a Code?' in L. Foxall and A.D.E. Lewis (eds) *Greek Law in its Political Setting: Justifications not Justice*, Oxford, Clarendon Press: 31–56.

—— (1997) 'The "Origins of the Greek *Polis*": Where should we be looking?' in L.G. Mitchell and P.J. Rhodes (eds) *The Development of the Polis in Archaic Greece* London, Routledge: 13–20.

—— (1998) 'Ancient Economies: Models and Muddles' in H. Parkins and C. Smith (eds) *Trade, Traders and the Ancient City*, London and New York: 225–56.

—— (2001) 'Hellenistic Economies in the post-Finley era' in Z. H. Archibald, J. Davies, V. Gabrielsen and G. J. Oliver (eds) *Hellenistic Economies*, London & New York, Routledge: 11–62.

—— (2005) 'The Gortyn Laws' in Michael Gagarin and David Cohen (eds) *The Cambridge Companion to Ancient Greek Law*, Cambridge, Cambridge University Press: 305–27.

—— (2006) 'Hellenistic Economies' in G. Bugh (ed.) *Cambridge Companion to the Hellenistic World*, New York, Cambridge University Press: 73–92.

—— (2007a) 'Classical Greece: Production' in W. Scheidel, I. Morris and R. Saller, (eds) *Cambridge Economic History of the Greco-Roman World*, Cambridge, Cambridge University Press: 333–61.

—— (2007b) 'Pythios and Python: The Spread of a Cult', *Mediterranean Historical Review* 22 (1): 57–69.

De Sanctis, G. (1901) 'The Startus in the Cretan Inscriptions', *American Journal of Archaeology* 5 (3): 319–27.

De Souza, P. (1998) 'Late Hellenistic Crete and the Roman Conquest' in W.G. Cavanagh and M. Curtis (eds) *Post-Minoan Crete* BSA Studies 2, London, British School at Athens: 112–16.

—— (2000) *Piracy in the Graeco-Roman World*, Cambridge, Cambridge University Press.

—— (2008) 'Rome's Contribution to the Development of Piracy' in R. Hohlfelder (ed.) *The Maritime World of Ancient Rome*, Ann Arbor, University of Michigan Press.

Demargne, J. (1901) 'Fouilles de Goulas', *Bulletin de Correspondance Hellénique* 25: 282–307.

—— (1903) 'Fouilles de Goulas', *Bulletin de Correspondance Hellénique* 27: 206–32.

Demargne, P. (1929) 'Terres-cuites archaïques de Lato', *Bulletin de Correspondance Hellénique* 53: 382–429.

—— (1931) 'Recherches sur le site de l'Anavlochos', *Bulletin de Correspondance Hellénique* 55: 365–407.

—— (1947). *La Crète dédalique: Études sur les origines d'une renaissance*, Paris, E. de Boccard.

Demargne, P. and H. van Effenterre (1937a) 'Recherches à Dréros I', *Bulletin de Correspondance Hellénique* 61: 5–32.

—— (1937b) 'Recherches à Dréros II', *Bulletin de Correspondance Hellénique* 61: 333–48.

Desborough, V.R. d'A., (1964) *The Last Mycenaeans and their Successors*, Oxford, Oxford University Press.

Detorakis, T.E. (1994) *History of Crete*, Iraklion, Detorakis.

Diodorus Siculus *History.*

Driessen, F. (2006) 'Pression sociale et descente vers la mer en Crète à la période hellénistique', *Actes du IXème congrès crétologique*, Heraclion: 179–88.

—— (2009) 'Paul Faure 1916–2007', *Aegean Archaeology* 8: 137–139.

Driessen, J. (2010) 'Spirit of Place – Minoan *Houses* as Major Actors' in D. Pullen (ed.) *Political Economies of the Aegean Bronze Age*, Oxford, Oxbow Books.

Driessen, J. and A. Farnoux (1991) 'Recherches sur l'Anavlochos', *Bulletin de Correspondance Hellénique* 115: 749–50.

Ducrey, P. (1970) 'Nouvelles remarques sur deux traités attalides avec des cités crétoises', *Bulletin de Correspondance Hellénique* 94: 637–59.

Ducrey, P. and O. Picard (1969) 'Recherches à Lató', *Bulletin de Correspondance Hellénique* 93: 792–822.

—— (1970) 'Recherches à Lató II: Le Grand Temple', *Bulletin de Correspondance Hellénique* 94: 567–90.

—— (1971) 'Recherches à Lató IV: Le Théâtre', *Bulletin de Correspondance Hellénique* 95: 515–92.

—— (1972) 'Recherches à Lató V: Le Prytanée', *Bulletin de Correspondance Hellénique* 96: 567–90.

Dunn, J. (1994) *Democracy: the Unfinished Journey 508 BC–1993 AD*, Oxford, Oxford University Press.

—— (2007) 'Capitalist Democracy: Elective Affinity or Beguiling Illusion?', *Daedalus* 136: 5–13.

Durkheim, E. (1961) *Elementary Forms of the Religious Life*, New York, Collier.

Eder, W. (2005) 'The Political Significance of the Codification of Law in Archaic Societies: An Unconventional Hypothesis' in Kurt A. Raaflaub (ed.) *Social Struggles in Archaic Rome: New Perspectives on the Conflict of the Orders*, Malden, MA and Oxford, Blackwell: 239–67.

Ehrenberg, V. (1937) 'When did the Polis Rise', *Journal of Hellenic Studies* 57: 147–59.

—— (1943) 'An Early Source of Polis-Constitution', *The Classical Quarterly* 37 (1/2): 14–18.

Eiring, J., M-C. Boileau and I.K. Whitbread (2002) 'Local and Imported Transport Amphorae from a Hellenistic Kiln Site at Knossos: the Results of Petrographic Analysis' in F. Blondé, P. Ballet and J-F. Salles (eds) *Céramiques hellénistiques et romaines: Production et diffusion en Méditerranée orientale*, Lyons, Travaux de la Maison de l'Orient Méditerranéen: 59–65.

Empereur, J-Y., S. Markoulaki and A.A. Marangou (1989) 'Recherches sur les centres de fabrication d'amphores de Crète occidentale', *Bulletin de Correspondance Hellénique* 113 (2): 551–80.

Empereur, J-Y., A.A. Marangou and C.B. Kritzas (1991) 'Recherches sur les amphores crètoises II: les centres de fabrication d'amphores en Crète centrale', *Bulletin de Correspondance Hellénique* 115 (1): 481–523.

Epstein, S.R. (2000) *Freedom and Growth: The Rise of States and Markets in Europe, 1300–1750*, London, Routledge.

Ercek, R., D. Viviers and N. Warzée1 (2010) '3D Reconstruction and Digitalization of an Archeological Site, Itanos, Crete', *Virtual Archaeology Review* 1 (1): 74–78.

Erickson, B.L. (2000) 'Archaic and Classical Crete: Island Pottery Styles in an Age of Historical Transition, ca. 600–400 B.C.' unpublished PhD dissertation, Classical Archaeology, University of Texas at Austin.

—— (2002) 'Aphrati and Kato Syme: Pottery, Continuity, and Cult in Late Archaic and Classical Crete', *Hesperia* 71: 41–90.

—— (2004) 'Eleutherna and the Greek World in the Sixth and Fifth Centuries, B.C.' in *Crete beyond the Palaces: Proceedings of the Crete 2000 Conference, INSTAP Press*: 199–212.

—— (2005) 'Archaeology of Empire: Athens and Crete in the Fifth Century B.C.', *American Journal of Archaeology* 109: 619–63.

—— (2010) 'Priniatikos Pyrgos and the Classical Period in Eastern Crete: Feasting and Island Identities', *Hesperia* 79: 305–349.

Evans, T.S., C. Knappett and R.J. Rivers (2007) 'Using Statistical Physics to Understand Relational Space: A Case Study from Mediterranean Prehistory', in D. Lane, S. Pumain, G. van der Leeuw and G. West (eds) *Complexity Perspectives on Innovation and Social Change*, Springer Methodos Series.

Falkener, E. (1854) *A Description of Some Important Theatres and Other Remains in Crete* (from an MS entitled a 'History of Candia' by Onorio Belli completed in 1596), London, Trübner and Co.

—— (1860) 'La Descrizione dell' Isola di Candia: A MS of the Sixteenth Century on the Antiquities of Candia (1538)' in *The Museum of Classical Antiquities*, London, Longman, Green, Longman and Roberts: 263–310.

Faraguna, M. (2007) 'Guest Editor's Preface: Nomos Despotes: Law and Legal Procedures in Ancient Greek Society', special issue *Etica & Politica / Ethics & Politics* 9 (1): 5–9.

Farenga, V. (2006) *Citizen and Self in Ancient Greece: Individuals Performing Justice and the Law*, Cambridge, Cambridge University Press.

Faure, P. (1959) 'La Crète aux cent villes', *Kretika Chronika* 13: 171–217.

—— (1960) 'La Crète aux cent villes', *BAssBudé*, ser. 4: 228–49.

—— (1962) 'Cavernes et sites aux deux extrémités de la Crète', *Bulletin de Correspondance Hellénique* 86 (1): 36–56.

—— (1963) 'Nouvelles localizations de ville crétoises', *Kretika Chronika* 17: 16–26.

—— (1965a) 'Sept nouvelles villes de la Crète antique', *Kretika Chronika* 19: 222–30.

—— (1965b) 'Recherches sur le peuplement des montagnes de Crète : sites, cavernes et cultes', *Bulletin de Correspondance Hellénique*, 89: 27–63.

—— (1967a) 'Aux frontières de l'Etat de Lato: 50 toponymes,' in W.C. Brice (ed.), *Europa. Studien zur Geschichte und Epigraphik der früher Aegaeis. Festschrift für E. Grumach*, Berlin, De Gruyter: 94–112.

—— (1967b) 'Toponymes préhelléniques dans la Crète moderne', *Kadmos: Zeitschrift für vor- und frühgriechische Epigraphik* 6 (1): 41–79.

—— (1970) 'Nouveaux Toponymes Préhelléniques dans la Crète Moderne', *Kadmos: Zeitschrift für vor- und frühgriechische Epigraphik* 9 (1): 75–92.

—— (1978) 'Chronique des cavernes crétoises (1972–1977)', *Bulletin de Correspondance Hellénique* 102 (2): 629–40.

—— (1984) 'Hydronymes crétoises', *Kretologia* 16: 30–61.

—— (1988) 'Cités antiques de la Crète de l'ouest', *Cretan Studies* 1: 83–96.

—— (1989) *Recherches de Toponymie Crétoise: Opera Selecta*, Amsterdam, Hakkert.

—— (1993) 'Nouvelles identifications d'antique localités Crétoises', *Kadmos: Zeitschrift für vor- und frühgriechische Epigraphik* 32 (1): 67–74.

Feng, Y. (2003) *Democracy, Governance and Economic Performance: Theory and Evidence*, Boston, Mass., MIT Press.

Figueira, T. (1998) *The Power of Money: Coinage and Politics in the Athenian Empire*, Philadelphia, University of Pennsylvania Press.

Finley, M.I. (1951) 'Some Problems of Greek Law' (review of Pringsheim, *The Greek Law of Sale*, 1950), *Seminar* 9: 72–91.

—— (1966) 'The Problem of the Unity of Greek Law' in *La Storia del diritto nel quadro delle scienze storiche (Atti del primo Congresso Internazionale della Società Italiana di Storia del Diritto)*, Florence: 129–42. (Reprinted in *The Use and Abuse of History*, London 1986: 134–52, 236–7).

—— (1981) *Economy and Society in Ancient Greece*, London, Chatto and Windus.

—— (1999) *The Ancient Economy*, Berkeley, University of California Press.

Fleck, R. K. & F.A. Hanssen (2006) 'The Origins of Democracy: A Model with Application to Ancient Greece', *Journal of Law and Economics* 49: 115–145.

Fleming, N.C. and P.A. Pirazzoli (1988) 'Archéologie des côtes de la Crète', *Histoire et Archéologie* 50: 66–81.

Forrest, W.G. (2000) 'The Pre-polis Polis' in R. Brock and S. Hodkinson (eds) *Alternatives to Athens: Varieties of Political Organization and Community in Ancient Greece*, Oxford, Oxford University Press: 280–92.

Forsdyke, S. (2005) *Exile, Ostracism, and Democracy: The Politics of Expulsion in Ancient Greece*, Princeton, Princeton University Press.

Foxhall, L. (2007) *Olive Cultivation in Ancient Greece: Seeking the Ancient Economy*, Oxford, Oxford University Press.

Foxall, L. and A.D.E. Lewis (eds) (1996) *Greek Law in its Political Setting: Justifications not Justice*, Oxford, Clarendon Press.

French, A. (1991) 'Economic Conditions in Fourth-century Athens', *Greece & Rome* 38: 24–40.

Fried, C. (2000) 'Markets, Law and Democracy', *Journal of Democracy* 11 (3): 5–18.

Frost, F.J. (1989) 'The Last Days of Phalasarna', *Ancient History Bulletin* 3 (1): 15–18.

Frost, F.J. and E. Hadjidaki (1990) 'Excavations in the Harbor of Phalasarna in Crete', *Hesperia* 59: 513–27.

Gabrielsen, V. (2001) 'Economic Activity, Maritime Trade and Piracy in the Hellenistic Aegean', *Revue des Etudes Anciennes* 103 (1–2): 219–40.

—— (2003) 'Piracy and the Slave Trade' in A. Erskine (ed.) *A Companion to the Hellenistic World*, Oxford, Blackwell: 389–404.

Gagarin, M. (1995) 'The First Law of the Gortyn Code Revisited', *Greek Roman and Byzantine Studies* 36: 7–15.

—— (1999) 'Rhétorique et anti-rhétorique à Gortyne' in Catherine Dobias-Lalou (ed.) *Des dialectes grecs aux lois de Gortyne*, Paris, de Boccard: 65–74.

—— (2001) 'The Gortyn Code and Greek Legal Procedure', *Symposion 1997. Akten der Gesellschaft für griechische und hellenistische Rechtsgeschichte*, 13: 41–52.

—— (2004) 'The Rule of Law in Gortyn' in Edward M. Harris and Lene Rubinstein (eds) *The Law and the Courts in Ancient Greece*: 173–83.

—— (2005a) 'The Unity of Greek Law' in Michael Gagarin and David Cohen (eds) *The Cambridge Companion to Ancient Greek Law*, Cambridge, Cambridge University Press: 29–40.

—— (2005b) 'Early Greek Law' in M. Gagarin and D. Cohen (eds) *Cambridge Companion to Ancient Greek Law*, Cambridge, Cambridge University Press: 82–94.

—— (2008) *Writing Greek Law*, New York and Cambridge, Cambridge University Press.

Gantzel, K.J. and T. Schwinghammer (1999) *Warfare since the Second World War*, New York, Transaction.

Gardiakos, S. (1969) *The Coinage of Modern Greece, Crete, the Ionian Islands, and Cyprus*, Oak Park, Ill., Obol International.

Garlan, Y. (1987) 'War, Piracy and Slavery in the Greek world', *Slavery & Abolition*, 8 (1): 7–21.

Gavrilaki, I. and Y. Tzifopoulos (1998) 'An "Orphic-Dionysiac" Gold Epistomion from Sfakaki near Rhethymno', *Bulletin de Correspondance Hellénique* 122: 343–56.

Gehrke, H.-J. (1997) 'Gewalt und Gesetz. Die soziale und politische Ordnung Kretas in der Archaischen und Klassischen Zeit', *Klio* 79: 23–68.

—— (2009) 'States' in K. A. Raaflaub and H. van Wees (eds) *A Companion to Archaic Greece*, Oxford, Wiley-Blackwell: 395–410.

Gere, C. (2006) 'Cretan Psychoanalysis and Freudian Archaeology: H.D.'s Minoan Analysis with Freud in 1933' in Y. Hamilakis and N. Momigliano (eds) *Archaeology and European Modernity: Producing and Consuming the 'Minoans.' Creta Antica (Rivista annuale di studi archeologici, storici ed epigrafici, Centro di Archaeologica Cretese, Università di Catania)*, 7, Padua: Bottega d'Erasmo.

—— (2009) *Knossos and the Prophets of Modernism*, University of Chicago Press.

Gillin, J.L. (1919) 'The Origin of Democracy', *American Journal of Sociology* 24: 704–14.

Gkiasta, M. (2008) 'The Historiography of Landscape Research on Crete', PhD dissertation Universiteit Leiden. (https://openaccess.leidenuniv.nl/dspace/bitstream/1887/12855/16/).

Glytsos, N.P. (1993) 'Measuring the Income Effects of Migrant Remittances: A Methodological Approach Applied to Greece', *Economic Development and Cultural Change* 42 (1): 131–68.

Gondicas, D. (1988) *Recherches su la Crète occidentale, de l'époque géométrique à la conquête romaine: Inventaire des sources archéologiques et textuelles, position du problème*, Amsterdam: Adolph M. Hakkert.

Gorlin, C.E. (1988) 'The Spensithios Decree and Archaic Cretan Civil Status', *Zeitschrift für Papyrologie und Epigraphik*, Bd. 74: 159–65.

Gorokhovich, Y. (2005) 'Abandonment of Minoan Palaces on Crete in Relation to the Earthquake Induced Changes in Groundwater Supply', *Journal of Archaeological Science* 32 (2): 217–22.

Grandjean, C. (2006) 'Athens and Bronze Coinage' in Peter van Alfen (ed.) *Agoranomia: Studies in Money and Exchange Presented to John H. Kroll*, New York: The American Numismatic Society.

Granovetter, M. (1973) 'The Strength of Weak Ties', *American Journal of Sociology*, 78: 1360–80.

—— (1983) 'The Strength of Weak Ties: A Network Theory Revisited', *Sociological Theory* 1: 201–33.

Greco, E., Th. Kalpaxis, A. Schnapp and D. Viviers (1996) 'Itanos (Crète Orientale)', *Bulletin de Correspondance Hellénique* 120: 941–52.

—— (1997) 'Itanos (Crète Orientale)', *Bulletin de Correspondance Hellénique* 121: 809–24.

—— (1999) 'Itanos (Crète Orientale)', *Bulletin de Correspondance Hellénique* 123: 515–30.

Greco, E. and Mario Lombardo (2005) *La Grande Iscrizione di Gortyna. Centoventi anni dopo la scoperta. Atti del Convegno*, Atene-Haghii Deka 25–28 maggio 2004, Atene.

Greco, E., T. Kalpaxis, N. Papadkis, A. Schnapp and D. Viviers (2001) 'Itanos (Crète orientale)', *Bulletin de Correspondance Hellénique* 125 (2): 637–644.

Gruen, E. (1984) *The Hellenistic World and the Coming of Rome*, Berkeley, University of California Press.

Guarducci, M. (ed.) (1935–1950) *Inscriptiones creticae, opera et consilio Friderici Halbherr collectae*, I, *Tituli Cretae mediae praeter Gortynios* (1935); II, *Tituli Cretae occidentalis* (1939); III, *Tituli Cretae orientalis* (1942); IV, *Tituli Gortynii* (1950), Rome.

Guizzi, F. (2001) *Hierapytna. Storia di una polis cretese dalla fondazione alla conquista Romana.* (Memorie, Serie 9, Vol. 13, Fasc. 3.), Rome, Accademia Nazionale dei Lincei.

Haarman, H. (1995) *Early Civilization and Literacy in Europe: An Inquiry into Cultural Continuity in the Mediterranean World*, Amsterdam, Mouton de Gruyter.

Hadjidaki, E. (1987) 'Excavations at the Classical/Hellenistic Harbour of Phalasarna, Western Crete, Greece', *International Journal of Nautical Archaeology* 16 (3): 254–56.

—— (1988a) 'The Classical and Hellenistic Harbor at Phalasarna: A Pirate's Port?' Unpublished PhD dissertation, University of California, Santa Barbara.

—— (1988b) 'Preliminary Report of Excavations at the Harbor of Phalasarna in West Crete', *American Journal Archaeology* 92: 463–79.

—— (2000) 'Hellenistic Ceramics from Phalasarna Found from 1986–1990', *Ancient Worlds* 31 (1): 54–73.

—— (2001) 'The Roman Destruction of Phalasarna' in N.J. Higham (ed.) *Archaeology of the Roman Empire*, BAR International Series 940: 155–66.

Hadjimichali, V. (1971) 'Recherches à Latô III: Maisons', *Bulletin de Correspondance Hellénique* 95: 167–222.

Haggard, S.M., A. MacIntyre and L.B. Tiede (2008) 'The Rule of Law and Economic Development', *Annual Review of Political Science* 11: 205–34.

Haggis, D.C. (2002) 'Integration and Complexity in the Late Pre-Palatial Period: A View from the Countyside in Eastern Crete' in Y. Hamilakis (ed.) *Labyrinth Revisited: Rethinking 'Minoan' Archaeology*, Oxford, Oxbow: 120–42.

Halbherr, F. (1891) 'Researches in Crete', *Antiquary* 24: 241–245.

—— (1893) 'Researches in Crete', *Antiquary* 27: 10–14.

—— (1896) 'Cretan Expedition. 1. Inscriptions from Various Cretan Cities', *The American Journal of Archaeology and of the History of the Fine Arts*, 11 (4): 539–601.

—— (1897) 'Cretan Expedition III. Epigraphical Researches in Gortyna', *American Journal of Archaeology*, 1 (3): 159–238.

—— (1898) 'Cretan Expedition X. Addenda to the Cretan Inscriptions', *American Journal of Archaeology*, 2 (1/2): 79–94.

Hall, J.M. (2002) *Hellenicity: Between Ethnicity and Culture*, Chicago, University of Chicago Press.

—— (2007) *A History of the Archaic Greek World ca. 1200–479 BCE*, Oxford, Blackwell.

Hallager, P. et al. (1997) 'Archaic to Byzantine Periods: Stratigraphy and Catalogues' in E. Hallager and B.P. Hallager (eds), *The Greek-Swedish Excavation at the Agia Aikateri Square Kastelli, Khania 1970–87*, Stockholm, Svenska Instituet i Athen/Paul Astoms Forlag: 202–8.

Hamilakis, Y. (ed.) (2002) *Labyrinth Revisited: Rethinking 'Minoan' Archaeology*, Oxford, Oxbow.

Hamilakis, Y. and N. Momigliano (eds) (2006) *Archaeology and European Modernity: Producing and Consuming the 'Minoans.' Creta Antica (Rivista annuale di studi archeologici, storici ed epigrafici, Centro di Archaeologica Cretese, Università di Catania)*, 7, Padua: Bottega d'Erasmo.

Hamilakis, Y. and E. Yalouri (1996) 'Antiquities as Symbolic Capital in Modern Greek Society', *Antiquity* 70: 117–29.

Hansen, M.H. (1983) *The Athenian Ecclesia: A Collection of Articles, 1976–83* Copenhagen, Museum Tusculum Press.

—— (1987) *The Athenian Assembly in the Age of Demosthenes*, Oxford, Blackwell.

—— (2003) '95 Theses about the Greek "Polis" in the Archaic and Classical Periods. A Report on the Results Obtained by the Copenhagen Polis Centre in the Period 1993–2003', *Historia: Zeitschrift für Alte Geschichte* 52 (3): 257–82.

—— (2006a) *Polis: An Introduction to the Ancient Greek City-State*, Oxford, Oxford University Press.

—— (2006b) *The Shotgun Method: The Demography of the Ancient Greek City-State Culture.* Columbia and London, University of Missouri Press.

Hansen, M.H. and T.H. Nielsen (eds) (2004) *An Inventory of Archaic and Classical Poleis* Oxford University Press.

Harris, E.M. (2000) 'Open Texture in Athenian Law', *Dike* 3: 27–79.

—— (2005) 'Feuding or the Rule of Law? The Nature of Litigation in Classical Athens: An Essay in Legal Sociology' in M. Gargarin and R.W. Wallace (eds) *Symposion 2001: Vorträge zur griechischen und hellenistischen Rechtsgeschichte*, Vienna Austrian Academy of Sciences: 125–42.

—— (2006) *Democracy and the Rule of Law in Classical Athens: Essays on Law, Society, and Politics*, Cambridge, Cambridge University Press.

Harris, W. V. (1979) *War and Imperialism in Republican Rome, 327–70 BC*, Oxford, Oxford University Press.

—— (ed.) (2005) *Rethinking the Mediterranean*, Oxford, Oxford University Press.

Harrison, G.W. (1993) *The Romans and Crete*, Amsterdam, Hakkert

—— (1998) 'Crete the Ordinary', in W. Cavanagh & M. Curtis (eds) *Post-Minoan Crete*, London, British School at Athens: 129–34.

Hart, H.L.A. (1961) *The Concept of Law*, Oxford, Oxford University Press.

Harvey, D. (1973) *Social Justice and the City*, London: Edward Arnold.

—— (1996) *Justice, Nature and the Geography of Difference*, Oxford, Blackwell.

Havelock, E. (1978) *The Greek Concept of Justice: From Its Shadow in Homer to Its Substance in Plato*, Boston, Mass., Harvard University Press.

Hayden, B.J., J.A. Moody and O. Rackham (1992) 'The Vrokastro Survey Project, 1986–1989: Research Design and Preliminary Results', *Hesperia* 61: 293–353.

Hayden, B. with H. Dierckx, G. Harrison, J. Moody, G. Postma, O. Rackham, A. Stallsmith (2004) *The Vrokastro Reports, Vol. 2: The Settlement History of the Vrokastro Region from the Final Neolithic through the Early Modern Periods, with Supplementary Studies* University Museum Monograph 119 Philadelphia: University of Pennsylvania Museum of Archaeology and Anthropology.

Headlam, J.W. (1892–93) 'The Procedure of the Gortynian Inscription', *Journal of Hellenic Studies* 13: 48–69.

Held, D. (1996) *Models of Democracy* (2nd Edition), Stanford, Stanford University Press.

Herodotus *Histories.*

Hetherington, K. (1996) 'Identity Formation, Space and Social Centrality', *Theory, Culture & Society*, 13: 33–52.

Hetherington, K. (1997) 'In Place of Geometry: the Materiality of Place' in K. Hetherington and R. Munro (eds) *Ideas of Difference: Social Spaces and the Labour of Division* Oxford, Blackwell: 183–99.

Hirsch, E. (1995) 'Landscape: between Place and Space', in E. Hirsch and M. O'Hanlon (eds) *The Anthropology of Landscape: Perspectives on Place and Space* Oxford, Clarendon Press: 1–30.

Hodkinson, S. (2009) *Property and Wealth in Classical Sparta*, Swansea, Classical Press of Wales.

Hoffman, G.L. (1997) *Imports and Immigrants: Near Eastern Contacts with Iron Age Crete*, Ann Arbor, University of Michigan Press.

Hölkeskamp, K-J. (1990) 'City and Territory, War and Trade in the Ancient Mediterranean', *Mediterranean Historical Review* 5 (1): 72–81.

—— (1992a) 'Arbitrators, Lawgivers and the "Codification of Law" in Archaic Greece', *Mètis: Anthropologie des mondes grecs anciens* 7: 49–81.

—— (1992b) 'Written Law in Archaic Greece', *Proceedings of the Cambridge Philological Society* 38: 87–117.

—— (2005) 'What's in a Code? Solon's Laws between Complexity, Compilation and Contingency', *Hermes* 133: 280–93.

Holloway, R.R. (1971) 'An Archaic Hoard from Crete and the Early Aeginetan Coinage', *American Numismatic Society – Museum Notes* 17: 1–23.

Homer *Odyssey*.

—— *Iliad*.

Homolle, T. (1879) 'Convention entre trois villes crétoises', *Bulletin de Correspondance Hellénique* 3 (1): 290–315.

Hood, M.S.F. (1965) 'Minoan Sites in the Far West of Crete', *Annual of the British School at Athens* 60: 99–113.

—— (1967) 'Some Ancient Sites in South-west Crete', *Annual of the British School at Athens* 62: 47–56.

Hood, M.S.F. and J. Boardman (1957) 'A Hellenic Fortification Tower on the Kefala Ridge at Knossos', *Annual of the British School at Athens* 52: 224–30.

Hood, M.S.F. and J. Boardman (1961) 'Early Iron Age Tombs at Knossos (Knossos Survey 25)', *Annual of the British School at Athens*, 56: 68–80.

Hood, M.S.F. and P. Warren (1966) 'Ancient Sites in the Province of Ayios Vasilios, Crete', *Annual of the British School at Athens* 61: 163–89.

Hood, M.S.F., P. Warren and G. Cadogan (1964) 'Travels in Crete, 1962', *Annual of the British School at Athens* 59: 50–99.

Hood, M.S.F. and D. Smyth (1981) *Archaeological Survey of the Knossos Area*, British School at Athens Supplement 14, 2nd ed., London, BSA.

Hopkins, K. (1980) 'Taxes and Trade in the Roman Empire (200 B.C. – A.D. 400)', *Journal of Roman Studies* 70: 101–25.

—— (1981) *Conquerors and Slaves*, Sociological Studies in Roman History 1, Cambridge, Cambridge University Press.

—— (2002) 'Rome, Taxes, Rents and Trade' in W. Scheidel and S. Von Reden (eds) *The Ancient Economy*, New York, Routledge: 190–230.

Horden, P. and N. Purcell (2000) *The Corrupting Sea: A Study of Mediterranean History*, Oxford, Blackwell.

Horowitz, Donald L. (1993) 'Democracy in Divided Societies', *Journal of Democracy* 4 (4): 18–38.

Hunter, V. (2000) 'Policing Public Debtors in Classical Athens', *Phoenix* 54 (1/2): 21–38.

Inglis, D. and R. Robertson (2004) 'Beyond the Gates of the Polis: Reconfiguring Sociology's Ancient Inheritance', *Journal of Classical Sociology* 4, 2: 165–89.
—— (2005) 'The Ecumenical Analytic: "Globalization", Reflexivity and the Revolution in Greek Historiography', *European Journal of Social Theory* 8 (2): 99–122.
—— (2006) 'From Republican Virtue to Global Imaginary: Changing Visions of the Historian Polybius', *History of the Human Sciences* 19 (1): 1–18.
Ion, T.P. (1910) 'The Cretan Question', *American Journal of International Law*, 4 (2): 276–284.

Jackson, A. (1971) 'The Chronology of the Bronze Coins of Knossos', *Annual of the British School at Athens* 66: 283–95.
Jannaris, A.N. (1907) 'Another Prehistoric City in Crete', *Contemporary Review*, 92 (July / December): 22–24.
Jeffery, L.H. (1990) *The Local Scripts of Archaic Greece. A Study of the Origin of the Greek Alphabet and its Development from the Eighth to the Fifth Centuries B.C.* revised edition with a supplement by A.W. Johnston, Oxford Monographs on Classical Archaeology, Oxford, Clarendon Press.
Jeffery, L.H. and A. Morpurgo-Davies (1971) 'An Archaic Greek Inscription from Crete', *British Museum Quarterly* 36, 1/2: 24–9.
Jensen, E.G. and T.C. Heller (2003) *Beyond Common Knowledge: Empirical Approaches to the Rule of Law*, Stanford, Stanford University Press.
Johannowsky, W. (2002) *Il Sanctuario sull'Acropoli di Gortina*. Vol. 2. Monografie della Scuola Archeologica Italiana di Atene e delle Missioni Italiane in Oriente 16 Athens, Scuola Archeologica Italiana di Atene.
Jones, N.F. (1980) 'The Order of the Dorian Phylai', *Classical Philology* 75 (3): 197–215.
—— (1987) *Public Organization in Ancient Greece: A Documentary Study*, Philadelphia, American Philosophical Society.
—— (1990) 'The Organization of the Kretan City in Plato's *Laws*', *Classical World* 83: 473–92.
—— (1995) 'The Athenian Phylai as Associations: Disposition, Function, and Purpose', *Hesperia* 64: 503–42.

Kagan, D. (1982) 'The Dates of the Earliest Coins', *American Journal of Archaeology* 86, 3: 343–60.
—— (1991) *Pericles of Athens and the Birth of Democracy*, New York, Free Press.
Kallet-Marx, R.M. (1995) *Hegemony to Empire. The Development of the Roman Imperium in the East from 148 to 62 B.C.* Hellenistic Culture and Society, volume 15, Berkeley, University of California Press.
Kalpaxis, A. (1999) 'Le città cretesi' in Greco, E. (ed.) *La Città Greca Antica: Istituzioni, Società e Forme Urbane*, Rome, Donzelli editore: 111–27.
Kalpaxis, T., Schnapp, A., and Viviers, D. (1995) 'Itanos', *Bulletin de Correspondance Hellénique* 119: 713–36.
Karafolas, S. (1998) 'Migrant Remittances in Greece and Portugal: Distribution by Country of Provenance and the Role of the Banking Presence', *International Migration* 36 (3): 357–81.

Karafotias, A. (1997) 'Crete and International Relationships in the Hellenistic Period', unpublished PhD thesis, University of Liverpool.

Kardulias, P.N. (ed.) (1999) *Leadership, Production and Exchange: World-Systems Theory in Practice*, New York, Rowman and Littlefield.

Katsonas, A. (2002) 'The Rise of the Polis in Central Crete', *Eulimeme* 3: 37–74.

—— (2008) 'The Discovery of Eleutherna from the Formation of the Modern Cretan State to Humfry Payne's Excavations (1899–1929)', *Annual of the British School at Athens* 103: 275–98.

Keane, J. (2009) *The Life and Death of Democracy*, London, Simon and Schuster.

King, R.J., S.S. Özcan, T. Carter, E. Kalfoğlu, S. Atasoy, C. Triantaphyllidis, A. Kouvatsi, A.A. Lin, C-E. T. Chow, L.A. Zhivotovsky, M. Michalodimitrakis, P.A. Underhill (2008) 'Differential Y-chromosome Anatolian Influences on the Greek and Cretan Neolithic', *Annals of Human Genetics* 72: 205–14.

Kirsten, E. (1942) *Das dorische Kreta*. Pt. 1, *Die Insel Kreta im fünften und vierten Jahrhundert*. Warzburg: K. Triltsch.

Kitchell, K.F. (1977) 'Topographica Cretica: 'Topoi' of Classical Crete with Testimonia', unpublished dissertation, Loyola University of Chicago.

—— (1983) 'New Evidence for the Cretan *Ariaioi* Coinage', *American Journal of Archaeology* 87: 216–20.

Knappett, C. (1999) 'Assessing a Polity in Protopalatial Crete: the Malia-Lasithi State', *American Journal of Archaeology* 103: 615–39.

—— (2007) 'Materials with Materiality?' *Archaeological Dialogues* 14: 20–3.

Knappett, C. and I. Nikolakopoulou (2005) 'Exchange and Affiliation Networks in the MBA Southern Aegean: Crete, Akrotiri and Miletus' in R. Laffineur and E. Greco (eds) *Emporia: Aegeans in East and West Mediterranean* (Liège: Aegaeum 25): 175–84.

Knappett, C. and I. Nikolakopoulou (2007) 'Colonialism without Colonies? A Bronze Age Case Study from Akrotiri, Thera', *Hesperia* 77: 1–42.

Knappett, C. and I. Schoep (2000) 'Continuity and Change in Minoan Palatial Power' *Antiquity* 74: 365–71.

Kolodny, E-Y. (1968) 'La Crète: mutations et évolution d'une population insulaire grecque', *Revue de Géographie de Lyon* 43 (3): 227–290.

Kosso, P. and C. Kosso (1995) 'Central Place Theory and the Reciprocity between Theory and Evidence', *Philosophy of Science* 62 (4): 581–98.

Kotsonas, A. (2006) 'Wealth and Status in Iron Age Knossos', *Oxford Journal of Archaeology* 25 (2): 149–72.

Kristensen, K.R. (2007) 'Inheritance, property and management: Gortynian family law revisited' *Symposion 2005*, Akten der Gesellschaft für griechische und hellenistische Rechtsgeschichte 19: 89–100.

Kristiansen, K.R. and T.B. Larsson (2005) *The Rise of Bronze Age Society: Travels, Transmissions and Transformations*, Cambridge, Cambridge University Press.

Kraay, C.M. (1964) 'Hoards, Small Change and the Origin of Coinage', *Journal of Hellenic Studies* 84: 76–91.

Kroll, J.H. and N.M. Waggoner (1984) 'Dating the Earliest Coins of Athens, Corinth and Aegina', *American Journal of Archaeology* 88: 325–40.

Kuzmin, A.V. (2001) 'The Celestial Map: The Symbolism of Historical Eras and Reflection of the World Model', *Astronomical & Astrophysical Transactions* 20 (6): 1045–64.

Kvist, K. (2005) 'Cretan Grants of Asylia: Violence and Protection as Interstate Relations', *Classica et Mediaevalia* 54: 185–222.

Kyriakidis, E. (2005) *Ritual in the Bronze Age Aegean: The Minoan Peak Sanctuaries*, London, Duckworth.

Lanni, A. (2005) 'Relevance in Athenian Courts' in M. Gagarin and D. Cohen (eds) *Cambridge Companion to Ancient Greek Law*, Cambridge, Cambridge University Press: 112–28.

—— (2006) *Law and Justice in the Courts of Classical Athens*, Cambridge, Cambridge University Press.

—— (2009) 'Social Norms in the Courts of Ancient Athens', *Public Law & Legal Theory Working Paper Series*, Paper No. 09–58, Harvard Law School.

Lapatin, K. (2000) 'Journeys of an Icon: The Provenance of the "Boston Goddess"', *Journal of Mediterranean Archaeology* 13: 127–54.

—— (2002) *Mysteries of the Snake Goddess: Art, Desire, and the Forging of History*, Boston, Houghton Mifflin.

La Rosa, V. (1992) 'Phaistos' in Meyers, J. W., E.E. Myers and G. Cadogan (eds) *The Aerial Atlas of Ancient Crete*, Berkeley and Los Angeles, University of California Press: 232–43.

Larsen, J.A.O. (1936) 'Perioeci in Crete', *Classical Philology*, 31 (1): 11–22.

Le Rider, G. (1966) *Monnaies crétoises, du Ve au Ier siècle* Paris, Ecole Française d'Athènes, Étude crétoises 15.

—— (1968) 'Un groupe de monnaies crétoises a types athéniens' in *Humanisme actif: Mélanges d'art et de littérature offerts à Julien Cain*, Paris.

Lefebvre, H. (1991) *The Production of Space*, Oxford, Blackwell.

Leigh Fermor, P. (2007) 'Foreword' to I. Grundon, *The Rash Adventurer: A Life of John Pendlebury* London, Libri Publications.

Levi, D. (1930–31) 'I bronzi di Axos', *ASAtene* 13–14: 43–146.

—— (1945) 'Early Hellenic Pottery of Crete', *Hesperia* 14 (1): 1–32.

Lévy, E. (2000) 'La cohérence du code de Gortyne' in Lévy, E. (ed.) *La codification des lois dans l'antiquité: Actes du Colloque de Strasbourg 27–29 novembre 1997* Strasbourg: 185–214.

Lianos, T.P. (1997) 'Factors Determining Migrant Remittances: The Case of Greece', *International Migration Review* 31 (1): 72–87.

Lijphart, A. (1969) 'Consociational Democracy', *World Politics* 21: 207–25.

—— (1977) *Democracy in Plural Societies: A Comparative Explanation*, New Haven, Yale University Press.

—— (1999) *Patterns of Democracy: Government Forms and Performance in Thirty-Six Countries*, New Haven, Yale University Press.

Link, S. (1994) *Das griechische Kreta. Untersuchungen zu seiner staatlichen und gesellschaftlichen Entwicklung vom 6, biz zum 4*, Stuttgart, Franz Steiner Verlag.

Link, S. (2003) 'Kosmoi, Startoi und Iterationsverbote: Zum Kampf um das Amt des Kosmos auf Kreta', *Dike* 6: 139–49.

Lintott, A. (2002) 'Aristotle and the Mixed Constitution' in R. Brock and S. Hodgkinson *Alternatives to Athens: Varieties of Political Organisation and Community in Ancient Greece* Oxford University Press: 152–66.

Low, P. (2007) *Interstate Relations in Classical Greece: Morality and Power*, Cambridge, Cambridge University Press.

Ma, J. (2003) 'Peer Polity Interaction in the Hellenistic Age', *Past and Present* 180: 9–40.

MacDonald, C. (1995) *The Lost Battle: Crete 1941*, London, MacMillan.

Macdonald, G. (1919) *The Silver Coinage of Crete: A Metrological Note*, Proceedings of the British Academy 9, London, Oxford University Press.

MacGillivray, A. (2000) 'The Great Kouros in Cretan Art' in A. MacGillivray, J.M. Driessen and L.H. Sackett (eds) *The Palaikastro Kouros: a Minoan Chryselephantine Statuette and its Aegean Bronze Age Context* BSA Studies 6, London, British School at Athens: 122–30.

McGuire, R.H. (1996) 'The Limits of World-Systems Theory for the Study of Prehistory' in P.N. Peregrine and G.M. Feinman (eds), *Pre-Columbian World Systems* Monographs in World Prehistory No. 26, Madison, Prehistory Press: 51–64.

McKee, S. (2000) *Uncommon Dominion: Venetian Crete and the Myth of Ethnic Purity* Philadelphia, University of Pennsylvania Press.

Mackil, E. (2003) 'Koinon and Koinonia: Mechanisms and Structures of Political Collectivity in Classical and Hellenistic Greece', unpublished PhD dissertation, Princeton University.

—— (2004) 'Wandering Cities: Alternatives to Catastrophe in the Greek Polis', *American Journal of Archaeology* 108 (4): 493–516.

Mackil, E. and Peter van Alfen (2006) 'Cooperative Coinage' in P. van Alfen (ed.) *Agoranomia: Studies in Money and Exchange Presented to J.H. Kroll*, New York, American Numismatic Society: 201–46.

Makrypoulias, C. G. (2000) 'Byzantine Expeditions against the Emirate of Crete c. 825–949', *Graeco-Arabica* (7–8): 347–362.

Madison, J. (1996) *The Federalist Papers, No. 10*, London: Everyman.

Malkin, I. (2003) 'Networks and the Emergence of Greek Identity', *Mediterranean Historical Review* 18: 56–74.

—— (ed.) (2005) *Mediterranean Paradigms and Classical Antiquity*, London and New York, Routledge.

Malkin, I., C. Constantakopoulou and K. Panagopoulou (2007) 'Networks in the Ancient Mediterranean', Preface to a Special Issue of *Mediterranean Historical Review* 22: 1–9.

Marangou-Lerat, A. 1995 *Le Vin et les amphores de Crète*. Études Crétoises 30, Paris, École Française d'Athènes.

Marginesu, G. (2005) *Gortina di Creta: Prospettive epigrafiche per lo studio della forma urbana*, Athens, Scuola Archeologica Italiana di Atene.

Marinatos, S. (1936) 'Le temple géométrique de Dréros', *Bulletin de Correspondance Hellénique* 60: 214–85.

Mariani, L. (1895) 'Antichità Cretesi', *Monumenti Antichi* 6: 153–348.

Martin, T.R. (1996) 'Why Did the Greek "Polis" Originally Need Coins?', *Historia: Zeitschrift für Alte Geschichte* 45 (3): 257–83.

Martínez Fernández, A. (2006) *Epigramas Helenísticos de Creta* Madrid, Consejo Superior de Investigaciones Científicas.

Mastrocinque, A. (2009) 'The Antikythera Shipwreck and Sinope's Culture during the Mithridatic Wars' in Jakob Munk Højte (ed.) *Mithridates VI and the Pontic Kingdom* Danish National Research Foundation, Centre for Black Sea Studies, Aarhus University Press: 313–20.

Matz, F. (1951) *Forschungen auf Kreta, 1942* (Deutsches Archäologisches Institut), Berlin, W. de Gruyter.

Meadows, A. and K. Shipton (eds) (2001) *Money and Its Uses in the Ancient Greek World*, Oxford, Oxford University Press.

Merriam, A.C. (1885) 'Law Code of the Kretan Gortyna (I)', *American Journal of Archaeology and of the History of the Fine Arts* 1, 4: 324–50.

—— (1886) 'Law Code of the Kretan Gortyna (II)', *American Journal of Archaeology and of the History of the Fine Arts* 2, 1: 24–45.

Merrill, W.P. (1991) 'Τὸ πλεθος in a Treaty concerning the Affairs of Argos, Knossos and Tylissos', *The Classical Quarterly*, New Series, 41: 16–25.

Meyer-Laurin, H. (2007) 'Law and Equity in the Attic Trial' in E. Carawan (ed.) *The Attic Orators* (Oxford Readings in Classical Studies) Oxford, Oxford University Press: 116–39.

Meyers, J. W., E.E. Myers and G. Cadogan (eds) (1992) *The Aerial Atlas of Ancient Crete*, Berkeley and Los Angeles, University of California Press.

Migeotte, L. (2009) *The Economy of the Greek Cities from the Archaic Period to the Early Roman Empire*, Berkeley, Los Angeles, London, University of California Press.

Miles, G.C. (1964) 'Byzantium and the Arabs: Relations in Crete and the Aegean Area', *Dumbarton Oaks Papers* 18: 1–32.

Mill, J.S. (1951) 'Considerations on Representative Government' in H.B. Acton (ed.) *Utilitarianism, Liberty, and Representative Government*, London, Dent.

Millard, A.R. (1986) 'The Infancy of the Alphabet', *World Archaeology* 17, 3: 390–98.

Miller, F. D. (2009) 'The Origins of Rights in Ancient Political Thought' in S. Salkever (ed.) *The Cambridge Companion to Ancient Greek Political Thought*, New York, Cambridge University Press: 301–30.

Mitchiner, M. (2004) *Ancient Trade and Early Coinage*, 2 vols, London, Spink.

Moody, J.A. (1987) 'The Environmental and Cultural Prehistory of the Khania Region of West Crete: Neolithic through Late Minoan III', unpublished PhD dissertation, University of Minnesota.

Moody, J., O. Rackham and G. Rapp (1996) 'Environmental Archaeology of Prehistoric NW Crete', *Journal of Field Archaeology* 23: 273–97.

Moore, D. (2010) *Dawn of Discovery: The Early British Travellers to Crete. Richard Pocoke, Robert Pashley and Thomas Spratt, and their Contribution to the Island's Bronze Age Archaeological Heritage* (BAR International Series 2053), Oxford, Archaeopress.

Morgan, C. (2003) *Early Greek States beyond the Polis*, London, Routledge.

Mørkholm, O. (1991) *Early Hellenistic Coinage from the Accession of Alexander to the Peace of Apamea*, Cambridge, Cambridge University Press.

Morkot, R.G. (2005) *The Egyptians: an Introduction*, London and New York, Routledge.

Morley, N. (2007) *Trade in Classical Antiquity*, Key Themes in Ancient History, Cambridge, Cambridge University Press.

Morris, C. (2006) 'From Ideologies of Motherhood to "Collecting Mother Goddesses"' in Y. Hamilakis and N. Momigliano (eds) *Archaeology and European Modernity: Producing and Consuming the 'Minoans.' Creta Antica (Rivista annuale di studi archeologici, storici ed epigrafici, Centro di Archaeologica Cretese, Università di Catania), 7*, Padua, Bottega d'Erasmo: 69–78.

Morris, I. (1990) 'The Gortyn Code and Greek Kinship', *Greek Roman and Byzantine Studies* 31: 233–54.

—— (1991) 'The Early Polis as City and State' in J. Rich and A. Wallace-Hadrill (eds), *City and Country in the Ancient World*, London, Routledge: 25–58.

—— (1994) 'The Athenian Economy Twenty Years after *The Ancient Economy*', *Classical Philology* 89: 351–66.

—— (1999) 'Foreword' to M.I. Finley, *The Ancient Economy*, updated ed. Berkeley, Los Angeles and London, University of California Press: ix–xxxvi.

—— (2003) 'Mediterraneanization', *Mediterranean Historical Review* 18: 30–55.

—— (2004) 'Economic Growth in Ancient Greece', *Journal of Institutional and Theoretical Economics* 160: 709–42.

—— (2005a) 'Archaeology, Standards of Living, and Greek Economic History' in J.G. Manning and I. Morris (eds) *The Ancient Economy: Evidence and Models*, Stanford, Stanford University Press: 91–126.

—— (2005b) 'Greek Traders' (review), *The Classical Review* 55: 575–77.

—— (2006) 'The Growth of Greek Cities in the First Millennium B.C.' in G. Storey (ed.) *Urbanism in the Preindustrial World: Cross-cultural Approaches*, Tuscaloosa, AL: 27–51.

Morris, I. and B.R. Weingast (2004) 'Views and Comments on Institutions, Economics, and the Ancient Mediterranean World: Introduction', *Journal of Institutional and Theoretical Economics* 160: 702–08.

Morris, I., R.P. Saller and W. Scheidel (2007) 'Introduction' in W. Scheidel, I. Morris and R. Saller, *The Cambridge Economic History of the Greco-Roman World*, Cambridge, Cambridge University Press: 1–14.

Mueller, K. (2007) *Settlements of the Ptolemies: City Foundations and New Settlement in the Hellenistic World*, Leuven, Peeters Publishing.

Murray, O. (1990) 'Cities of Reason' in O. Murray and S. Price (eds) *The Greek City: From Homer to Alexander*, Oxford, Clarendon Press: 1–28.

—— (2000) 'What is Greek about the *Polis*?' in P. Flensted-Jensen, T.H. Nielsen and L. Rubinstein (eds) *Polis & Politics: Studies in Ancient Greek History, Presented to Mogens Herman Hansen on his 60th Birthday*, Copenhagen, Museum Tusculanum Press: 231–44.

Nafplioti, A. (2008) '"Mycenaean" political domination of Knossos following the Late Minoan IB destructions on Crete: negative evidence from strontium isotope ratio analysis ($^{87}Sr/^{86}Sr$)', *Journal of Archaeological Science* 35: 2307–17.

Negbi, O. (1992) 'Early Phoenician Presence in the Mediterranean Islands: A Reappraisal', *American Journal of Archaeology*, 96, 4: 599–615.

Niniou-Kindeli, V. (1990) 'Ανασκαφικές εργασίες, Νομός Χανίων (Απτέρα)', *ArchDelt B2 Χρονικά*, 45: 443.

—— (1993) 'Ανασκαφικές εργασίες, Νομός Χανίων (Απτέρα)', *ArchDelt B2 Χρονικά*, 48: 473–74.

—— (1994) 'Ανασκαφικές εργασίες, Νομός Χανίων', *ArchDelt B2 Χρονικά*, 49: 721.

—— (1995) 'Ανασκαφικές εργασίες, Νομός Χανίων', *ArchDelt B2 Χρονικά*, 50: 733.

—— (1999) 'Αρχαιολογικές Ειδήσεις 1995–1997, Νομός Χανίων, Επαρχία Αποκορώνου, Απτέρα (Απτάρα)', *Κρητική Εστία*, ΠΕΡΙΟΔΟΣ Δ΄-ΤΟΜΟΣ 7: 167–75.

Nixon, L., J. Moody and O. Rackham (1988) 'Archaeological Survey in Sphakia, Crete', *Echos du Monde Classique / Classical Views* 32, n.s. 7: 159–73.

Nördquist, G. and H. Whittaker (2007) 'Comments on Kristian Kristiansen and Thomas B. Larsson (2005): *The Rise of Bronze Age Society: Travels, Transmissions and Transformations*, Cambridge, Cambridge University Press, *Norwegian Archaeological Review* 40: 75–84.

North, D. (1981) *Structure and Change in Economic History*, New York, W.W. Norton.

—— (1990) *Institutions, Institutional Change and Economic Performance*, Cambridge, Cambridge University Press.

—— (2005) *Understanding the Process of Economic Change*, Princeton, Princeton University Press.

North D. and R. Thomas (1973) *The Rise of the Western World: A New Economic History*, New York, Cambridge University Press.

Nowicki, K. (1996) 'Arvi Fortetsa and Loutraki Kandilioro: Two Refuge Settlements in Crete', *Annual of the British School at Athens* 91: 253–85.

—— (2000) *Defensible Sites in Crete ca. 1200–800 B.C.*, Liège, Université de Liège.

Ober, J. (2008) 'What the Ancient Greeks Can Tell Us About Democracy', *Annual Review of Political Science* 11: 67–91.

Olivier, J-P. (1986) 'Cretan Writing in the Second Millennium B.C.', *World Archaeology* 17, 3: 377–89.

Ormerod, H.A. (1997) *Piracy in the Ancient World: an Essay on Mediterranean History*, Baltimore, Johns Hopkins University Press (originally published 1924).

Osborne, R. (1991) 'Pride and Prejudice, Sense and Substance: Exchange and Society in the Greek City' in J. Rich and A. Wallace-Handrill (eds) *City and Country in the Ancient World*, London and New York, Routledge: 119–45.

—— (1985) 'Law in Action in Classical Athens', *Journal of Hellenic Studies* 105: 40–58.

—— (1996a) *Greece in the Making: 1200–479 BC*, Abingdon, Oxon, Routledge.

—— (1996b) 'Pots, Trade and the Archaic Greek Economy', *Antiquity* 70, 31–44.

Ostwald, M. (1969) *Nomos and the Beginnings of Athenian Democracy*, Oxford, Oxford University Press.

Papadakis, N. and B. Rutkowski (1985) 'New Research at Skales Cave near Praisos', *Annual of the British School at Athens* 80: 129–37.

Papadopoulos, G.A., E. Daskalaki, A. Fokaefs and N. Giraleas (2010) 'Tsunami Hazard in the Eastern Mediterranean Sea: Strong Earthquakes and Tsunamis in the West Hellenic Arc and Trench System', *Journal of Earthquakes and Tsunamis* 4 (3): 145–79.

Papadopoulos, J. (2005) 'Inventing the Minoans: Archaeology, Modernity and the Quest for European Identity', *Journal of Mediterranean Archaeology* 18: 87–149.

Papakonstantinou, Z. (1996) 'The Cretan *Apokosmos*', *Zeitschrift für Papyrologie und Epigraphik* 111: 93–6.

—— (2002) 'Written Law, Literacy and Social Conflict in Archaic and Classical Crete', *Ancient History Bulletin* 16: 135–50.

—— (2008) *Lawmaking and Adjudication in Archaic Greece*. London, Duckworth.

Papazarkadas, N. and P. Thonemann (2008) 'Athens and Kydonia: Agora I 7 602', *Hesperia* 77 (1): 73–87.

Parkinson, W.A. and M.L. Galaty (2007) 'Secondary States in Perspective: An Integrated Approach to State Formation in the Prehistoric Aegean', *American Anthropologist* 109: 113–29.

Pashley, R. (1837) *Travels in Crete* (two vols) London, John Murray (fasc. ed. Athens, Karavias, 1989).

Pausanias *Description of Greece.*

Peacock, M.S. (2006) 'The Origins of Money in Ancient Greece: the Political Economy of Coinage and Exchange', *Cambridge Journal of Economics* 30: 637–650.

Pendlebury, J.D.S. (1965) *Archaeology of Crete: An Introduction*, London, Methuen.

Peregrine, P. (1996) 'Introduction: World-Systems Theory and Archaeology' in P.N. Peregrine and G.M. Feinman (eds) *Pre-Columbian World Systems*, Monographs in World Prehistory No. 26, Madison, Prehistory Press: 1–10.

Perlman, P. (1992) 'One Hundred-Citied Crete and the 'Cretan *Politeia*', *Classical Philology* 87 (3): 193–205.

—— (1994) 'Inscriptions from Crete I', *Zeitschrift für Papyrologie und Epigraphik*, Bd. 100: 123–25.

—— (1995) 'ΘΕΩΡΟΔΟΚΟΥΝΤΕΣ ΕΝ ΤΑΙΣ ΠΟΛΕΣΙΝ: Panhellenic *Epangelia* and Political Status' in Mogens Herman Hansen (ed.) *Sources for the Ancient Greek City State*, Acts of the Copenhagen Polis Centre Volume 2, Copenhagen, Muntsgaard, 113–64.

—— (1996) '*Polis Upikoos*: The Dependent Polis and Crete' in M.H. Hansen (ed.) *Introduction to an Inventory of Poleis: Symposium August, 23–26, 1995*, Acts of the Copenhagen Polis Centre 3, Copenhagen, Munksgaard: 233–87.

—— (2000) 'Gortyn: The First Seven Hundred Years (Part 1)' in P. Flensted-Jensen, T.H. Nielsen, and L. Rubinstein (eds) *Polis and Politics: Studies in Ancient Greek History Presented to Mogens Herman Hansen on His Sixtieth Birthday*, Copenhagen, Museum Tusculanum Press, University of Copenhagen: 60–89.

—— (2002) 'Gortyn. The first Seven Hundred Years Part II: The Laws from the Temple of Apollo Pythios', *CPCPapers* 6: 187–227.

—— (2004a) 'Crete' in Hansen, M.H. and Nielsen, T.H. (eds) *An Inventory of Archaic and Classical Poleis* Oxford, Oxford University Press: 1144–95.

—— (2004b) 'Tinker, Tailor, Soldier, Sailor: The Economies of Archaic Eleutherna, Crete', *Classical Antiquity* 23 (1): 95–137.

—— (2004c) 'Writing on the Walls. The Architectural Context of Archaic Cretan Laws' in Leslie P. Day, Margaret S. Mook and James D. Muhly (eds) *Crete beyond the Palaces: Proceedings of the Crete 2000 Conference*, Philadelphia: 81–97.

—— (2005) 'Imagining Crete' in M.H. Hansen (ed.) *The Imaginary Polis: Acts of the Copenhagen Polis Centre*, Volume 7, Copenhagen, The Royal Danish Academy of Science and Letters: 282–334.

—— (2010) 'Of Battle, Booty, and (Citizen) Women: A "New" Inscription from Archaic Axos, Crete', *Hesperia* 79: 79–112.

Petropoulou, A. (1985) *Beiträge zur Wirtschafts- und Gesellschaftsgeschichte Kretas in hellenistischer Zeit*, Frankfurt.

Pirazzoli, P.A., J. Ausseil-Badie, P. Giresse, E. Hadjidaki and M. Arnold (1992) 'Historical Environmental Changes at Phalasarna Harbor, West Crete', *Georchaeology* 7: 371–92.

Plassart, A. (1921) 'Inscriptions de Delphes, la liste des Théorodoques', *Bulletin de Correspondance Helléneique* 45 (1): 1–85.

Plato *Laws*.

Platon, N. (1966) *Crete*, London, Frederick Muller.

—— (1992) 'Lisos' in Myers et al. (eds) *The Aerial Atlas of Ancient Crete*, Berkeley, University of California Press: 68–71.

Pliny *Natural History*.

Pococke, R. (1745) *A Description of the East and Some other Countries* Vol. II, London, W. Boyer.

Polányi, K. (1957) *The Great Transformation: The Political and Economic Origins of our Time*, Boston, Beacon Press.

—— (1963) 'Ports of Trade in Early Societies', *Journal of Economic History* 23: 30–45.

Polányi, K., C.M. Arensbert, and H.W. Pearson (eds) (1957) *Trade and Market in Early Empires*, New York, Free Press.

Polybius *Histories*.

Polignac, F. de (1995) *Cults, Territory, and the origins of the Greek City State*, Chicago and London, University of Chicago Press.

Powell, B.B. (1977) 'The Significance of the so-called "Horns of Consecration"', *Kadmos* 16 (1): 70–82.

Prent, M. (2005) *Cretan Sanctuaries and Cults: Continuity and Change from Late Minoan IIIC to the Archaic Period*, Leiden, Leiden University Press.

Preziosi, D. (2002) 'Archaeology as Museology: Re-thinking the Minoan Past' in Y. Hamilakis (ed.) *Labyrinth Revisited: Rethinking 'Minoan' Archaeology*, Oxford, Oxbow Books: 30–9.

Price, S., T. Higham, L. Nixon and, J. Moody (2002) 'Relative Sea-Level Changes in Crete: Reassessment of Radiocarbon Dates from Sphakia and West Crete', *Annual of the British School at Athens*, 97: 171–200.

Pseudo-Skylax *Periplous*.

Purcell, N. (2005) 'A View from the Customs House' in W.V. Harris (ed.) *Rethinking the Mediterranean*, Oxford, Oxford University Press: 200–32.

Raab, H.A. (2001) *Rural Settlement in Hellenistic and Roman Crete*, Oxford, Archaeopress.

Raaflaub, K.A., J. Ober and R.W. Wallace (2007) *Origin of Democracy in Ancient Greece*, Berkeley, University of California Press.

Rackham, O. (1990) 'Ancient Landscapes' in Murray, O. and Price, S. (eds) *The Greek City from Homer to Alexander*, Oxford, Oxford University Press: 108–9.

Rackham, O. and J. Moody (1996) *The Making of the Cretan Landscape*, Manchester and New York, Manchester University Press.

Rauh, N.K. (2003) *Merchants, Sailors & Pirates in the Roman World*, Stroud, Tempus Publishing.

Ray, J.D. (1986) 'The Emergence of Writing in Egypt', *World Archaeology* 17: 307–16.

Reinach, A.J. (1911) 'Inscriptions d'Itanos', *Revue des Etudes Grecques* 24: 377–425.

Reed, C.M. (2003) *Maritime Traders in the Ancient Greek World*, Cambridge, Cambridge University Press.

Reger, G. (2003) 'The Economy' in A. Erskine (ed.) *A Companion to the Hellenistic World*, Oxford, Blackwell: 331–353.

Renfrew, C. (1969) 'Trade and Culture Process in European Prehistory', *Current Anthropology* 10 (2/3): 151–69.

—— (1996) 'Who were the Minoans? Towards a Population History of Crete', *Cretan Studies* 5: 1–22.

—— (2001) 'Commodification and Institution in Group-Oriented and Individualizing Societies' in W.G. Runciman (ed.) *The Origin of Human Social Institutions* London, British Academy: 93–117.

Renfrew, C. and J. Cherry (eds) (1986) *Peer-Polity Interaction and Socio-Political Change*, Cambridge, Cambridge University Press.

Richardson, M.B. (2000) 'The Location of Inscribed Laws in Fourth-Century Athens. IG II2 244, on Rebuilding the Walls of Peiraieus' in P. Flensted-Jensen, T. Heine Nielsen, and L. Rubinstein (eds) *Polis & Politics: Studies in Ancient Greek History Presented to Mogens Hansen on His Sixtieth Birthday*, Copenhagen, CPSC.

Rizza, G. (1967–1968) 'Le terrecotte di Axòs', *ASAtene* New Series 29–30: 211–302.

Rizza, G. and S.M.V. Scrinari (1968) *Il sanctuario sull'acropoli di Gortina 1. Monografie della Scuola Archeologica di Atene e della missioni italiana in Oriente* 2 Rome, Istituto Poligrafico dello Stato.

Rizza, G. and M.A. Rizzo (1985) 'Prinias' in *Ancient Crete: A Hundred Years of Italian Archaeology (1884–1984)*, Rome, De Luca Editione: 143–67.

Rizza, G., D. Palermo and F. Tomasello (1994) *Priniàs 2: Mandra di Gipari: Una officina di vasai nel territorio di Priniàs*, Catania, Studi e Materiali di Archaeologia Greca 5.

Roberts, E.S. (1888) 'Archaic Inscriptions from Crete', *Classical Review* 2: 9–12.

Robinson, E.W. (1997) *The First Democracies: Early Popular Government outside Athens*, Stuttgart, F. Steiner.

—— (2007) 'The Sophists and Democracy Beyond Athens', *Rhetorica* 25 (1): 109–22.

Rocchetti, L. (ed.) (1994) *Sybrita: La Valle di Amari fra Bronzo e Ferro*, Rome, Gruppo Editoriale Internazionale.

Rodrik, D. and R. Rigobon (2005) 'Rule of Law, Democracy, Openness, and Income: Estimating the Interrelationships', *Economics of Transition* 13 (3): 533–64.

Roessel, D. (2006) 'Happy Little Extroverts and Bloodthirsty Tyrants: Minoans and Mycenaeans in Literature in English after Evans and Schliemann' in Y. Hamilakis and N. Momigliano (eds) *Archaeology and European Modernity: Producing and Consuming the 'Minoans.' Creta Antica (Rivista annuale di studi archeologici, storici ed epigrafici, Centro di Archaeologica Cretese, Università di Catania)*, 7, Padua: Bottega d'Erasmo 197–208.

Rostovtzeff, M.I. (1926) *Social and Economic History of the Roman Empire*, Oxford, Oxford University Press

Rousseau, J.J. (1968) *The Social Contract*, Harmondsworth, Penguin.

Roy, J. (1998) 'The Threat from the Piraeus' in Cartledge, P.P. Millett and S. von Reden (eds) *Kosmos: Essays in Order, Conflict and Community in Classical Athens*, Cambridge, Cambridge University Press: 191–202.

Runciman, W.G. (1982) 'Origins of States: The Case of Archaic Greece', *Comparative Studies in Society and History* 24 (3): 351–77.

—— (1990) 'Doomed to Extinction: The *Polis* as an Evolutionary Dead-End' in O. Murray and S. Price (eds) *The Greek City: From Homer to Alexander*, Oxford, Clarendon Press: 347–67.

—— (1998) 'Greek Hoplites, Warrior Culture, and Indirect Bias', *Journal of the Royal Anthropological Institute* 4 (4): 731–51.

—— (2005) 'Stone Age Sociology', *Journal of the Royal Anthropological Institute* 11: 129–42.

—— (2009) *The Theory of Cultural and Social Selection*, Cambridge, Cambridge University Press.

Sackett, L.H. (ed.) (1992) *Knossos from Greek City to Roman Colony*, Oxford, Oxford University Press.

Sadler, M.T. (1830) *The Law of Population: A Treatise, in Six Books; in Disproof of the Superfecundity of Human Beings, and Developing of the Real Principle of Their Increase*, London, John Murray.

Sanders, I.F. (1982) *Roman Crete*, Warminster, Aris and Phillips.

Sassen, S. (1991) *Global City: New York, London, Tokyo*, Princeton, Princeton University Press.

Sauer, E.W. (ed.) (2004) *Archaeology and Ancient History: Breaking Down the Boundaries*, London and New York, Routledge.

Savignoni, L. and G. de Sanctis (1901) 'Esplorazione archaeologica delle Provincie occidentali de Creta', *Monumenti Antichi* 11: 285–550.

Saxonhouse, A.W. (1992) *Fear of Diversity: The Birth of Political Science in Ancient Greek Thought*, Chicago, University of Chicago Press.

—— (1993) 'Athenian Democracy: Modern Mythmakers and Ancient Theorists', *PS: Political Science and Politics* 26: 486–90.

Schachermeyr, F. (1938) 'Vorbericht über eine Expedition nach Ostkreta', *AA* 53: 466–80.

Schäfer, J. (ed.) (1992) *Amnisos: nach den archäologischen, historischen und epigraphischen Zeugnissen des Altertums und der Neuzeit*, Berlin, Deutsches Archaologisches Institut, Abeteilung Aten.

Schaps, D. (1975) 'Women in Greek Inheritance Law', *Classical Quarterly* 25, 1: 53–7.

Schaps, D.M. (2004) *The Invention of Coinage and the Monetization of Ancient Greece*, Ann Arbor, Michigan University Press.

—— (2008) 'What was Money in Ancient Greece' in W.V. Harris (ed.) *The Monetary Systems of the Greeks and Romans*, Oxford, Oxford University Press: 38–48.

Scheffers, A. and S. Scheffers (2007) 'Tsunami Deposits on the Coastline of West Crete (Greece)', *Earth & Planetary Science Letters* 259: 613–624.

Scheidel, W. (2007) 'Demography' in Scheidel, W., Morris, I. and Saller, R. (eds) *The Cambridge Economic History of the Greco-Roman World*, Cambridge, Cambridge University Press: 38–86.

Scheidel, W., I. Morris, and R. Saller (eds) (2007) *The Cambridge Economic History of the Greco-Roman World*, Cambridge, Cambridge University Press.

Schlager, N. (1991) *Archäologische Geländeprospektion Südostkreta. Erste Ergebnisse*, Vienna, Schindler.

Schmitt-Pantel, P. (1990) 'Collective Activities and the Political in the Greek City' in O. Murray and S. Price (eds) *The Greek City: From Homer to Alexander*, Oxford, Clarendon Press: 199–213.

Schoenberger, E. (2008) 'The Origins of the Market Economy: State Power, Territorial Control, and Modes of War Fighting', *Comparative Studies in Society and History* 50 (3): 663–91.

Seaford, R. (1994) *Reciprocity and Ritual: Homer and Tragedy in the Developing City-State* Oxford, Clarendon Press.

Sealey, Raphael (1994) *The Justice of the Greeks*, Ann Arbor, University of Michigan.

Segre, S. (2004) 'A Durkheimian Network Theory', *Journal of Classical Sociology* 4: 215–35.

Sekunda, N.V. (2000) 'Land-use, Ethnicity, and Federalism in West Crete' in R. Brock and S. Hodkinson (eds) *Alternatives to Athens: Varieties of Political Organization and Community in Ancient Greece* Oxford, Clarendon Press: 327–47.

—— (2004–2009) 'The Date and Circumstances of the Construction of the Fortifications at Phalasarna', *Horos* 17–21: 595–600.

—— (2007) 'Land Forces' in P. Sabin, H. van Wees and M. Whitby (eds) *Cambridge History of Greek and Roman Warfare* Volume 1 *Greece, the Hellenistic World and the Rise of Rome*, Cambridge, Cambridge University Press: 325–56.

Shaw, B., N.N. Ambraseys, P.C. England, M.A. Floyd, G.J. Gorman, T.F.G. Higham, J.A. Jackson, J.M. Nocquet, C.C. Pain and M.D. Piggott (2008) 'Eastern Mediterranean Tectonics and Tsunami Hazard Inferred from the AD 365 Earthquake', *Nature Geoscience* 1 (4): 268–76.

Sherk, R. (1990) 'The Eponymous Officials of Greek Cities: Mainland Greece and the Adjacent Islands', *Zeitschrift für Papyrologie und Epigraphik* 84: 231–95.

Sherratt, A. (2006) 'Crete, Greece, and the Orient in the Thought of Gordon Childe (with an Appendix on Toynbee and Spengler: The Afterlife of the Minoans in European Intellectual History)' in Y. Hamilakis and N. Momigliano (eds) *Archaeology and European Modernity: Producing and Consuming the 'Minoans'. Creta Antica (Rivista annuale di studi archeologici, storici ed epigrafici, Centro di Archaeologica Cretese, Università di Catania)* 7, Padua, Bottega d'Erasmo: 107–126.

Shipton, K. (2000) *Leasing and Lending: The Cash Economy in Fourth Century BC Athens*, London.

Sjögren, L. (2003) *Cretan Locations Discerning Site Variations in Iron Age and Archaic Crete (800–500 B.C.)* BAR –S1185, Oxford, Archaeopress.

—— (2006) 'Minoan Wannabees: The Resurrection of Minoan Influences in Scandinavian Archaeology' in Y. Hamilakis and N. Momigliano (eds) *Archaeology and European Modernity: Producing and Consuming the 'Minoans.' Creta Antica (Rivista annuale di studi archeologici, storici ed epigrafici, Centro di Archaeologica Cretese, Università di Catania), 7,* Padua, Bottega d'Erasmo: 127–142.

—— (2008) *Fragments of Archaic Crete: Archaeological Studies on Time and Space*, Uppsala Studies in Ancient Mediterranean and Near Eastern Civilizations 31, Uppsala, Acta Universitatis Upsaliensis.

Smith, G. (1922) 'Early Greek Codes', *Classical Philology* 17 (3): 187–201.

Smith, M.E. (2004) 'The Archaeology of Ancient State Economies', *Annual Review of Anthropology* 33: 73–102.

Smith, W. (1854) *Dictionary of Greek and Roman Geography*, Boston, Little, Brown and Co.

Snodgrass, A.M. (1980) *Ancient Greece: The Age of Experiment*, Berkeley and London, University of California Press.

—— (1986) 'Interaction by Design: the Greek City State' in C. Renfrew and J.F. Cherry (eds) *Peer-Polity Interaction and Socio-Political Change*, Cambridge, Cambridge University Press: 47–58.

—— (1993) 'The Rise of the Polis: The Archaeological Evidence' in M.H. Hansen (ed.) *The Ancient Greek City-State*, Copenhagen, CSP: 30–40.

Sporn, K. (2001) 'The Topography of and a Votive Hoard from Rhaukos on Crete' in Johannes Bergemann (ed.) *Science with Enthusiasm: Contributions to Portraits in Antiquity and Regional Historical Studies Dedicated to Klaus Fittschen*, Internationale Archäologie – Studia honoraria, Rahden / Westf: 49–77.

—— (2002) *Heiligtümer und Kulte Kretas in klassischer und hellenistischer Zeit (Studien zu antiken Heiligtümern, 3)*, Heidelberg, Verlag Archäologie und Geschichte.

Spratt, T.B. (1865) *Travels and Researches in Crete*, London, van Voorst (fasc. ed. Elibron Classics 2005).

Spyridakis, S. (1969) 'Aristotle on the Election of Kosmoi', *La Parola del Passato* 24: 265–68.

—— (1970a) *Ptolemaic Itanos and Hellenistic Crete*, Berkeley, University of California Press.

—— (1970b) 'A Delian Inscription and the Cretan Koinon', *Hermes* 98: 254–56.

—— (1976) 'Salamis and the Cretans', *La Parola del Passato* 31: 345–55.

—— (1977) 'Cretans and Neocretans', *Classical Journal* 72, 4: 299–307.

—— (1979) 'Aristotle on Cretan πολυτεχνία', *Historia: Zeitschrift für Alte Geschichte* 28 (3): 380–84.

—— (1992) *Cretica: Studies on Ancient Crete*, Athens, Aristide D. Caratzas.

Stahl, M. and U. Walter (2009) 'Athens' in K.A. Raaflaub and H. van Wees (eds) *A Companion to Archaic Greece* Oxford, Wiley-Blackwell: 138–61.

Stampolidis, N. (1990) 'Eleutherna on Crete: An Interim Report on the Geometric-Archaic Cemetery', *Annual of the British School at Athens* 85: 375–403.

—— (1993) *Ελεύθερνα. Vol 3, pt 1. Γεωμετρικά-αρχαϊκά χρόνια και οδηγός στην έκθεση ΄Το γεωμετρικό΄ αρχαίκο νεκροταφείο της ορθής Πέτρας*, Heraklion, University of Crete Press.

—— (1994) *Ελεύθερνα. Vol 3, pt 2. Από τη γεωμετρική και αρχαϊκη νεκρόπολη*, Rethymnon, University of Crete.

—— (1996) *Reprisals: Contributions to the Study of Customs of the Geometric-Archaic Period*, Rethymno, University of Crete.

—— (1998) 'Imports and Agalmata: The Eleuthernian Experience' in V. Karageorghis and N. Chr. Stampolidis (eds) *Eastern Mediterranean: Cyprus–Dodecanese–Crete 16th–6th cent. B.C.* Iraklio, University of Crete and Ministry of Culture: 175–84.

—— (ed.) (2004) *Eleutherna: Polis-Acropolis-Necropolis*, Athens, University of Crete.

Stampolidis, N.C. and V. Karageorghis (eds) (2003), *Sea Routes: Interconnections in the Mediterranean: 16th–6th c. BC, Proceedings of the International Symposium held at Rethymnon, Crete, 29th September – 2nd October 2002*, Athens, Orion Press.

Stampolidis, N.C. and A. Kotsonas (2006) 'Phoenicians in Crete' in Sigrid Deger-Jalkotzy and Irene S. Lemos (eds) *Ancient Greece: From the Mycenaean Palaces to the Age of Homer* Edinburgh Leventis Studies 3, Edinburgh, Edinburgh University Press: 337–60.

Stavrinos, M. (1992) 'Palmerston and the Cretan Question, 1839–1841', *Journal of Modern Greek Studies* 10 (2): 249–269.

Stefanaki, V.E. (2001) 'Sur deux monnaies de bronze inédites d'Hiérapytna: Monnayage Hiéraptynian et timbres amphoriques à l'époque hellénistique', *Eulimene* 2: 129–42.

—— (2005) 'Le monnayage d'Hierapytna (Crète orientale) de la fin de l'époque classique à l'époque impériale', unpublished PhD dissertation, Université Paris Sorbonne-Paris IV.

—— (2009) 'Le monnayage de bronze de Viannos et de Malla en Crète orientale', Κερμάτια φιλίας. Τιμητικός τόμος για τον Ιωάννη Τουράτσογλου. Α: Νομισματική-Σφραγιστική: 271–283.

Stefanakis, E.I. (1996a) 'Ptolemaic Coinage and Hellenistic Crete' in A. Karetsos (ed.) Κρητη και Αίγυπτος Μελέτες Athens, Ministry of Culture: 195–207.

—— (1996b) 'Polichne' in E.I. Stefanakis (ed.) *In Memory of Martin Jessop Price*, Greek Numismatic Series 5: 152–156.

—— (1997) 'Studies in the Coinages of Crete with Particular Reference to Kydonia', unpublished PhD dissertation, University of London.

—— (1998) 'A Mid-fourth Century BC Alliance Coinage on Crete? The Case of Kytaion Reassessed' in W.G. Cavanagh and M. Curtis (eds) *Post-Minoan Crete* British School at Athens, Studies 2, London, BSA: 96–104.

—— (1999) 'The Introduction of Coinage in Crete and the Beginning of Local Minting' in A. Chaniotis (ed.) *From Minoan Farmers to Roman Traders: Sidelights on the Economy of Ancient Crete* Heidelberger Althistorische Beiträge und episraphische Studien 29, Stuttgart, Franz Steiner: 247–68.

Stefanakis, M.I. (2000a) 'Kydon the Oikist or Zeus Cretagenes Kynotraphes? The Problem of Interpreting Cretan Coin Types', *Eulimene* 1: 79–90.

—— (2000b) 'Πολυρρήνια, Όρειοι και Κάνδανος. Μια σχέση του δευτέρου μισού του τρίτου αιώνα π.Χ.', *Πεπραγμένα του Η' Διεθνούς Κρητολογικού Συνεδρίου, Ηράκλειο 1996*, Ηράκλειο 2000, τ. Α3: 249–261.

—— (2002) 'Η τέχνη και οι καλλιτέχνες των Κρητικών νομισμάτων', *Κρητική Εστία* 9: 43–57.

—— (2005a) 'The "Chania 1922" Hoard (IGCH 254 & CH VII 104): A Reassessment', *Cretan Studies* 7: 231–248.

—— (2005b) 'Counter-stamping Coins in Hellenistic Crete: First Approaches', *XIII Congreso Internacional de Numismatica* 1: 383–94.

—— (2006a) 'Natural Catastrophes in the Greek and Roman World: Loss or Gain? Four Cases of Seaquake-Generated Tsunamis', *Mediterranean Archaeology and Archaeometry* 6 (2): 5–22.

—— (2006b) 'Phalasarna: un port antique, un space d'échanges en Méditerranée' in F. Clément, J. Tolan and J. Wilgaux (eds) *Espaces d'échanges en Méditerranée: Antiquité et Moyen Âge*, Rennes, Presses Universitaires de Rennes: 41–75.

—— (2007) 'Two Argive Triobols and Notes on Argive Coinage in Crete', Appendix 1 in D.C. Haggis, M.S. Mook, R.D. Fitzsimmons, C.M. Scarry and L.M. Snyder 'Excavations at Azoria, 2003–2004', *Hesperia* 76: 243–321.

—— (2010) 'Western Crete: From Captain Spratt to Modern Archaeoseismology' in M. Sintubin, I.S. Stewart, T.M. Niemi and E. Altunel (eds) *Ancient Earthquakes*, Geological Society of America Special Paper 471: 67–79.

Stefanakis, M.I. and V.E. Stefanaki (2006) 'Ρόδος και Κρήτη: Νομισματικές συναλλαγές, επιρροές και αντιδράσεις στις αρχές του 2ου αι. π.Χ.', *Το νόμισμα στα Δωδεκάνησα και τη Μικρασιατική τους Περαία, Δ´ Επιστημονική Συνάντηση*, Κως 30 Μαΐου–2 Ιουνίου 2003, *Οβολός* 8: 165–190.

Stein, G.J. (1998) 'World Systems Theory and Alternative Modes of Interaction in the Archaeology of Culture Contact' in J.G. Cusick (ed.) *Studies in Culture Contact: Interaction, Culture Change and Archaeology*, Center for Archaeological Investigations, Occasional Paper No. 25, Carbondale: 220–55.

Stiros, S.C. (2009) 'The 8.5þ Magnitude, AD365 Earthquake in Crete: Coastal Uplift, Topography Changes, Archaeological and Historical Signature', *Quaternary International* 30: 1–10.

Stiros, S.C. and S. Papageorgiou (2001) 'Seismicity of Western Crete and the Destruction of the Town of Kisamos at A D 365: Archaeological Evidence', *Journal of Seismology* 5: 381–397.

Stoddart, S. and J. Whitley (1988) 'The Social Context of Literacy in Archaic Greece and Etruria', *Antiquity* 62: 761–72.

Strabo *Geography*.

Strataridaki, A. (1988–89) 'The Historians of Ancient Crete: A Study in Regional Historiography', *Kretika Chronika* 28–29: 137–93.

—— (2009) 'Orphans at Cretan *Syssitia*', *Greek, Roman, and Byzantine Studies* 49: 335–42.

Svoronos, J-N. (1890) *Numismatique de la Crète ancienne*, Macon, Imprimerie Protat Frères.

Talbert, R.J.A. (ed.) (2000) *Barrington Atlas of the Greek and Roman World*, Princeton, Princeton University Press.

Tandy, D. (1997) *Warriors into Trade: The Power of the Market in Early Greece*, Berkeley, University of California Press.

Tamanaha, B. (2004) *On the Rule of Law*, Cambridge, Cambridge University Press.

Taramelli, A. (1899) 'Ricerche archeologiche cretesi', *Monumenti Antichi* 9: 286–428.

Thenon, L. (1867) 'Fragments d'une description de l'ile de Crète: Forteresses de la Vallée du Vlithias et ruines de Téménia les Archéens', *Revue Archéologique* ns. 16: 104–15.

Thomas, J. (2004) *Archaeology and Modernity*, London, Routledge.

Thomas, R. (1996) 'Written in Stone? Liberty, Equality, Orality, and the Codification of Law' in Foxall, L. and A.D.E. Lewis (eds) *Greek Law in its Political Setting: Justifications not Justice*, Oxford, Clarendon Press: 9–31.

—— (2005) 'Writing, Law, and Written Law' in M. Gagarin and D. Cohen (eds) *Cambridge Companion to Ancient Greek Law*, Cambridge, Cambridge University Press: 41–60.

Thrift, N. (1996) *Spatial Formations*, London, Sage.

—— (2006) 'Space', *Theory Culture and Society* 23 (2–3): 139–46.

Thucydides *History*.

Thür, G. (2005) 'The Role of the Witness in Athenian Law' in M. Gagarin and D. Cohen (eds) *Cambridge Companion to Ancient Greek Law*, Cambridge, Cambridge University Press: 146–69.

Tilley, C. (1994) *A Phenomenology of Landscape: Places, Paths and Monuments*, Oxford, Berg.

—— (2004) *The Materiality of Stone: Explorations in Landscape Phenomenology*, Oxford, Berg.

—— (2006) 'Introduction: Identity, Place, Landscape and Heritage', *Journal of Material Culture* 11: 7–32.

Todd, S.C. (2005) 'Law and Oratory at Athens' in M. Gagarin and D. Cohen (eds) *Cambridge Companion to Ancient Greek Law*, Cambridge, Cambridge University Press: 97–111.

Treadgold, W.T. (1997) *A History of the Byzantine State and Society*, Stanford, Stanford University Press.

Tsonis, A.A., K.L. Swanson, G. Sugihara and P.A. Tsonis (2010) 'Climate Change and the Demise of Minoan Civilization', *Climate of the Past* 6: 525–530.

Tzedakis, Y. (1970) 'Ἀρχαιότηες καὶ μνημεία Δντικῆς Κρήτης', *ArchDelt* 25: 465–78.

Tzedakis, Y. and A. Kanta. (1978) *Καστέλι Χανίων: Ἀναλυτική μελέτη τῆς κεραμικῆς ἀπό τῆ στρωματογραφημένη τάφρο Β καὶ τὸ πηγάδι*, Incunabula Graeca 66, Rome, Edizione dell'Ateneo and Bizzarri.

van der Mijnsbrugge, M. (1931) *The Cretan Koinon*, New York, G.E. Stechert and Co.

van der Muhll, G. (1977) 'Robert A. Dahl and the Study of Contemporary Democracy: A Review Essay', *American Political Science Review* 71: 1070–96.

van Effenterre, H. (1937) 'A propos du serment des Drériens', *Bulletin de Correspondance Hellénique* 61: 327–32.

—— (1946) 'Inscriptions archaïques crétoises', *Bulletin de Correspondance Hellénique* 70: 588–606.

—— (1948) *La Crète et le monde grec de Platon à Polybe*, Paris, E. de Boccard.

—— (1961) 'Pierres inscrites de Dréros', *Bulletin de Correspondance Hellénique* 85: 544–68.

—— (1973) 'Le contrat de travail du scribe Spensithios', *Bulletin de Correspondance Hellénique* 97: 31–46.

—— (1991) 'E3-E4. Les deux inscriptions de Nési' in H. Van Effenterre, Th. Kalpaxis, A.B. Petropoulou and E. Stavrianopoulou (eds) *Ἐλεύθερνα, ii.1: Ἐπιγραφές ἀπό τὸ Πυργί καὶ τὸ Νῆσι*, Rethymnon, University of Crete Press: 24–30.

van Effenterre, H. and M. van Effenterre (1985) 'Nouvelles lois archaïques de Lyttos', *Bulletin de Correspondance Hellénique* 109: 157–88.

van Effenterre, H., A.-M. Liesenfelt, and I. Papaoikonomou (1983) 'Base inscrite de Kydonia', *Bulletin de Correspondance Hellénique* 107: 405–19.

van Effenterre, H. and M. van Effenterre (2000) 'La codification Gortynienne, mythe ou réalité?' in E. Lévy (ed.) *La codification des lois dans l'antiquité: Actes du Colloque de Strasbourg 27-29 novembre 1997*, Strasbourg: 175–84.

van Effenterre, H. and F. Ruzé (1994-5) *Nomima: recueil d'inscriptions politiques et juridiques de l'archaïsme grec*, 2 vols, Rome.

van Wees, H. (2009) 'The Economy' in Kurt A. Raaflaub and Hans van Wees (eds) *A Companion to Archaic Greece*, Oxford, Wiley-Blackwell: 444–67.

Vasilakis, A.T. (2000) *The 147 Cities of Ancient Crete*, Herakleion, Kairatos Editions.

Verdieck, A.F. (2004) 'The Gortyn Crisis and the Creation of the Gortyn Code', unpublished thesis, Colorado State University (Ft. Collins).

Vidal-Naquet, P. and M. Austin (1977) *Economic and Social History of Ancient Greece*, Berkeley and Los Angeles, University of California Press.

Viviers, D. (1994) 'La cité de Dattalla et l'expansion territoriale de Lyktos en Crète centrale', *Bulletin de Correspondance Hellénique* 118: 229–59.

—— (1995) 'Hérodote et la neutralité des crétois en 480 avant notre ère: La trace d'un débat athénien?', *Hermes* 123: 257–69.

—— (1999) 'Economy and Territorial Dynamics in Crete from the Archaic to the Hellenistic Period' in A. Chaniotis (ed.) *From Minoan Farmers to Roman Traders. Sidelights on the Economy of Ancient Crete*, Heidelberger Althistorische Beiträge und Episraphische Studien 29, Stuttgart, Franz Steiner: 221–33.

—— (2006): 'Itanos: archéologie d'une cite crétoise' (L'archéologie à l'Université Libre de Bruxelles (2001–2005): Matériaux pour une histoire des milieux et des pratiques humaines) *Etudes d'Archéologie* 1: 97–108.

Vlassopoulos, K. (2007a) 'Beyond and Below the Polis: Networks, Associations, and the Writing of Greek History', *Mediterranean Historical Review* 22: 11–22.

—— (2007b) *Unthinking the Greek Polis: Ancient Greek History beyond Eurocentrism*, Cambridge, Cambridge University Press.

Vogeikoff-Brogan, N. and S. Apostolakou (2004) 'New Evidence of Wine Production in East Crete in the Hellenistic Period' in J. Eiring and J. Lund (eds) *Transport Amphorae and Trade in the Eastern Mediterranean*, Monographs of the Danish Institute at Athens 5, Aarhus, Aarhus University Press: 417–27.

Vollgraff, W. (1913) 'Inscription d'Argos (Traité entre Knossos et Tylissos)' *Bulletin de Correspondance Hellénique* 37: 279–308.

von Reden, S. (1995) 'The Piraeus – a World Apart', *Greece & Rome* (Second Series) 42: 24–37.

—— (1997) 'Money, Law and Exchange: Coinage in the Greek Polis', *Journal of Hellenic Studies* 117: 154–76.

—— (2002a) *Exchange in Ancient Greece*, London, Duckworth.

—— (2002b) 'Money in Classical Antiquity: a Survey of Recent Literature', *Klio* 84: 141–74.

Wagstaff, J.M. (ed.) (1987) *Landscape and Culture: Geographical and Archaeological Perspectives*, Oxford, Blackwell.

Walbank, F.W. (2002) *Polybius, Rome and the Hellenistic World: Essays and Reflections*, Cambridge, Cambridge University Press.

Wallace, R.W. (1987) 'The Origin of Electrum Coinage', *American Journal of Archaeology* 91, 3: 385–97.

Wallace, S.A. (1997–2000) 'Case Studies of Settlement Change in Early Iron Age Crete (c. 1200–700 BC): Economic Models of Cause and Effect Reassessed', *Aegean Archaeology*, 4: 61–99.

—— (2003) 'The Perpetuated Past: Re-use or Continuity in Material Culture and the Structuring of Identity in Early Iron Age Crete', *Annual of the British School at Athens* 98: 251–77.

—— (2005) 'Last Chance to See? Karfi (Crete) in the Twenty-First Century: Presentation of New Archaeological Data and their Analysis in the Current Context of Research', *Annual of the British School at Athens* 100: 215–74.

—— (2007) 'Why We Need New Spectacles: Mapping the Experiential Dimension in Prehistoric Cretan Landscapes', *Cambridge Archaeological Journal*, 17 (3): 249–70.

—— (2010) *Ancient Crete: From Successful Collapse to Democracy's Alternatives, 12th–5th Centuries BC*, Cambridge, Cambridge University Press.

Wallerstein, I. (1974) *The Modern World System: Capitalist Agriculture and the Origins of the European World Economy in the Sixteenth Century*, London, Academic Press.

Warren, P. (1972) *Myrtos: An Early Bronze Age Settlement in Crete* (B.S.A. Supplementary Volume 7), London, Thames and Hudson.

Watrous, L.V., D. Hadzi-Vallianou and H. Blitzer (2004) *The Plain of Phaistos: Cycles of Social Complexity in the Mesara Region of Crete*, Monumenta Archaeological 23, Cotsen Institute of Archaeology, University of California Press.

Watrous, L.V. and D. Hadzi-Vallianou (2004) 'The Polis of Phaistos: Development and Destruction' in L. Vance Watrous, D. Hadzi-Vallianou and H. Blitzer, *The Plain of Phaistos: Cycles of Social Complexity in the Mesara Region of Crete*, Monumenta Archaeological 23, Cotsen Institute of Archaeology, University of California Press: 307–38.

Weber, M. (1958) *The City*, New York, The Free Press.

—— (1961) *General Economic History*, New York, Collier.

—— (1976) *The Agrarian Sociology of Ancient Civilisations*, London, New Left Books.

Weinberg, G.D. (1959) 'Glass Manufacture in Ancient Crete', *Journal of Glass Studies* 1: 10–21.

—— (1960) 'Excavations at Tarrha, 1959', *Hesperia* 29 (1): 90–108.

Weingast, B. (1997) 'The Political Foundations of Democracy and the Rule of Law', *American Political Science Review* 91 (2): 245–63.

Westermann, W.L. (1974) *Slave Systems of Greek and Roman Antiquity*, Philadelphia, American Philosophical Society.

Westgate, R. (2007a) 'House and society in Classical and Hellenistic Crete: a case study in regional variation', *American Journal of Archaeology* 111: 423–57.

—— (2007b) 'The Greek House and the Ideology of Citizenship', *World Archaeology*, 39 (2): 229–45.

Whitley, J. (1992–1993) 'Praesos', *Archaeological Report* 39: 77–9.

—— (1997) 'Cretan Laws and Cretan Literacy', *American Journal of Archaeology* 101 (4): 635–61.

—— (1998a) 'Literacy and Lawmaking: The Case of Archaic Crete' in N.R.E. Fisher and H. van Wees (eds) *Archaic Greece: New Approaches and New Evidence*, London, Duckworth: 311–32.

—— (1998b) 'From Minoan to Eteocretans: the Praisos region, 1200–500 BC' in W.G. Cavanagh, M. Curtis, A.W. Johnston, and J.N. Coldstream (eds) *Post-Minoan Crete. Proceedings of the First Colloquium BSA* Studies 2, London, British School at Athens: 27–39.

—— (1998c) 'Review Article: Knossos without Minos', *American Journal of Archaeology*, 102 (3): 611–13.

—— (2001) *Archaeology of Ancient Greece*, Cambridge, Cambridge University Press.

—— (2002a) 'Objects with Attitude: Biographical Facts and Fallacies in the Study of Late Bronze Age and Early Iron Age Warrior Graves', *Cambridge Archaeology Journal* 12: 217–32.

—— (2002b) 'Too Many Ancestors', *Antiquity*, Vol. 76: 119–26.

—— (2002–2003) 'Archaeology in Greece 2002–2003', *Archaeological Reports* 49 BSA, Athens: 1–88.

—— (2006a) 'Praisos: Political Evolution and Ethnic Identity in Eastern Crete, c.1400–300 B.C.' in S. Deger-Jalkotsy and I.S. Lemos (eds) *Ancient Greece from the Mycenaean Palaces to the Age of Homer*, Edinburgh, Edinburgh University Press: 597–617.

—— (2006b) 'The Minoans – a Welsh Invention? A View from East Crete' in Y. Hamilakis and N. Momigliano (eds) *Archaeology and European Modernity: Producing and Consuming the 'Minoans', Creta Antica (Rivista annuale di studi archeologici, storici ed epigrafici, Centro di Archaeologica Cretese, Università di Catania), 7*, Padua, Bottega d'Erasmo: 55–68.

—— (2009) 'Crete' in K.A. Raaflaub and H. van Wees (eds) *A Companion to Archaic Greece* Oxford, Wiley-Blackwell: 273–93.

Whitley, J., K. O'Conor and H. Mason (1995) 'Praisos III: a Report on the Architectural Survey Undertaken in 1992', *Annual of the British School at Athens* 90: 405–28.

Whitley, J., M. Prent, and S. Thorne (1999) 'Praisos IV: a Preliminary Report on the 1993 and 1994 Survey Seasons', *Annual of the British School at Athens* 94: 215–64.

Wiedemann, T. (1988) *Greek and Roman Slavery*, London, Routledge.

Will, E. (1955) *Korinthiaka*, Paris, Éditions E. de Boccard.

Willetts, R.F. (1955) *Aristocratic Society in Ancient Crete*, London, Routledge and Kegan Paul.

—— (1965) *Ancient Crete: A Social History*, London, Routledge and Kegan Paul.

—— (1967) *The Law Code of Gortyn*, Berlin, Walter De Gruyter and Co.

—— (1975) 'The Cretan Koinon: Epigraphy and Tradition', *Kadmos* 14 (2): 143–53.

—— (1976) *The Civilization of Ancient Crete*, London, Batsford.

—— (1990) 'Aspects of Land Tenure in Dorian Crete', *Cretan Studies* 2: 221–30.

Wilson, J-P. (2009) 'Literacy' in K.A. Raaflaub and H. van Wees (eds) *A Companion To Archaic Greece*, Oxford, Wiley-Blackwell: 542–63.

Woudhuizen, F.C. (2006) 'The Ethnicity of the Sea Peoples', unpublished PhD dissertation, Erasmus University, Rotterdam.

Wroth, W. (1886) *A Catalogue of the Greek Coins of Crete and the Aegean Islands*, London, Longmans and Co.

Xanthoudidis, S.A. (1898) 'Cretan Expedition IX. Inscriptions from Gortyna, Lyttos, and Lató Pros Kamara', *American Journal of Archaeology*, 2 (1/2): 71–8.

Yangaki, A.G. (2004–5) 'Amphores crétoises: le cas d'Éleutherna en Crète', *Bulletin de Correspondance Hellénique*, 129: 503–23.

Yunis, H. (2005) 'The Rhetoric of Law in Fourth-century Athens' in M. Gagarin and D. Cohen (eds) *Cambridge Companion to Ancient Greek Law*, Cambridge, Cambridge University Press: 191–208.

Zalloua, P.A., D.E. Platt, M. El Sibai, J. Khalife, N. Makhoul, M. Haber, Y. Xue, H. Izaabel, E. Bosch, S.M. Adams, E. Arroyo, A.M. López-Parra, M. Aler, A. Picornell, M. Ramon, M.A. Jobling, D. Comas, J. Bertranpetit, R.S. Wells, C. Tyler-Smith and The Genographic Consortium (2008) 'Identifying Genetic Traces of Historical Expansions: Phoenician Footprints in the Mediterranean', *The American Journal of Human Genetics* 83: 633–642.

Index

Pagination in bold refers to an entry in the Gazetteer.

.